Adulthood in Britain and the United States from 1350 to Generation Z

Adulthood in Britain and the United States from 1350 to Generation Z

Edited by
Maria Cannon and Laura Tisdall

Available to purchase in print or download
for free at https://uolpress.co.uk

First published 2024 by
University of London Press
Senate House, Malet St, London WC1E 7HU

© the Authors 2024

The right of the authors to be identified as authors of this Work has been asserted by them in accordance with sections 77 and 78 of the Copyright, Designs and Patents Act 1988.

This book is published under a Creative Commons Attribution-NonCommercial-NoDerivatives 4.0 International (CC BY-NC-ND 4.0) license.

Please note that third-party material reproduced here may not be published under the same license as the rest of this book. If you would like to reuse any third-party material not covered by the book's Creative Commons license, you will need to obtain permission from the copyright holder.

A CIP catalogue record for this book is available from The British Library.

ISBN 978-1-908590-82-4 (hardback)
ISBN 978-1-908590-83-1 (paperback)
ISBN 978-1-908590-85-5 (.epub)
ISBN 978-1-908590-84-8 (.pdf)
ISBN 978-1-915249-84-5 (.html)

DOI https://doi.org/10.14296/vjit1721

Cover image: Boy dressed in father's clothes holding attaché.
Photo by Camerique/Mary Evans

Cover design for University of London Press by Nicky Borowiec.
Series design by Nicky Borowiec.
Book design by Nigel French.
Text set by Westchester Publishing Services UK in Meta Serif and Meta, designed by Erik Spiekermann.

Contents

List of figures	vii
Notes on contributors	ix
Acknowledgements	xiii

Introduction   1
Maria Cannon and Laura Tisdall

1. 'Middle age' in the Middle Ages of western Europe, 1300–1500   25
Deborah Youngs

2. 'The most constant and settled part of our life'?:
Adulthood and the ages of man in early modern England   45
Maria Cannon

3. Spiritual maturity and childishness in Protestant
England, c.1600–60   67
Emily E. Robson

4. The rising generation and the fogram: Locating adulthood
in eighteenth-century England   89
Barbara Crosbie

5. Seduction suits and gendered adulthood in the civil court
systems of the early United States, 1820–50   111
Holly N.S. White

6. 'They're not children anymore': Juveniles as adult
defendants in US criminal justice, 1786–2000   127
Jack Hodgson

7. 'Childish, adolescent and recherché': Psychoanalysis and
maturity in psychological selection boards, c.1940s–60s   149
Grace Whorrall-Campbell

8. 'The Pill for an unmarried girl is hardly going to improve her
character': The impact of changing sexual behaviours on the
construction of adulthood in Scotland, c.1968–80   171
Kristin Hay

9. African-Caribbean and South Asian adolescents, adulthood
and the 'generation gap' in late Cold War Britain, c.1970–89   193
Laura Tisdall

vi CONTENTS

10. Marriage, intimacy and adulthood in disabled people's lives
and activism in twentieth-century Britain   215
Lucy Delap

11. A road of one's own: The rejection of standard adulthood in
US emerging adult films   239
Andrea Sofía Regueira Martín

Afterword: Against adulthood   259
Kristine Alexander

Index   267

List of figures

2.1 Ages of man: third stage, from the age of thirty-two to forty-eight, and the classical orders of architecture: ionic. Engraving by J. Wierix, 1577, after J. Vredeman de Vries. Wellcome Collection. ⓢ Source: Wellcome Collection.　49

2.2 The ages of man represented as a step scheme. Reproduction of an engraving by C. Bertelli. Wellcome Collection. ⓢ Source: Wellcome Collection.　53

4.1 'A speedy and effectual preparation for the next world' (1777). © The Trustees of the British Museum. Shared under a Creative Commons Attribution-NonCommercial-ShareAlike 4.0 International (CC BY-NC-SA 4.0) licence.　97

4.2 "_____" *"And catch the living Manners as they rise"* (1794). © National Portrait Gallery, London.　103

4.3 'An agreeable group of young gentlemen, otherwise old bachelors turn'd asses' (1797). Courtesy of The Lewis Walpole Library, Yale University.　104

Notes on contributors

Kristine Alexander is an associate professor of history at the University of Lethbridge, which is located on Blackfoot Territory in southern Alberta, Canada. Her publications include *Guiding Modern Girls: Girlhood, Empire, and Internationalism in the 1920s and 1930s* (UBC Press, 2017) and the edited volumes *Small Stories of War: Children, Youth, and Conflict in Canada and Beyond* (McGill-Queen's University Press, 2023) and *A Cultural History of Youth in the Modern Age* (Bloomsbury, 2022). Her current research analyses concepts of age, race and development in the history of the Canadian settler state.

Maria Cannon is a senior lecturer in history at the University of Portsmouth, UK. Her research interests are family, gender, emotions and the life cycle in early modern England. Her current project, 'Blending the Family: Affection, Obligation and Dynasty in Early Modern English Stepfamilies', explores emotion and authority in blended families. She is a co-convener of the Life Cycles seminar at the Institute of Historical Research and a committee member of the Children's History Society.

Barbara Crosbie is an associate professor in the Department of History, Durham University, UK. She specialises in British social and cultural history with a particular interest in age relations and the process of historical change. Her first monograph, *Age Relations and Cultural Change in Eighteenth-Century England* (2020), follows an age cohort from the nurseries and schoolrooms of the 1740s through the volatile terrain of adolescence and into the adult world, tracing the roots of a generational divide that spilled into the political arena in the 1770s. She is currently working on a second book that complements this macro approach with a micro study of the life cycle, *At Home with Ralph Jackson 1749–1791: Age and Masculinity in Georgian England*.

Lucy Delap teaches modern history at the University of Cambridge, UK and is a fellow of Murray Edwards College. She has published widely on the history of feminism, gender, sexuality, labour and religion, including the prize-winning *The Feminist Avant-Garde: Transatlantic Encounters of the Early Twentieth Century* (2007), *Knowing Their Place: Domestic Service in Twentieth Century Britain* (2011) and *Feminisms: A Global History* (2020). Her current research is in disability history and includes 'Slow Workers: Labelling and Labouring in Britain, c. 1909–1955' (*Social History of Medicine*, 2023).

Kristin Hay (she/her) is a historian of gender and medicine, with a particular focus on women's reproductive health and rights and oral history. She is a recipient of the Neil Rafeek Oral History Prize and the Leah Leneman (Runner Up) Essay Prize. Her recent research examined the impact of changing birth control practices in Scotland between 1965 and 1980, exploring how heterosexual men and women learned about, accessed and accepted birth control following the so-called 'sexual revolution', and the subsequent impact it had on their lives.

Jack Hodgson is a lecturer in history at the University of Roehampton, London, UK. He received his PhD from Northumbria University in 2022 and was previously awarded the Scottish Association for the Study of America's Ellen Craft Prize. His research primarily examines the history of children's rights and children's political agency in American history. His first book, *Young Reds in the Big Apple: The New York Young Pioneers of America, 1923–1934*, is forthcoming with Fordham University Press.

Andrea Sofía Regueira Martín is a lecturer in the Department of English and German at the University of Zaragoza, Spain. She received her PhD from the University of Zaragoza in 2022. Her research focuses on filmic representations of the transition to contemporary adulthood and on virtual spaces of girlhood in contemporary film. She is a member of the research project 'From Social Space to Cinematic Space: Mise-en-Scènes of the Transnational in Contemporary Cinema'.

Emily E. Robson is a PhD candidate at the University of Cambridge, UK. Her doctoral research explores early modern English representations of male prophets, as well as the blurred boundaries between extraordinary prophecy and exegesis. She is currently working on an article examining the activities of William Juniper, the 'Gosfield Seer'. Emily's research interests include ecclesiastical reform, early modern Protestantism and the interrelation of gender and religion.

Laura Tisdall is a senior lecturer in history at Newcastle University, UK. She is a historian of childhood, adolescence, adulthood and chronological age in modern Britain and the United States. Her first book, *A Progressive Education?*, was published by Manchester University Press in 2020, and her most recent publication is a 'state of the field' article on the history of childhood in *History* (2022). She is currently working on a book on age and adulthood in Britain between c.1956 and c.1989, which is under contract with Yale University Press London.

Holly N.S. White is an adjunct professor of history at William & Mary, Williamsburg, VA, USA. She specialises in the history of age, childhood and youth in the early United States. She is the co-editor of *Engaging Children in Vast Early America* (Routledge, 2024). Her first authored book, *Negotiating American Childhood: Age-Based Laws and the Illusion of Protection in the Early United States*, is forthcoming from the University of Virginia Press in 2025.

Grace Whorrall-Campbell is a Junior Research Fellow at Corpus Christi College, Oxford, UK. Her doctoral research examined the application of psy-science to management and the workplace in postwar Britain. Grace's work has been published in the edited collection *Feelings and Work in Modern History: Emotional Labour and Emotions about Labour* (Bloomsbury, 2022). Grace's research interests include the history of labour, gender, sexuality, mental health and the psychosocial in modern Britain.

Deborah Youngs is a professor of late medieval and early Tudor British history who has published widely on gender, law, ageing and the life course in women's experiences, 1350–1550. Her latest publications explore women's litigation in the central law courts of Tudor England including (with Teresa Phipps) the edited book *Litigating Women: Gender and Justice in Europe, c.1300–c.1800* (Routledge, 2021). She is currently Pro-Vice Chancellor (Education) at Swansea University, UK.

Acknowledgements

We are grateful for the support of the Leverhulme Trust in funding the original workshop from which this edited collection emerged.

Introduction

Maria Cannon and Laura Tisdall[1]

In twenty-first-century Britain and the United States, we are often told that adulthood is under threat. Its demise is blamed on millennials, the generation born between 1981 and 1996, as the oldest of this group are now reaching their early forties without necessarily acquiring traditional markers of maturity. There is no shortage of assertions, in both popular media and academic texts, that millennials are infantilised, immature and incapable.[2] In their turn, millennials have struck back, challenging the relevance and value of traditional adulthood. Journalist Catherine Baab-Muguira explored 'Why so many American millennials feel that adulthood is a lie' in July 2018, while fellow millennial Whizy Kim similarly asserted in *Refinery29* in May 2021 that 'For millennials, the dream of adulthood is dead – and that's OK'.[3] These challenges highlight the social and economic difficulties faced by this generation, coming of age shortly before, during or after the financial crisis of 2008, with rising rent and house prices, precarious unemployment and, especially for Americans, skyrocketing student debt.

The next generation down, Generation Z, born between 1997 and 2012, are often portrayed, in contrast to 'lazy' millennials, as 'old before their time', missing out on the life experiences that ought to define youth.[4] A British psychotherapist recently quoted in a *Guardian* article said: 'I do have the sense that [this generation] are possibly missing out on making mistakes and the sense of being young', citing evidence that Gen Z drink less alcohol and tend to have a smaller number of close friends rather than meeting lots of people in clubs and bars.[5] Both millennial 'childishness' and Gen Z's 'premature maturity' are framed as problems, underlining the idea that there is a 'right kind' of adulthood that can only be experienced at a specific chronological age. Meanwhile, sociologists, policymakers, psychologists and neuroscientists increasingly suggest that adulthood begins later than we thought and ends earlier than we expected. 'Brain science' purports to show that our frontal lobes, seat of our executive functioning, are not fully mature until age twenty-five or thirty, then begin to decline again after age forty.[6]

The current tensions between the ideal of adulthood and the reality of 'adulting' are nothing new. Although 'adulthood' is under intense scrutiny in contemporary Britain and the United States, this is not a uniquely turbulent period, nor does it represent the overturning of norms that were previously settled and unquestioned. Adulthood has a history. Expectations for adults have altered across time, just as other age categories such as childhood, adolescence and old age have been shaped by cultural and social contexts. In the past, just as in the present, historical actors have wrestled with the contrast between their own experiences and the life-stage markers they were expected to meet. Older generations have feared that younger generations will never be ready to assume the full responsibilities of maturity. Adulthood has been presented as the idealised peak of the life cycle, a period of life that is often very brief or impossible to achieve before the slide into middle and old age begins.

Both Britain and the United States developed a range of chronological ages linked to the achievement of adulthood in the modern period. However, individuals, just as they had done in the pre-modern period, were more likely to associate adulthood with individual roles or qualities, whether that was getting married, holding property or becoming an 'independent' and 'responsible' person. This created an inevitable contradiction between theoretical definitions of adulthood and people's actual experiences of it. In this way, even those who were firmly defined as adults might experience the limiting nature of adulthood, which relied on stereotypes about how one should be, feel and act at a given age or life stage. For this reason, historicising adulthood should mean not just demonstrating the unfairness of the exclusion of non-adults from this category but also questioning the usefulness of the category itself.

Adulthood is relational; it makes sense only when defined in opposition to those who are excluded from it. While children and adolescents, or 'dependent subjects', represent the principal group of non-adults, they are by no means the only one. Adulthood is intersectional: class, race, gender, sexuality and disability, including the disabilities of old age, might affect your access to it. It can operate as both a burden and a benefit, as groups can be framed as both 'adultified' and 'childlike'. This makes adulthood an important historical category, even for scholars who do not focus on chronological age or the life cycle. Since the late seventeenth century, the category of adult has been used to define citizenship in both Britain and the United States, and hence who is allowed to hold political authority; it is the foundation of the modern state.[7] Prior to that, adulthood was a stage of life associated with suitability for governance through the values of maturity and wisdom, albeit with a less clearly defined identity around the term 'adult'. Understanding adulthood is crucial to truly understanding the dynamics of power.

Historicising adulthood

Historians have rarely thought directly about adulthood, despite the fact that it is the yardstick by which ideas of what it means to be 'childish', 'elderly' or 'adolescent' are measured. Even modern Global North concepts such as the 'midlife crisis' presume the existence of a healthy kind of adulthood that exists before you hit middle age. But in the same way as an analysis of femininity is incomplete without understanding what is meant by masculinity, we cannot really understand how concepts of childhood, adolescence or old age have changed without thinking about how adulthood is also given different meanings in different societies at different times. Without this empirical knowledge, we cannot fully use age as a category of historical analysis.[8]

Scholars of childhood have recognised this problem. As Sari Edelstein writes, we should not 'subject childhood to scholarly analysis without attending to age more generally' as 'age is the larger paradigm in which childhood belongs'.[9] Stephanie Olsen asked recently, 'Why has childhood been so extensively historicized but adulthood has not? After all, aren't humans at every stage in the life cycle always in a state of becoming as well as being?'[10] However, a limited amount of historical work on adulthood has emerged.[11] Most existing histories focus on 'middle age' or the 'midlife crisis' rather than earlier stages of social maturity – work that is significant in its own right, but which does not historicise healthy adulthood.[12] Literary scholars of Britain and the United States have done important work on the presentation of adulthood in specific texts and on the emergence of a separate category of children's literature – which entailed the production of a category of 'adult literature' – but these texts focus solely on nineteenth-century literary culture.[13]

There is currently no single historical text that considers the history of adulthood in Britain and the United States across a longer chronological span, allowing us to attend to how ideas about this life stage changed and how they stayed the same. Steven Mintz's *The Prime of Life* (2015) comes closest to offering a history of adulthood itself, but this survey text, which focuses solely on the United States, is deeply flawed: rather than historicising adulthood, it reinscribes a sequence of modern stereotypes about what it means to be 'grown up', connecting adulthood to life-cycle markers such as marriage, paid employment and home ownership.[14] Mintz unquestioningly accepts modern Global North assumptions about the capabilities of children and adults, writing that 'adulthood is consequential in ways that childhood and adolescence are not ... Adulthood is the time of life when individuals achieve emotional and intellectual maturity and support themselves and others'.[15] This description highlights the key qualities that we often associate with twenty-first-century adulthood – independence, responsibility and psychological maturity – but assumes that this is actually what adults are like and takes the universal relevance of these qualities for granted.

For the medieval and early modern periods, research that could be described as focusing on adulthood in fact considers values associated with masculinity and femininity, and how they complemented each other in the patriarchal household.[16] To some degree this reflects pre-modern ideas of adulthood that were closely linked with other status-conferring concepts including social status and gender. Rites of passage that conferred status on individuals were significant in medieval society, but not necessarily linked to chronological age.[17] One exception is the recent work of Jacob W. Doss, which opens up a discussion of medieval adulthood by considering how twelfth-century Cistercian monks understood the ideal monk as 'mature and masculine', explicitly challenging earlier work on monkhood that focused solely on gender. Doss argues that the education of the Cistercian recruit, regardless of the recruit's chronological age, was about making 'boys' into 'men'.[18]

Marriage has been singled out by medieval and early modern historians as the most significant event in the lives of both men and women.[19] Marriage and the associated status of householder conferred a degree of stability and responsibility on individuals that marked their entry into adulthood.[20] Women who never married could find it especially difficult to obtain householding status as independent work was often denied to never-married women by the authorities.[21] Deborah Youngs notes that even after marriage, adults were required to continually demonstrate their new status as successful householders, spouses and parents.[22] Similarly, modern historians have considered changing ideas of 'womanhood' and 'manhood', and marked the significance of marriage and parenthood as a rite of passage, especially for women.[23] Nevertheless, this important work is not primarily a history of adulthood. These historians use gender, not age, as their primary category of historical analysis. They analyse 'girls and women' and 'boys and men' through this lens, rather than considering how chronological age shapes the disempowerment of children, young people and older people, and hence the valorisation of adulthood.

Adulthood and chronological age

The category of adulthood has long been used as a tool of power.[24] Holly Brewer argues that, from the late seventeenth century onwards, political understandings of childhood and adulthood fundamentally changed in the Anglo-American world. As ideas of government focused more on the ability to 'consent', children were no longer viewed as legitimate political actors. This contrasted with older patriarchal norms, where those who inherited young wielded power by virtue of their status rather than their age. This move 'from status to contract' meant children were the only group explicitly excluded from legal rights.[25] In political terms, age and maturity did not directly correlate until into the eighteenth century.[26] After this major shift, chronological age became increasingly important in Britain and the United States: first as a way of designating who had access to certain rights, and then, through the expansion of mass age-graded schooling from the late nineteenth century, as a way of separating childhood and adolescence into increasingly smaller units.[27]

However, age-markers and laws conferring legal majority existed in various forms in medieval and early modern England. The legal age of marriage was twelve for girls and fourteen for boys. Fourteen was also the age individuals were liable to pay the poll tax in medieval England as this age 'presumed increasing economic activity' in rural areas where many of this age earned money in service or labour placements outside of their family homes.[28] There was no single age of majority and these laws were primarily guidelines by which to judge individual cases.[29] As noted by Miriam Müller, adulthood was not fixed by chronological age and laws indicating legal majority used age 'to judge other factors of social maturity against'.[30] Most people in medieval society would not have known their birthdate or exact chronological age and so relied on collective, community knowledge to ascertain how old they were.[31]

The community also had a role in deciding whether the individual was mature enough to be granted independent 'adult' status. As age was not usually known, it could be amended to suit an individual's circumstances.[32] Thus, age and social maturity could be defined and altered depending on whether the individual was deemed to have sufficient qualities to be conferred an 'adult'. Historians of old age have noted the importance of 'functional' age as individuals were often deemed to be

elderly when they were no longer able to support themselves independently.[33] This dependence was largely dictated by circumstance and
social context. Similar caveats were applied to those with disabilities
who may not have been granted legal adulthood.[34] This definition could
be flexible: for example, those with mental health issues could move in
and out of legal wardship depending on the level of support they needed
to manage their affairs.[35]

Furthermore, even after the rise of 'chronological age' as a marker of
adulthood in the modern period, it did not reign supreme. As Sarah
Mulhall Adelman has recently argued in reference to nineteenth-century
New York orphan asylums, institutions wanted to use precise chronological ages, but record-keeping took some time to catch up to their ambition,
as dates of birth were often still unknown.[36] Holly N.S. White and Julia M.
Gossard show that concepts of 'double age' were in play in the nineteenth-
and twentieth-century United States, with functional age still privileged
above chronological age when it suited those who wanted to either grant,
or remove, certain protections.[37]

In both Britain and the United States, different and internally contradictory age-markers were constructed across the modern period to mark
out precise chronological ages when individuals entered 'adulthood'. In
the nineteenth century, twenty-one was often used as the age of majority,
despite the fact that many individuals remained uncertain of their age.[38]
This was the age at which all white men in the United States gained voting rights, and the age at which those men who were able to vote under
successive extensions of the franchise in Britain in 1832, 1867 and 1885
became legally qualified to do so. In Britain, this age was formalised by
the 1832 Great Reform Act, based on the minimum age of property ownership. The United Kingdom was the first democracy to lower its voting age
to eighteen, in 1969; the United States followed in 1971, as the World War II
slogan 'old enough to fight, old enough to vote' gained further currency
in the context of the Vietnam War.[39]

This, however, did not signal a single legal age of adulthood: the age
of sexual consent moved from ten to thirteen and finally to sixteen in
Britain between 1860 and 1885.[40] And as Ishita Pande has recently argued,
age of consent laws were amended across the British Empire in the last
two decades of the nineteenth century but did not reach consensus. In
India, for example, the age was raised to twelve; in the Cape of Good
Hope, to fourteen; and in New Zealand, to sixteen.[41] In the United States,
ages of sexual consent and statutory marriage ages, which might be different from each other, were set by individual states: if no legislation was
passed, marriage ages were supposed to be the common-law ages of fourteen for boys and twelve for girls. Different marriage ages based on sex

often persisted until the 1970s, when states equalised them.[42] The age of consent was sixteen or eighteen in all states after 1918 except Georgia, where it remained at fourteen until 1995. Meanwhile, Britain set a legal drinking age of eighteen in 1923, whereas in the United States, states instituted their own drinking age laws after the end of Prohibition in 1933, and a national minimum drinking age of twenty-one was established in 1984.[43]

Oppressed and marginalised groups marked different legal paths to adulthood in modern Britain and the United States. African-American men did not gain the (theoretical) right to vote in the United States until 1868, and women of any race until 1919. Native Americans were not guaranteed voting rights in every state until 1962, despite the 1924 Indian Citizenship Act supposedly giving them rights to full citizenship. In Britain, the Representation of the People Act of 1918 established a universal male franchise but restricted the female vote to property-owning women or female graduates over thirty; the franchise was not equalised until 1929. In the British Empire, colonised subjects had even fewer rights: for example, despite the expansion of opportunities for Indians over twenty-one to vote in provincial elections from the early twentieth century onwards, especially after the Government of India Act 1935, the franchise was based on property qualifications until independence in 1947 and so only about a sixth of Indian adults could vote.[44] The age of consent, meanwhile, was set at twenty-one for men who had sex with men after the Sexual Offences Act of 1967 in England and Wales (sex between men was not legalised until 1980 in Scotland). It was lowered to eighteen in 1994 and equalised at sixteen in 2000. As this shows, even in the modern period, concepts of adulthood were used to oppress those who would otherwise have been defined as adults by virtue of their chronological age, further challenging its neutrality.

Chronological age clearly became a more significant legal and social marker in modern Britain and the United States during the nineteenth century, although it was neither insignificant before this period nor totally dominant thereafter.[45] However, when we look at individuals' own concepts of adulthood, these are not always tied tightly to chronological age, even in the modern period. As this collection will show, adulthood is often viewed as an individual attitude, situation or state of mind. This reflects a key division in the limited historiography on age: those who focus on 'age grading' versus those who focus on 'age consciousness'.[46] Although little has been written on adulthood on both sides of this divide, 'age consciousness' seems especially ill-served, with historians often focusing on legal ages of majority rather than on how people themselves thought about adulthood. This approach can be distorting: for example,

Britain technically established the legal age of majority at eighteen in 1969, but British teenagers and young adults reflecting on adulthood in the 1970s and 1980s very rarely refer to chronological age, instead highlighting life-cycle markers like leaving school, getting a job and getting married.[47]

Adulthood through time: static, idealised, oppressive

Adulthood has been seen as a static state both throughout history and during the human life span. Patrick Alexander, John Lowenthal and Graham Butt argue that relatively new sociological concepts, such as Jeffrey Arnett's 'emerging adulthood', imply that adulthood is changing over time but actually still fix adulthood as a coherent, unchanging category that is ultimately achieved.[48] Even in medieval and early modern ages of man schemata which could allow for multiple stages of adulthood, it was still positioned as the apex of the life cycle. This reflects what Bernadette Baker has called 'the developmental conception of the child', which positions childhood and adolescence as an ever-changing journey and adulthood as their fixed destination.[49] As Valerie Walkerdine has written, modern developmental psychology understands 'adulthood as a stable state of being' and 'childhood as unstable', but the stability of adulthood is 'fictional'.[50] A number of scholars have also pointed out that, if adulthood is understood in this way, elderly people risk becoming non-adults again as they age past reliable independence.[51] As the radical American children's rights campaigner and educator, John Holt, wrote in *Escape from Childhood* (1974), 'we are more and more coming to think of human life as a series of crises – the crisis of puberty, the crisis of adolescence, the crisis of middle age, the crisis of old age. It is almost as if the only age to be is between twenty-one and thirty-five'.[52]

The term 'adult' was not used in medieval literature, but other categories such as 'full' or 'perfect' age were used to indicate the apex of the human life course. Historians have analysed written and visual depictions of the 'ages of man', the different life stages man could expect to experience from birth to death.[53] Simple schema contained three or four stages but they could depict up to twelve stages. By the sixteenth century, the 'seven ages' had become the most popular and were increasingly presented in a step form with adulthood at the pinnacle.[54] These schemes were mainly an intellectual exercise intended 'to integrate the life of man into the larger order of the natural world'.[55] They were idealised depictions and did not represent all men's (and certainly not women's) experiences. They nevertheless show that medieval people thought intellectually about the physical and mental changes that men could expect to experience through their life course. Adulthood could be a stage on its own in a three- or four-stage schema, or made up of multiple stages in a larger schema, but it usually functioned as an apex where physical strength and mental capacity were ideally balanced.

In the modern period, the creation of increasingly complex stages of development to map childhood and adolescent experience coupled with the assumption that adulthood is a fixed end-point led to the idealisation of psychological adulthood.[56] Teresa Michals argues that this modern view of adulthood emerged only from the late eighteenth century onwards, as adulthood became more associated with personal qualities than for-mal power, and that this introduced a fundamental contradiction into the term: 'The psychological sense of adulthood as an age-leveled norm ... is in tension with its meaning as an aspirational ideal.'[57] Teri Chettiar echoes the idea of the modernity of this kind of adulthood in her history of the growing political significance of emotional intimacy in postwar Britain, writing that, after World War II, adulthood 'increasingly became an emotional category rather than a demographic designation'.[58] However, Michals and Chettiar fail to recognise that adulthood was associated with personal qualities as well as social status in the medieval and early mod-ern period as well; the same tension between norm and ideal existed before the eighteenth century, despite chronological age being much less significant.

A central component of the 'ages of man' was an examination of the qualities associated with each life stage. Children and the elderly were understood to have different physical constitutions and mental capaci-ties compared to adults who, as in modern concepts of adulthood, were capable of shouldering responsibility and behaving moderately and rationally. It was possible for people to exhibit qualities of a different life stage with positive and negative effects. For instance, many saints were described as exhibiting mature levels of wisdom and intelligence during their childhoods, but people who behaved youthfully in old age were criticised. Even in these idealised depictions, developmental stages were linked to wider societal understandings of adult maturity.[59]

Despite the clear association of certain characteristics with the broad life stage of adulthood, pre-modern concepts of political and social status perhaps explain the lack of a general term for 'adult'. Although marriage and heading a household conferred a degree of maturity and independence, dependence/independence and youth/adulthood did not always correlate directly. Lower-status people were not deemed politically mature by those in power, even if they were economically independent. Alexandra Shepard has shown that dependence was linked more closely to social status than age in early modern English society. When accounting for their own wealth, those of elite social ranks were more likely to be financially reliant on their parents, even at an adult chronological age, than poorer social groups who supported themselves. Shepard sums up the contradiction that 'paradoxically, for those in the "fast stream" to adulthood, dependence on parental patronage was much longer lasting'.[60] The young adults of elite families could expect to be conferred with political maturity in the future, despite the fact that poorer people of the same chronological age might have already been financially independent for years. This complicates Michals's assertion that, in the pre-modern period, 'those who remained economically dependent had to remain perpetual children'.[61]

Excluding a physically mature group of people from adulthood was one way it might be used as a tool of oppression. In the British Empire, colonised subjects were often framed as both effeminate and childlike to justify the 'necessity' of British domination; discourse about 'tutelage' was used to refer to both colonised countries and their native elites.[62] In the nineteenth-century United States, Corinne T. Field has shown how both white women and formerly enslaved black people had to fight for equal recognition as 'adults'.[63] Across Britain, western Europe and the United States, Freudian psychology framed homosexual people as developmentally arrested from the late nineteenth century onwards, unlikely to achieve 'adult' milestones such as marrying or having children.[64] Working-class children in twentieth-century Britain were not expected to meet the same milestones of intellectual development as their middle-class peers.[65] As Patrick McKearney has explored, disabled people in the Global North have been understood as 'childlike' because of their inability to live 'independent lives'; this fails to recognise how all humans are ultimately interdependent.[66]

While these exclusions made adulthood seem like a privilege, the conferral of premature adulthood could also be used as a tool of oppression within both colonial and domestic contexts. Satadru Sen argues that 'delinquent' native children in British India were framed as 'small, perverse adults'; unlike their white counterparts, they were seen as unamenable to reform, needing punishment rather than education.[67] Danielle Kinsey builds on these assertions by examining the earlier British fascination with child maharajas in the 1840s; these child rulers were seen as a symbol of India's corrupt state, a reversal of the natural order of things.[68] Historians of eighteenth- and nineteenth-century slavery in Jamaica and the United States have claimed that enslaved children had their childhoods 'stolen' as they were pressed into labour or used as 'breeding wenches' early in adolescence.[69] Tera Eva Agyepong has shown how this 'adultification' of black children extended into the twentieth century within the US juvenile court system, a theme explored further in Jack Hodgson's chapter in this collection.[70]

However, historians can recognise these dynamics of exploitation without framing childhood falsely as a desirable identity. As Sen goes on to argue, by stripping childhood from native children in India, British colonisers also ensured these children could never be considered true adults, as 'the premature adult is frozen in a permanently unreasoning, childish state'.[71] In his consideration of black childhood in the United States in two different historical eras – the antebellum period and the twenty-first century – Jacob Breslow reaches similar conclusions.[72] He argues that black people were viewed in both eras as 'childlike'. Black minors were not treated as children because, in João Costa Vargas and Joy A. James's words, they were 'already framed by the image of the menacing black [adult]', but nor were black adults considered genuinely grown-up.[73] Neither the category of childhood nor of adulthood protected black people because they were positioned as outside the normal trajectories of maturation accessible to whites.

Chapter summaries and conclusion

The eleven chapters in this collection, alongside the Afterword, examine how adulthood has been both persistent and highly mutable in Britain and the United States since c.1350. It compares these two major imperial nation-states, although due to its chronological span, there are fewer chapters that focus on the United States, as it did not become a formal entity until later in the time period covered by this book. This comparative approach has been chosen for three reasons. First, this comparison allows us to consider two countries that share much of the same international psychological and sociological influences via the language of 'progressivism', but still are sometimes differentiated quite sharply in their approaches to adulthood.[74] Second, these two countries have some of the most developed historiographies of childhood and adolescence, which allow us to situate our assertions about adulthood. Third, as imperialist nations, both countries exported their ideas about adulthood – Britain throughout its formal and informal empire, and the United States to its indigenous and formerly enslaved populations and to other geographical areas where it exercised influence, such as Central and South America.[75]

This collection does not directly consider the wider empires of Britain and the United States, but it does explore how colonialism shaped the experiences of those living within those nation-states. Hodgson looks at the experiences of both Native Americans and Mexican Americans, as well as African Americans, within juvenile courts, exploring the impact of imperialism and colonisation both within the USA and its expansion into Central America. Laura Tisdall's chapter shows how second-generation immigrant African-Caribbean and South Asian adolescents in Britain were profoundly impacted by their countries' histories of colonial exploitation, and this changed how they understood age and generation, as their parents gave them a direct, experiential link to these histories that they themselves lacked.

By using 1900 as a rough halfway point in our chronology, this collection critically engages with the idea that adulthood is a late eighteenth-century invention. Both Deborah Youngs's and Maria Cannon's chapters argue that adulthood was constructed as part of the 'ages of man' in medieval and early modern England and western Europe, but that it was not a single, unchanging state. Medieval and early modern concepts of the life cycle allowed for different stages of adulthood, considering a variety of midlife transitions. Emily E. Robson's chapter on English Protestant conceptions of 'childishness' and 'spiritual maturity' builds on these discussions of the 'ages of man' by exploring competing conceptions of adulthood that valorised old age as the pinnacle of spiritual maturity; however, in order to make this rhetorical move, they had to reckon with the realities of physical decline. Barbara Crosbie's chapter on adulthood in eighteenth-century England further exposes how many of our concerns about adulthood are not new. Crosbie explores the kind of conflict between the 'young' and the 'old' that is sometimes associated solely with modernity, considering definitions of adulthood as a battle fought between generations.

As Robson's and Cannon's chapters show, individuals who had attained adulthood might be denied the status of adults as a way of limiting their power and agency. This is a theme that continues into the modern period, as White's chapter on the late eighteenth- and early nineteenth-century United States demonstrates. Adult daughters in this period never achieved true legal adulthood, and were expected to pass from their father's authority to their husband's. In this context, gender trumped age, despite the existence of statutes that defined adulthood chronologically. Kristin Hay's chapter explores how these gendered ideas about adulthood and women's sexual and marital agency played out in the very different context of late twentieth-century Scotland, where unmarried women were treated as 'girls' in relation to their reproductive choices. While possessing far more power over their own lives than their earlier counterparts, their freedom was still restricted by assumptions about their maturity and the need to control their sexuality. Meanwhile, Lucy Delap argues that disabled adults had to claim the right to sex and marriage in twentieth-century Britain; society's ableism excluded them from stereotypical ideas about adulthood, but also allowed them to explore new kinds of intimacy and family formations, challenging the idea of a linear trajectory.

Similarly, other oppressed and socially marginalised groups have been unable to achieve the stereotypical qualities that would define them as 'adults'. Grace Whorrall-Campbell explores how applicants to the War Office Selection Boards, the Civil Service Selection Boards and the Unilever Company Management Development Scheme in wartime and postwar Britain underwent psychological selection processes that could flag them as 'immature' or 'childish'. Whorrall-Campbell argues that this coded language allowed employers to identify candidates who were suspected to be homosexual because homosexuality was viewed at the time as a form of arrested development. The treatment of adolescents of colour in Cold War Britain also indicates how certain groups struggled to prove their 'maturity', as Tisdall considers in her chapter. African-Caribbean and South Asian adolescents were aware that they had to perform adulthood to higher standards than their white counterparts to be taken seriously, while sometimes rejecting the conventional norms that defined hegemonic concepts of adulthood.

Adulthood is not always a desirable state, nor one that is pursued by those who are excluded from it. Hodgson's chapter explores how children of colour have been more likely to be treated as adult defendants than their white counterparts since the inception of juvenile courts in the US since 1899, and even children of colour who are treated legally as children are less likely to be judged leniently. Meanwhile, more privileged adolescents and young people may seek to extend adolescence and defer adulthood, perhaps conceptualising 'young adulthood' as a new life stage in its own right due to the associations of adulthood with responsibility, duty and limited freedoms. Andrea Sofía Regueira Martín suggests that twenty-first-century US 'emerging adulthood' films present a rejection of standard adulthood, foregrounding protagonists who avoid commitment and stability in search of 'new ways' of being an adult. But these responses are conditioned by a worsening economic background since the financial crisis of 2008, making traditional milestones of modern adulthood less attainable for both millennials and Generation Z.

Adulthood is a contradictory state: both burden and benefit, static and ever-changing, relational and individual. Even those who managed to successfully 'achieve' adulthood, a status that has historically not been available to all, found themselves negotiating different sets of expectations during this 'perfect age'. And as Kristine Alexander argues in her Afterword, Anglo-American ideas of adulthood are not the only ones, even as they were forcibly imposed upon other peoples through colonialisation and imperialism. This collection is only the beginning of the many different histories of adulthood that could be written once we no longer treat it as an invisible, or a desirable, norm.

Notes

1. Tisdall's research for this chapter was funded by the Leverhulme Trust, grant number ECF-2017-369.

2. Frank Furedi, *Why Borders Matter: Why Humanity Must Relearn the Art of Drawing Boundaries* (Abingdon: Routledge, 2020); Kyle Smith, 'Millennials Need to Put Away the Juice Boxes and Grow Up', *New York Post*, 21 March 2016.

3. Catherine Baab-Mugeira, 'Failure to Launch: Why So Many American Millennials Feel That Adulthood Is a Lie', *NBC News*, 8 July 2018; Whizy Kim, 'For Millennials, the Dream of Adulthood Is Dead – And That's OK', *Refinery29*, 21 May 2021.

4. Barbara Herman, 'Gen Z: Nonrebels with a Cause', *FutureVision*, 21 February 2021.

5. David Batty, '"Generation Sensible" Risk Missing Out on Life Experiences, Therapists Warn', *The Guardian*, 19 August 2022.

6. Sarah-Jayne Blakemore, *Inventing Ourselves: The Secret Life of the Teenage Brain* (London: Penguin, 2018); Moya Sarner, *When I Grow Up: Conversations with Adults in Search of Adulthood* (London: Scribe UK, 2022).

7. Holly Brewer, *By Birth or Consent: Children, Law and the Anglo-American Revolution in Authority* (Chapel Hill, NC: North Carolina University Press, 2005).

8. Corinne T. Field and Nicholas L. Syrett, 'Chronological Age: A Useful Category of Historical Analysis', *American Historical Review*, 125, no. 2 (2020), 371–84.

9. Sari Edelstein, *Adulthood and Other Fictions: American Literature and the Unmaking of Age* (Oxford: Oxford University Press, 2018).

10. Zsuzsa Millei, 'Temporalizing Childhood: A Conversation with Erica Burman, Stephanie Olsen, Spyros Spyrou, and Hanne Warming', *Journal of Childhood Studies*, 46, no. 4 (2021), 64.

11. Jennine Hurl-Eamon, 'Youth in the Devil's Service, Manhood in the King's: Reaching Adulthood in the Eighteenth-Century British Army', *Journal of the History of Childhood and Youth*, 8, no. 2 (2015), 163–90; Aaron William Moore, 'Reversing the Gaze: The Construction of "Adulthood" in the Wartime Diaries of Japanese Children and Youth' in Sabine Frühstück and Anne Walthall (eds.), *Child's Play: Multi-Sensory Histories of Children and Childhood in Japan* (Berkeley, CA: University of California Press, 2017), 141–59; Laura Tisdall, '"What a Difference It Was to Be a Woman and Not a Teenager": Adolescent Girls' Conceptions of Adulthood in 1960s and 1970s Britain', *Gender and History* 34, no. 2 (2022), 495–513; Teri Chettiar, *The Intimate State: How Emotional Life Became Political in Welfare-State Britain* (Oxford: Oxford University Press, 2023).

12. John Benson, *Prime Time: A History of the Middle Aged in Twentieth Century Britain* (London: Routledge, 1997); Kay Heath, *The Emergence of Midlife in Victorian Britain* (Albany, NY: SUNY Press, 2009); Sue Niebrzydowski (ed.), *Middle-Aged Women in the Middle Ages* (Woodbridge: Boydell and Brewer, 2011); Patricia Cohen, *In Our Prime: The Invention of Middle Age* (New York: Scribner, 2012); Suzanne

Schmidt, *Midlife Crisis: The Feminist Origins of a Chauvinist Cliché* (Chicago, IL: University of Chicago Press, 2020); Ben Hutchinson, *The Midlife Mind: Literature and the Art of Ageing* (London: Reaktion Books, 2020); Ella Sbaraini, '"Those That Prefer the Ripe Mellow Fruit to Any Other": Rethinking Depictions of Middle-Aged Women's Sexuality in England, 1700–1800', *Cultural and Social History*, 17, no. 2 (2020), 165–87; Mark Jackson, *Broken Dreams: An Intimate History of the Midlife Crisis* (London: Reaktion Books, 2021).

13. Edelstein, *Adulthood and Other Fictions*; Claudia Nelson, *Precocious Children and Childish Adults: Age Inversion in Victorian Literature* (Baltimore, MD: Johns Hopkins University Press, 2012); Teresa Michals, *Books for Children, Books for Adults: Age and the Novel from Defoe to James* (Cambridge: Cambridge University Press, 2014).

14. Steven Mintz, *The Prime of Life: A History of Modern Adulthood* (Cambridge, MA: Harvard University Press, 2015).

15. Mintz, *The Prime of Life*, x–xi.

16. Elizabeth Foyster, *Manhood in Early Modern England: Honour, Sex and Marriage* (London: Routledge, 1999); Alexandra Shepard, *Meanings of Manhood in Early Modern England* (Oxford: Oxford University Press, 2003); Barbara Harris, *English Aristocratic Women, 1450–1550: Marriage and Family, Property and Careers* (Oxford: Oxford University Press, 2002); Jeffrey Jerome Cohen and Bonnie Wheeler (eds.), *Becoming Male in the Middle Ages* (London: Routledge, 2000).

17. J.A. Burrow, *The Ages of Man: A Study in Medieval Writing and Thought* (Oxford: Oxford University Press, 1986), 93.

18. Jacob W. Doss, 'Making Masculine Monks: Gender, Space, and the Imagined "Child" in Twelfth-Century Cistercian Identity Formation', *Church History*, 91, no. 3 (2022), 467–8.

19. Ilana Krausman Ben-Amos, *Adolescence and Youth in Early Modern England* (New Haven: Yale University Press, 1994), 208; Deborah Youngs, *The Life Cycle in Western Europe, c. 1300–1500* (Manchester: Manchester University Press, 2006), 132; Shepard, *Meanings of Manhood*, 73–4; David Cressy, *Birth, Marriage, and Death: Ritual, Religion, and the Life-Cycle in Tudor and Stuart England* (Oxford: Oxford University Press, 1997), 288; Hurl-Eamon, 'Youth in the Devil's Service', 163.

20. Lucy Underwood, *Childhood, Youth and Religious Dissent in Post-Reformation England* (London: Palgrave, 2014), 4, acknowledges that transitions to adulthood were 'gradual and various' but does exclude married people from her source base, even if they were still chronologically young.

21. Amy M. Froide, *Never Married: Singlewomen in Early Modern England* (Oxford: Oxford University Press, 2005).

22. Youngs, *The Life Cycle*, 157; Susan D. Amussen and David E. Underdown, *Gender, Culture and Politics in England, 1560–1640: Turning the World Upside Down* (London: Bloomsbury, 2017), also show that men and women used various means to uphold their place in the patriarchal order of society.

23. For example, Barbara Ehrenreich, *The Hearts of Men: American Dreams and the Flight from Commitment* (London: Pluto Press, 1983); Michael Roper and John Tosh (eds.), *Manful Assertions: Masculinities in Britain since 1800* (Abingdon: Routledge, 1991); Nancy F. Cott, *No Small Courage: A History of Women in the United States* (Oxford: Oxford University Press, 2000); Lynn Abrams, *Feminist Lives: Women, Feelings and the Self in Post-War Britain* (Oxford: Oxford University Press, 2023).

24. Satadru Sen, *Colonial Childhoods: The Juvenile Periphery of India, 1850–1945* (New York, 2005); Field and Syrett, 'Chronological Age'; Ishita Pande, *Sex, Law and the Politics of Age: Child Marriage in India, 1891–1937* (Cambridge: Cambridge University Press, 2019).

25. Brewer, *By Birth or Consent*.

26. Michals, *Books for Children*, 81.

27. Howard P. Chudacoff, *How Old Are You? Age Consciousness in American Culture* (Princeton, NJ: Princeton University Press, 1989); Corinne T. Field and Nicholas L. Syrett (eds.), *Age in America: The Colonial Era to the Present* (New York: New York University Press, 2015); Kathryn M. Anderson-Levitt, 'The Schoolyard Gate: Schooling and Childhood in Global Perspective', *Journal of Social History*, 38, no. 4 (2005), 987–1006; Stephen Lassonde, 'Age, Schooling, And Development' in Paula Fass (ed.), *The Routledge History of Childhood in the Western World* (Abingdon: Routledge, 2013).

28. Miriam Müller, *Childhood, Orphans and Underage Heirs in Medieval Rural England* (London: Palgrave Macmillan, 2019), 59.

29. Müller, *Childhood, Orphans and Underage Heirs*, 59; Youngs, *The Life Cycle*, 127.

30. Müller, *Childhood, Orphans and Underage Heirs*, 59.

31. Joel T. Rosenthal, *Social Memory in Late Medieval England: Village Life and Proofs of Age* (Oxford: Oxford University Press, 2018); Müller, *Childhood, Orphans and Underage Heirs*, 59.

32. Müller, *Childhood, Orphans and Underage Heirs*, 59.

33. Lynn Botelho and Pat Thane (eds.), *Women and Ageing in British Society since 1500* (Harlow: Routledge, 2001), 4; Albrecht Classen (ed.), *Old Age in the Middle Ages and the Renaissance: Interdisciplinary Approaches to a Neglected Topic* (Berlin: De Gruyter, 2007), 12.

34. Irina Metzler, 'Reflections on Disability in Medieval Legal Texts: Exclusion – Protection – Compensation', in Cory James Rushton (ed.), *Disability and Medieval Law: History, Literature, Society* (Newcastle: Cambridge Scholars Publishing, 2013), 19–53; Anne Digby and David Wright (eds.), *From Idiocy to Mental Deficiency: Historical Perspectives on People with Learning Disabilities* (London: Routledge, 1997).

35. Wendy J. Turner, *Care and Custody of the Mentally Ill, Incompetent, and Disabled in Medieval England* (Turnhout: Brepols, 2013); Wendy J. Turner, 'Angry Wives of Madmen: The Economic Constraints of Families under Royal Guardianship in England' in Wendy J. Turner and Tory Vandeventer Pearman (eds.), *The Treatment of Disabled Persons in Medieval Europe: Examining Disability in the Historical, Legal, Literary, Medical, and Religious Discourses of the Middle Ages* (Lewiston, NY: The Edwin Mellen Press, 2010), 51–69.

36. Sarah Mulhall Adelman, '"How This Occurred I Cannot Say": Record-Keeping and Double Age in Nineteenth-Century New York City Orphan Asylums', *Journal of the History of Childhood and Youth*, 3, no. 15 (2022), 363–75.

37. Holly N.S. White and Julia M. Gossard, 'Considering "Double Age" in the History of American Childhood and Youth: An Introduction', *Journal of the History of Childhood and Youth*, 15, no. 3 (2022), 355–61.

38. Corinne T. Field, *The Struggle for Equal Adulthood: Gender, Race, Age and the Fight for Citizenship in Antebellum America* (Durham, NC: North Carolina Press, 2014), 7.

39. Thomas Loughran, Andrew Mycock and Jonathan Tonge, 'A Coming of Age: How and Why the UK Became the First Democracy to Allow Votes for 18-Year-Olds', *Contemporary British History*, 35, no. 2 (2021), 284–313.

40. Louise Jackson, 'The Child's Word in Court: Cases Of Sexual Abuse in London, 1870–1914' in Meg Arnot and Cornelie Usborne (eds.), *Gender and Crime in Modern Europe* (Abingdon: Routledge, 1999), 223.

41. Ishita Pande, 'Vernacularizing Justice: Age of Consent and a Legal History of the British Empire', *Law and History Review*, 38, no. 1 (2020), 267–79.

42. Nicholas L. Syrett, 'Statutory Marriage Ages and the Gendered Construction of Adulthood in the Nineteenth Century', in Field and Syrett (eds.), *Age in America*, 103–23.

43. Timothy Cole, '"Old Enough to Live": Age, Alcohol and Adulthood in the United States, 1970–1984', in Field and Syrett (eds.), *Age in America*, 238, 242.

44. John Darwin, 'Imperialism in Decline? Tendencies in British Imperial Policy between the Wars', *Historical Journal*, 23, no. 3 (1980), 657–79.

45. Chudacoff, *How Old Are You?*; Corinne T. Field and Nicholas L. Syrett, 'Introduction' in Field and Syrett (eds.), *Age in America*, 6.

46. Field and Syrett, *Age in America*, 5.

47. Loughran et al., 'A Coming of Age'; Tisdall, '"What a Difference It Was to Be a Woman"'; Frank Coffield, Carol Borrill and Sarah Marshall, *Growing Up at the Margins: Young Adults in the North East* (Milton Keynes: Open University Press, 1986), 183; Susan Hutson and Richard Jenkins, *Taking the Strain: Families, Unemployment and the Transition to Adulthood* (Milton Keynes: Open University Press, 1989), 89–90, 95, 107.

48. Jeffrey Jensen Arnett, *Emerging Adulthood: The Long and Winding Road from the Late Teens through the Twenties* (Oxford: Oxford University Press, 2004); Patrick Alexander, John Lowenthal and Graham Butt, '"Fuck It, Shit Happens (FISH)": A Social Generations Approach to Understanding Young People's Imaginings of Life after School in 2016–2017', *Journal of Youth Studies*, 23, no. 1 (2020), 109–26.

49. Bernadette Baker, 'The Dangerous and the Good? Developmentalism, Progress, and Public Schooling', *American Educational Research Journal*, 36, no. 4 (1999), 813.

50. Valerie Walkerdine, 'Developmental Psychology and the Study Of Childhood' in M.J. Kehily (ed.), *An Introduction to Childhood Studies* (New York: Open University Press, 2008), 117.

51. Edelstein, *Adulthood and Other Fictions*, 15, 126–7; Jenny Hockey and Allison James, *Growing Up and Growing Old: Ageing and Dependency in the Life Course* (London: Sage, 1993), 5; Jane Pilcher, *Age and Generation in Modern Britain* (Oxford: Oxford University Press, 1995); Botelho and Thane (eds.), *Women and Ageing in British Society since 1500*, 3.

52. John Holt, *Escape from Childhood: The Needs and Rights of Children* (Boston, MA: E.P. Dutton, 1974), 18.

53. Elizabeth Sears, *The Ages of Man: Medieval Interpretations of the Life Cycle* (Cambridge, MA: Harvard University Press, 1986); Burrow, *The Ages of Man*.

54. Mary Dove, *The Perfect Age of Man's Life* (Cambridge: Cambridge University Press, 1986), 11; Sears, *The Ages of Man*, 153.

55. Burrow, *The Ages of Man*, 2.

56. Clementine Beauvais, 'Ages and Ages: The Multiplication of Children's "Ages" in Early Twentieth-Century Child Psychology', *History of Education*, 45, no. 3 (2015), 304–18.

57. Michals, *Books for Children*, 10.

58. Chettiar, *The Intimate State*, 5.

59. Müller, *Childhood, Orphans and Underage Heirs*, 61.

60. Alexandra Shepard, *Accounting for Oneself: Worth, Status, and the Social Order in Early Modern England* (Oxford: Oxford University Press, 2015), 206.

61. Michals, *Books for Children*, 81.

62. Uday Singh Mehta, *Liberalism and Empire: A Study in Nineteenth-Century British Liberal Thought* (Chicago, IL: University of Chicago Press, 1999); Sen, *Colonial Childhoods;* Shirleene Robinson and Simon Sleight (eds.), *Children, Childhood and Youth in the British World* (Basingstoke: Palgrave Macmillan, 2016).

63. Field, *The Struggle for Equal Adulthood.*

64. Kate Fisher and Jana Funke, 'The Age of Attraction: Age, Gender and the History of Modern Male Homosexuality', *Gender and History*, 31, no. 2 (2019), 266–83.

65. Laura Tisdall, *A Progressive Education? How Childhood Changed in Mid-Twentieth-Century English and Welsh Schools* (Manchester: Manchester University Press, 2020).

66. Patrick McKearney, 'L'Arche, Learning Disability, and Domestic Citizenship: Dependent Political Belonging in a Contemporary British City', *City and Society*, 29, no. 2 (2017), 260–80; Hockey and James, *Growing Up and Growing Old*, 5.

67. Sen, *Colonial Childhoods*, 1.

68. Danielle Kinsey, 'Atlantic World Mining, Child Labor, and the Transnational Construction of Childhood in Imperial Britain in the Mid-Nineteenth Century', *Atlantic Studies*, 11, no. 4 (2014), 455.

69. Colleen A. Vasconcellos, *Slavery, Childhood and Abolition in Jamaica, 1788–1838* (Athens, GA: University of Georgia Press, 2015); Wilma King, *Stolen Childhood: Slave Youth in Nineteenth-Century America* (Bloomington, IN: Indiana University Press, 1995).

70. Tera Eva Agyepong, *The Criminalization of Black Children: Race, Gender and Delinquency in Chicago's Juvenile Justice System, 1899–1945* (Chapel Hill, NC: North Carolina University Press, 2018).

71. Sen, *Colonial Childhoods*, 33.

72. Jacob Breslow, 'Adolescent Citizenship, or Temporality and the Negation of Black Childhood in Two Eras', *American Quarterly*, 71, no. 2 (2019), 473–94.

73. Breslow, 'Adolescent Citizenship', 483.

74. Daniel T. Rodgers, *Atlantic Crossings: Social Politics in a Progressive Age* (Cambridge, MA: Harvard University Press, 1998); Alan Petigny, *The Permissive Society: America, 1941–1965* (New York: Cambridge University Press, 2009); Emily Robinson, *The Language of Progressive Politics in Modern Britain* (Basingstoke: Palgrave, 2017).

75. Robin D.G. Kelley and Stephen Tuck (eds.), *The Other Special Relationship: Race, Rights and Riots in Britain and the United States* (New York: Palgrave, 2015), 4, explores Britain as a site of 'overlapping African diasporas' of primarily first-generation immigrants in comparison to the United States.

References

Abrams, Lynn. *Feminist Lives: Women, Feelings and the Self in Post-War Britain*. Oxford: Oxford University Press, 2023.

Adelman, Sarah Mulhall. '"How This Occurred I Cannot Say": Record-Keeping and Double Age in Nineteenth-Century New York City Orphan Asylums', *Journal of the History of Childhood and Youth*, 3, no. 15 (2022), 363–75.

Agyepong, Tera Eva. *The Criminalization of Black Children: Race, Gender and Delinquency in Chicago's Juvenile Justice System, 1899–1945*. Chapel Hill, NC: North Carolina University Press, 2018.

Alexander, Patrick, Lowenthal, John and Butt, Graham. '"Fuck It, Shit Happens (FISH)": A Social Generations Approach to Understanding Young People's Imaginings of Life after School in 2016–2017', *Journal of Youth Studies*, 23, no. 1 (2020), 109–26.

Amussen, Susan D. and Underdown, David E. *Gender, Culture and Politics in England, 1560–1640: Turning the World Upside Down*. London: Bloomsbury, 2017.

Anderson-Levitt, Kathryn M. 'The Schoolyard Gate: Schooling and Childhood in Global Perspective', *Journal of Social History*, 38, no. 4 (2005), 987–1006.

Arnett, Jeffrey Jensen. *Emerging Adulthood: The Long and Winding Road from the Late Teens through the Twenties*. Oxford: Oxford University Press, 2004.

Baab-Mugeira, Catherine. 'Failure to Launch: Why So Many American Millennials Feel That Adulthood Is a Lie', *NBC News*, 8 July 2018, www.nbcnews.com/think/opinion/failure-launch-why-so-many -millennials-feel-adulthood-lie-ncna889466, accessed 17 July 2024.

Baker, Bernadette. 'The Dangerous and the Good? Developmentalism, Progress, and Public Schooling', *American Educational Research Journal*, 36, no. 4 (1999), 797–834.

Batty, David. '"Generation Sensible" Risk Missing Out on Life Experiences, Therapists Warn', *The Guardian*, 19 August 2022, www .theguardian.com/society/2022/aug/19/generation-sensible-risk -missing-out-life-experiences-therapists, accessed 17 July 2024.

Beauvais, Clementine. 'Ages and Ages: The Multiplication of Children's "Ages" in Early Twentieth-Century Child Psychology', *History of Education*, 45, no. 3 (2015), 304–18.

Ben-Amos, Ilana Krausman. *Adolescence and Youth in Early Modern England*. New Haven, CT: Yale University Press, 1994.

Benson, John. *Prime Time: A History of the Middle Aged in Twentieth Century Britain*. London: Routledge, 1997.

Blakemore, Sarah-Jayne. *Inventing Ourselves: The Secret Life of the Teenage Brain*. London: Penguin, 2018.

Botelho, Lynn and Thane, Pat, eds. *Women and Ageing in British Society since 1500*. Harlow: Routledge, 2001.

Breslow, Jacob. 'Adolescent Citizenship, or Temporality and the Negation of Black Childhood in Two Eras', *American Quarterly*, 71, no. 2 (2019), 473–94.

Brewer, Holly. *By Birth or Consent: Children, Law and the Anglo-American Revolution in Authority*. Chapel Hill, NC: North Carolina University Press, 2005.

Burrow, J.A. *The Ages of Man: A Study in Medieval Writing and Thought*. Oxford: Oxford University Press, 1986.

Chettiar, Teri. *The Intimate State: How Emotional Life Became Political in Welfare-State Britain*. Oxford: Oxford University Press, 2023.

Chudacoff, Howard P. *How Old Are You? Age Consciousness in American Culture*. Princeton, NJ: Princeton University Press, 1989.

Classen, Albrecht, ed. *Old Age in the Middle Ages and the Renaissance: Interdisciplinary Approaches to a Neglected Topic*. Berlin: De Gruyter, 2007.

Coffield, Frank, Borrill, Carol and Marshall, Sarah. *Growing Up at the Margins: Young Adults in the North East*. Milton Keynes: Open University Press, 1986.

Cohen, Patricia. *In Our Prime: The Invention of Middle Age*. New York: Scribner, 2012.

Cohen, Jeffrey Jerome and Wheeler, Bonnie, eds. *Becoming Male in the Middle Ages*. London: Routledge, 2000.

Cole, Timothy. '"Old Enough to Live": Age, Alcohol and Adulthood in the United States, 1970–1984' in *Age in America: The Colonial Era to the Present*. New York: New York University Press, 2015, 237–58.

Cott, Nancy F. *No Small Courage: A History of Women in the United States*. Oxford: Oxford University Press, 2000.

Cressy, David. *Birth, Marriage, and Death: Ritual, Religion, and the Life-Cycle in Tudor and Stuart England*. Oxford: Oxford University Press, 1997.

Darwin, John. 'Imperialism in Decline? Tendencies in British Imperial Policy between the Wars', *Historical Journal*, 23, no. 3 (1980), 657–79.

Digby, Anne and Wright, David, eds. *From Idiocy to Mental Deficiency: Historical Perspectives on People with Learning Disabilities*. London: Routledge, 1997.

Doss, Jacob W. 'Making Masculine Monks: Gender, Space, and the Imagined "Child" in Twelfth-Century Cistercian Identity Formation', *Church History*, 91, no. 3 (2022), 467–91.

Dove, Mary. *The Perfect Age of Man's Life*. Cambridge: Cambridge University Press, 1986.

Edelstein, Sari. *Adulthood and Other Fictions: American Literature and the Unmaking of Age*. Oxford: Oxford University Press, 2018.

Ehrenreich, Barbara. *The Hearts of Men: American Dreams and the Flight from Commitment*. London: Pluto Press, 1983.

Field, Corinne T. *The Struggle for Equal Adulthood: Gender, Race, Age and the Fight for Citizenship in Antebellum America*. Durham, NC: North Carolina Press, 2014.

Field, Corinne T. and Syrett, Nicholas L., eds. *Age in America: The Colonial Era to the Present*. New York: New York University Press, 2015.

Field, Corinne T. and Syrett, Nicholas L. 'Chronological Age: A Useful Category of Historical Analysis', *American Historical Review*, 125, no. 2 (2020), 371–84.

Fisher, Kate and Funke, Jana. 'The Age of Attraction: Age, Gender and the History of Modern Male Homosexuality', *Gender and History*, 31, no. 2 (2019), 266–83.

Foyster, Elizabeth. *Manhood in Early Modern England: Honour, Sex and Marriage*. London: Routledge, 1999.

Froide, Amy M. *Never Married: Singlewomen in Early Modern England*. Oxford: Oxford University Press, 2005.

Furedi, Frank. *Why Borders Matter: Why Humanity Must Relearn the Art of Drawing Boundaries*. Abingdon: Routledge, 2020.

Harris, Barbara. *English Aristocratic Women, 1450–1550: Marriage and Family, Property and Careers*. Oxford: Oxford University Press, 2002.

Heath, Kay. *The Emergence of Midlife in Victorian Britain*. Albany, NY: SUNY Press, 2009.

Herman, Barbara. 'Gen Z: Nonrebels with a Cause', *FutureVision*, 21 February 2021, https://rga.com/futurevision/articles/genz-nonrebels -with-a-cause, accessed 17 July 2024.

Hockey, Jenny and James, Allison. *Growing Up and Growing Old: Ageing and Dependency in the Life Course*. London: Sage, 1993.

Holt, John. *Escape from Childhood: The Needs and Rights of Children*. Boston, MA: E.P. Dutton, 1974.

Hurl-Eamon, Jennine. 'Youth in the Devil's Service, Manhood in the King's: Reaching Adulthood in the Eighteenth-Century British Army', *Journal of the History of Childhood and Youth*, 8, no. 2 (2015), 163–90.

Hutchinson, Ben. *The Midlife Mind: Literature and the Art of Ageing*. London: Reaktion Books, 2020.

Hutson, Susan and Jenkins, Richard. *Taking the Strain: Families, Unemployment and the Transition to Adulthood*. Milton Keynes: Open University Press, 1989.

Jackson, Louise. 'The Child's Word in Court: Cases of Sexual Abuse in London, 1870–1914' in Meg Arnot and Cornelie Usborne, eds., *Gender and Crime in Modern Europe*. Abingdon: Routledge, 1999, 222–37.

Jackson, Mark. *Broken Dreams: An Intimate History of the Midlife Crisis*. London: Reaktion Books, 2021.

Kelley, Robin D.G. and Tuck, Stephen, eds. *The Other Special Relationship: Race, Rights and Riots in Britain and the United States*. New York: Palgrave, 2015.

Kim, Whizy. 'For Millennials, the Dream of Adulthood Is Dead – And That's OK', *Refinery29*, 21 May 2021, www.refinery29.com/en-us/2021/05/10482901/millennials-adulthood-dream-money, accessed 17 July 2024.

King, Wilma. *Stolen Childhood: Slave Youth in Nineteenth-Century America*. Bloomington, IN: Indiana University Press, 1995.

Kinsey, Danielle. 'Atlantic World Mining, Child Labor, and the Transnational Construction of Childhood in Imperial Britain in the Mid-Nineteenth Century', *Atlantic Studies*, 11, no. 4 (2014), 449–72.

Lassonde, Stephen. 'Age, Schooling, and Development' in Paula Fass, ed., *The Routledge History of Childhood in the Western World*. Abingdon: Routledge, 2013, 211–28.

Loughran, Thomas, Mycock, Andrew and Tonge, Jonathan. 'A Coming of Age: How and Why the UK Became the First Democracy to Allow Votes for 18-Year-Olds', *Contemporary British History*, 35, no. 2 (2021), 284–313.

McKearney, Patrick. '*L'Arche*, Learning Disability, and Domestic Citizenship: Dependent Political Belonging in a Contemporary British City', *City and Society*, 29, no. 2 (2017), 260–80.

Mehta, Uday Singh. *Liberalism and Empire: A Study in Nineteenth-Century British Liberal Thought*. Chicago, IL: University of Chicago Press, 1999.

Metzler, Irina. 'Reflections on Disability in Medieval Legal Texts: Exclusion – Protection – Compensation' in Cory James Rushton, ed., *Disability and Medieval Law: History, Literature, Society*. Newcastle: Cambridge Scholars Publishing, 2013, 19–53.

Michals, Teresa. *Books for Children, Books for Adults: Age and the Novel from Defoe to James*. Cambridge: Cambridge University Press, 2014.

Millei, Zsuzsa. 'Temporalizing Childhood: A Conversation with Erica Burman, Stephanie Olsen, Spyros Spyrou, and Hanne Warming', *Journal of Childhood Studies*, 46, no. 4 (2021), 59–73.

Mintz, Steven. *The Prime of Life: A History of Modern Adulthood*. Cambridge, MA: Harvard University Press, 2015.

Moore, Aaron William. 'Reversing the Gaze: The Construction of "Adulthood" in the Wartime Diaries of Japanese Children and Youth' in Sabine Frühstück and Anne Walthall, eds., *Child's Play: Multi-Sensory Histories of Children and Childhood in Japan*. Berkeley, CA: University of California Press, 2017, 141–59.

Müller, Miriam. *Childhood, Orphans and Underage Heirs in Medieval Rural England*. London: Palgrave Macmillan, 2019.

Nelson, Claudia. *Precocious Children and Childish Adults: Age Inversion in Victorian Literature*. Baltimore, MD: Johns Hopkins University Press, 2012.

Niebrzydowski, Sue, ed. *Middle-Aged Women in the Middle Ages*. Woodbridge: Boydell and Brewer, 2011.

Pande, Ishita. *Sex, Law and the Politics of Age: Child Marriage in India, 1891–1937*. Cambridge: Cambridge University Press, 2019.

Pande, Ishita. 'Vernacularizing Justice: Age of Consent and a Legal History of the British Empire', *Law and History Review*, 38, no. 1 (2020), 267–79.

Petigny, Alan. *The Permissive Society: America, 1941–1965*. New York: Cambridge University Press, 2009.

Pilcher, Jane. *Age and Generation in Modern Britain*. Oxford: Oxford University Press, 1995.

Robinson, Emily. *The Language of Progressive Politics in Modern Britain*. Basingstoke: Palgrave, 2017.

Robinson, Shirleene and Sleight, Simon, eds. *Children, Childhood and Youth in the British World*. Basingstoke: Palgrave Macmillan, 2016.

Rodgers, Daniel T. *Atlantic Crossings: Social Politics in a Progressive Age*. Cambridge, MA: Harvard University Press, 1998.

Roper, Michael and Tosh, John, eds. *Manful Assertions: Masculinities in Britain since 1800*. Abingdon: Routledge, 1991.

Rosenthal, Joel T. *Social Memory in Late Medieval England: Village Life and Proofs of Age*. Oxford: Oxford University Press, 2018.

Sarner, Moya. *When I Grow Up: Conversations with Adults in Search of Adulthood*. London: Scribe UK, 2022.

Sbaraini, Ella, '"Those That Prefer the Ripe Mellow Fruit to Any Other": Rethinking Depictions of Middle-Aged Women's Sexuality in England, 1700–1800', *Cultural and Social History*, 17, no. 2 (2020), 165–87.

Schmidt, Suzanne. *Midlife Crisis: The Feminist Origins of a Chauvinist Cliché*. Chicago, IL: University of Chicago Press, 2020.

Sears, Elizabeth. *The Ages of Man: Medieval Interpretations of the Life Cycle*. Cambridge, MA: Harvard University Press, 1986.

Sen, Satadru. *Colonial Childhoods: The Juvenile Periphery of India, 1850–1945*. London: Anthem Press, 2005.

Shepard, Alexandra. *Meanings of Manhood in Early Modern England.* Oxford: Oxford University Press, 2003.

Shepard, Alexandra. *Accounting for Oneself: Worth, Status, and the Social Order in Early Modern England.* Oxford: Oxford University Press, 2015.

Smith, Kyle. 'Millennials Need to Put Away the Juice Boxes and Grow Up', *New York Post*, 21 March 2016, https://nypost.com/2016/03/21/millennials-need-to-put-away-the-juice-boxes-and-grow-up, accessed 17 July 2024.

Tisdall, Laura. *A Progressive Education? How Childhood Changed in Mid-Twentieth-Century English and Welsh Schools.* Manchester: Manchester University Press, 2020.

Tisdall, Laura. '"What a Difference It Was to Be a Woman and Not a Teenager": Adolescent Girls' Conceptions of Adulthood in 1960s and 1970s Britain', *Gender and History*, 34, no. 2 (2022), 495–513.

Turner, Wendy J. 'Angry Wives of Madmen: The Economic Constraints of Families under Royal Guardianship in England' in Wendy J. Turner and Tory Vandeventer Pearman, eds., *The Treatment of Disabled Persons in Medieval Europe: Examining Disability in the Historical, Legal, Literary, Medical, and Religious Discourses of the Middle Ages.* Lewiston, NY: The Edwin Mellen Press, 2010, 51–69.

Turner, Wendy J. *Care and Custody of the Mentally Ill, Incompetent, and Disabled in Medieval England.* Turnhout: Brepols, 2013.

Underwood, Lucy. *Childhood, Youth and Religious Dissent in Post-Reformation England.* London: Palgrave, 2014.

Vasconcellos, Colleen A. *Slavery, Childhood and Abolition in Jamaica, 1788–1838.* Athens, GA: University of Georgia Press, 2015.

Walkerdine, Valerie. 'Developmental Psychology and the Study of Childhood' in M.J. Kehily, ed., *An Introduction to Childhood Studies.* New York: Open University Press, 2008, 112–23.

White, Holly N.S. and Gossard, Julia M. 'Considering "Double Age" in the History of American Childhood and Youth: An Introduction', *Journal of the History of Childhood and Youth*, 15, no. 3 (2022), 355–61.

Youngs, Deborah. *The Life Cycle in Western Europe, c. 1300–1500.* Manchester: Manchester University Press, 2006.

Chapter 1

'Middle age' in the Middle Ages of western Europe, 1300–1500

Deborah Youngs

For several decades, historians have used age as a category of analysis to understand the culturally constructed nature of life's course in medieval Europe. This has generated a wealth of detailed studies on different age groups in villages, towns and cities across the globe. However, the concept of adulthood, and what it means to be an adult, has received far less critical attention. There are several likely reasons, reflecting various assumptions. There has been a sense that once adulthood has been reached, 'age' becomes less important as an identifier. Adulthood has been treated as unchanging: while childhood and adolescence are marked by development and old age as a period of decline, adulthood, once achieved, is a period of sameness. It is considered a period of standing still, of stasis.[1] As a result, there has been little historical analysis of adulthood as a stage and one that incorporates within itself substages or turning points, or an understanding of how individuals experience different economic, social or spiritual transitions in their lives. As a step to address this lacuna, this chapter considers medieval adulthood through the lens of one such 'sub' stage and marker of change: middle age. While work has been undertaken on entry points (age of majority for young adulthood) and on exit points in the case of old age, very little has been written on the period in the middle. In order to do so, evidence will be drawn from medieval literary sources (poetry and prose) and literary writers who reflected on the journey of life and the development of an individual's progress through it. Attention will largely focus on English sources from the fourteenth and fifteenth centuries, but the chapter will also consider several writings from across western Europe, which demonstrate some of the shared intellectual assumptions about ageing in the Middle Ages.

Historiography

Academic interest in adulthood is relatively recent across all disciplines and periods, as the Introduction to this volume has outlined, and for middle age or middle adulthood the historiography has moved in fits and starts. In the 1990s, developmental psychologists were describing middle age as the 'last uncharted territory in human development'.[2] Echoing that sentiment in *Prime Time* (1997), the historian John Benson outlined his purpose 'to rescue the history of middle age from the deadly combination of neglect and condescension with which it has been treated'. While by 2005 the picture was changing, contributors to the study *Middle Adulthood: A Lifespan Perspective* still commented that 'it seems as if the historical analysis of the concept of middle adulthood has not been of much interest'.[3] For the medieval period, where the concept of adulthood has received no such lengthy scrutiny, discussions of mature adulthood have generally appeared in studies of ageing and old age. Within the last decade there has been important work undertaken on middle age (as discussed below), although the focus has been entirely on middle-aged women.[4]

Part of the problem has lain with imprecise definitions and a lack of agreed entry and exit points. The *Oxford English Dictionary* defines middle age as 'the period of life between young adulthood and old age, now usually regarded as between about forty-five and sixty. Also figurative'. The 'now usually' is telling and acknowledges imprecision. In contemporary society the complexities are evident in uncertainties over what criteria one should use, such as chronological age (thirty-five? Forty? Fifty? Sixty? Seventy?), biological markers (reproduction/menopause?), familial or societal events (children growing up, leaving home?), or psychological approaches (how old do you feel?). Middle age has been variously described as 'defying straightforward definition', 'hard to pin down' and a 'changeling'.[5]

Nevertheless, these concerns have not prevented modern commentators recognising middle age as a distinct category of development with notable characteristics. All describe it as a period of transition, a turning point, a bridge, a liminal age. The scientist David Bainbridge, for example, described middle age as 'the time when the forces of creation and destruction compete on an equal footing'.[6] Strikingly, in the case of modern

Europe and America, middle age has regularly been judged to mark a period of decline: it is a narrative of lost youth, failing vitality and increasing trepidation with mortality. This view of midlife is often associated with 'midlife crisis', an idea commonly attributed to the psychoanalyst Elliot Jaques. In an article published in 1965, Jaques explained the midlife crisis in psychological and sociological terms as individuals tried to adjust to new and multiple responsibilities (such as family and work) on their path to a mature and independent adulthood.[7] Such an idea became popularised from the 1970s onwards in works such as Gail Sheehy's *Passages*, and is now a staple of modern publishers.[8] Yet the theory has not gone unchallenged and, in turn, has spawned an industry of those discrediting it. Its detractors have condemned it as a Western invention, a wholly male construction and a 'cultural fiction'.[9] Others, like David Bainbridge, have drawn out the advantages of middle age and the benefits of a period of plateauing for cognitive development. Alongside this academic output there has been an explosion of popular works on contemporary middle age and how individuals and groups have responded to it. Whatever it means to twenty-first-century Western society, being 'middle-aged' is a well-used descriptor.

These modern narratives have heavily influenced scholarly investigations into historical middle age. For some writers, the focus on how a particular (i.e. modern) middle age came into existence occludes other possible earlier middle ages; they simply did not exist. Hans-Werner Wahl and Andreas Kruse argued that in societies where few people reached old age and where young adults had little freedom from societal obligations, 'there was simply no need for a social construction of middle age as a separate and unique period of life'. In their view, 'people rarely considered what we would call middle age ... until around the beginning of the nineteenth century'.[10] Others see the cultural construction of midlife as a distinct stage 'originating only in the twentieth century', linked to increasing longevity and declining fertility.[11] Among modern British historians it is not so much middle age as a concept they consider a modern invention, but the ideology of midlife decline. John Benson argued that the twentieth century witnessed a transformation in how middle age was defined, when it became 'associated unambiguously with decay and collapse'.[12] If this concept of a midlife crisis came to fruition in Britain during the twentieth century, for historians like Kay Heath, its origins lay in the nineteenth century as 'midlife anxiety became fully expressed as a regular part of the life course' and as the beginning of 'an inevitable and calamitous decline'. She points out that 'midlife' first entered English-language dictionaries in 1895.[13] In other words, midlife and midlife crises are considered entirely modern inventions.

Conceptualising middle age in the Middle Ages

How then to respond as a pre-modern historian, and for a period where we lack the types of data, particularly first-hand accounts, that assist explorations of modern-day adulthood and middle age? The first point to make is that there were, of course, adults and middle-aged people in the Middle Ages. Indeed, they dominated society. It is undoubtedly true that life expectancy was low in the medieval world, and infant mortality notoriously high. Nevertheless, studies on a number of defined communities suggest that once the hazards of childhood were over, a long midlife was a real prospect. Adult life expectancy would differ greatly depending on gender and social status; for women, childbirth was a particularly dangerous time. Looking at the data for men, calculations of life expectancy made among working communities in both northern and southern England, the Italian city states and urban areas of France in the later Middle Ages indicate that those reaching their twenties could expect another three decades of life.[14] Other studies show communities filled with adults and those in middle age appear to dominate England's medieval dead. In Roberta Gilchrist's study of medieval cemeteries in England, particularly in London and York, adults (those calculated as aged twenty-six to forty-five) represented 'the largest group buried in most cemeteries'.[15] While fewer would reach old age, therefore, middle adulthood was a real probability.

The more appropriate question, then, is how these individuals were described in the Middle Ages; were they identified as a single age group? The answer is far from straightforward. Let us first consider the term 'adult', which does not appear in its modern meaning in any medieval vernacular language.[16] It derives from the Latin *adultus/a* meaning 'full grown' or mature.[17] In medieval England, where Latin was the language of the Church and government, *adultus* is found in a number of Latin texts circulating at that time. The twelfth-century historian William of Malmesbury, for example, uses it on several occasions, yet always when he is describing someone as 'growing up' or 'grown up' and never as an age descriptor.[18] This was how it was deployed when it first made its transition into European vernacular languages: a term that indicated the process of physical development had been completed.[19] It was not until the sixteenth century that 'adult' as a life-stage term entered the English language. The first known recorded use was in 1531 when Sir Thomas Elyot in *The Boke Named the Governour* referred to 'suche persones beinge nowe adulte, that is to saye passed theyr childehode as well in maners as in yeres'.[20] It is a simple explanation that classifies an adult as 'not a child' and does so in reference to both biological age ('yeres') and in terms of behaviour ('maners').

'MIDDLE AGE' IN THE MIDDLE AGES OF WESTERN EUROPE 29

That Elyot needed to gloss the word suggests he did not expect his readers to know unequivocally what he meant by 'adult'. Nevertheless, the attributes he used to define the age stage were far from new. The conceptual framing of ageing as a series of stages or age groupings was widespread in the Middle Ages. A well-known schema – drawn from the classical world – was that of the 'ages of man' (and it was almost exclusively male), which characterised life as a series of sequential stages. They numbered anywhere between two and twelve and featured in a wide range of media.[21] They reveal an awareness of ageing as a gradual process, with the accumulation or reduction of responsibilities over time. Different qualities were associated with each stage, along with corresponding age expectations. It is also worth underlining that, despite low life expectancies, medieval commentators always wrote in terms of the full life span, commonly referencing the biblical threescore years and ten. Yet, while terms such as 'infant', 'child', 'adolescent' and 'old age' were used in describing human development, it is immediately obvious that 'adult' does not appear as a fixed stage that is consistent in terminology or appearance, and the range of chronological ages selected varied considerably. As Michael Goodich noted in his study of the stages of life, 'following adolescence the pattern tended to break down'.[22]

What can be discerned, however, is a transition period between youth and old age. In writers preferring the four-stage schema, one can locate 'adulthood' as either the second or third stage of life. In the work of the Arabic philosopher and physician Ibn Sīnā (widely known to the West as Avicenna, 980–1037) it appears to be the second stage of life – those in their thirties – and described by medieval Latin translators as the *aetas consistendi*.[23] In *Les Quatre Âges de l'Homme*, written in the thirteenth century by Philippe de Novare, the adult years might be considered to span the second age *jovant* (twenty to forty) and the third *moien age* (forty to sixty).[24] In the well-known and influential six stages of Isidore of Seville (d.636 CE), it was the fourth stage *iuventus* and spanned the ages from twenty-eight to fifty, with the thirtieth year 'the time of full maturity'.[25] This was echoed in the Middle English *Stanzaic Life of Christ* where 'The ferth elde is зouth calt / From eзt & twenty to fifty' (the fourth age is called youth, from twenty-eight to fifty).[26] In discussions of seven or more ages, where short periods are associated with planets or other natural phenomena, we can look to Thomas of Cantimpré (d.1272) who called the fourth of his seven stages *robor*, reflecting the perceived strength and vigour of the age group thirty-five to fifty. A final example to note is that of the French-writing author, Jean Froissart (1337–1410), who divided the years twenty-four to fifty into three, symbolised by the sun, Mars and Jupiter, respectively.[27]

In these examples, we see an attempt to describe a process whereby young men became mature men, but not yet old. In chronological age this stage accords with modern adulthood, but it is also a 'middle' phase of life and its position in these schemas is noteworthy: it is prioritised and celebrated; it is an aspiration. Drawing on the ancient writings of Aristotle, who had promoted the theory of a person's ideal moral mean, medieval writers saw middle age as the zenith of physical and rational development.[28] It was the prime of life. Physically it was the point where the body was in balance: it had all the advantages of youth (e.g. physical excellence) and old age (e.g. wisdom) but none of their excesses and defects. The Scottish poem *Ratis Raving* described the fifth stage of life (thirty to fifty years) as the age that incorporated within itself the good parts of youth and old age: it was a time that 'ringis the perfeccioune of resone and discreccion'.[29] In ways reminiscent of later descriptions, therefore, middle age bridges youth and old age, here in terms of incorporating within itself the good elements of both. In visual depictions of the age stage it was the apex of the wheel of life or the top of an arc; it was commonly visualised as a plateau and characterised as a stable, static period, neither climbing up nor down. It was the *aetas consistendi*, the age of standing still.

Alongside stability and balance, other qualities included strength, wisdom and sobriety or, as the *Stanzaic Life of Christ* put it, 'wit & strength most studfastlie'.[30] Much emphasis was placed on independence and responsibility, which could be gained legally, economically, socially or societally. When Thomas Elyot had first used the English word 'adult' back in 1531, it was to describe those 'when they firste recyve any great dignitie, charge, or governance of the weale publike'.[31] No longer being a dependant, those in middle age were now capable of managing or helping others. This was the explanation given by some writers, like Isidore of Seville, for the use of the descriptor *iuventus* from the Latin *iuvare* ('to help') or 'youth' in English, to describe adulthood.[32] There were other terms used in English to describe these middle years between childhood/ adolescence (growing up) and old age (in decline). They included 'middel age'/'elde', 'manhood', 'mannes age', 'ful age', 'mean age' and 'prime of life'. They all suggest a belief that a mature age stage existed, which began some years after the legal age of majority had been reached. It will be seen that all the terms are positive, powerful and 'manly'.[33] It is for this reason that, visually, middle age was commonly represented by a bearded man, often a king, alongside the status symbols of swords, sceptre or money bags.

It is with evidence of this kind that scholars of medieval literature have supported a distinction between a positive 'medieval' and a negative 'modern' middle age. Both John Burrow and Mary Dove hesitated to use the term 'middle age' in their explorations of medieval poetry because of the connotations attached to the word in their contemporary English society. In the 1980s Mary Dove wrote: 'our so-called "middle age" [has] almost entirely negative associations, whereas the medieval tendency was to exalt and glory in a middle age which ... was represented as being possessed of exuberance, strength and maturity'.[34] Similarly, John Burrow believed that the 'dim and negative' twentieth-century associations of middle age could not be applied to the 'vigorous' figures witnessed in Ricardian poetry 'who were no longer young, but not yet old'.[35] Both authors were focusing on male literary figures, but it is noteworthy that those exploring the lives of medieval women similarly do so using positive terms even if they are more likely to recognise the physical ageing of the middle aged. Anneke Mulder-Bakker and Renée Nip considered the age of forty as a turning point for women when they were post-productive and post-menopausal; their book's subtitle describes them as 'wise old women', which perhaps at first suggests a decline.[36] Similarly, Sue Niebrzydowski defined middle age as the 'liminal moment in a woman's life cycle, in which she is neither young nor old'. In turning to the four stages of life, she believed a medieval woman's middle age was closer to the autumn of life than its summer because the former is 'more evocative of middle age and is characterized by a lessening but not the outright loss in power or strength'.[37] Interestingly, the focus of these studies is not on possessing physical perfection but on women undertaking new opportunities and achieving their goals. In that context, these studies show the middle age stage as positive for women, when they too came into their prime.

A period of uncertainty?

There are many other examples of the supremacy of middle age as the prime of life. They support the view that a middle stage of life existed as a concept in the pre-industrial past and adds weight to those who see a negative middle age as a modern invention. However, it was by no means the only discourse on ageing circulating in the Middle Ages.

For one, the move to a more sober and serious stage of life was not always considered in positive terms. For Europe's poets, the midpoint in life was marked by the cooling of the passions, which was an unwelcome reminder of the physical ageing process when exuberant youth became boring middle age. The lament for lost youth as a philosophical and literary motif was widespread across medieval Europe. It can be found in both medieval Arabic and Jewish literature, as well as the Romance languages.[38] Several fourteenth-century poets bemoaned the transition from young, gallant lover to sensible, responsible older man, and the internal struggles that brought. Whether writing in Welsh (Dafydd ap Gwilym) or French (Jean Froissart and François Villon), poets expressed vividly their unhappiness at finding themselves 'past it' and with it the lost opportunities for love (poetry) making.[39] They all appear to have internalised specific age expectations that determined that they should no longer act in a particular youthful way, although they are still being tempted. Here there are familiar tropes that still come through strongly in modern understandings of midlife angst as 'the time when youthful aspirations crash into mature reality'.[40] It is perhaps not surprising then that modern writers are sometimes tempted to describe a medieval poet's farewell to youth as a 'midlife crisis', one in which the narrator is full of regrets.[41] For Europe's poets, such loss of youth was (and is) clearly considered a major life stage and turning point.

The desire to push back at middle age and resist sobriety is also visible in Middle English poems where a generational clash of youth and middle age helps drive the narrative. In the *Parlement of the Thre Ages* we are presented with the differing outlooks of Youthe, Medill Elde and Elde (Youth, Middle Age and Age). While Youthe shows off his fine clothes and enjoys hunting, dancing and women, Medill Elde is more soberly dressed and voices his concerns over money and property. Whereas Youthe sees the horse for pleasure-riding, Medill Elde sees it as a draught animal. The poet's own sympathies appear more aligned with carefree Youth than avaricious Middle Age; there is an implied criticism of money as motivation. In his analysis of the poem Thorlac Turville-Petre considered Middle Age far from the prime of life and rather 'another nail in the coffin' on the route to death.[42] Middle age is therefore a stage marking the loss of freedoms and passions characteristic of younger ages, to be replaced by the 'adult' gains of resources and responsibilities. While some poets resisted the coming of sobriety, the *Parlement* and other moral tales railed against the complacency of midlifers with money and power who, not yet old, failed to consider the end of life sufficiently and the prospect of what awaited them. In *The Parlement of the Thre Ages* it is Elde (Age) who closes the poem by demonstrating that neither Youth nor Middle Age is right because nothing matters in the end if they do not reflect on, and repent for, their sins.

It was during their middle years that other real and fictional poets received their calls to repent. A notable example is provided by the fourteenth-century *Piers Plowman*, a series of dream visions in which the main character 'Will' falls asleep and meets a number of allegorical

'MIDDLE AGE' IN THE MIDDLE AGES OF WESTERN EUROPE   33

characters who instruct him in leading a good Christan life. It is at the point where he had 'completed fyue and fourty wyntre' (age forty-five) that the character 'Ymaginitif' (Imaginative) arrives to remind him to repent while there is time. Following the 'wilde wantownesse' of youth, he is urged 'To amende it in þi myddel age'.[43] Medieval spiritual and allegorical literature reminded their audiences how temptations changed over the life course, and several were considered typical for those in their physical prime. *The Mirror of the Periods of Man's Life* presents a picture of the adult male as prey to pride, anger, gluttony and lechery. At thirty, 'Ful of manhode & of myʒt', he boasts of his powers, strength and youthful abilities. At fifty, when his hair loses colour, covetousness comes calling. It is only when he reaches sixty that he laments his past indiscretions and is taunted by youth.[44] 'Manhood' (who became so named at twenty-one) in the English morality play *Mundus and Infans* similarly enjoys the peak of his power by exhibiting a range of new sins. 'Manhood mighty am I', he claims and is described by the phrase 'stiff, strong, stalworth and stout' but also as the king of Pride, Lechery, Wrath, Covetise, Gluttony, Sloth and Envy.[45] Likewise, Manhood in the *Castle of Perserverence*, who is given great honours, a name, riches and power, spends his time with friends such as Lust-liking, Folly and Backbiting while sitting high on Fortune's wheel.[46] Nevertheless, they soon receive other visitors. In didactic literature, the arrival of Conscience or Penance in midlife appears to mark a new stage in a person's development, one that comes as young adulthood recedes. In *Mundus and Infans*, the dialogue between Manhood and Conscience charts the move from Manhood's preoccupation with power in the early scenes (and years) to the more sober questioning of his soul in the later ones. In this way, the process of becoming and demonstrating manliness (virility) was linked to the progress of spiritual life (becoming virtuous).

This is a spiritual and psychological journey without fixed chronological ages and there appears an implicit recognition that people develop at different rates. While medieval writers might adopt a regular order to the stages of life, they also recognised individual choice and circumstance. There are no clear rites of passage to mark the journey through adulthood: there would be births, deaths and marriages to witness or endure and challenges in relationships, health and wealth. All could lead to personal development and greater maturity, or not. Stability itself would be tested and perhaps hard fought.

These medieval English morality tales, therefore, did not want individuals to feel they should be standing still or become stuck in their ways. Questions would be asked of them and new responsibilities would confront them. Other evidence suggests that medieval society recognised the pressures and trials of midlife. One example can be found within a collection of Latin sermons on canon law, written in Cambridge in the 1480s, where the author describes the typical career of a canon law student in relation to the three stages of youth, middle age and old age. In contrast to the youthful beginner who tries to learn and advance too quickly, those in the next stage of life – who have achieved their qualification – are less sure of themselves. To quote Donald Logan who examined the manuscript: 'the student of canon law can, in mid-life, find himself beset by a different danger: he can now become uncertain of himself, timorous, hesitant, reluctant to commit himself, vacillating intellectually from one position to another'.[47] That academic life could bring uncertainties in middle age can also be seen in the real-life example of Jean Gerson (b.1363) who became a canon of Notre-Dame de Paris in 1395 and was elected chancellor of the university. It was a post that weighed heavily on him and in 1399 (at the age of thirty-six) he underwent a spiritual crisis and attempted to resign. In 1400 he was so ill that he arranged his final will and testament, although his writings continue to show a keen, vigorous mind. Earlier that year he had written a letter reflecting on his decision to leave his post, which was rooted in his loss of confidence in academic life: he had grown sick of gossip; having to write inane sermons; working with ill-mannered men; and being forced to promote the ignorant and morally corrupt. To those who might accuse him of 'changeableness if now I so passionately flee that which I once diligently pursued, let them know that my knowledge has grown with age and experience, and my hopes have been greatly frustrated. One thing, indeed, is certain: the wise man changes his ways with the times'.[48]

Gerson feared being described as changeable, a characteristic usually associated with fickle youth (or women). Instead, he linked his decision to maturity; growing older could mean changing paths. For him, as for others, middle age was a time of possibilities. By the 1400s there was a strong literary tradition that the onset of middle adulthood marked a time of crossroads and opportunities. This saw the early thirties as a period of spiritual development. In a Christian context it was, conveniently, midway through the biblical life span of threescore years and ten, and when Christ had been crucified (thirty-three). The history of Christianity is filled with conversion stories, of (literally) damascene moments where adult lives changed; St Augustine's famous transformation and conversion to Christianity occurred in his early thirties. Indeed, Peter Brown described Augustine's *Confessions* as an 'act of therapy' for a man who was 'entering middle age' and was 'forced to come to terms with himself'. Other modern historians have taken the analysis further and been tempted to cast such spiritual acts as midlife crises. In studying adult conversions in monastic communities, for example, Constance Berman explored those who entered the monasteries 'at mid-career, or founded a new religious community after experiencing a mid-life crisis and conversion'.[49] There is a questionable assumption here that modern manifestations and terms for a life-stage event are easily transposed to pre-modern society. But what is recognised is that adulthood was far from a long period of sameness.

Outside the religious context, we also find examples of those who saw their thirties as the starting point of a new, inner journey, the point where they took stock of life thus far experienced. The Florentine poet Dante is by far the best known for embarking on his literary descent into hell 'in the middle of the journey of our life' at the age of thirty-five/thirty-six. The narrator is a man who has lost his way, in a state of despair; he no longer knows where he is going. It was Dante's journey that had influenced Elliot Jaques in his 1965 article on the midlife crisis as a period of self-assessment and reappraisal, and Dante regularly appears as an example of medieval attitudes to midlife.[50] He was not alone, however, in seeing the midlife as a point for reflection, for soul-searching. Francesco Petrarch (b.1304), the great Renaissance scholar, underwent a spiritual crisis in the early 1340s, following a close reading of the Church fathers, notably St Augustine. Indeed he seems to have cast his life to mirror that of Augustine's, for instance dating his realisation of a new perspective to 1336 when he was thirty-two, the age Augustine is said to have achieved his conversion. *The Secretum* of 1347–53, when Petrarch was in his middle years, is often viewed as the work in which he lays bare his anxiety at the prospect of change. It comprises imaginary dialogues with St Augustine where Petrarch begins questioning his pursuit of love and fame, seeing them as the goals of youth and 'empty pleasures'. Augustine advises Petrarch to 'put away the childish things of infancy; quench the burning desires of youth; think not all the time of what you are going to be and do next; look carefully at what you are now'.[51] The emphasis is on reflection as Petrarch looks back over his early life and its vigour, while the march of time and his own experience are forging a more mature vision. It charts his change of direction in life and writing: from celebrating the glories of the classical past (as a means to grow his reputation) towards a more personal, creative, moral and philosophical writing. It is a message that also comes through strongly in medieval Jewish literature where several writers saw forty as the age of transition from lust to sobriety and hence an ideal age to pursue wisdom.[52]

These voices are male, and the idea of men's lives marked by turning points, crises and conversions is well attested in a range of medieval literature.[53] Female writers, however, also borrowed from this tradition. The fourteenth-century anchoress Julian of Norwich wanted to experience sickness and suffering as part of her spiritual growth 'when I ware 30 yeare olde'.[54] The writer Christine de Pizan (b.1364) began her semi-autobiographical *Vision* around the age of forty when 'I had already finished half of my pilgrimage'.[55] She is at the midpoint in her life where she wishes to assess her reputation and sees herself as a traveller who looks back over paths trodden and ahead to the inevitable end. It was a new and transformative phase. Her *Vision* is a journey out of chaos as she traces her education and her spiritual and intellectual development. Christine's love of learning meant that she saw ageing largely in terms of intellect and reasoning. In contrast to those male writers of love poetry mentioned earlier, Christine saw youth as an immature state, riotous and reckless, with sobriety to be welcomed. Reaching the midpoint in her life meant that 'my age had brought me in due course to a certain degree of understanding'.[56] As an author, it allowed her to write the kind of serious works she had always wished to write but had been unable to do while young.[57] Christine was also well versed in the key writers of her day and the traditions on which they drew; she was inspired by Dante and Petrarch. All were consciously constructing narratives that would trace a path for others. They existed within a rich allegorical and didactic literature that warned of the need to reflect on one's journey through life. While one cannot see here the decline associated with middle age in the modern world, the possibility that a person's fortunes may go either way was well understood.

What also links Dante, Petrarch, Julian and Christine is that they had all experienced real crises before or at the point when they wrote their narratives. Christine, for instance, was writing during a period of political turmoil for France, which was on the verge of civil war. She had also faced years of adversity following the death of her husband when she had raised her family as a single mother. What further links them – and the authors of numerous books in the twenty-first century reflecting on midlife – is that they were also writing during their own middle adulthood. The lens through which we view the Middle Ages (and much of our distant past) is one almost wholly fashioned by adults. They are the ones, after all, who dominate history and direct its course. Most individuals only come to our attention in medieval documents once they have reached adulthood, and many others only when they achieved their goals in midlife. These include those who changed paths as mature adults, particularly the case of women who embarked on a new stage after child-bearing and -rearing. We can see this in the writings of holy women, when they turned their attention to a different type of creativity – and hence came to the attention of those who would later write their biographies. In 1341, when she was forty, Birgitta of Sweden went with her husband on a pilgrimage to Santiago de Compostella. It was on her return that she had her first divine vision and receive her new calling from God.[58] While unusual in her path and eventual fame, she was one of many women who embraced middle age as a new beginning.

Conclusion

This examination of middle age began by pointing out that it is a stage of adult life that continually appears elusive, with its beginning and end often in the eyes of the beholder. We can look around in the twenty-first century and see that we live in a world of multiple middle ages. Midlife identity crises rub up against those living their best life; the means to stay looking young and healthy fight for publication space alongside those individuals praised for looking as nature intended. Several processes run alongside each other that are (re)formative: a person can be both old enough and young enough depending on the context. This chapter has argued that the concept of a middle stage of life was not a modern invention, even if the terms 'adult', 'midlife' and 'midlife crisis' are later additions to the English language (and their equivalents in many other languages). Medieval society similarly had a more capacious understanding of middle age than is commonly assumed. There was a recognition that power, knowledge and responsibilities accumulated over time, and that wisdom came through experience.

Reading Middle English literature reveals some familiar concerns about decisions made, paths taken, responsibilities shouldered and the regrets carried during the middle years of life. This is why – as pointed out throughout this chapter – some modern scholars have chosen to use modern conceptions of midlife to analyse past subjects; there is a recognition of shared concerns. Nevertheless, how individuals in medieval England (and medieval Europe more broadly) actually explained these challenges to themselves and how they developed their version of middle age requires further work. How much did they adhere to the moral and spiritual tales reminding them to reflect on the passage of time? How many listened wistfully to poets recounting their younger years? While we will never achieve complete answers, by asking these questions we are more sensitive to how individuals in past times performed their adulthood and middle years, what they wanted to hold on to and what experience told them were 'childish' things they needed to put away.

Notes

1. See my earlier survey on the reasons in Deborah Youngs, 'Adulthood in Medieval Europe: The Prime of Life or Midlife Crisis?', in Isabelle Cochlin and Karen Smyth, eds., *Medieval Life Cycles: Continuity and Change* (Turnhout: Brepols, 2013), 239–64.

2. Orville Gilbert Brim, *Ambition: How We Manage Success and Failure Throughout Our Lives* (New York: Basic Books, 1992), 171.

3. John Benson, *Prime Time: A History of the Middle Ages in Twentieth-Century Britain* (Harlow: Longman, 1997), 4; Hans-Werner Wahl and Andreas Kruse, 'Historical Perspectives of Middle Age within the Life Span', in Sherry L. Willis and Mike Martin, *Middle Adulthood: A Lifespan Perspective* (Thousand Oaks, CA: Sage, 2005), 3–4.

4. Anneke B. Mulder-Bakker and Renée Nip, eds., *The Prime of Their Lives: Wise Old Women in Pre-Industrial Europe* (Leuven: Peeters, 2004); Sue Niebrzydowski, ed., *Middle-Aged Women in the Middle Ages* (Cambridge: D.S. Brewer, 2011).

5. Summarised in Patricia Cohen, *In Our Prime: The Invention of Middle Age* (New York: Scribner, 2012), 8: 'our ideas of middle age are continually evolving, which is one reason it remains elusive, a changeling with no fixed entry or end point, clinging to youth and spilling over into old age'.

6. David Bainbridge, *Middle Age: A Natural History* (London: Portobello Books Ltd., 2013), 36. For early discussions of middle age as a bridge, see, for example, Bernice L. Neugarten, 'The Awareness of Middle Age', in Bernice L. Neugarten, ed., *Middle Age and Aging: A Reader in Social Psychology* (Chicago, IL: The University of Chicago Press, 1968), 93–8.

7. Elliot Jaques, 'Death and the Mid-Life Crisis', *International Journal of Psychoanalysis*, 46 (1965): 502–14, particularly 502, 506.

8. Gail Sheehy, *Passages: Predictable Crises of Adult Life* (New York: Dutton, 1976); David Levinson, *The Seasons of Man's Life* (New York: Ballantine Books, 1979).

9. For example, Suzanne Schmidt, *Midlife Crisis: The Feminist Origins of a Chauvinist Cliché* (Chicago, IL: The University of Chicago Press, 2020); Richard A. Schweder, ed., *Welcome to Middle Age! (And Other Cultural Fictions)* (Chicago, IL: The University of Chicago Press, 1998). Summaries of the midlife crisis can also be found in: Stanley D. Rosenberg, Harriet J. Rosenberg and Michael P. Farrell, 'The Midlife Crisis Revisited', in Sherry L. Willis and James D. Reid, eds., *Life in the Middle: Psychological and Social Development in Middle Age* (San Diego, CA: Academic Press, 1999), 47–73; Ben Hutchinson, *The Midlife Mind: Literature and the Art of Ageing* (London: Reaktion Books, 2020), ch. 1; Mark Jackson, *Broken Dreams: An Intimate History of the Midlife Crisis* (London: Reaktion Books, 2021), 19.

10. Wahl and Kruse, 'Historical Perspectives', 9, 17.

11. Phyllis Moen and Elaine Wethington, 'Midlife Development in a Life Course Context', in Sherry Willis and James D. Reid, eds., *Life in the Middle: Psychological and Social Development in Middle Age* (San Diego, CA: Academic Press, 1999), 3.

12. Benson, *Prime Time*, 12.

13. Kay Heath, *Aging by the Book: The Emergence of Midlife in Victorian Britain* (Albany, NY: State University of New York Press, 2009), 1–3. See, however, Barbara Crosbie's chapter in this volume, which argues against Heath's central thesis.

14. Deborah Youngs, *The Life Cycle in Western Europe, c. 1300–c. 1500* (Manchester: Manchester University Press, 2006), 26.

15. Roberta Gilchrist, *Medieval Life: Archaeology and the Life Course* (Woodbridge: The Boydell Press, 2012), 59.

'MIDDLE AGE' IN THE MIDDLE AGES OF WESTERN EUROPE   39

16. Compare Sara Elin Roberts's exploration of Welsh terms for those 'in-between' young and old: 'Seeking the Middle-Aged Women in Medieval Wales', in Niebrzydowski, ed., *Middle-Aged Women*, 25–36, particularly 27 ('there is no precise term').

17. In classical Latin, *adultus, -a, -um* is a participial adjectival form (perfect participle passive) from the fourth principal part of the third conjugation verb *adolesco, adolescere* 'to grow'. In Britain it was found in medieval Latin sources as *adultus* = to grow up, mature: R.E. Latham, *Dictionary of Medieval Latin from British Sources*, Fascicule 1 A-B (London: Oxford University Press, 1975), 35.

18. *William Malmesbury Gesta Regum Anglorum. The History of the English Kings*, vol. 1, ed. R.A.B. Mynors, R.M. Thomson and M. Winterbottom (Oxford: Oxford University Press, 1998), for example, chs. 140, 170, 188 and 239.

19. For example, Dante Alighieri, *The Divine Comedy*, trans. Charles Singleton (6 vols., Princeton, NJ: Princeton University Press, 1970–75): *Paradiso*, VII, 58–60.

20. Thomas Elyot, *The Boke Named the Governour*, edited from the 1531 edn by Henry Herbert Stephen Croft (2 vols, London: J.M. Dent & Co., 1883), vol. 2:1 (2).

21. Elizabeth Sears, *The Ages of Man: Medieval Interpretations of the Life Cycle* (Princeton, NJ: Princeton University Press, 1986); J.A. Burrow, *The Ages of Man: A Study in Medieval Writing and Thought* (Oxford: Clarendon Press, 1986); Michael E. Goodich, *From Birth to Old Age: The Human Life Cycle in Medieval Thought 1250–1350* (Lanham, MD: University Press of America, 1989); Youngs, *The Life Cycle*, ch. 1.

22. Goodich, *From Birth to Old Age*, 143. See too Maria Cannon's chapter in this volume on adulthood and the ages of man in the early modern period.

23. Hasan Shuraydi, *The Raven and the Falcon: Youth versus Old Age in Medieval Arabic Literature* (Leiden: Brill, 2014), 35; Burrow, *The Ages of Man*, 23.

24. Burrow, *The Ages of Man*, 25.

25. Stephen A. Barney, W.J. Lewis, J.A. Beach and Oliver Berghof, eds., *The Etymologies of Isidore of Seville* (Cambridge: Cambridge University Press, 2006), XI.ii, 5.

26. F.A. Foster, ed., *A Stanzaic Life of Christ* (EETS, os, 1987), 1.126 (5).

27. Youngs, 'Adulthood', 170.

28. Burrow, *The Ages of Man*, 5–10.

29. J. Rawson Lumby, ed., *Ratis Raving and Other Moral Religious Pieces in Prose and Verse* (EETS, os, 43, 1870), 65, 70.

30. Foster, *A Stanzaic Life of Christ*, 1.126 (5).

31. Elyot, *The Boke Named the Governour*.

32. *The Etymologies of Isidore of Seville*, XI, ii, 16. For the challenges posed by the use of 'iuventus' to mean mature adulthood, particularly in its English translation, see Mary Dove, *The Perfect Age of Man's Life* (Cambridge: Cambridge University Press 1986), 15–16.

33. Dove, *The Perfect Age*, 16.

34. Dove, *The Perfect Age*, 3.

35. J.A. Burrow, *Ricardian Poetry: Chaucer, Gower, Langland and the 'Gawain' Poet* (London: Routledge, 1971), 120.

36. Mulder-Bakker and Nip, *The Prime of Their Lives*.

37. Niebrzydowski, *Middle-Aged Women*, 6.

38. Shuraydi, *The Raven and the Falcon*, 41 and ch. 4; Elisha Russ-Fishbane, *Ageing in Medieval Jewish Culture* (Liverpool: Liverpool University Press, 2022), 38–40.

39. Youngs, 'Adulthood', 171.

40. Bainbridge, *Middle Age*, 128.

41. Peter F. Dembowski, *Jean Froissart and His Melidor: Context, Craft and Sense* (Lexington, KY: French Forum, 1983), 36–9; William W. Kibler, '*Le joli buisson de jonece*: Froissart's Midlife Crisis', in Donald Maddox and Sara Sturm-Maddox, eds., *Froissart across the Genres* (Gainesville, FL: University Press of Florida, 1998), 64–6.

42. Thorlac Turville-Petre, 'The Ages of Man in "The Parlement of the Thre Ages"', *Medium Ævum*, 46, no. 1 (1977): 66–76 (p. 67).

43. Elizabeth Robertson and Stephen H.A. Shepherd, eds., *Piers Plowman* by William Langland (New York: W.W. Norton, 2006), passus XII, 3–11; Dove, *The Perfect Age*, ch. 11.

44. 'The Mirror of the Periods of Man's Life', in F.J. Furnival, ed., *Hymns to the Virgin and Christ* (EETS, os, 24, 1867), 58–78.

45. G.A. Lester, ed., *Three Late Medieval Morality Plays: Mankind, Everyman, Mundus and Infans* (London: A&C Black Ltd., 1981), *Mundus and Infans*, lines 160–287.

46. 'The Castle of Perseverance', in Mark Eccles (ed.), *The Macro Plays: The Castle of Perseverance, Wisdom, Mankind* (EETS, os, 262, 1969).

47. F. Donald Logan, 'The Cambridge Canon Law Faculty: Sermons and Addresses from Cambridge Dating to the 1480s', in M.J. Franklin and Christopher Harper-Bill, eds., *Medieval Ecclesiastical Studies in Honour of Dorothy M. Owen* (Woodbridge: The Boydell Press, 1995), 157.

48. *Jean Gerson: Early Works*, trans. Brian Patrick McGuire (New York: Paulist Press, 1998), 167.

49. Peter Brown, *Augustine of Hippo: A Biography* (Berkeley, CA: University of California Press, 1967, 2000), 157–8; Constance H. Berman, 'Monastic and Mendicant Communities', in Carol Lansing and Edward D. English, eds., *A Companion to the Medieval World* (Oxford: Blackwell, 2013), 239.

50. Dante, *The Divine Comedy: Inferno*, canto 1:1.

51. *Petrarch's Secret or The Soul's Conflict with Passion*, trans. William H. Draper (London: Chatto & Windus, 1911), 160; *Francesco Petrarca: My Secret Book*, ed. and trans. Nicholas Mann (Cambridge, MA: Harvard University Press, 2016), xv–xvi.

52. Russ-Fishbane, *Ageing*, 39.

53. Rosalynn Voaden and Stephanie Volf, 'Visions of My Youth: Representations of the Childhood of Medieval Visionaries', *Gender and History*, 12 (2000): 665–84.

54. Edmund Colledge and James Walsh, eds., *A Book of Showings to the Anchoress Julian of Norwich* (Toronto: Pontifical Institute of Medieval Studies, 1978), 289, lines 38–9 (taken from the long text). The editors suggest that Julian's desire to suffer when she was thirty derived from her wish to associate with Christ: 204, n. 46.

55. Christine de Pizan, *The Vision*, trans. Glenda McLeod and Charity Cannon Willard (Cambridge: D.S. Brewer, 2005), bk I.1, 18.

56. De Pizan, bk 111.10, 104.

57. Renate Blumenfield-Kosinski, 'The Compensations of Aging: Sexuality and Aging in Christine de Pizan with an Epilogue on Collete', in Mulder-Bakker and Nip, *The Prime of Their Lives*, 10–11.

58. Blumenfield-Kosinski, 'The Compensations of Aging', 10–11.

References

Primary sources

Alighieri, Dante, *The Divine Comedy*, trans. Charles Singleton. 6 vols, Princeton, NJ: Princeton University Press, 1970–75.

Colledge, Edmund, and James Walsh, eds., *A Book of Showings to the Anchoress Julian of Norwich*. Toronto: Pontifical Institute of Medieval Studies, 1978.

de Pizan, Christine, *The Vision*, trans. Glenda McLeod and Charity Cannon Willard. Cambridge: D.S. Brewer, 2005.

Eccles, Mark, ed., *The Macro Plays: The Castle of Perseverance, Wisdom, Mankind*. EETS, os, 262, 1969.

Elyot, Thomas, *The Boke Named the Governour*, edited from the 1531 edn by Henry Herbert Stephen Croft. 2 vols, London: J.M. Dent & Co., 1883.

Foster, F.A., ed., *A Stanzaic Life of Christ*. EETS, os, 1987.

Furnival, F.J., ed., *Hymns to the Virgin and Christ*. EETS, os, 24, 1867.

Jean Gerson: Early Works, trans. Brian Patrick McGuire. New York: Paulist Press, 1998.

Langland, William, *Piers Plowman*, edited by Elizabeth Robertson and Stephen H.A. Shepherd. New York: W.W. Norton, 2006.

Lester, G.A., ed., *Three Late Medieval Morality Plays: Mankind, Everyman, Mundus and infans*. London: A&C Black Ltd., 1981.

Lumby, J. Rawson, ed., *Ratis Raving and other Moral Religious Pieces in Prose and Verse*. EETS, os, 43, 1870.

The Etymologies of Isidore of Seville, edited by Stephen A. Barney, W.J. Lewis, J.A. Beach and Oliver Berghof. Cambridge: Cambridge University Press, 2006.

William Malmesbury Gesta Regum Anglorum. The History of the English Kings, vol. 1, ed. R.A.B. Mynors, R.M. Thomson and M. Winterbottom. Oxford: Oxford University Press, 1998.

Secondary sources

Bainbridge, David. *Middle Age: A Natural History*. London: Portobello Books Ltd., 2013.

Benson, John. *Prime Time: A History of the Middle Aged in Twentieth-Century Britain*. Harlow: Longman, 1997.

Berman, Constance H., 'Monastic and Mendicant Communities', in Carol Lansing and Edward D. English, eds., *A Companion to the Medieval World*. Oxford: Blackwell, 2013: 231–56.

Blumenfield-Kosinski, Renate. 'The Compensations of Aging: Sexuality and Aging in Christine de Pizan with an Epilogue on Collete', in Anneke B. Mulder-Bakker and Renée Nip, eds., *The Prime of Their Lives: Wise Old Women in Pre-Industrial Europe*. Leuven: Peeters, 2004: 1–16.

Brim, Orville Gilbert. *Ambition: How We Manage Success and Failure Throughout Our Lives*. New York: Basic Books, 1992.

Brown, Peter. *Augustine of Hippo: A Biography*. Berkeley, CA: University of California Press, 1967, 2000.

Burrow, J.A. *Ricardian Poetry: Chaucer, Gower, Langland and the 'Gawain' Poet*. London: Routledge, 1971.

Burrow, J.A. *The Ages of Man: A Study in Medieval Writing and Thought*. Oxford: Clarendon Press, 1986.

Cohen, Patricia. *In Our Prime: The Invention of Middle Age*. New York: Scribner, 2012.

Dembowski, Peter F. *Jean Froissart and His Melidor: Context, Craft and Sense*. Lexington, KY: French Forum, 1983.

Dove, Mary. *The Perfect Age of Man's Life*. Cambridge: Cambridge University Press, 1986.

Elliot, Jaques. 'Death and the Mid-Life Crisis', *International Journal of Psychoanalysis*, 46 (1965): 502–14.

Francesco Petrarca: My Secret Book, ed. and trans. Nicholas Mann (Cambridge, MA: Harvard University Press, 2016).

Gilchrist, Roberta. *Medieval Life: Archaeology and the Life Course*. Woodbridge: The Boydell Press, 2012.

Goodich, Michael E. *From Birth to Old Age: The Human Life Cycle in Medieval Thought 1250–1350*. Lanham, MD: University Press of America, 1989.

Heath, Kay. *Aging by the Book: The Emergence of Midlife in Victorian Britain*. Albany, NY: State University of New York Press, 2009.

Hutchinson, Ben. *The Midlife Mind: Literature and the Art of Ageing*. London: Reaktion Books, 2020.

Jackson, Mark. *Broken Dreams: An Intimate History of the Midlife Crisis*. London: Reaktion Books, 2021.

Latham, R.E., *Dictionary of Medieval Latin from British Sources*, Fascicule 1 A-B. London: Oxford University Press, 1975.

Levinson, David. *The Seasons of Man's Life*. New York: Ballantine Books, 1979.

Logan, F. Donald. 'The Cambridge Canon Law Faculty: Sermons and Addresses from Cambridge Dating to the 1480s', in M.J. Franklin and Christopher Harper-Bill, eds., *Medieval Ecclesiastical Studies in honour of Dorothy M. Owen*. Woodbridge: The Boydell Press, 1995: 151–64.

Kibler, William W. '*Le Joli Buisson de Jonece*: Froissart's Midlife Crisis', in Donald Maddox and Sara Sturm-Maddox, eds., *Froissart across the Genres*. Gainesville, FL: University Press of Florida, 1998: 63–80.

Moen, Phyllis, and Elaine Wethington. 'Midlife Development in a Life Course Context', in Sherry Willis and James D. Reid, eds., *Life in the Middle: Psychological and Social Development in Middle Age*. San Diego, CA: Academic Press, 1999: 3–23.

Mulder-Bakker, Anneke B., and Renée Nip, eds. *The Prime of Their Lives: Wise Old Women in Pre-Industrial Europe*. Leuven: Peeters, 2004.

Neugarten, Bernice L. 'The Awareness of Middle Age', in Bernice L. Neugarten, ed., *Middle Age and Aging: A Reader in Social Psychology*. Chicago, IL: The University of Chicago Press, 1968, 93–8.

Niebrzydowski, Sue, ed. *Middle-Aged Women in the Middle Ages*. Cambridge: D.S. Brewer, 2011.

Petrarch's Secret or The Soul's Conflict with Passion, trans. William H. Draper (London: Chatto & Windus, 1911).

Rosenberg, Stanley D., Harriet J. Rosenberg, and Michael P. Farrell, 'The Midlife Crisis Revisited', in Sherry L. Willis and James D. Reid, eds., *Life in the Middle: Psychological and Social Development in Middle Age*. San Diego, CA: Academic Press, 1999: 47–73.

Russ-Fishbane, Elisha. *Ageing in Medieval Jewish Culture*. Liverpool: Liverpool University Press, 2022.

Schmidt, Suzanne. *Midlife Crisis: The Feminist Origins of a Chauvinist Cliché*. Chicago, IL: The University of Chicago Press, 2020.

Schweder, Richard A., ed. *Welcome to Middle Age! (And Other Cultural Fictions)*. Chicago, IL: The University of Chicago Press, 1998.

Sears, Elizabeth. *The Ages of Man: Medieval Interpretations of the Life Cycle*. Princeton, NJ: Princeton University Press, 1986.

Sheehy, Gail, *Passages: Predictable Crises of Adult Life*. New York: Dutton, 1976.

Shuraydi, Hasan. *The Raven and the Falcon: Youth versus Old Age in Medieval Arabic Literature*. Leiden: Brill, 2014.

Turville-Petre, Thorlac. 'The Ages of Man in "The Parlement of the Thre Ages"', *Medium Ævum*, 46, no. 1 (1977): 66–76.

Voaden, Rosalynn, and Stephanie Volf. 'Visions of My Youth: Representations of the Childhood of Medieval Visionaries', *Gender and History*, 12 (2000): 665–84.

Wahl, Hans-Werner, and Andreas Kruse, 'Historical Perspectives of Middle Age within the Life Span', in Sherry L. Willis and Mike Martin,

Middle Adulthood: A Lifespan Perspective. Thousand Oaks, CA: Sage, 2005.

Willis, Sherry L., and James D. Reid, eds. *Life in the Middle: Psychological and Social Development in Middle Age*. San Diego, CA: Academic Press, 1999.

Willis, Sherry L., and Mike Martin. *Middle Adulthood: A Lifespan Perspective*. Thousand Oaks, CA: Sage, 2005.

Youngs, Deborah. *The Life Cycle in Western Europe, c. 1300–c. 1500*. Manchester: Manchester University Press, 2006.

Youngs, Deborah. 'Adulthood in Medieval Europe: The Prime of Life or Midlife Crisis?', in Isabelle Cochlin and Karen Smyth, eds., *Medieval Life Cycles: Continuity and Change*. Turnhout: Brepols, 2013, 239–64.

Chapter 2

'The most constant and settled part of our life'?: Adulthood and the ages of man in early modern England

Maria Cannon

Introduction

The first use of the term 'adult' in English, according to the *Oxford English Dictionary*, was in *The Boke named The Governour* by Thomas Elyot, published in 1531. He described adults as 'soche persons ... passed theyr childehode'.[1] The term 'adult' was rarely used by writers in early modern England, but the concept of an adult life stage was understood, usually in terms of 'perfect', 'ripe' or 'full' age. The ages of man was a long-established model of 'universal, ahistorical and asocial' stages that set out an ideal life course in medieval Europe, as examined by Deborah Youngs in the previous chapter.[2] Life could be separated into any number of stages between three and twelve, with a seven-age scheme becoming more popular by the sixteenth century, perhaps most famously outlined by Shakespeare in the 'All the world's a stage' monologue from his late sixteenth-century comedy play *As You Like It*. The sixteenth century also saw a change in visual depictions of the ages of man from a wheel of stages to steps.[3] These steps represented life as a climb from birth and childhood to the pinnacle of adulthood before declining to old age and death. This chapter analyses ages of man texts and images to examine what those continuing to explore the ages of man tradition in sixteenth- and seventeenth-century England understood as the key features of adulthood. Elyot's definition of the newer term 'adult' as any person no longer a child reflects the complexity of thinking about how people moved through the life course. Adulthood could be seen as a pinnacle or perfect age, but could also incorporate a range of experiences as people moved out of their childhoods but still grew and changed.

Historians of youth and of family have followed Elyot's definition of adulthood as the stage that follows childhood, and considered the transition to adulthood in some depth.[4] Marriage is often singled out as a rite of passage that conferred adult status on men and women in early modern England, usually in conjunction with setting up an independent household.[5] Beyond this, historians do not generally consider the life stage of adulthood past this entry point. They frequently discuss the lives of adults in research on gender, family life and economic activities but do not always consider these experiences in the context of age.[6] Historians of the life cycle have spent more time on smaller divisions of other life stages, for example separating childhood into infancy, childhood and youth, or old age into 'green' and 'decrepit' or 'functional/chronological/cultural', than on the changes experienced by people between youth and old age.[7] Discussions of marriage and parenting stand in for research on adulthood even as historians acknowledge that not all adults took on these roles.[8] This chapter will begin by outlining some of the key features and activities associated with adulthood and then consider how the variety of ages of man schemes allowed for a nuanced understanding of what it meant to move through the life course in early modern society.

Ages of man schemes have been noted by many historians as exclusive – the phrase really did mean men for the majority of writers and artists.[9] This raises the question of whether a history of adulthood through these sources is, in fact, the same as a history of masculinity. Alexandra Shepard has written extensively about the relationship between masculinity and patriarchy in early modern England.[10] While the 'estate' of manhood was associated with adult age, she argues that marital status 'transcended hierarchies of age' in the according of status and privilege for men.[11] Adulthood and manhood were linked but should not be used interchangeably. This chapter will conclude by considering the inclusion of women in ages of man schemes and demonstrate that women could be included both as essential partners for adult men and for their own experiences of growth and development through the life course.

'Adulthood' as a stage of man's life

The nature of ages of man schemes was that they saw life as divided into equal segments, therefore adulthood was described and theorised equal to other stages. Writers and illustrators considered ageing from a variety of perspectives, often drawing on classical ideas and theories. Humorism was an enduring theory that explained the composition of the human body as balanced between the four humors: blood, phlegm, black bile and yellow bile. It also stated that the body could be at different levels of heat or cold, and of dryness or wetness. Ideally a body should be kept in a healthy balance, but this balance varied depending on a number of factors including age and gender. Classical scholar Henry Cuffe explained in his 1607 publication *The Differences of the Ages of Man's Life* that ages of man schemes set out by ancient thinkers were all based on this humoral understanding of the body.[12] Adulthood was the stage of life where the humors were at their most perfect balance:

> The next [stage] is our flourishing and middle age, and this is, when a man is come to the highest degree of perfection in the temper of his body ... without any notorious decay or im-pairing his heat, supplying the just quantity of moisture.[13]

Adult men had a good balance of heat and dryness compared to children (warm but moist) and the elderly (cold and moist). Adulthood was also associated with summer and the sun, as the four seasons were part of humoral theory. Thomas Fortescue, in a translation of a work by Spanish humanist writer Pedro Mexia, described this as follows:

> Of this Age the Sunne is chiefe Lorde and Governour ... This Age is the moste perfectst, and most excellent of the others, it is the bewtie and flowre of mans life. Duringe this Age, the forces and powres, bothe of the understandinge, and bodie, acquire, and retaine their vertue, and vigor. Man therefore in this time, well advised and hardy, becometh skilfull to knowe and choose, that is good for him, he seeketh and searcheth Honour and Ritches, he laboreth to be accompted greate and renowmed, he busieth him selfe in laudable and vertuous Actions.[14]

Adult men were well balanced in body and mind, thus they had the ability to embody the highest ideals of virtue and success. As can be seen here, one of the appealing aspects of humorism was that it could be used to explain many aspects of life and the natural world, so it offered a comprehensive explanation of the physical and behavioural expectations around ageing.

Physically, adulthood was associated with the apex of bodily health, largely measured by internal energy and aptitude. One of the only outwardly visual markers of male adulthood noted is the beard. Will Fisher argues that the beard was 'one of the primary ways in which masculinity was materialized' and 'therefore not simply a "secondary" sexual characteristic'.[15] He argues that growing a beard was so tied to masculinity that young boys were viewed as a different gender to men. Eleanor Rycroft considers this in the context of the early modern stage, suggesting that having a beardless boy play a female character was not a huge imaginative leap for the audience.[16] Indeed, the men in Shakespeare's 'All the world's a stage' fourth and fifth stages of life are described as having beards. Conduct literature also supports Fisher's statement that beard growth was the main visual marker of adult masculinity, for example German writer Hermannus Schottennius in a translation in 1566:

> The fifth age is called mannes age, when as a man is growen to his full rype age, and that his body is past growth, & his beard buddeth from out his chinne.[17]

And R. Hoper, published in 1580:

> at this time, both the person, age, and body of man is now fullye ripe and growen up: so that it hath ceassed to grow any further in youthfulnes: and that also the beard hath now appeared on his Chinne.[18]

These readings do not support the idea that adult men were perceived as a different gender to boys as these descriptions refer to the development of male youths into adult men, but it does appear that beards were a universal symbol of adulthood for men. A set of late sixteenth-century engravings of a five-age stage of life, copied from Dutch painter and architect Hans Vredeman de Vries (Figure 2.1), depicts the age range of thirty-two to forty-eight as its third stage. The men all have beards and wear doublets and breeches, clothing items associated with younger men. Catherine Richardson states that middling-sort men were likely to own fashionable and ceremonial clothes, with longer robes as more appropriate for carrying out civic responsibilities.[19] The man at the front of the image who is engaged in teaching or instructing children wears a longer robe. Civic responsibility would have increased with age so a longer robe could indicate an older man.

Adult men were the most capable of reasoned judgement as they were understood to be able to control their anger and desire more effectively than youths. Thus, they were well suited for heading households, state and military leadership, and setting an example to younger and older generations. Legally, men were seen as 'of ripe age' at twenty-one but generally the 'perfect' age of man was deemed in the thirties/forties. Adult men were linked by various writers with the Latin term 'vir', with its connotations of virility and virtue; a person with the bodily state to practise virtuous behaviour. Heroes of classical stories like Aeneas were the embodiment of the potential of adulthood for men as they had a natural

Figure 2.1. Ages of man: third stage, from the age of thirty-two to forty-eight, and the classical orders of architecture: ionic. Engraving by J. Wierix, 1577, after J. Vredeman de Vries. Wellcome Collection. © Source: Wellcome Collection.

combination of bravery and wisdom that enabled them to 'shoulder the burdens of leadership'.[20] Older men gained even more wisdom through their life experiences but sound judgement was linked to the strength of the body and other natural forces that were subject to decline as the body was.[21] Adult men were at an ideal stage of life to head society as they had both physical and mental strength, where older or younger men often had to prove they could transcend their age stage to display these qualities.[22] Alexandra Shepard argues that this 'othering' of youth and old age 'illustrates the importance of age as a determinant of early modern hierarchies of masculinity'.[23] Emily E. Robson's chapter in this collection demonstrates that the spiritual maturity of Protestant ministers could follow a different course and be associated with older chronological ages, albeit drawing on the language of youth and rejuvenation.

The adults in the De Vries images are distinguished by their activities, some of which correspond with the expected qualities of adult men set out in written ages of man texts, for instance Fortescue's 'laudable and vertuous Actions'.[24] The men of the third age are engaged in various activities that require reason and wise judgement, including the man instructing children, a married man talking to his wife and the military men standing guard over the scene. The Latin inscription indicates that this age is 'full of labours'. The couple are holding hands and talking, not kissing or embracing, so it seems they are intended to depict a more mature partnership of householders rather than young lovers. While those teaching and instructing are in the foreground, there are indications of violence in this scene. Background figures are engaging in sword-fighting, a man on horseback appears to be presiding over executions and a man looks to be under threat of theft or harm from a group of armed men. Men seem to be responsible for ensuring the policing of crime, but also capable of criminality themselves. This criminal and state-sponsored violence is almost completely absent from De Vries's fourth age depiction of men aged forty-eight to sixty-four years, except one ceremonially dressed soldier, and from the second age of men aged sixteen to thirty-two, except two men engaged in sword-fighting practice. This suggests that, although adult men were considered to have grown further into a state of rationality and wisdom, the balance of reason and physical strength could result in violence and the potential for criminality.

Adulthood as a stage had the potential for the ideal balance of humors, and of strength and wisdom, but the human body and mind did have potential for imbalance dependent on individual circumstance and experience. Karen Raber and Stephanie Tarbin assert that life-cycle texts 'intended to confer a degree of self-knowledge on individuals, giving them markers by which to measure themselves; [and] establish a set of common expectations for human beings as they negotiate the challenges of growing into adulthood, and then old age'.[25] This was certainly the case, but the above analysis demonstrates that texts did not skip over the stage of adulthood as one of growth and challenge. Even if idealised, these descriptions set out expected behaviour and activities for adult men, as well as hinting at the consequences for deviating from the ideal. A 'perfect' age was possible for adult men, but it was not inevitable that everyone would achieve it.

Achieving perfection? Adulthood as a stage of change and development

Many ages of man schemes allowed for adulthood to be seen as the pinnacle or 'prime' age of life, especially those with an odd number of stages, for example the simple three-age system – childhood, adulthood, old age. When early modern writers discussed the three or four age stages put forward by ancient thinkers like Aristotle and Pythagoras, they acknowledged that there were stages within these stages, and generally preferred seven-age schemes.[26] The 'perfect age', if it did exist at all, was not a lengthy stage of life, perhaps ten years, usually in the thirties. So this means that there were experiences of being an adult (a young adult and an older adult) that did not fit into this 'perfect age' neatly. Adult behaviour and experiences developed over a longer span of chronological age. In the De Vries images, the third age has a sense of continuity with the second and fourth ages as the men take part in similar activities and wear similar clothes. The engraving of the second age shows people aged sixteen to thirty-two engaging in various activities, mostly artistic – sculpting, music, painting, reading – but also sword-fighting, which is echoed in the depictions of fighting and criminal violence in the third-age image.[27] The educational activities of the second age are commensurate with youth but seem to be self-directed, unlike the children who are being educated by adults in the third-age picture. In the fourth age men continue to read and engage in discussion. The soldier in the foreground continues to echo the soldierly activities of men in the third age.[28]

This is a more unusual five-age depiction that marks the boundaries between age stages at different places. Writers acknowledged the confusion of different numbered schemes, for example Geffray Fenton who debated the value of the popular seven ages against the six ages posited by Isidore of Seville in Isidore's much-referenced and translated work on the ages of the world from the seventh century.[29] Fenton commented that Isidore's scheme did not separate virility (adult manhood) from youth as other writers did and so had the stage of 'youth' starting later at age twenty-nine.[30] Fenton preferred a three-age scheme but acknowledged smaller stages within those three ages.[31] Henry Cuff also acknowledged multiple stages of adulthood:

> the first is our youth, (for so the penurie of our English toong warranteth me to call it) when our growth is staied, and our naturall heat beginneth to be most flourishing; you may call it our Prime ...; it lasteth from the fiue and twenti-eth to the fiue and thirtieth or fortieth yeere of our life: the second part of our middle age, is our Manhood, the most constant and setled part of our life, as having our life-qualities most firme and in greatest mediocritie, wherein notwithstanding our naturall heat beginnes a little to decay and decline from its vigour; yet so, as it cannot by sense be perceived, and this lasteth oftentimes till we be fiftie yeeres old.[32]

He saw the 'prime' of life as a short one lasting between ten and fifteen years, but acknowledged youth and manhood as similar experience to this 'prime'. Although covering fifteen years between ages thirty-two and forty-eight, De Vries similarly describes his third age as 'short and swift'.[33] Cuff's theory relied on the understanding of balance that could be achieved as men reached adulthood. The 'prime' age was one of full bodily strength but 'greatest mediocrity', a positive description within humoral theory that saw balance as an ideal state, was reached in the following stage of 'manhood'. While the body began to decline in this stage, this decline was not yet evident and so men had the capacity to live in an ideal balanced and settled state. For Cuff, perfection appeared to apply only to physical strength in the stage he terms 'youth'.

Cuff's assertion that the English term 'youth' is not the ideal word to describe the young adult stage and Fenton's criticisms of Isidore's description of youth lasting until age fifty are likely comments on the ineffectual translation of the Latin *juventus*, which does indicate young chronological age but perhaps not as much as the English word 'youth' implies. As noted in the previous chapter, this was an unresolved issue from the medieval period where writers also struggled with their translations.[34] The same problem applied to the translation of the Latin *senectus* which translates most closely in English as an old man and in a three-age stage came directly after *juventus*. William Vaughan took issue with age schemes that too easily described men as old. When writing about the 'sixth age' that usually described men aged fifty to sixty-two, he stated that 'this age is termed (although improperly) old age'.[35] He considered this stage as more closely related to prime or manhood than old age in terms of shared qualities of moderation and temperance. Mary Dove suggests that men who described a 'stepping-stone' age between *juventus* and *senectus* were aiming to smooth over the transition between youth and old age and reassure men that the course of life 'would be a steady and measured progress'.[36] Those who wrote about a transitional age – usually forty to fifty – stressed the virtues of wisdom and moderation that men of this age continued to possess even though they had begun to decline physically.[37] It is perhaps worth noting that some writers would have been approaching this age stage themselves when writing these texts, for example Cuff was in his late thirties and Fenton likely in his mid-thirties when they chose to write about the topic of ageing.[38]

The imprecise nature of these translated terms meant that sometimes writers used the same terms to describe different age stages, for example youth and manhood could both be compared to the season of summer. And it is not always clear if youth or manhood/prime age was seen as the pinnacle of life. Authors known only as W.B. and E.P. describe the fourth age as formed of young men aged twenty-two to thirty-four who had begun 'to know he is a man' as they learned reason and discretion and exhaled 'the thicke mists of ignorance and follie' but describe the fifth 'virile or man's age' as one of decline where 'man begins to bee covetous, churlish, cholerick'.[39] Their seven-age scheme thus does not appear to have a pinnacle at all. As already seen, Cuff's work is unclear in its descriptions of two stages of adulthood: youth and manhood. He describes youth in terms of summer 'for that growen strength of the body and minde' and 'man-age' as autumn because 'the good giftes and indowments of our minde ... receive a kind of seasonable and timely ripeness'.[40] So although summer could be viewed as the prime and 'flowering' or 'flourishing' stage of adulthood, autumn was the 'ripening'. Both stages of adulthood could be described positively in this way and seen as a progression of learning and development.

These texts suggest that adulthood was not a period of sameness but one of change and growth. The links between different life stages can be seen in some of the steps-of-life imagery popular from the sixteenth century onwards. In an Italian engraving of nine age stages (Figure 2.2), the middle three 'adult' figures all engage with each other as if connected

Figure 2.2. The ages of man represented as a step scheme. Reproduction of an engraving by C. Bertelli. Wellcome Collection. © Source: Wellcome Collection.

by their life experiences. The fourth-step military figure looks up at the statesman-like figure seated on the fifth step. The sixth-step figure is clearly in decline and has an hourglass next to him as a reminder. He seems to be looking back to the fourth figure, suggesting that the fourth stage between youth and manhood is in fact the perfect age, not the man at the pinnacle of the steps. Research on the behaviour of young men reflects the overlap many would have experienced between their youth and adult life stages when they were functionally adults in their capacity for work but had not achieved all the markers of adulthood like marriage or political authority.[41] Rachel Moss describes adolescence in the fifteenth century as a 'significant life cycle stage' when youths 'were expected to be laying the foundations of their adult lives' but also indulging 'in activities particular to their age'.[42] The adolescents she refers to are largely unmarried men in their twenties who could have been considered adults, or certainly close to adult in their ability to work and relocate independently. Historians of male youth culture have noted that men who had achieved the adult marker of becoming a patriarchal householder, and thus considered in their 'prime age', continued to engage in youthful masculine behaviours, for example alehouse socialising and misogynistic humour.[43] Ages of man descriptions, although idealised texts aimed at providing moral ideals for men, included an awareness of the personal development young men should aim for.

At the other end of the adult stage, men who were past their physical 'prime age' could be seen at their most suited to taking on significant roles of authority and civic responsibility, having had more time to learn the qualities associated with adult masculinity. For Shakespeare, it was during the fifth age of seven that man took on the role of the wise 'justice', a development from the fourth-age 'soldier' who had a more volatile temperament: 'jealous in honor, sudden and quick in quarrel'. The men in De Vries's fourth age aged forty-eight to sixty-four – past their 'prime' but by no means in the decrepit elderly stage – engage in multiple activities including instructing a soldier, reading and discussion, and using scientific instruments. Writers did warn of the dangers of old men who continued to behave youthfully. Puritan minister John Reading's published sermons on ageing explained that this was understandable, as for many physical signs of old age might arrive unexpectedly: 'clouded with pleasures and businesse, ... when it seemeth farre off, it layeth hand on vs'.[44] This unexpected advance to old age, while men were busy with the adult concerns of both 'pleasures and businesse', explained why there were 'so many youthfull old men' who had not 'put off our youthfull mind' and indicates the blurred line between the positive mental qualities of adulthood and the negative physical deterioration of old age.

Despite focusing on ideals, ages of man texts acknowledged that positive development in adulthood was not inevitable. In a 1700 publication, John Bunyan cited the common (and 'perhaps true') saying that 'he who is not Handsome at Thirty, nor Strong at Forty, nor Wise at Fifty, will never be either Handsome, Strong or Wise', demonstrating both the ideal qualities of these ages and the sense that those qualities would endure through the rest of the man's life, or not.[45] For Reading, one key aspect of adulthood was to form 'the foundation of a comfortable old age', demonstrating an understanding that adulthood was a time of necessary development as one moved through the life course, but warning that wickedness in youth would endure through life. He also noted similarities across life stages for individuals, including how 'young men blame the aged for speaking much when their owne eares itch to be running out into their tongues'.[46] Although there were identifiable qualities associated with ideal adulthood for early modern writers, it was not always clear exactly what age range or stage they applied to. The overlapping terms and descriptions appear to reflect the understanding that even the ideal life course was one where development and experience could be complex.

Ages of woman?

In the majority of ages of man schemes, 'man' is not an inclusive term. As has been seen so far, they were idealised depictions used to understand the ageing process and instruct on how best to navigate it, but they were almost always aimed at understanding and instructing men. Humoral theory was behind many of the descriptions of ageing and women had a different humoral balance to men. Cuff explained as follows:

> the male according vnto Aristotle in euerie kinde almost, is by nature better fitted for long life than the female, hauing greater force of heat, and the moisture more firm & better able to resist than the fluid substance of the female; and thence it is that women for the most part are sooner perfected than men, being sooner fit for generation, sooner in the flower and prime of their age, and finally, sooner old, for their heat though little, yet sooner preuaileth ouer that fluid thinne substance and moisture of theirs, than it possibly can ouer that solid and compact humiditie which is in man.[47]

Women's colder and wetter balance of humors meant that they reached adulthood and old age earlier than men. As Philippa Maddern and Stephanie Tarbin have noted, men and women were most alike at the age extremes of the life cycle, in the wetter and cooler stages of infancy and old age.[48] It was the stage of adulthood where men and women were physiologically most different, and so women are explicitly not included in many ages of man schemes.

The way women's biological experiences shaped their lives has been a focus for some historians seeking alternative ways of schematising the female life cycle and offering an alternative 'ages of woman'. Sara Read uses 'occasions of bleeding', including first menstruation and postpartum flow, to conceptualise the female life cycle, stating that these biological experiences were significant as transitional stages in sociocultural experience.[49] This reflects writing about women by men in the early modern period; for example, Cuff's quote above references the humoral balance of women that meant they were 'fit for generation' sooner than men. However, in the De Vries engravings, the third age of thirty-two to forty-eight includes a woman breastfeeding an infant and surrounded by other small children, suggesting that marriage and childrearing would take place at a similar age for women and men.

The 'close association' between women's biology and their culturally idealised roles as wives and mothers has also led historians to consider female life cycles in uxorial terms – daughter, wife, widow.[50] The justification of this approach is often that woman's status as daughter, wife or widow was a significant factor shaping her life experience, even more so than the associated bodily experiences.[51] Research has highlighted how crucial marriage was for the lives and careers of women of different social ranks.[52] Tim Reinke-Williams has combined these approaches and shown that women's concerns about their physical appearance were closely connected to the life cycle, especially when linked to securing marriage.[53] However, solely considering women in the context of marriage and childbearing creates a separate life cycle for them, ignoring any possible similarities to the life cycle of men.

Marriage was a significant moment in attaining full adult status for men, as well as women. Youngs describes it as 'close to a universal rite of passage' in late medieval Europe.[54] Ideal qualities of male adulthood were also the ideal qualities of a husband and householder. Some depictions of the ages of man include women and indicate this shared aspect of ideal adulthood. In an engraving by German artist Paul Fürst depicting the three ages of man, although the childhood images depict two boys playing, the adulthood and old age images show couples; the younger couple embracing and the older couple dining together.[55] As already noted, the De Vries image of the third age depicts a man and woman who look to be in a marital partnership, walking together (although it does seem to be the man who is talking). Even if the women are not the

'THE MOST CONSTANT AND SETTLED PART OF OUR LIFE'?   57

primary focus of this ages of man scheme, it is clear that men's relationships with women were key to their experience of adult life.

The children's textbook *Orbis Sensualium Pictus*, written by Czech educationalist John Amos Comenius in 1658 and translated into English the following year by cleric and teacher Charles Hoole, includes a seven-step ages of man scheme depicting both sexes at each stage. Apart from the stage of infancy, represented by a single infant in a crib, each step has a male and female figure with corresponding descriptions. Stage four, the top of the step, is represented by the 'young man' and 'maid', with the fifth step held by simply 'man' and 'woman'. These distinctions are largely drawn from the gendered Latin terms 'iuvenis' and 'vir' for men and 'virgo' and 'mulier' for women. It is only on the top step where the young man and maid interact with each other by holding hands in a courting-lovers pose typically associated with this stage. But the parallels drawn between men and women in schemes such as this indicate the possibility for women to be included and their journey through the life course seen on comparable terms.

This chapter has considered the question of how far the 'perfect' age of a man's life corresponded with adulthood. It is also possible to ask this question of the more limited depictions of women's life cycles. Mary Dove argues that a 'perfect' age was one that only men could achieve.[56] Indeed, according to humoral theory, women were never able to achieve the perfect balance that men could, but they could still reach a perfect age for their sex. Cuff refers to women being 'sooner perfected than men'.[57] Nicholas Culpepper indicates that women's 'ripe' age was after they had begun menstruation and thus were fertile.[58] This also indicates a younger age of 'perfection' than anticipated for men. However, as has been seen, when writers considered the transitional stages from youth to adulthood and the qualities that made up an ideal adult man, there was not complete agreement on whether the younger adult or older adult stage was the most 'perfect'. Authors and artists varied on this depending on the number of age stages they chose. For the step-age system put forward by Comenius, the top step was occupied by a youthful man and woman. This suggests a similar degree of nuance from writers considering the qualities that constituted adulthood for women as well.

Similarly to men, women did not move straight from their 'perfect' age with its associations of youth and fertility to old and decrepit. Historiography on women and the life cycle in medieval and early modern England reflects the experience many had of adulthood as a stage that included biological and cultural changes, and some historians have used the term 'middle aged' to indicate this moment in the female life cycle. Niebrzydowski's work on the Middle Ages states that women's middle age was understood to 'be marked by the loss of beauty and fertility, and the onset of sterility and the menopause', but acknowledges that this might begin in 'the latter part of one's summer time' in accordance with a four-age ages of man scheme.[59] When considering female perceptions of their own physical attractiveness across the life cycle in the seventeenth century, Reinke-Williams considers stages where women were in their twenties and looking to secure marriages and forties when they began to experience physical signs of ageing as significant moments.[60] This suggests a middle period for women in their thirties, and perhaps a pinnacle where they had achieved the main marker of adulthood as married women, but did not yet look old, similar to Cuff's description of men whose natural heat had declined but 'it cannot by sense be perceived'.[61] However, it would seem premature by contemporary descriptions of adulthood to describe women in their forties as 'old'. As Reinke-Williams notes, women began to notice and seek remedies for physical and mental ageing at around this age, and this suggests a change that adult women experienced as part of this stage of life.

Thus, women also underwent a transitional stage of later adulthood when they began to notice the signs of ageing, but were not really considered to be old. Ella Sbaraini defines middle age for women in the eighteenth century as between the ages of thirty and fifty, especially sexually, as they 'were often seen as not as attractive as they once were, yet neither were they old or undesirable'.[62] These women were ideally 'settled' as wives and mothers, and thus clearly adults, in much the same way as men moved through their adulthoods by gaining wisdom and experience as householders. Of course, not all women were wives and mothers, as not all men were husbands and fathers, but the existence of multiple stages of adulthood, or an in-between adult stage between youth and elderly, indicates that adulthood was a stage of life where men and women acquired qualities and capabilities to ensure they were the age group most appropriate for taking responsibility at home and in wider society.

Conclusion

Male adulthood in early modern England was characterised by qualities of reason and strength. By around the fourth decade of life, men's bodies were deemed to be in their perfect state and they had acquired sufficient wisdom and virtue to take on and excel at important societal roles. They had crucially grown out of the sins of youth like lust and vanity, but not yet begun to physically decline. While each stage of the ages of man was presented as static and with a set of fixed characteristics, the existence of multiple age schemes reveals that writers and artists understood change, progress and decline as features of adulthood. Ages of man schemes were divided equally so those who chose to separate into more than three or four stages acknowledged several stages of adulthood that a man could move through. Women featured alongside men as they fulfilled their adult roles of husbands and householders, but could also be seen to have a separate journey through adulthood and a different moment of 'ripe' or 'full' age. Change and growth defined this stage as much as earlier or later stages.

The increasing visual emphasis on adulthood as the pinnacle of man's life in visual depictions of 'the steps of life' indicates a shift in thinking about adulthood in the sixteenth century. Walsham's recent work on generations highlights that while 40–50 per cent of England's population was under the age of twenty-one, society was also gerontocratic where obedience to elders was expected.[63] In this context, it is not surprising that there was an interest in giving young men an ideal to look towards for moral guidance. Shepard argues that patriarchal privileges were increasingly related to 'distinctions of social position rather than divisions of age or marital status' by the mid-seventeenth century, which perhaps explains the examination of the qualities of men at all stages of adulthood.[64] Men *could* achieve 'fullness' in body and spirit but were not automatically entitled to the associated privileges. Alexandra Walsham's work on age, generation and the Reformation highlights the 'complex interconnections between the spiritual life cycle and its biological counterpart', as those following the new, Reformed faith might see themselves as spiritual children who needed, and wanted, to develop their spiritual understanding.[65] As Robson shows in this collection, spiritual maturity could certainly be achieved later in life.[66] This research supports the interpretation of adulthood as a period of potential growth or decline dependent on individual action as presented by the early modern English writers discussed here.

The impact of demographic change and new spiritual outlooks makes the sixteenth and seventeenth centuries an interesting moment at which to consider what it meant to be an adult. Indeed, these social and cultural changes led to the coining of the term adult itself. For writers and illustrators, the concept of the ages of man provided a flexible framework to debate and explore exactly how one might change and grow in the identity of adulthood, setting a moral example for those taking on positions of responsibility in an ever-changing society.

Notes

1. 'adult, adj. and n.'. *OED Online*. June 2021. Oxford University Press. www.oed.com /view/Entry/2821?isAdvanced=false&result=1&rskey=vcsmQc& (accessed 22 August 2021).

2. Deborah Youngs, *The Life Cycle in Western Europe, c. 1300–c. 1500* (Manchester: Manchester University Press, 2006), 34.

3. Elizabeth Sears, *The Ages of Man: Medieval Interpretations of the Life Cycle* (Princeton, NJ: Princeton University Press, 1986), 153.

4. Ilana Krausman Ben-Amos, *Adolescence and Youth in Early Modern England* (New Haven, CT: Yale University Press, 1994); Henry French and Mark Rothery, '"Upon your entry into the world": Masculine values and the threshold of adulthood among landed elites in England 1680–1800', *Social History*, 33, no. 4 (2008), 402–22; Jennine Hurl-Eamon, 'Youth in the devil's service, manhood in the king's: Reaching adulthood in the eighteenth-century British army', *Journal of the History of Childhood and Youth*, 8, no. 2 (2015), 163–90; Rachel E. Moss, 'An orchard, a love letter and three bastards: The formation of adult male identity in a fifteenth-century family' in John Arnold and Sean Brady eds., *What Is Masculinity? Historical Dynamics from Antiquity to the Contemporary World* (Basingstoke: Palgrave, 2011), 226–44.

5. David Cressy, *Birth, Marriage, and Death: Ritual, Religion, and the Life-Cycle in Tudor and Stuart England* (Oxford: Oxford University Press, 1997), 288; Alexandra Shepard, *Meanings of Manhood in Early Modern England* (Oxford: Oxford University Press, 2003), 74, 246; Hurl-Eamon, 'Youth in the devil's service', 163.

6. K. Tawny Paul, 'Accounting for men's work: Multiple employments and occupational identities in early modern England', *History Workshop Journal*, 85, no. 1 (2018), 26–46; Mark Hailwood, '"The honest tradesman's honour": Occupational and social identity in seventeenth-century England', *Transactions of the Royal Historical Society*, 24 (2014), 79–103; Tim Reinke-Williams, 'Misogyny, jest-books and male youth culture in seventeenth-century England', *Gender and History*, 21, no. 2 (2009), 324–39; Anne F. Sutton, '"Serious money": The benefits of marriage in London, 1400–1499', *The London Journal*, 38, no. 1 (2013), 1–17.

7. Ben-Amos, *Adolescence and Youth*; Mary Abbott, *Life Cycles in England 1560–1720* (London: Routledge, 1996); Lynn Botelho and Pat Thane, 'Introduction' in Lynn Botelho and Pat Thane eds., *Women and Ageing in British Society since 1500* (Harlow: Longman, 2001), 4; Anna French ed., *Early Modern Childhood: An Introduction* (London: Routledge, 2019).

8. Amy Froide, *Never Married: Singlewomen in Early Modern England* (Oxford: Oxford University Press, 2007); Helen Berry, 'Childless men in early modern England' in Helen Berry and Elizabeth Foyster eds., *The Family in Early Modern England* (Cambridge: Cambridge University Press, 2007), 158–83.

9. Mary Dove, *The Perfect Age of Man's Life* (Cambridge: Cambridge University Press, 1986), 20; Karen Raber and Stephanie Tarbin, 'The life cycle' in Karen Raber ed., *A Cultural History of Women in the Renaissance, volume 3* (London: Bloomsbury, 2013), 27; Katie Barclay, Rosalind Carr, Rose Elliot and Annmarie Hughes, 'Introduction: Gender and generations – Women and life cycles', *Women's History Review*, 20, no. 2 (2011), 176.

10. Shepard, *Meanings of Manhood*, 7.

11. Shepard, *Meanings of Manhood*, 75.

12. Paul E.J. Hammer, 'Cuffe [Cuff], Henry (1562/3–1601), classical scholar and secretary to the earl of Essex'. *Oxford Dictionary of National Biography*, 23 September 2004. www.oxforddnb.com/view/10.1093/ref:odnb/9780198614128.001 .0001/odnb-9780198614128-e-6865 (accessed 9 August 2023).

'THE MOST CONSTANT AND SETTLED PART OF OUR LIFE'? 61

13. Henry Cuff, *The differences of the ages of mans life* (London, 1607, 2nd edition), 118–19.

14. Thomas Fortescue, *The Foreste or Collection of histories* (London, 1571) from a French version by Claude Gruget of an Italian translation of Pedro Mexia, 46.

15. Will Fisher, 'The Renaissance beard: Masculinity in early modern England', *Renaissance Quarterly*, 54, no. 1 (2001), 184.

16. Eleanor Rycroft, 'Facial hair and the performance of adult masculinity on the early modern English stage' in Helen Ostovich, Holger Schott Syme and Andrew Griffin eds., *Locating the Queen's Men, 1583–1603: Material Practices and Conditions of Playing* (Farnham: Ashgate, 2009), 217–28.

17. Hermannus Schottennius, *The government of all estates, wherein is contayned the perfect way to an honest life* (London, 1566).

18. R. Hoper, *The instruction of a Christian man* (London, 1580?), 64.

19. Catherine Richardson, 'Status' in Elizabeth Currie ed., *A Cultural History of Dress and Fashion in the Renaissance, volume 3* (London: Bloomsbury, 2017), 129.

20. J.A. Burrow, *The Ages of Man: A Study in Medieval Writing and Thought* (Oxford: Clarendon Press, 1986), 119–20.

21. Geffray Fenton, *Golden epistles* (London, 1575), 155.

22. Shepard, *Meanings of Manhood*, 46.

23. Shepard, *Meanings of Manhood*, 23.

24. Fortescue, *The Foreste*, 46.

25. Raber and Tarbin, 'The life cycle', 25.

26. Dove, *The Perfect Age*, 11.

27. Ages of man: second stage, from the ages of sixteen to thirty-two, and the classical orders of architecture: Corinthian. Engraving by J. Wierix, 1577, after J. Vredeman de Vries. Wellcome Collection. https://wellcomecollection.org/works /dz6rnz5j/items (accessed 12 October 2023).

28. Ages of man: fourth stage, from the age of forty-eight to sixty-four years and the classical orders of architecture: doric. Engraving by J. Wierix, 1577, after J. Vredeman de Vries. Wellcome Collection. https://wellcomecollection.org/works/dh3tkb8r/ items (accessed 12 October 2023).

29. Sears, *The Ages of Man*, 17–18, 59–61.

30. Fenton, *Golden epistles*, 150–51.

31. Fenton, *Golden epistles*, 157.

32. Cuff, *The differences*, 118–19.

33. Ages of man: third stage J. Wierix, 1577, after J. Vredeman de Vries. https:// wellcomecollection.org/works/k7gxqq6m/items (accessed 12 October 2023).

34. See Youngs's Chapter 1 in this collection.

35. William Vaughan, *Naturall and Artificial Directions for health* (London, 1600), 54.

36. Dove, *The Perfect Age*, 27.

37. Shepard, *Meanings of Manhood*, 41.

38. It is perhaps worth noting that I turned thirty-five while writing this chapter so understand the intellectual impulse to assess adulthood as a transitional stage.

39. W.B. and E.P., *A Helpe to Discourse. Or A Miscelany of Merriment* (London, 1619), 234–5.

40. Cuff, *The differences*, 116.

41. Maria Cannon, 'Conceptualising childhood as a relational status: Parenting adult children in sixteenth-century England', *Continuity and Change*, 36, no. 3 (2021), 309–30.

42. Moss, 'An orchard, a love letter and three bastards', 239.

43. Hailwood, 'The honest tradesman's honour', 96; Reinke-Williams, 'Misogyny, jest-books and male youth culture', 331–5.

44. John Reading, *The old mans staffe* (London, 1621), 5.

45. John Bunyan, *Meditations of the several ages of man's life* (London, 1700), 43.

46. Reading, *The old mans staffe*, 11.

47. Cuff, *The differences*, 106–107.

48. Philippa Maddern and Stephanie Tarbin, 'Life cycle' in Sandra Cavallo and Silvia Evangelisti eds., *A Cultural History of Childhood and Family in the Early Modern Age, volume 3* (London: Bloomsbury, 2013), 25–44.

49. Sara Read, *Menstruation and the Female Body in Early Modern England* (Basingstoke: Palgrave Macmillan, 2013).

50. Barclay et al., 'Introduction: Gender and generations', 176.

51. Raber and Tarbin, 'The life cycle', 43–4; Cordelia Beattie, 'The life cycle: The ages of medieval women' in Kim M. Philips ed., *A Cultural History of Women in the Middle Ages, volume 2* (London: Bloomsbury, 2013), 37.

52. For example: Barbara Harris, *English Aristocratic Women 1450–1550: Marriage and Family, Property and Careers* (Oxford: Oxford University Press, 2002), 43; Barbara A. Hanawalt, *The Wealth of Wives: Women, Law, and Economy in Late Medieval London* (Oxford: Oxford University Press, 2007), 69; and Diana O'Hara, *Courtship and Constraint: Rethinking the Making of Marriage in Tudor England* (Manchester: Manchester University Press, 2000), in addition to numerous textbooks on the lives of women in early modern England.

53. Tim Reinke-Williams, 'Physical attractiveness and the female life-cycle in seventeenth-century England', *Cultural and Social History*, 15, no. 4 (2018), 469–85.

54. Youngs, *The Life Cycle in Western Europe*, 132.

55. The three ages of man: a couple embrace, children play with hoops and toys and an old couple eat at a table. Engraving by P. Fürst, 1652. Wellcome Collection. https://wellcomecollection.org/works/t4bt4n89/items (accessed 12 October 2023).

56. Dove, *The Perfect Age*, 20.

57. Cuff, *The differences*, 106–107.

58. Nicholas Culpeper, *Directory for midwives: or, a guide for women* (London, 1676), 95.

59. Sue Niebrzydowski, 'Introduction: "Becoming bene-straw" – The middle-aged woman in the Middle Ages' in Sue Niebrzydowski ed., *Middle-Aged Women in the Middle Ages* (Woodbridge: Boydell and Brewer, 2011), 7.

60. Reinke-Williams, 'Physical attractiveness', 470.

61. Cuff, *The differences*, 119.

62. Ella Sbaraini '"Those that prefer the ripe mellow fruit to any other": Rethinking depictions of middle-aged women's sexuality in England, 1700–1800', *Cultural and Social History*, 17, no. 2 (2020), 166.

63. Alexandra Walsham, *Generations: Age, Ancestry, and Memory in the English Reformations* (Oxford: Oxford University Press, 2023), 27. This statistic does not take

into account the high infant mortality rate of early modern England but does indicate a youthful society.

64. Shepard, *Meanings of Manhood*, 7.

65. Walsham, *Generations*, 76.

66. See Chapter 3 of this collection.

References

Primary sources

Bunyan, John. *Meditations of the several ages of man's life* (London, 1700).

Cuff, Henry. *The differences of the ages of mans life* (London, 1607, 2nd edition).

Culpeper, Nicholas. *Directory for midwives or, a guide for women* (London, 1676).

Fenton, Geffray. *Golden epistles* (London, 1575).

Fortescue, Thomas. *The Foreste or Collection of histories* (London, 1571).

Hoper, R. *The instruction of a Christian man* (London, 1580?).

Reading, John. *The old mans staffe* (London, 1621).

Schottennius, Hermannus. *The government of all estates, wherein Is contayned the perfect way to an honest life* (London, 1566).

Vaughan, William. *Naturall and Artificial Directions for health* (London, 1600).

W.B. and E.P. *A Helpe to Discourse. Or A Miscelany of Merriment* (London, 1619).

Secondary sources

Abbott, Mary. *Life Cycles in England 1560–1720*. London: Routledge, 1996.

Barclay, Katie, Carr, Rosalind, Elliot, Rose and Hughes, Annmarie. 'Introduction: Gender and generations – Women and life cycles', *Women's History Review*, 20, no. 2 (2011), 175–88.

Beattie, Cordelia. 'The life cycle: The ages of medieval women' in Kim M. Philips ed., *A Cultural History of Women in the Middle Ages, volume 2*. London: Bloomsbury, 2013, 15–38.

Ben-Amos, Ilana Krausman. *Adolescence and Youth in Early Modern England*. New Haven, CT: Yale University Press, 1994.

Berry, Helen. 'Childless men in early modern England' in Helen Berry and Elizabeth Foyster eds., *The Family in Early Modern England*. Cambridge: Cambridge University Press, 2007, 158–83.

Botelho, Lynn and Thane, Pat. 'Introduction' in Lynn Botelho and Pat Thane eds., *Women and Ageing in British Society since 1500*. Harlow: Longman, 2001, 1–4.

Botelho, Lynn and Thane, Pat eds. *Women and Ageing in British Society since 1500*. Harlow: Longman, 2001.

Burrow, J.A. *The Ages of Man: A Study in Medieval Writing and Thought*. Oxford: Clarendon Press, 1986.

Cannon, Maria. 'Conceptualising childhood as a relational status: Parenting adult children in sixteenth-century England', *Continuity and Change*, 36, no. 3 (2021), 309–30.

Cressy, David. *Birth, Marriage, and Death: Ritual, Religion, and the Life-Cycle in Tudor and Stuart England*. Oxford: Oxford University Press, 1997.

Dove, Mary. *The Perfect Age of Man's Life*. Cambridge: Cambridge University Press, 1986.

Fisher, Will. 'The Renaissance beard: Masculinity in early modern England', *Renaissance Quarterly*, 54, no. 1 (2001), 155–87.

French, Anna ed. *Early Modern Childhood: An Introduction*. London: Routledge, 2019.

French, Henry and Rothery, Mark. '"Upon your entry into the world": Masculine values and the threshold of adulthood among landed elites in England 1680–1800', *Social History*, 33, no. 4 (2008), 402–22.

Froide, Amy. *Never Married: Singlewomen in Early Modern England*. Oxford: Oxford University Press, 2007.

Hailwood, Mark. '"The Honest Tradesman's Honour": Occupational and social identity in seventeenth-century England', *Transactions of the RHS*, 24 (2014), 79–103.

Hammer, Paul E.J. 'Cuffe [Cuff], Henry (1562/3–1601), classical scholar and secretary to the earl of Essex'. *Oxford Dictionary of National Biography*, 23 September 2004. www.oxforddnb.com/view/10.1093 /ref:odnb/9780198614128.001.0001/odnb-9780198614128-e-6865 (accessed 9 August 2023).

Hanawalt, Barbara A. *The Wealth of Wives: Women, Law, and Economy in Late Medieval London*. Oxford: Oxford University Press, 2007.

Harris, Barbara. *English Aristocratic Women 1450–1550: Marriage and Family, Property and Careers*. Oxford: Oxford University Press, 2002.

Hurl-Eamon, Jennine. 'Youth in the devil's service, manhood in the king's: Reaching adulthood in the eighteenth-century British army', *Journal of the History of Childhood and Youth*, 8, no. 2 (2015), 163–90.

Maddern, Philippa and Tarbin, Stephanie. 'Life cycle' in Sandra Cavallo and Silvia Evangelisti eds., *A Cultural History of Childhood and Family in the Early Modern Age, volume 3*. London: Bloomsbury, 2013, 25–44.

Moss, Rachel E. 'An orchard, a love letter and three bastards: The formation of adult male identity in a fifteenth-century family' in John Arnold and Sean Brady eds., *What Is Masculinity? Historical Dynamics from Antiquity to the Contemporary World*. Basingstoke: Palgrave, 2011, 226–44.

Niebrzydowski, Sue, 'Introduction: "Becoming bene-straw" – The middle-aged woman in the Middle Ages' in Sue Niebrzydowski ed.,

Middle-Aged Women in the Middle Ages. Woodbridge: Boydell and Brewer, 2011, 1–7.

Niebrzydowski, Sue ed. *Middle-Aged Women in the Middle Ages*. Woodbridge: Boydell and Brewer, 2011.

O'Hara, Diana. *Courtship and Constraint: Rethinking the Making of Marriage in Tudor England*. Manchester: Manchester University Press, 2000.

Paul, K. Tawny. 'Accounting for men's work: Multiple employments and occupational identities in early modern England', *History Workshop Journal*, 85, no. 1 (2018), 26–46.

Raber, Karen and Tarbin, Stephanie. 'The life cycle' in Karen Raber ed., *A Cultural History of Women in the Renaissance*. London: Bloomsbury, 2013, 25–44.

Read, Sara. *Menstruation and the Female Body in Early Modern England*. Basingstoke: Palgrave Macmillan, 2013.

Reinke-Williams, Tim. 'Misogyny, jest-books and male youth culture in seventeenth-century England', *Gender and History*, 21, no. 2 (2009), 324–39.

Reinke-Williams, Tim. 'Physical attractiveness and the female life-cycle in seventeenth-century England', *Cultural and Social History*, 15, no. 4 (2018), 469–85.

Richardson, Catherine. 'Status' in Elizabeth Currie ed., *A Cultural History of Dress and Fashion in the Renaissance, volume 3*. London: Bloomsbury, 2017, 117–34.

Rycroft, Eleanor. 'Facial hair and the performance of adult masculinity on the early modern English stage' in Helen Ostovich, Holger Schott Syme and Andrew Griffin eds., *Locating the Queen's Men, 1583–1603: Material Practices and Conditions of Playing*. Farnham: Ashgate, 2009, 217–28.

Sbaraini, Ella. '"Those that prefer the ripe mellow fruit to any other": Rethinking depictions of middle-aged women's sexuality in England, 1700–1800', *Cultural and Social History*, 17, no. 2 (2020), 165–87.

Sears, Elizabeth. *The Ages of Man: Medieval Interpretations of the Life Cycle*. Princeton, NJ: Princeton University Press, 1986.

Shepard, Alexandra. *Meanings of Manhood in Early Modern England*. Oxford: Oxford University Press, 2003.

Sutton, Anne F. '"Serious money": The benefits of marriage in London, 1400–1499', *The London Journal*, 38, no. 1 (2013), 1–17.

Walsham, Alexandra. *Generations: Age, Ancestry, and Memory in the English Reformations*. Oxford: Oxford University Press, 2023.

Youngs, Deborah. *The Life Cycle in Western Europe, c. 1300–c. 1500*. Manchester: Manchester University Press, 2006.

Chapter 3

Spiritual maturity and childishness in Protestant England, c.1600–60[1]

Emily E. Robson

In early modern England, ideas surrounding growth and maturation carried connotations which extended into individuals' spiritual lives. Protestant theology, especially that stemming from a Calvinistic outlook, imagined all people as starting their lives as inherently sinful beings, tarnished by the actions of Adam and Eve in the Garden of Eden. The elect, through God's irresistible grace, were saved and destined for heaven, while the reprobate were condemned to hell. Yet while redemption ultimately lay in the hands of God, the truly faithful were believed to embark on a process of spiritual discovery and maturation, revealing their elect status. Spiritual maturity was a measure of a person's theological awareness, as well as how well they applied this awareness within their everyday lives. Spiritual growth existed alongside and overlapped with other important determinants of age, such as numerical age and physical development. It is therefore an important concept to explore in order to understand what it meant to be an adult in the early modern world.

The chronological range of this chapter covers a period of widespread religious and political turmoil. Despite the efforts of a generation of reformers, many clergymen believed that the English populace had failed to fully absorb Protestant doctrine. Richard Kilby, writing in 1618, lamented that 'even where learned preachers have killed themselves with sore labours, the greater number of people are grossely ignorant'.[2] Godly ministers also grappled with perceived failings within the English Church. On the one hand, the continuation of 'popish' traditions, such as kneeling before the altar, frustrated those leaning in a more Reformed direction. On the other side of the conversation, religious conservatives were alarmed by repeated pushes for further reform. The Civil War polarised religious debate by allowing differing opinions to clash on a physical as well as a polemical battlefield.

This fraught situation was compounded by what Anthony Milton has called the 'second Reformation'.[3] The emergence of new sectarian groups in the 1640s and 1650s contributed to an already fissiparous Protestant landscape. Prominent examples included the Quakers, who rejected formal ministry, and Fifth Monarchists, who believed in Christ's imminent return and a thousand-year rule of saints. These sects were nonconformist – they refused to follow the tenets laid down by the established Church. They were therefore thorns in the sides of the ecclesiastical hierarchy. Against this backdrop of religious turmoil, spiritual maturity took on a special relevance as various groups vied to define themselves as the pinnacle of earthly religious achievement.

This chapter brings spiritual maturation into dialogue with biological growth. It builds upon the work of Alexandra Walsham, who has argued that biological and religious age were closely intertwined in the early modern world. Conceptions of physical and religious age were open to reinterpretation and shifted in line with wider changes in the English ecclesiastical landscape. Furthermore, these shifts were indicative of generational struggles as young Protestants came into conflict with their elders.[4] This chapter builds upon Walsham's work by exploring the Protestant minister as the pinnacle of spiritual maturity. Ministers justified their monopoly of the pulpit by associating themselves with the best qualities of various life stages. Yet these flattering depictions were challenged by negative age-based stereotypes.

Published sermons form the evidential backbone of this chapter. These didactic texts addressed a range of topics and spoke into a divisive and often polemical Protestant landscape. The testimonies offered by funeral sermons portrayed deceased ministers as spiritual exemplars, while larger martyrologies, such as Samuel Clarke's *Lives*, cemented patterns of representation.[5] Theological commentaries defended contentious viewpoints and often used polemic to denounce religious rivals. As Arnold Hunt has demonstrated, printed sermons were different beasts to oral exegeses. Sermons might be fine-tuned for the print marketplace, with old commentaries updated and controversial material defended.[6] What appears to the historian is therefore a carefully curated representation of spirituality rather than a reflection of everyday attitudes. These representations were produced by and described a relatively small group of educated men. Female spirituality is therefore not the focus of this chapter. These sources cannot offer unmediated access into the lives of their subjects, yet they do reveal the importance of age as a cultural concept, as well as how this concept might be manipulated to serve various agendas.

Measuring age

In early modern Protestant rhetoric, those with little understanding of scripture, or who lived ungodly lives, were described as children. The Lancashire minister William Harrison, writing in 1625, argued that anyone unmoved by the promises of the gospel 'wee may compare, as Christ did the Iewes, vnto little children'.[7] This language had scriptural precedents. In his first letter to the Corinthians, Saint Paul identified the Corinthians as 'babes in Christ', who required meat rather than milk.[8] In Paul's analogy, meat stands for complex matters of scripture, while milk describes the most elementary knowledge. This biblical passage was often used in didactic literature to express the spiritual needs of the most unenlightened Christians. William Crashaw, writing in 1618, promised that his catechism would provide 'either the Milke, or the Meate fit for their soules'.[9] Catechisms were elementary didactic texts often written in the form of a dialogue. According to Crashaw, milk was appropriate for those that are 'vnskilfull in the Word of Righteousnesse, for he is a Babe. But strong Meate belongeth to them that are of full age'.[10] In this context, spiritual childishness was an undesirable state denoting a dangerous lack of understanding.

Accusations of spiritual childishness were often levelled by Protestant writers lamenting the benighted state of ordinary people. In a 1636 treatise explaining the steps to salvation, Independent preacher Thomas Goodwin complained that insecure Christians were 'like children, when their mother is gone aside a little, you fall a crying, as if you were undone'. Goodwin encouraged his readers to meditate on the 'great deale of trouble your childishnesse put the Spirit of God unto'.[11] Catholic polemicists also utilised the language of spiritual infancy. According to the priest Richard Broughton, the truth of Catholic doctrine was so 'plaine & prespicious that euen children may be able to finde & walkein'.[12] Those who failed to grasp this truth were like 'children wauering with euerie winde of doctrine'.[13] Accusations of spiritual infancy were not therefore a Protestant monopoly. Similar language was also used outside of a spiritual context to describe undesirable or inferior peoples. *An exact description of the West-Indies*, published in 1655, described South American peoples as 'savage and barbarous, going for the most part naked, eating Mans-flesh ... hairy all over like bruit beasts, from whom they seem but little to differ'.[14]

Beastliness was akin to childishness – both states denoted a shameful lack of reason and self-control. Negative depictions of immaturity therefore had a broad currency in the early modern world.

While everybody began life as a spiritual babe, the faithful were expected to grow in piety and understanding into a state of spiritual maturity. A fully grown Christian was associated with standard moral virtues. In a 1622 treatise on spiritual growth, Thomas Cooper identified mature Christians as 'moderate in our affections, more sober in our iudgments, cōcerning indifferent things; more charitable in iudging others, more wise in prouiding necessary things & auoiding vnnecessary troubles'.[15] The process of spiritual growth was captured in the Protestant conversion narrative. Conversion narratives developed in the seventeenth century and charted a person's progression from spiritual ignorance into a new appreciation and understanding of the gospel. Donatella Pallotti has identified what she has termed a 'morphology of conversion' – the faithful could expect to pass through stages of sin, false confidence, doubt, conviction, faith, temptation and assurance.[16] This sense of spiritual maturation was grounded in scripture. In his letter to the Ephesians, Saint Paul stated that followers of God's word would 'henceforth be no more children' but would grow 'unto a perfect man, unto the measure of the stature of the fulnes of Christ'.[17] Those who progressed through the stages of conversion, and lived with piety and wisdom, were described as fully grown, perfect and ripe in years. For example, William Negus, a minister from Lee in Essex, likened the mature Christian to a mighty oak tree. Such trees are 'longer a growing and slower in attaining to their full growth ... but being once growne they will stand any storme'.[18] The slow growth of Negus's oak tree suggests a lengthy process of maturation for the truly righteous.

The stages of spiritual maturity often corresponded with chronological age. Childhood was a time of inchoate development. An anonymous text published in 1595, which translated Aristotle's medical theories into English, suggested that boys began to acquire the features of adulthood at age fourteen. At that point a boy's shoulders would broaden, his voice deepen, his genitalia enlarge and his whole body increase in size.[19] Physical immaturity was accompanied by nascent mental development. In *Passions of the Mind*, first published in 1600, recusant Thomas Wright commented that children 'lacke the vse of reason, and are guided by an internall imagination, following nothing else but that pleaseth their sences, even after the same maner as bruite beastes doe'.[20] Children were therefore physically and mentally inferior to their adult counterparts.

The inchoate nature of childhood negatively impacted a child's spiritual security. In a 1658 treatise on original sin, the preacher Anthony

Burgess warned of 'the danger that will accrew even to the godly, *if they live after the flesh, they shall die*'. Believers must therefore 'study and abound in holiness' in a manner that reflected their elect status.[21] Living a holy life was particularly difficult for children, as they lacked an adult capacity for reason – 'children have not understanding to serve God with, and therefore their memory, which is easily quickned in them, must be the more drawn out, that so they may serve God as they are able'.[22] This lack of reason made children particularly vulnerable to sinful temptations. According to Richard Kilby, the souls of children who delight in scornful, mocking words 'are died in the blacke colour of hell'.[23] Even newborns were tainted with original sin. The puritan minister Sampson Price wrote in 1624 that infants entered the world 'bathed in bloud, an image of sinne, his first song is the Lamentation of a sinner, weeping and sobbing'.[24] As a result, infancy was nothing but 'an Apprentiship of seuen yeares infirmity', while childhood, which lasted until the tenth year, was characterised as 'an vntoward phantasticall toying'.[25] The young were therefore viewed as ill-equipped to resist the many faces of the Devil.

Commentators disagreed upon the exact chronological age which marked the end of childhood and the beginning of adolescence. While Price identified ten as the beginning of '*Mans* estate', the gentleman David Papillion argued that this transition took place at age fifteen.[26] This conceptual slippage was compounded by the observation that individuals matured at different rates. The physician William Clever noted that adolescence 'is commonly knowen by hayres, eyther about the chin, or priuie partes', which might appear at any time between the ages of twelve and fourteen.[27] Yet while commentators diverged on matters of chronology, they agreed that a person's earliest years were often characterised by a dangerous proclivity for sin. Papillion posited a relatively late transition into adolescence, yet he concurred with his peers that the young were full of 'malice, obstinacy and disobedience'.[28] There was therefore a strong vein in early modern Protestant thought which saw the young as spiritually and morally undeveloped.

On the other side of the life span, older individuals were often envisaged as fully grown in the spirit. Unlike other age classification schemas, which located the 'perfect' age in midlife, spiritual adulthood was often achieved in a person's latter years. This laudable state was partially grounded in the physical changes associated with advanced age. In a ballad decrying the various sins of youth, court poet Francis Lenton looked forward to the day when boys are grown, and 'manly Reason doth controle the vagrant VVill, and thirsting Appetite'.[29] Those in the final stages of life were the furthest divorced from youthful passions. Presbyterian preacher William Jenkyn, in a 1654 funeral sermon lauding old age, stated that 'old age is highly commendable for its safety. An old Saint hath passed through those dangerous storms and difficulties that a poor young one is now sailing toward ... he is by death beyond the temptations, the difficulties, the passions, that a young man lies ingaged to'.[30] Senescence was often viewed as a time of pitiable weakness and decrepitude, yet here physical decline was viewed in a positive light. Spiritual maturity was therefore a context in which usually emasculating or undesirable qualities could be given a new meaning.[31]

Old age might also be lauded for the experience and wisdom accumulated over a lifetime. Alexandra Shepard has pointed out that the elderly were repositories of memory, making them valuable resources in customs disputes.[32] Furthermore, Lynn Botelho has shown that old men, unlike old women, were often positively depicted in woodcut images as regal kings and wise, bearded seers.[33] Aged wisdom also had currency within a religious context. William Jenkyn argued that maturity 'brings *wisdom* and *experience*, and therefore makes men more able to give wise and wholesome counsel to others'.[34] As a result, old age was 'an age of the greatest growth and perfection of grace ... Old men (if godly) are spiritual hoarders; they have been laying up grace all of their dayes'.[35] The correlation between old age and spiritual maturity was a frequent theme in Protestant funeral sermons. For example, in a sermon from 1652, puritan minister Thomas Hodges encouraged his readers to treat the elderly with respect, as 'the longer and greater experience any one hath had in religion, he is the more wise, and therefore more honourable'.[36] The concept of adulthood cannot therefore be reduced to chronological 'middle age' because in situations where culminated experience and education were relevant, the later years might represent a more 'perfect' state of maturation.

The immaturity of childhood and wisdom of the elder suggests that the stages of spiritual growth largely correlated with chronological milestones. Yet there were exceptions to this rule. Studies of childhood have shown that even the youngest members of society might exhibit strong faith. For example, Hannah Newton has shown that sick children drew strength from God's promises and the examples set by Protestant martyrs.[37] Children were also viewed as potentially less sinful than their adult counterparts. According to Anthony Burgess, 'comparatively to grown persons they [children] are innocent, having not the pride and other sins as men of age have'.[38] This vision of childhood piety was part of a pre-Reformation inheritance which posited that, once baptised, a child was washed clean of sin and became sweet, innocent and pure.[39] Protestant doctrine cast doubt on the efficacy of baptism, yet this sense of childish innocence lingered on within the early modern imagination.

SPIRITUAL MATURITY AND CHILDISHNESS IN PROTESTANT ENGLAND   73

In special situations, the gerontocracy was turned on its head and the young commanded the old. Anna French has demonstrated how early modern society carved a niche for children to act as prophets of God's word.[40] These inspired youths took on an adult role by preaching God's word to an older audience. For example, Thomas Darling, a thirteen-year-old boy who experienced symptoms of possession in 1586, was praised by his exorcist John Darrell for completing pious exercises which 'might well have beseemed one of riper yeares'.[41] This sense of childhood spiritual authority was grounded in scripture. Acts 2:17 stated that 'in the last days, saith God, I will pour out my Spirit upon all flesh; and your sons and daughters shall prophesy, and your young men shall see visions, and your old men shall dream dreams'.[42] Childhood was therefore both a hazard and an advantage; it made children less capable of resisting sin while also enhancing their relationship with the divine.

Just as children could act with spiritual maturity, so old men might be accused of spiritual childishness. A 1634 ballad warned its readers that that while 'child-hood is a wonderfull simple thinge, yet time and old age more wisdome will bring. Yet some men in age are so Childish grone, as if that true man-hood they had neuer known'.[43] In this context childishness was seen as a sinful state. William Jenkyn warned his readers against 'recollecting former youthfull follies with delight', while the godly minister John Reading suggested that 'youth in age is but a second childishnesse of the old; there being nothing more vnreasonable, than to loathe that state and age to which with wishes and feare of failing we haue attained'.[44] The childishness of old age was also associated with contemptible ignorance. William Jenkyn lamented how 'shamefull it is to see a man whose hairs and wrinckles speak him an hundred, but his knowledge of Christ speaks him not ten'.[45] Similarly, influential Arminian churchman Simon Patrick claimed that old men who did nothing positive with their lives were 'Childish in their desires, as weak in their fears, as unreasonable in their hopes, as impertinantly and vainly imployed, as if they were but newly come into the world, and had not attained to the use of their Reason'.[46] These commentators were critical of their subjects' lack of spiritual investment, which brought them down to the level of uneducated children.

This picture of spiritual infancy can be subsumed into a broader stereotype linking old age to terminal decline. The physical realities of an ageing body were often noted and lamented by contemporary commentators. In a treatise on sight, translated into English in 1594, French physician André du Laurens stated that old men suffered from stiff joints, weeping eyes and runny noses, which caused them to constantly spit, cough and drool. Physical symptoms were accompanied by mental degradation. Old people suffered from a loss of memory and judgement, 'so that they become as they were in their infancie'.[47] Men who had passed their physical prime were often deemed outmoded and overworn. French theologian Simon Goulart stated in a 1621 treatise that old age was accounted 'miserable, in regard it makes vs vnseruicable men, and vnfit to manage and meddle with worldy affaires, enfeebles our bodies ... being moreouer the next neighbour to death'.[48] Old bodies lost their youthful strength and vigour and gradually descended into feebleness and incapability. Therefore 'all men agree in this point, that old age is miserable, being as it were the very sinke of all extreme miseries, where they settle'.[49] Venerable old age therefore co-existed with narratives which associated longevity with pitiable incapability and weakness.[50] As Maria Cannon's contribution to this collection demonstrates, a 'perfect' balance of physical and mental prowess was associated with middle age rather than youth or longevity.

This section has suggested that spiritual maturity was not a simple facet of physical and mental development. Growing in the spirit was a lifelong process ideally culminating in a pious old age. Old men became childish when they failed to heed spiritual advice, and young children, if blessed by God, could be mature. Unlike other age classification schemas, which saw middle age as the 'perfect age', spiritual maturity was often located at the end of the life span. Yet this developmental pattern was complicated by alternative narratives which saw pitiable decline as the inevitable consequence of longevity. These contradictory notions of advanced age shaped representations of those ideally embodying the pinnacle of spiritual maturity – the ordained ministry.

The mature minister

Spiritual maturity and the ministerial vocation were inextricably linked in the early modern imagination. According to William Perkins, the 'holy Ministerie in it selfe is so high and excellent a calling ... whose honour and excellencie is such, that as we see here scarce one of a thousand attaines unto it'.[51] According to Perkins, a minister is called 'a Messenger, or an Angel'.[52] Such honorifics were common in Protestant sermons. The minister might also be an 'ambassador', a 'shepherd' and a 'husband'.[53]

Ministers emphasised their vocational uniqueness by associating themselves with the advanced age which denoted spiritual maturity. Precocious development signifies the value of the moral virtues related to advanced age, as ministers presented themselves as 'old' despite their chronological youth. Eminent preachers were often said to have been

SPIRITUAL MATURITY AND CHILDISHNESS IN PROTESTANT ENGLAND   75

unusually mature from childhood. For example, John Murcot was described as exceptionally diligent and industrious during his schooldays: 'Time was not mispent and prodigally expanded in the eager pursuite of childish vanities.'[54] Samuel Clarke also pointed to examples of childhood piety in his martyrological accounts of deceased Protestant divines. For example, Clarke described Herbert Palmer as a wonderfully pious child who, at the tender age of four or five, delighted to receive godly instruction.[55] Similarly, Miles Coverdale, former bishop of Exeter, was characterised by Clarke as one who 'from his childhood was much given to learning, and by his diligence and industry profited exceedingly therein'.[56] The early maturation of pious ministers suggests that children were capable of drawing on their spiritual education, especially when their actions were appraised with the benefit of hindsight.

Attitudes towards early maturation were dependent on context. Precocious physical development was viewed with suspicion. A translation of a Latin text entitled *The cabinet of Venus unlocked* noted that in the Americas there are people who 'have among them an herb which hath such a mysterious quality, as that it will dilate girles privy members, and magnifie and longifie their boys members ... that they may the sooner be capable for to exercise them'.[57] This was achieved to satisfy their supposedly voracious lust. The transition from childhood to adulthood was therefore tied to numerical age – achieving physical milestones prematurely was viewed as unnatural and undesirable.[58] Yet early spiritual maturation was viewed in a positive light, revealing a divergence in attitudes towards different developmental schemas.

As well as being precocious in childhood, ministers also emphasised the great numerical ages attained by many in their vocation. The three biblical patriarchs – Abraham, Isaac and Jacob – were all said to have lived to well over 100. The antediluvian patriarchs lived even longer lives. Adam lived to be 930, Noah reached 950 and Methuselah, the longest-lived of them all, finally died at 969. According to Francis Bacon, commenting in 1638, 'A *Life* led in *Religion*, and in *Holy Exercises*, seemeth to conduce to long Life.'[59] Many of the ministers described by Clarke also enjoyed long life spans. For example, Arthur Hildersham lived to the 'great age' of sixty-eight years, Hugh Clark died at seventy-one and Laurence Chaderton reached the impressive age of ninety-four.[60] Samuel Clarke also saw fit to include that it was 'no disparagement' to John Preston that he died young.[61]

Outer appearance might reflect inner maturity, and some ministers were described as seemingly older than they were. Thomas Gataker and William Gouge, both of whom died in the 1650s, were described as prematurely aged in their funeral sermons. Like his illustrious companions,

Thomas Gataker had a 'lovely gravity' in his youth.[62] Furthermore, as he grew, he became 'grey betimes, that made him to be thought elder than he was, because he had long appeared ancient in the eye of the world'.[63] William Gouge actively cultivated the impression of advanced age. He grew a long beard, and in doing so 'did much resemble the Picture that is usually made for Moses. Certainly he was the exact Effiges of Moses his spirit, and in this resembled him to the life'.[64] Old age and spiritual maturity were therefore intertwined in the early modern imagination.

Ministers who achieved great ages were often presented as having been spared the physical and mental tribulations of senescence. For example, Arthur Hildersham 'out-lived not his parts, but as his graces increased towards his end, so his abilities of invention, judgement, memory, elocution decayed not in his age'.[65] Similarly, the minister Samuel Collins was able to live to seventy-seven years without any significant physical or mental decline. In his funeral sermon, Matthew Newcomen expressed his amazement and admiration that Collins was able to preach twice every Sabbath even in his old age. He

> [w]ondred that he had the strength of body to do it, being almost four-score years old ... but God had vouchsafed him a singular blessing, that even in his old age he was *fat and flourishing* ... His *Understanding, Invention, Memory, Utterance* and other Ministerial parts, they were as lively, as fresh and nimble now in his old age as in the prime of his years.[66]

Newcomen and his sprightly peers transcended many of the negative qualities associated with old age and continued in their physical prime. A distinction was therefore drawn between 'green' old age, in which physical and mental functions remained largely intact, and 'decrepit' old age, when the body and mind began to weaken. The physician Thomas Newton noted in 1586 that some old men remain 'lustie in bodie, constant in mind and in strength seruicable and actiue'.[67] These fortunate men are 'not much tainted, nipped, or bitten with yeeres', yet they stand at the threshold of 'reuerend stowping Age: and it seazeth and catcheth some bodies sooner, and some later'.[68] In was in a similar vein that the politician Henry Cuffe noted in 1607 that while some old men retain 'a will and readinesse to bee doing', their slightly older counterparts were 'so farre decaied, that not onely all abilitie is taken away, but euen all willingnesse, to the least strength and motion of our bodie'.[69] Old age was therefore divided into at least two stages – the first characterised by minor decline, the second suffering from the full infirmity of senescence. Spiritual maturity was associated with 'green' old age, which can be viewed as an extension of adulthood, while 'decrepit' age bore the brunt of physical and mental decline.

God's ministers were presented as enjoying the advantages of 'green' old age even as they entered their seventies and eighties. This extended period of good health was often interpreted as a sign of divine approval. Elderly Protestant martyrs were depicted as unusually healthy and strong as they approached their place of execution. John Foxe's influential *Acts and Monuments*, first published in 1563, described how the martyred evangelist Rawlins White appeared 'crooked, through the infirmity of age, having a sad countenance and a very feeble complexion' as he approached the pyre. Yet as he stood at the stake he stretched 'bolt upright, but also bare withall a most pleasant and comfortable countenaunce'. White embodied the best of both worlds – his posture resembled that of a younger man, yet he also appeared exceedingly old. The hair in his beard and on his head seemed 'more inclined to white then to grey, whiche gave such a shewe and countenaunce to his whole person, that he seemed to be altogether angelicall'.[70] White's unusual health and vigour was portrayed as a blessing from heaven, bringing spiritual maturity into dialogue with physical strength. Foxe's *Acts and Monuments* went through multiple editions and remained an important framework influencing depictions of Protestant exemplars into the seventeenth century.

Physical rejuvenation often corresponded with an inner spiritual revitalisation. The culmination of the conversion experience, when the sinner was transformed into a true believer, was sometimes spoken of as a second birth. This foundational transition led some Protestant writers to count their age from the date of their conversion. For example, Ignatius Jurdian, the puritan mayor of Exeter, died in 1640 in his seventy-ninth year, yet was also said to be sixty-five 'according to his account for the New-birth'.[71] In this context, youthfulness was a descriptor of spiritual maturity rather than childish ignorance, as the spirit was renewed and refreshed through a close relationship with the divine. Fulk Bellers, a 'preacher of the gospel', likened the faithful Christian to a 'renewed Eagle, inabled to mount up in duties with winges as Eagles, to run in the ways of Gods Commandments ... his flesh was restored as the flesh of a little Childe, and hee became clean'.[72] Comparisons between the faithful Christian and the eagle come from Isaiah 40:31, which in the King James Bible states 'they that wait upon the Lord shall renew their strength; they shall mount up with wings as eagles; they shall run, and not be weary; and they shall walk, and not faint'.[73] The analogy of the renewed eagle suggests that while spiritual youth might denote dangerous ignorance, it could also describe an exalted spiritual state, revealing the complex relationship between spiritual growth and chronological age.

Representations of spiritual maturity were further complicated when praiseworthy ministers moved from 'green' to 'decrepit' old age. Not every early modern minister was as fortunate as Newcomen – many elderly ministers suffered from the infirmities of age. In his later years, William Gouge experienced 'the bitternesse of his pains and sharpnesse of urine, and ... Asthma or difficulty of breathing'.[74] Similarly, Daniel Featley, who died in his sixties, was towards the end of his life 'very ill affected with the *Asthma in saburra stomachi*, and with the Dropsie'.[75] It was also suspected that 'he was distracted of his wits'.[76] These ailments were not unique to the elderly. Robert Daniel has pointed out that godly ministers were often laid low by sickness, sometimes as a result of their unrelenting preaching.[77] Yet infirmity was particularly associated with advanced age, when the body lost its youthful resilience and the mind began to weaken.

Ministers dealt with the problem of physical decline by emphasising the continuing ability of sick ministers to fulfil their pastoral functions. Samuel Clarke's martyrologies contained multiple examples of sick and suffering elderly ministers. For example, Thomas Cartwright suffered in his later years from the stone and gout, yet he would 'not intermit his labours, but continued preaching when many times he could scarce creep to the pulpit'. Those without the strength to stand and preach continued to minister from their sickbeds. When ninety-six-year-old John Dod lay on his deathbed, he spent his time 'breathing out such speeches, as tended to the praise of God, and to the edification of those who attended him'.[78] Rather than an unwelcome sign of physical decline, these representations used the infirmities of age to emphasise the commitment and perseverance of God's ministers.

Commentators also stressed that while these men might have weakened bodies, their mental faculties were still acute. Gouge retained his mental acumen even as his body decayed: 'the blade of his mind was too sharp for the sheath of his body, the wine too strong for the cask, and his abilities of minde to vigerous for his weak diseased carkass'.[79] Therefore, while he may have suffered 'craziness of body', no one could accuse him of craziness of mind.[80] Similarly, William Loe was quick to dismiss rumours that Daniel Featley had lost his mental sharpness. Rather than descend into elderly senility, Featley continued to produce lucid and didactic tracts during his sickness, showing that he 'was ever the same man' up to the point of death.[81] These representations suggest that it was possible to remain spiritually engaged even when the body was in decline.

SPIRITUAL MATURITY AND CHILDISHNESS IN PROTESTANT ENGLAND   79

Elderly decline complicated attempts by ministers to use the behaviours and qualities associated with chronological age to bolster their claims to a perfect spiritual age. When youth and old age were brought into conflict, the multiple narratives lurking behind a long life span were thrown into relief. In the 1640s Thomas Gataker, then in his seventies, became embroiled in a published dispute with John Saltmarsh, a younger man. In 1646 Gataker published *A mistake, or misconstruction, removed*, in which he criticised a recent treatise by Saltmarsh. Gataker used his own advanced years to justify his condemnation. Despite being 'one wel nigh spent with age', Gataker compared himself to an 'old steed' who 'bestirs him as wel as he can, and by his neying and prancing incites others of his kind and rank to that imployment of service, which himself is unable to perform'.[82] Gataker's self-effacement was a common rhetorical convention. His choice to focus on his own advanced age also resonates with contemporary tracts, including Clarke's *Lives*, in which elderly ministers heroically bestirred themselves to advance God's cause.

Saltmarsh published an answer to Gataker's comments that same year. Unlike Gataker, who saw his advanced age as a spur to those younger than him to take up their pens, Saltmarsh took Gataker's age as proof of his incapability. He stated that 'I should not rebuke your yeers, but that I find you Comicall and Poeticall ... though I am young, having tasted straines of a more glorious Spirit, how much more you that are old, and call your selfe a Divine, ought not to have any fruit in those things?'[83] According to Saltmarsh, while Gataker's age should have made him wiser than a younger writer, in reality it had landed him on the other side of the semantic divide by making him into a weak, comical old man. Saltmarsh claimed that Gataker had 'too much of that which Solomon calls frowardnesse in old men'. His 'frowardnesse' was directly linked to his age, as it was a reminder 'of your disease, rather than your judgement; and the infirmity of your body, not the strength of your spirit'. Saltmarsh asked why Gataker 'chose you not a better time to trie Truth in, when you were not so much in the body?'[84] For Saltmarsh, Gataker was too old to be engaging in theological debate. As a result, many of his words amounted 'not to any thing of, substance, but of quarrelsome and humerous exceptions'. The 'Old steed which neighs and prances, but is past service' did not therefore validate Gataker's words, but explained their inadequacy.[85]

Conflicting attitudes towards different life stages have been explored by Alexandra Walsham, who has argued that generational conflict inflected linguistic choices. Young men might mock the apparent senility of the elderly and highlight their own spiritual youth. In contrast, old men frowned on childish impulsivity while pointing to their own patriarchal authority and wisdom.[86] In his response to Saltmarsh's criticism, Gataker reminded his young rival to 'scof not at old age: you may live if God pleas, to come to it your self'.[87] Gataker sought to prove that he was a wise, venerable old man, while Saltmarsh pulled on the other side of the semantic thread, employing the language of age-based foolishness to discredit his opponent. Spiritual maturity was therefore a flexible concept that could be reworked and reformed to fit different agendas.

Conclusion

In the early modern world, spiritual development followed a pattern of maturation mirroring chronological growth. Everyone began life as a spiritual infant, yet with education and experience, God's children might grow into a state of spiritual maturity. Spiritual age was closely tied to biological age. As a person grew in bodily stature and mental capacity, so their understanding of the gospel also increased. Old age was therefore a time of piety and understanding, while children were unable to resist Satan's temptations. Yet this narrative was open to reinterpretation. Precocious children could demonstrate unusual spiritual development, while sinful old men were viewed as pitifully childish. Spiritual maturity correlated with markers of adulthood – the fully grown Christian was sober, moderate and, when ordained, an authoritative preacher of the gospel. Yet unlike most chronological schemas, a perfect spiritual age was often located at the end of the life span. Adulthood was not therefore always grounded in 'middle age'.

The close association between spiritual adulthood and longevity shaped portrayals of Protestant ministers. Ideally, ministers represented the pinnacle of spiritual growth and wielded a patriarchal authority which brought religious maturity into dialogue with other markers of adulthood. Ministers presented themselves as prematurely aged and long-lived, bringing their appearance in line with biblical precedents. Many ministers also apparently enjoyed an extended 'green' old age characterised by physical and mental competency. Yet others suffered from symptoms of elderly decline which conflicted with their exalted state. Furthermore, spiritual maturity was often captured in the language of youth and rejuvenation, revealing a semantic flexibility within depictions of religious growth. This conceptual malleability gave the language of spiritual maturation a cross-denominational, intergenerational appeal, revealing its importance within early modern religious debate.

Notes

1. This research was partially funded by the Archbishop Cranmer studentship and by the Belmont Education Trust.

2. Richard Kilby, *Hallelu-iah: praise yee the Lord* (Cambridge, 1618), p. 82. See also Christopher Haigh, 'Success and Failure in the English Reformation', *Past and Present* 173, no. 1 (2001), 28–49.

3. Anthony Milton, *England's Second Reformation: The Battle for the Church of England, 1625–1662* (Cambridge: Cambridge University Press, 2021).

4. Alexandra Walsham, 'The Reformation of the Generations: Youth, Age and Religious Change in England, c. 1500–1700', *Transactions of the Royal Historical Society* 21 (2011), 93–121; Alexandra Walsham, 'Second Birth and the Spiritual Life Cycle in Protestant England', in Caroline Bowden, Emily Vine and Tessa Whitehouse eds., *Religion and Life Cycles in Early Modern England* (Manchester: Manchester University Press, 2021), 17–39; Alexandra Walsham, *Generations: Age, Ancestry, and Memory in the English Reformations* (Oxford: Oxford University Press, 2013), especially chapter 1, 'Youth and Age', 22–96.

5. For Clarke's influence on Puritan self-representation, see Peter Lake, 'Reading Clarke's Lives in Political and Polemical Context', in Kevin Sharpe and Steven N. Zwicker eds., *Writing Lives: Biography and Textuality, Identity, and Representation in Early Modern England* (Oxford: Oxford University Press, 2008), 293–318.

6. Arnold Hunt, *The Art of Hearing: English Preachers and Their Audiences, 1590–1640* (Cambridge: Cambridge University Press, 2010), 147–63.

7. William Harrison, *A plaine and profitable exposition* (London, 1625), 53.

8. 1 Corinthians 3:1–2, King James version.

9. William Crashaw, *Milke for babes, or, a north-countrie catechisme* (London, 1618), sig. A2v.

10. Crashaw, *Milke for babes*, sig. A6r.

11. Thomas Goodwin, *A childe of light walking in darknesse* (London, 1636), 12.

12. Richard Broughton, *The conuiction of noueltie* (Douai, 1632), 158–49.

13. Broughton, *The conuiction of noueltie*, 152.

14. N.N., *America: or an exact description of the West-Indies* (London, 1655), 441.

15. Thomas Cooper, *The vvonderful mysterie of spirituall growth* (London, 1622), 47.

16. Donatella Pallotti, '"Out of their owne mouths"? Conversion Narratives and English Radical Practice in the Seventeenth Century', *Journal of Early Modern Studies* 1, no. 1 (2012), 73–95, 76.

17. Ephesians 4:13–14, King James version.

18. William Negus, *Mans actiue obedience* (London, 1619), 166.

19. Anon., *The problemes of Aristotle with other philosophers and phisitions* (Edinburgh, 1595), sig. M9v.

20. Thomas Wright, *Passions of the minde in generall* (London, 1604), 7.

21. Anthony Burgess, *A treatise of original sin* (London, 1658), 105.

22. Burgess, *A treatise of original sin*, 267.

23. Kilby, *Hallelu-iah: praise yee the Lord* (London, 1618), 29.

24. Sampson Price, *The two twins of birth and death* (London, 1624), 8. See also Anna French, '"All Things Necessary for Their Saluation"? The Dedham Ministers and the "Puritan" Baptism Debates', in Tali Berner and Lucy Underwood eds.,

Childhood, Youth and Religious Minorities in Early Modern Europe (Cham: Palgrave Macmillan, 2019), 75–98, 93–5.

25. Price, *The two twins of birth and death*, 9.

26. David Papillion, *The vanity of the lives and passions of men* (London, 1651), 4–5.

27. William Clever, *The flower of phisicke* (London, 1590), 69.

28. Papillion, *The vanity of the lives and passions of men*, 7.

29. Francis Lenton, *The young gallants whirligigg* (London, 1629), 17.

30. William Jenkyn, *A shock of corn coming into its season* (London, 1654), 28.

31. For more on alternative depictions of undesirable attributes, see Anu Korhonen, 'Strange Things Out of Hair: Baldness and Masculinity in Early Modern England', *Sixteenth Century Journal* 41, no. 2 (2010), 371–91.

32. Alexandra Shepard, *Meanings of Manhood in Early Modern England* (Oxford: Oxford University Press, 2003), 221–30.

33. Lynn Botelho, 'Images of Old Age in Early Modern Cheap Print: Women, Witches, and the Poisonous Female Body', in Susannah R. Ottaway, Lynn A. Botelho and Katharine Kitteridge eds., *Power and Poverty: Old Age in the Pre-Industrial Past* (Westport, CT: Greenwood Press, 2002), 225–46, 231–3.

34. Jenkyn, *A shock of corn*, 27.

35. Jenkyn, *A shock of corn*, 26.

36. Thomas Hodges, *The hoary head crowned* (Oxford, 1652), 18.

37. Hannah Newton, *The Sick Child in Early Modern England* (Oxford: Oxford University Press, 2012), 204–208.

38. Burgess, *A treatise of original sin*, 415.

39. See Alexandra Walsham, *Providence in Early Modern England* (Oxford: Oxford University Press, 2001), 209–10.

40. Anna French, *Children of Wrath: Possession, Prophecy and the Young in Early Modern England* (Farnham: Ashgate, 2015).

41. John Darrell, *The most wonderfull and true storie* (London, 1597), 2.

42. Acts 2:17, King James version.

43. I.D., *The praise of brotherhood* (London, 1634).

44. Jenkyn, *A shock of corn*, 31; John Reading, *The old mans staffe, two sermons shewing the onely way to a comfortable old age* (London, 1631), 13.

45. Jenkyn, *A shock of corn*, 30–1.

46. Simon Patrick, *Divine arithmetick* (London, 1659), 35.

47. André du Laurens, *A discourse of the preservation of the sight* (London, 1599), 175–6, at p. 175.

48. Simon Goulart, *The wise vieillard, or old man* (London, 1621), 49.

49. Goulart, *The wise vieillard*, 44–5.

50. For more on the benefits and tribulations of old age, see Keith Thomas, 'Age and Authority in Early Modern England', *Proceedings of the British Academy* 62 (1976), 205–48.

51. William Perkins, *The works of that famous and worthy minister of Christ* (London, 1631), vol. 3, part 2, 434.

52. Perkins, *The works of that famous and worthy minister*, 430.

SPIRITUAL MATURITY AND CHILDISHNESS IN PROTESTANT ENGLAND   83

53. See Tom Webster, *Godly Clergy in Early Stuart England: The Carline Puritan Movement, c.1620–1643* (Cambridge: Cambridge University Press, 1997), 102.

54. John Murcot, *Several works of Mr. Iohn Murcot* (London, 1657), 4.

55. Samuel Clarke, *The lives of two and twenty English divines* (London, 1660), 218. Clarke was not the original author of many of these martyrological accounts. His drew much of his material from existing work, including published funeral sermons and Foxe's *Acts and Monuments*.

56. Clarke, *The lives of two and twenty English divines*, 4.

57. Giovanni Benedetto Sinibaldi, *Rare verities. The cabinet of Venus unlocked* (London, 1658), 21.

58. See Sarah Toulalan, '"Unripe" Bodies: Children and Sex in Early Modern Europe', in Kate Fisher and Sarah Toulalan eds., *Bodies, Sex and Desire from the Renaissance to the Present* (Basingstoke: Palgrave Macmillan, 2011), 131–50. For precocious childhood development in a modern context, see Laura Tisdall's contribution to this volume.

59. Francis Bacon, *Historie naturall and experimentall* (London, 1638), 159–60.

60. Clarke, *The lives of two and twenty English divines*, 156, 165, 170.

61. Clarke, *The lives of two and twenty English divines*, 140.

62. Simeon Ashe, *Grey hayres crowned with grace* (London, 1654), 42.

63. Ashe, *Grey hayres crowned with grace*, 62.

64. Samuel Clarke, *The lives of thirty-two English divines* (London, 1677), 242.

65. Clarke, *The lives of two and twenty English divines*, 156.

66. Matthew Newcomen, *A sermon preached at the funerals of the reverend and faithful servant of Jesus Christ in the work of the gospel Mr. Samuel Collins* (London, 1658), 54.

67. Thomas Newton, *The old mans dietarie* (London, 1586), sig. B3r.

68. Newton, *The old mans dietarie*, sig. B3v.

69. Henry Cuffe, *The differences of the ages of mans life* (London, 1607), 120.

70. John Foxe, *Actes and monuments of matters most speciall and memorable* (London, 1583), 1559 – original pagination.

71. Samuel Clarke, *A collection of the lives of ten eminent divines* (London, 1662), 487.

72. Fulk Bellers, *Abrahams internment, or, the good old-mans buriall in a good old age opened in a sermon* (London, 1656), 21.

73. Isaiah 40:31, King James version.

74. Jenkyn, *A shock of corn*, 37.

75. William Loe, *A sermon preached at Lambeth* (London, 1645), 25–6.

76. Loe, *A sermon preached at Lambeth*, 28.

77. Robert W. Daniel, 'Godly Preaching, in Sickness and Ill-Health, in Seventeenth-Century England', *Studies in Church History* 58 (2022), 134–49.

78. Clarke, *The lives of two and twenty English divines*, 25, 211.

79. Clarke, *The lives of two and twenty English divines*, 45–6.

80. Clarke, *The lives of two and twenty English divines*, 45.

81. Loe, *A sermon preached at Lambeth*, 28.

82. Thomas Gataker, *A mistake, or a misconstruction, removed* (London, 1646), 43.

83. John Saltmarsh, *Reasons for vnitie, peace, and love, with an answer (called shadowes flying away) to a book of Mr Gataker* (London, 1646), 127.

84. Saltmarsh, *Reasons for vnitie, peace, and love*, 130.

85. Saltmarsh, *Reasons for vnitie, peace, and love*, 141.

86. See Walsham, 'The Reformation of the Generations'.

87. Thomas Gataker, *Shadowes without substance* (London, 1646), 15.

References

Primary sources

Anon. *The problemes of Aristotle with other philosophers and phisitions* (Edinburgh, 1595).

Ashe, Simeon. *Grey hayres crowned with grace* (London, 1654).

Bacon, Francis. *Historie naturall and experimentall* (London, 1638).

Bellers, Fulk. *Abrahams internment, or, the good old-mans buriall in a good old age opened in a sermon* (London, 1656).

Broughton, Richard. *The conuiction of noueltie* (Douai, 1632).

Burgess, Anthony. *A treatise of original sin* (London, 1658).

Clarke, Samuel. *The lives of two and twenty English divines* (London, 1660).

Clarke, Samuel. *A collection of the lives of ten eminent divines* (London, 1662).

Clarke, Samuel. *The lives of thirty-two English divines* (London, 1677).

Clever, William. *The flower of phisicke* (London, 1590).

Crashaw, William. *Milke for babes, or, a north-countrie catechisme* (London, 1618).

Cuffe, Henry. *The differences of the ages of mans life* (London, 1607).

Darrell, John. *The most wonderfull and true storie* (London, 1597).

Du Laurens, André. *A discourse of the preservation of the sight* (London, 1599).

Foxe, John. *Actes and monuments of matters most speciall and memorable* (London, 1583).

Gataker, Thomas. *A mistake, or a misconstruction, removed* (London, 1646).

Gataker, Thomas. *Shadowes without substance* (London, 1646).

Goodwin, Thomas. *A childe of light walking in darknesse* (London, 1636).

Harrison, William. *A plaine and profitable exposition* (London, 1625).

Hodges, Thomas. *The hoary head crowned* (Oxford, 1652).

I.D. *The praise of brotherhood* (London, 1634).

Jenkyn, William. *A shock of corn coming into its season* (London, 1654).

Kilby, Richard. *Hallelu-iah: praise yee the Lord* (Cambridge, 1618).

Lenton, Francis. *The young gallants whirligigg* (London, 1629).

Loe, William. *A sermon preached at Lambeth* (London, 1645).

Murcot, John. *Several works of Mr. Iohn Murcot* (London, 1657).

Negus, William. *Mans actiue obedience* (London, 1619).

Newcomen, Matthew. *A sermon preached at the funerals of the reverend and faithful servant of Jesus Christ in the work of the gospel Mr. Samuel Collins* (London, 1658).

Newton, Thomas. *The old mans dietarie* (London, 1586).

N.N. *America: or an exact description of the West-Indies* (London, 1655).

Papillion, David. *The vanity of the lives and passions of men* (London, 1651).

Patrick, Simon. *Divine arithmetick* (London, 1659).

Perkins, William. *The works of that famous and worthy minister of Christ* (London, 1631), vol. 3.

Price, Sampson. *The two twins of birth and death* (London, 1624).

Reading, John. *The old mans staffe, two sermons shewing the onely way to a comfortable old age* (London, 1631).

Saltmarsh, John. *Reasons for vnitie, peace, and love, with an answer (called shadowes flying away) to a book of Mr Gataker* (London, 1646).

Sinibaldi, Giovanni Benedetto. *Rare verities. The cabinet of Venus unlocked* (London, 1658).

Secondary sources

Botelho, Lynn. 'Images of Old Age in Early Modern Cheap Print: Women, Witches, and the Poisonous Female Body', in Susannah R. Ottaway, Lynn A. Botelho and Katharine Kitteridge eds., *Power and Poverty: Old Age in the Pre-Industrial Past* (Westport, CT: Greenwood Press, 2002), 225–46.

Daniel, Robert W. 'Godly Preaching, in Sickness and Ill-Health, in Seventeenth-Century England', *Studies in Church History* 58 (2022), 134–49.

French, Anna. *Children of Wrath: Possession, Prophecy and the Young in Early Modern England* (Farnham: Ashgate, 2015).

French, Anna. '"All Things Necessary for Their Saluation"? The Dedham Ministers and the "Puritan" Baptism Debates', in Tali Berner and Lucy Underwood eds., *Childhood, Youth and Religious Minorities in Early Modern Europe* (Cham: Palgrave Macmillan, 2019), 75–98.

Haigh, Christopher. 'Success and Failure in the English Reformation', *Past and Present* 173, no. 1 (2001), 28–49.

Hunt, Arnold. *The Art of Hearing: English Preachers and Their Audiences, 1590–1640* (Cambridge: Cambridge University Press, 2010).

Korhonen, Anu. 'Strange Things Out of Hair: Baldness and Masculinity in Early Modern England', *Sixteenth Century Journal* 41, no. 2 (2010), 371–91.

Lake, Peter. 'Reading Clarke's Lives in Political and Polemical Context', in Kevin Sharpe and Steven N. Zwicker eds., *Writing Lives: Biography* and Textuality, Identity, and Representation in Early Modern England (Oxford: Oxford University Press, 2008), 293–318.

Milton, Anthony. *England's Second Reformation: The Battle for the Church of England, 1625–1662* (Cambridge: Cambridge University Press, 2021).

Newton, Hannah. *The Sick Child in Early Modern England* (Oxford: Oxford University Press, 2012).

Pallotti, Donatella. '"Out of their owne mouths"? Conversion Narratives and English Radical Practice in the Seventeenth Century', *Journal of Early Modern Studies* 1, no. 1 (2012), 73–95.

Shepard, Alexandra. *Meanings of Manhood in Early Modern England* (Oxford: Oxford University Press, 2003).

Thomas, Keith. 'Age and Authority in Early Modern England', *Proceedings of the British Academy* 62 (1976), 205–48.

Toulalan, Sarah. '"Unripe" Bodies: Children and Sex in Early Modern Europe', in Kate Fisher and Sarah Toulalan eds., *Bodies, Sex and Desire from the Renaissance to the Present* (Basingstoke: Palgrave Macmillan, 2011), 131–50.

Walsham, Alexandra. *Providence in Early Modern England* (Oxford: Oxford University Press, 2001).

Walsham, Alexandra. 'The Reformation of the Generations: Youth, Age and Religious Change in England, c. 1500–1700', *Transactions of the Royal Historical Society* 21 (2011), 93–121.

Walsham, Alexandra. *Generations: Age, Ancestry, and Memory in the English Reformations* (Oxford: Oxford University Press, 2013).

Walsham, Alexandra. 'Second Birth and the Spiritual Life Cycle in Protestant England', in Caroline Bowden, Emily Vine and Tessa Whitehouse eds., *Religion and Life Cycles in Early Modern England* (Manchester: Manchester University Press, 2021), 17–39.

Webster, Tom. *Godly Clergy in Early Stuart England: The Carline Puritan Movement, c.1620–1643* (Cambridge: Cambridge University Press, 1997).

Chapter 4

The rising generation and the fogram: Locating adulthood in eighteenth-century England

Barbara Crosbie

Adulthood is surprisingly hard to locate in histories of eighteenth-century England. The historiography might be dominated by those between childhood and old age, but this reflects an unconscious bias in which the middle stage of life is an implicit norm, the default object of study. This obscures the diverse and frequently contested nature of adult status, and not only in the eighteenth century, as other chapters in this collection demonstrate. But more than this, the predominance of inadvertently adult-centric history has relegated the young and old to the sidelines, left to be investigated as discrete categories. This is to underestimate the relational, or co-defined, nature of life stages. As a consequence, the role intergenerational relations play in changing attitudes towards phases of the life cycle tends to be overlooked.[1] Again, such oversights are not confined to the eighteenth century. This investigation therefore has broad-ranging relevance regardless of place and time, not simply in locating adulthood within the life cycle but also in demonstrating the importance of age relations (both inter- and intragenerational) as a lived experience and an analytical category.

The eighteenth century has long been associated with the 'invention of childhood' or the 'birth of the modern child'.[2] The later century has also been linked to an increasingly negative view of old age.[3] It will be argued here that the middle phase of life was also being reconceptualised as part of an intergenerational process of change. More specifically, the generation that came of age in the early decades of the century adopted explicitly youthful fashions that reflected a conscious rejection of the seventeenth-century values of their elders, but their adulation of youth took on new connotations as this cohort aged and had to contend with their own children and grandchildren entering the adult world.[4] Investigating this process of transition exposes some of the ways in which adulthood was conceived in relation to other stages of the life cycle and, importantly, how the relationships between age cohorts acted as a driver of change.

Eighteenth-century adulthood was not, of course, a homogenous phase of the life cycle. Yet one of the few places that this is brought into sharp focus is in histories of gender, where adults pass through stages from bachelor to householder/husband and father, or from virgin/spinster to wife/mother to menopause. Although this presents a very binary and fecund perspective on gender, it demonstrates distinct phases in the middle stage of life.[5] Nonetheless, even in the history of the family, there is limited recognition that intergenerational relationships might be central to framing perceptions of the life cycle, as Lynn Botelho points out in relation to old age.[6] There is also a need to acknowledge the possibility of conscious generational distinctions in people's experiences of life stages and, crucially, to remember that individuals progressed through the life cycle, taking earlier experiences with them as they aged. As I have argued elsewhere, age is a particularly powerful category of historical analysis precisely because it obliges us to recognise that people lived *through* and not *in* the past.[7]

Age is not, however, a simple question of counting birthdays. Botelho refers to three types of age: chronological, functional and cultural.[8] It is the changing interplay between these aspects of age and ageing that lies at the heart of this exploration of eighteenth-century adulthood. After establishing the ways 'adult' was defined in relation to other life stages, attention will shift to the cultural discourse surrounding age relations, and in particular the social censure faced by those who failed to age gracefully. Placing this often cruel commentary in an intergenerational context exposes the complex ways in which the boundaries of adulthood were being reshaped as age-appropriate behaviours were contested. Inevitably, the timing of an individual's transition from one life stage to the next was influenced by factors such as gender, class, occupation and specific life circumstances. But the focus here is the cultural expectations surrounding the life cycle that such experiences were measured against.

Language and the life cycle

The language used in relation to the life cycle was (and still is) imprecise. In the eighteenth century, various markers for the end of childhood could be offered: when a young person left home and/or started work, when they reached the age of discretion or when they established an independent household and/or married.[9] If we ask instead when adulthood began, the evidence takes on a slightly different hue. Is it possible to see someone as an adult at ten or twelve because they had left the parental home to become a servant or apprentice? Can they be described as a juvenile at thirty (or older) if they remained unmarried? The same ambiguity can be seen when considering what it meant to be old. There might, for instance, be a period of healthy or green old age prior to senescence (physical deterioration due to age) setting in. Moreover, can it be assumed that adult status was lost with the coming of aged dependence for men or the menopause for women?[10]

In looking to answer these questions, it makes sense to begin in a logical order with the transition from juvenile to adult, and the age of legal responsibility is an apposite place to start. However, this exposes a bewildering complexity of legal precedent when it comes to the age at which adult rights and culpabilities were thought to commence. According to *The Infants Lawyer* (1726), fourteen was 'the Age of Discretion' when an 'infant' could be 'privileged, punished or chargeable', but they remained an infant. It was only at eighteen that a will could be made for goods and chattels, and not until twenty-one could this will include land. To add further complication, twenty-one was 'the full Age in our [common] Law', whereas this was 'Twenty five by the Civil Law'.[11] Matthew Hale's *Historia Placitorum Coronæ* (1736) also described twenty-one and twenty-five as the 'complete full age' in matters of contract law (common and civil respectively), even if 'at seventeen years a man is said to be of full age to be procuirator or an executor', and in marriage contracts 'the full age of consent in males is fourteen years, and of females twelve' (the average age at first marriage was in fact mid-twenties).[12] It is interesting that Hale referred to seventeen-year-old males as men but not those of fourteen. It is also noteworthy that, after the passing of Hardwick's Marriage Act in 1753, to marry under the age twenty-one required the consent of a guardian.[13] Evidently, 'full age' in legal terms was contextual and was not synonymous with adulthood. It is, nonetheless, possible to say that those under twenty-one/twenty-five were not considered to be entirely legally independent.

The term adult was rarely used prior to the second quarter of the seventeenth century, as earlier chapters have noted. Moreover, as will become clear, it is only towards the end of the eighteenth century that adult was fully disentangled from the concept of adolescence. Turning to dictionary definitions both adds to our understanding of contemporary usage and helps to pinpoint the timing of this change. In John Kersey's *A*

New English Dictionary (1702) adult was defined as 'grown to full age', which presumably related to the age of legal maturity that might range from twelve to twenty-five.[14] Unfortunately, this dictionary had no entry for adolescent, which would have offered a useful comparator. By contrast, *Cocker's English Dictionary* (1704) chose not to include the term adult, while giving a very specific definition of 'Adolocency' as 'from Fifteen years to Twenty five', making it tempting to assume adulthood came after this.[15] In 1721 Nathan Bailey's definition of adolescence introduced a gender distinction and extended the timeframe for males, describing it as 'the Flower of Youth: the State from Fourteen to Twenty-five or Thirty in Men, and from Twelve to Twenty-one in Women'. Bailey also included a definition for adult, which was imprecisely rendered as 'grown, or come to full ripeness of Age'.[16] This ripeness clearly referred to physical maturity and could be linked to the idea of a fully grown or fully fledged adult, as Maria Cannon suggests in her chapter in this volume. However, it could also be linked to puberty (or the ability to reproduce), which would make Bailey's definitions of adult and adolescence somewhat indistinguishable.[17]

This ambiguity was perpetuated in the middle decades of the century by Samuel Johnson in his *Dictionary of the English Language* (1755), which defined adult as 'A person above the age of infancy, or grown to some degree of strength' but, crucially, only 'sometimes full grown'. His entry for adolescence is only slightly clearer: 'The age succeeding childhood, and succeeded by puberty; more largely, the part of life in which the body has not yet reached its full perfection.' His entry for pubescent helpfully explained women arrived at puberty when they were 'menstruent' and men were 'pubescent at the years of twice seven'.[18] So, those in their early to mid-teens were described as past the stage of adolescence, although it is not clear if this is also what Johnson meant by 'grown to some degree of strength' in his definition of adult. Again, in Daniel Fenning's *Royal English Dictionary* (1761) adolescence was described as the years between infancy and 'full growth', but this was indistinguishable from his definition of adult, which was rendered as either 'grown up; arrived at the age of discretion' or 'one who is arrived at the intermediate age between infancy and manhood'.[19]

In later decades these terms were becoming more distinct. The entries in John Ash's *New and Complete Dictionary* (1775) still lacked a clear divide, with adult described as 'grown up, arrived to the age of puberty' and adolescence 'the time between childhood and manhood, youth'.[20] By contrast, the definitions in John Bentick's *Spelling and Explanatory Dictionary* (1786) were rather cursory, but they were much less entangled than earlier offerings; here adolescence was rendered as 'youth' and

THE RISING GENERATION AND THE FOGRAM   93

adult as 'mature, full grown'.[21] Again, in 1790 William Perry's *General Dictionary of the English Language* offered definitions much more akin to those of the twenty-first century, adolescence being 'youth, the time between childhood and manhood' and adult 'a person grown to years of maturity'.[22] Even if it was not entirely clear what was meant by 'years of maturity', or when they might be reached, the difference between adolescence and adult was less vague by this time.

The definitions of 'man' and 'woman' presented an even greater imprecision in relation to adulthood. For most of the century woman was simply defined as a 'female man' or 'the Female of the Human Race'. In his entry for age in 1755, Johnson used woman in reference to a seven-year-old and man in relation to a fourteen-year-old; and demonstrating just how co-relational understandings of the life cycle (and gender) could be, Johnson's definitions for man included 'not a woman' and 'not a boy'. Only Ash (1775) linked definitions of both man and woman to a life stage, rendering man as the 'male of the human species' and 'one arrived to a state of maturity' while a woman was 'a female of the human race, a marriageable female'. Even here, while the terms were presented as age dependent, they were not age specific.

Most of these dictionaries included an entry for middle age defined as 'the middle of life'. Only Fenning placed it at an 'equal distance between childhood and old age', and only he added any qualitative detail describing it as 'a moderate age'. According to Kay Heath, it was not until the nineteenth century that midlife came to be seen as 'the beginning of the end', and prior to this middle age was associated with the prime of life rather than an anxiety about ageing that we now associate with the midlife crisis.[23] But Amanda Vickery has argued that 'what is middle-aged by most definitions today was definitively old for the Georgians'. More specifically, she concludes that for women 'there was an alarming hemorrhage of youth' from their late twenties as they hurtled to old age by fifty, and it was only eighteenth-century men who were thought to be in their prime in their fourth and fifth decades.[24] Ella Sbaraini emphasises the continued sexual attractiveness of eighteenth-century women in midlife. Nevertheless, she also sets the boundary of middle age at fifty, after which women were simply old.[25] As will become apparent, paying close attention to how the terminology surrounding middle age was used cautions against assuming cultural old age always began later for men, or that the midlife crisis was predominantly faced by women.

To fully appreciate this last point, it is necessary to first consider the dictionary definitions of old and elderly, and how these related to each other. For Kersey (1702), old was 'aged or ancient', whereas Bailey (1721) added an element of decrepitude, defining it as 'stricken in age, stale, worn'.

In 1775, Johnson's definition lacked any reference to decrepitude, simply being 'past the middle part of life; not young'. Elderly was also described by Johnson as 'No longer young'; although strikingly, this was qualified as 'bordering on old age'. This notion of elderly as a life stage prior to old age was surely related to his definition of elder as 'Persons whose age gives them a claim to credit and reverence'; and Johnson's definitions imply that reaching old age was to lose this claim. As late as 1775, Ash defined elderly as 'past the time of youth, bordering on old age'. Yet, by the close of the century the entries of both Bentick (1786) and Perry (1795) suggest elderly had, in the eyes of the dictionary writer, become more synonymous with being 'advanced in years' without any sense of this being distinct from old age. Again, then, there was some level of change over time, even if these definitions present an inexact sense of the later stages of life.

Looking beyond the dictionaries, elderly was mostly used ambiguously to describe a person of an unspecified age, and it was sometimes used as synonymous with the equally vague term old. It is therefore difficult to draw any clear conclusion from the occasions when a chronological age was apparent; for instance, when a fictional character was called an elderly woman at fifty-two or an elderly gentleman of about sixty.[26] But tellingly, *The Diseases of Women with Child* (1710) repeatedly used elderly in relation to older pregnant women in order to distinguish them from younger mothers-to-be, and by any definition the pre-menopausal could not be said to have reached old age.[27] Clearly, at the beginning of the century the terms old and elderly could be more distinct than might be expected, but this distinction was being blurred in later decades. This was in contrast to adolescent and adult, where there was a level of overlap before dictionary definitions began to emphasise a clearer distinction towards the end of the century.

Age-appropriate behaviour

The language used during the eighteenth century to describe adulthood makes it clear that life stages were framed in relation to one another, and this was not a static relationship. Particularly telling evidence of this shifting cultural landscape can be found in the prevalent commentary on age-appropriate behaviour. There was criticism of the young, who were accused of assuming the wisdom of age.[28] However, the more audible, and much crueller, contributions to this discourse were centred on those beyond the midpoint of the life cycle, and it is perhaps unsurprising that this social censure often came from younger voices. In 1699, for instance, at the age of thirty-one, Jonathan Swift penned a set of resolutions entitled

'When I Come to Be Old', which provide some very revealing prejudices about older men. He resolved

> Not to keep young company, unless they really desire it ... Not to scorn present ways, or wits, or fashions, or men, or wars, &c. ... Not to tell the same story over and over to the same people ... Not to be too free of advice, nor trouble any but those who deserve it. ... Not to boast of my former beauty, or strength, or favour with the ladies, &c.

The continuing resonance of these criticisms can be seen in their uncredited inclusion in the periodical *The Berwick Museum* in 1787.[29] However, notably, Swift did not specify when someone might become old, and this ambiguity gave his comments durability even as ideas about the onset and duration of life stages changed.

Others were more chronologically specific in their ridicule, which meant their comments lacked this longevity. Thomas Gordon was in his thirties when he included an essay in *The Humourist* (1724) mocking the habits of the older generation. The claimed intention was to disprove the notion that modern times were 'miserably inferior to the Ancients in Genius and Invention'. His older contemporaries were not, he asserted, to be beaten in the art of 'Restoring old Age to Youth'. The wide range of products that rejuvenated diminishing youth, which were advertised in the 'Fag-End of our News-Papers', were certainly less magical than Ovid's *Metamorphoses* but they were surely no less miraculous in outcome. The trade in such goods was said to employ 'Fifteen Hundred to Two Thousand Souls' in London alone, and to prove the efficacy of these products it was claimed that there were 'blooming Toasts' who were in fact old enough to be grandmothers and 'old Boys' of seventy 'that rake about Town' as if they were only twenty-three.[30] In this case, Gordon was clearly talking about men who, by contemporary definitions, were old and masquerading as young rakes. By contrast, while a grandmother might also be in her seventies, she could just as easily be several decades younger (given that average age at first marriage was mid-twenties), which would fit with the idea that women reached a cultural old age sooner than men. The terminology also hints at life-cycle expectations for women (daughter-wife-mother-grandmother) that are mostly absent in the description of older men.

The sentiment remained the same half a century later, but it was no longer men in their seventies and grandmothers who were the target of the anonymous contribution to Henry Mackenzie's periodical paper *The Lounger* (1786). When it came to men, it was complained that 'We see every day sexagenary beaux, and grey-haired rakes, who mix with the gay and the dissipated of the present time.'[31] It is noteworthy that Mackenzie, who wrote most of the content for his magazine, was in his early forties at this time, and this might explain the tone of disapproval for both the older and the younger generations. What can be said for certain is that whoever wrote this thought that a man in his sixties was no longer of the present times. This chimes with the laments of Horace Walpole (1717–97), whose correspondence was littered with examples of how he measured his experiences of ageing against cultural expectations. Katarzyna Bronk-Bacon concludes that Walpole did not think himself old until he reached sixty.[32] Yet, he evidently considered himself to be knocking on the door of old age at fifty-eight, when he complained he would be laughed at by young men if he were to claim he was 'still in the fashionable world ... for old and old-fashioned are synonymous in the vocabulary of mode, alas!'[33]

Mackenzie also disapproved of female 'rebels against time, who wish to extend the period of their youth beyond its natural duration', but while he harshly condemned grey-haired rakes, he thought more allowances could be made in the case of 'the other sex'. This is in stark contrast to the conclusions drawn by Vickery, who argues that it was women who were under the most social pressure to avoid accusations of feigning youth.[34] However, Mackenzie's indulgence was only extended 'to those who have no other part to perform'. Meanwhile,

> She who is a wife or a mother, has other objects to which her attention may be turned, from which her respectability may be drawn. I cannot therefore easily pardon those whom we see at the public places, the rivals of their daughters, with their airy gait, the sauntering dress, and the playful giggle of fifteen.[35]

So, just as the septuagenarian rake had been transformed into the sexagenarian beau, the grandmothers masquerading as blooming toasts had been replaced by mothers acting like their teenage daughters. The targets of this caustic indignation were therefore much more likely to be women in their forties or fifties than their sixties. This is not to say older spinsters and grandmothers were never lampooned by satirists; they most certainly were with regularity and often obtuse cruelty. Nonetheless, those ridiculed as 'superannuated coquettes'[36] possibly included younger women as the century progressed. Either way, both Gordon and Mackenzie can be read as presenting women as past their prime sooner than men, although care should be taken in assuming this always meant these women were seen as having reached old age as opposed to being middle-aged.

The growing censure of feigning youth was very often targeted at those in the middle decades of life. The satirical print 'A speedy and effectual preparation for the next world' (Figure 4.1), published in 1777, is a good example of this. Here the historian Catherine Macaulay, who was at this time in her mid-forties, is depicted sitting at her dressing table applying

Figure 4.1. 'A speedy and effectual preparation for the next world' (1777). © The Trustees of the British Museum. Shared under a Creative Commons Attribution-NonCommercial-ShareAlike 4.0 International (CC BY-NC-SA 4.0) licence.

make-up while sporting an exaggeratedly large wig adorned with a horse-drawn hearse. Behind her stands a skeleton with an hourglass and the sand of time has not only run out but is spilling onto the table. Macaulay did apparently wear a notable amount of rouge, and she was evidently not embracing a sober middle age given that a year after this print was published she married a man half her age. The mocking cruelty in this image is only heightened by the knowledge that the credited artist, Mattina Darly, was in her teens.[37]

The disdain for middle age felt by those with youth on their side is the theme of two letters included in Eliza Haywood's *Epistles for the Ladies* (1750), and here there is an unmistakable anxiety about ageing that would seem to refute any suggestion that the midlife crisis was a nineteenth-century invention. Haywood was almost sixty at the time of publication, while her fictional correspondents were both women in their early thirties. The first of these women expressed alarm at being seen to be ageing after a peddler tried to sell her spectacles. She mused on why everyone shared this concern but 'few of us desire to die young'. Rather, she thought, 'we would live forever if we could, and yet be always young; we would have a Gap in Time from fifteen to sixty; and even then not be content perhaps to be thought on as in the Decline'. Clearly, her main concern was the process of gradual ageing in midlife, even if she thought old age would still be intolerable at sixty. She was fully aware that the physiological signs of ageing did not neatly fit with this chronology. It might be that everyone had 'a natural Aversion for Grey Hairs and Wrinkles' but this could not be because old age was 'the forerunner of death' and 'attended by infirmities', as neither death nor infirmity were exclusive to old people. In fact, she claimed, 'most people would rather chuse *Deformity* with *Youth*, than *Comeliness* with *old Age*'. In response, her friend suggested that 'the true Motive which makes People afraid of growing old' was 'being treated with Contempt by every one who is a few Years younger than ourselves'. She agreed that 'a long Life is a Blessing every one is desirous of attaining', noting 'we all do every Thing in our Power, in order to preserve it'. Here, she thought, 'lies the Absurdity, to despise that in others, which we take so much Pains to be one Day ourselves'.[38] Despite their relative youth, these fictional women were expressing midlife anxieties about their current position as well as their futures. They were of course also ventriloquising Haywood's views, and she was in that stage of life described by Samuel Johnson as elderly; at very nearly sixty she seemingly considered herself on the cusp of old age. Interestingly, despite the claims that women were seen as socially old earlier in life than men, we see in Haywood's construction of these letters the same anxiety as was felt by Horace Walpole when he was about to turn sixty.

Three decades after Haywood voiced her disquiet about ageing, Vicesimus Knox appeared to concur with her reflections in his essay entitled 'On the Fear of Growing Old'. However, Knox was not on the cusp of old age as he penned his essay; he was about to turn thirty and so was almost the same age as Haywood's fictional correspondents. Knox reiterated the sense of anxiety that this relatively youthful stage of life brought, noting that 'After a certain age, every returning birth-day is saluted with silent sorrow, and we conceal the number of our years with as much solicitude as the consciousness of an atrocious crime.' He went on to complain that 'middle age' was when 'all the powers of mind and body are in complete perfection' but it was now 'loathed as if it were the age of decrepitude'. Then, providing a specific chronology, he lamented that 'The boundaries of life, by nature sufficiently circumscribed, are still further contracted by the empty votary of fashion, and from threescore and ten it shrinks to thirty.' What is more, unlike Haywood who in 1750 thought it a truism that everyone desired a long life, Knox claimed 'It has been currently reported, that many fashionable beauties have expressed a devout wish, that they might not survive their thirtieth birth-day.' He conceded that in truth 'they and their many imitators will probably be inclined to live on, even when they arrive at the formidable age of thrice ten years'. Nevertheless, while the idea that you were young in your twenties remained unchanged, the anxiety of leaving this youth behind appears (at least in the eyes of Knox) more acute than it was a generation earlier. Echoing Mackenzie, and so again at odds with prevailing historiographic assumptions, Knox thought an 'excessive dread of old age' was 'more excusable' in women. It would be wrong to assume women were necessarily afforded more leeway in such matters, as others have demonstrated this was certainly not the case.[39] These examples do, however, serve to modify the idea that women always suffered the greater vilification for feigning youth. According to Knox, it was men who forfeited their dignity by such behaviour. For them it was 'a mark of weakness, want of principle, and want of sense'. Consequently, those men who decorated 'their walking skeletons with every cosmetic art, and haunt[ed] every scene of vice and vanity, with all the wantonness of a strippling of eighteen' simply rendered themselves ridiculous.[40] It is worth noting that the eighteen-year-old stripling presented by Knox was a full five years younger than the twenty-three-year-old rake described by Thomas Gordon in 1724; so, like the giggling fifteen-year-old females cited by Mackenzie in 1786, the example used by Knox suggests perceptions of youthfulness were getting younger.

Knox wanted to believe that getting older was not inevitably wretched. There was, he thought, 'a natural dignity, authority, and beauty, in old age honourably supported', which fits with Helen Yallop's conclusion that the later eighteenth century witnessed a growing sense that ageing was 'something to be managed and controlled'.[41] While some turned to the ever-expanding range of consumer goods aimed at staving off the physical appearance of ageing, Knox emphasised a more rational (or cerebral) approach, advising 'For the enjoyment of the space between thirty to threescore, it will be necessary to have laid a stock of good humour', and this needed to be cultivated at an early age. Here then, despite the title of his essay, 'On the Fear of Growing Old', his main concern was not to improve experiences of old age but of middle age, specifically placed between thirty and sixty. Moreover, he was directing his advice to those who had not yet reached this formidable stage of life.

Knox's essay challenges the assumption that only women dreaded the termination of youth in midlife, while concurring with Heywood's fictional females that thirty was the age at which this transition occurred. It also casts doubt on the idea that old age always came at least a decade earlier for women than their male counterparts. Instead, Knox presents the stage of the life course between thirty and sixty as a time when both men and women felt increasing anxieties about ageing even though they had not yet reached old age. Like Heywood, Knox thought the eulogising of youth lay at the heart of the problem. 'They who have never been taught to consider any thing valuable but youth, beauty, and dissipating pleasure, will naturally feel themselves reduced to a state of dependency, when they behold all, for which life appears worth possessing, on the eve of departure.'[42]

This adoration of youth was a central tenet of eighteenth-century cultural mores. In particular, the cosmopolitan politeness that first gained prominence during the early decades of the century was at its inception a youthful innovation, a conscious rejection of the attitudes and habits of the older (seventeenth-century) generations.[43] As the century progressed, maintaining a youthful appearance became more of a social imperative for those who had used their youth as a symbol of their modern, enlightened credentials. It was as this cohort found themselves having to cope with first middle age and then, God forbid, old age that the censure of those feigning youth increased in volume and gained an ever-harsher tone. This was the context in which Horace Walpole expressed concern about no longer being part of 'the present times'. Like others of his age, Walpole struggled to reconcile his self-image as part of the youthful enlightened generation of the early century with his new-found status as old. As Bronk-Bacon notes, Walpole's copious correspondence 'reveals how much his own definition and perception of late life are built on his private ageist suppositions of how old age is perceived by the generalized construct of young(er) people'.[44] He was, in effect, projecting his own prejudices against the older generations of his youth onto the new rising generation.

The rising generation

Briefly turning to the other side of the conversation, and looking at the censure directed towards the young, helps to pinpoint this generational process. In a polemic *'complaint against the brutality of the present age'* made in 1726, Daniel Defoe, who was then sixty-seven, described himself as an 'Old Man' of 'small Health ... almost worn out with Age and Sickness'. His ire was targeted at *'the pertness and insolence of our youth to aged persons'*, and he railed at the ways old men and women were 'derided, and ill used ... and thought to stand in the way of the present Generation'. He cautioned the 'young Ladies of this Age' against sneering at 'sober Matrons, and elderly Ladies' who were once as young and beautiful. It was not just in terms of fashion and beauty that the young were said to feel superior; the 'present Generation ... ascribe no Merit to the Virtue and Experience of Old Age, but assume to themselves the Preference in all things'.[45] Such grumbling could be said to reflect a perennial intergenerational tension, and it was the very behaviour that Swift targeted in his 1699 resolutions 'when I become old' as he promised 'Not to scorn present ways'. Yet, while it might be expected that the older generation should disapprove of the habits of the rising youth, the rhetoric at this time marked a particularly pronounced generational schism.

These generational tensions were humorously played out in Bernard Mandeville's *The virgin unmask'd: or, female dialogues betwixt an elderly maiden lady and her niece* in 1709. The fictional niece was nineteen, while the aunt was that ambiguous 'elderly' stage, so at least middle-aged. Mandeville, who was about to turn forty, took neither side in the argument that ensued in his first dialogue when the aunt asked her niece to 'cover her Nakedness' as she could not abide to see her 'Naked Breast heaving up and down'. The fictional niece argued her stays were not cut any lower than was the fashion. Moreover, if something was fashionable, and so prevalent in society, then she claimed it could not be said to be immodest. This young woman did, however, concede that 'when I am as Old as you Aunt, perhaps I will do as you do'.[46] But, as the century progressed, this generation of women were increasingly ridiculed for failing to do just that.

Interestingly, when the fifty-two-year-old Christopher Anstey published *An Election Ball* in 1776 he referred to the same generational divide in fashion that Mandeville had critiqued in 1709. This satire was presented as a series of letters from the fictional Mr Inkle to his wife, keeping her abreast of events in Bath where he and their daughter, Madge, were to attend an election ball. While describing the scene as they readied themselves for the evening's entertainments, Anstey's Mr Inkle declared:

> And now I must tell thee, dear Wife, how thy Daughter
> Makes a Progress in all the fine Things you hast taught her;
> Not like thy old Grandmother DOROTHY DISTOFF[47]

Anstey's Mrs Inkle had first caught her husband's eye in 1739, so she was at least late middle-aged.[48] However, in contrast to the elderly aunt in Mandeville's *Dialogues*, she actively encouraged the *risqué* dress of her daughter. And whatever the truth in the lowering of necklines, Mr Inkle went on:

> to make a young Lady a true polite Figure
> You must cramp up her Sides that her Breast may look bigger,
> And her's tho' a Chicken as yet, my dear DINAH,
> Stand forth full as plump, and as Jolly as thine are:
> And why should ye leave any Charm for Conjecture,
> Like the Figure you see in your Grandmother's Picture,
> With her Neck in a Ruff, and her Waist in a Girdle,
> ...

> You never as yet did those Beauties conceal,
> Which Nature intended your Sex to reveal;
> And I'm happy that MADGE has acquir'd such a Spice
> Of Your excellent Manners, and wholesome Advice[49]

Mr Inkle's mocking of his wife's grandmother was playing on a cultural trope. Firstly, given that the ruff had faded from fashion before 1650, it is unlikely that someone of Mrs Inkle's generation had portraits of their grandmother (as opposed to their great-grandmother) in such dated clothing. Moreover, it is evident that not all elderly women in the earlier decades of the eighteenth century were adopting the stance of the sober matrons described by Defoe and Mandeville. Nonetheless, the seventeenth-century generations were presented as being a world apart from those who had grown up with modern eighteenth-century habits.

This is not, of course, to say that these modern habits were impervious to the vagaries of fashion. As far as the bright young things of the 1760s and 1770s were concerned, Horace Walpole's generation, which included the fictional Mr and Mrs Inkle, had become thoroughly outdated.[50] In 1774, at the age of fifty-seven, Walpole admitted as much:

> not that I am apt to dislike young folks, whom I think everything becomes. ... In the world, one cannot help perceiving one is out of fashion. ... I, who see many young men with better parts than myself, submit with a good grace, or retreat hither to my castle, where I am satisfied with what I have done. ... I do not much invite the juvenile, who think my castle and me of equal antiquity.[51]

Likewise, despite claiming he still cut a fine figure, the gout-ridden Mr Inkle 'very much feared' his daughter thought him a 'fogram'; a newly coined term to describe 'a fusty old fellow'.[52] The rising generation at this time were rejecting the cultural mores of their parents and grandparents, something I have discussed at length elsewhere.[53] As a consequence, those who were middle-aged and old were seen by the younger generation as not simply unfashionable but entirely out of kilter with the present times, just as sober matrons had seemed at the beginning of the century. It was in this context that Horace Walpole felt increasingly out of step with what he saw as 'a world more and more governed by the younger members of society'.[54]

In keeping with Walpole's assertion, the youthfulness inherent in new trends had become ever more pronounced during the 1760s and 1770s, before fashions became positively juvenile towards the close of the century.[55] This was when fashionable young men rejected stockings in favour of long trousers, adopting a style akin to the skeleton suit; an item

THE RISING GENERATION AND THE FOGRAM   103

of nursery clothing first seen a decade or so earlier, when these young men had been children. And it was not only young men but also young women who were maintaining the styles they had worn in childhood when they reached adulthood during the 1790s, as the hoops and bustles of the eighteenth century were discarded. This adult adoption of children's clothing was not missed by the satirists, as can be seen in Gillray's print "_____" *"And catch the living Manners as they rise"* (1794), in which he presented a burlesque rendition of these latest styles (Figure 4.2).

Gillray, who was in his late thirties, evidently expected his audience to know the preceding line of poetry from Alexander Pope's *An Essay on Man* (despite his transposing of two words); the missing line being, 'Shoot folly as it flies'. Yet while this middle-aged satirist might have seen the

Figure 4.2. "_____" *"And catch the living Manners as they rise"* (1794). © National Portrait Gallery, London.

Figure 4.3. 'An agreeable group of young gentlemen, otherwise old bachelors turn'd asses' (1797). Courtesy of The Lewis Walpole Library, Yale University.

rising generation's new styles as ripe for ridicule, there was no turning back the fashions. And it was in this context that the censure became particularly unforgiving of those older women and men foolhardy enough to attempt to keep up with the juvenile styles of the day, a habit often cruelly associated with being left on the shelf. This is clearly seen in the comical print 'Maiden Ewe Drest Lamb Fashion', discussed by Vickery; an image depicting an older woman dressed in the same style of neo-classical empire-waist gown as seen in Figure 4.2.[56] Likewise, 'An agreeable group of young gentlemen, otherwise old bachelors turn'd asses' (Figure 4.3) presents a group of older men sporting the long-trousered hyper-juvenile fashions of the day despite the tell-tale signs of their lack of youth, including bald heads, old-fashioned wigs and spectacles. Clearly, such behaviour was seen as a joke regardless of gender.

Conclusion

Adulthood was evidently not a homogenous or stable category. Its boundaries with youth and old age were key to framing cultural understandings of this phase of the life cycle, and so too was the midlife point when both men and women began to see their young adulthood as behind them. Moreover, those in later middle age might have been described as old in comparison to those in their twenties and even thirties, but this is not to say they were necessarily thought to have reached old age. It is this relational nature of the life cycle that makes it so important to recognise adulthood as a historical category. To study adult society without doing so is to isolate historical actors from the inherent dynamism of the life course, and from the age relations that helped to shape their experiences. In a century that eulogised youth, those entering the adult world were repeatedly framing new youthful ideas about what it meant to be an adult, and as they aged their own youthful prejudices against the older generations almost inevitably helped to shape their experience of growing older themselves. It is noteworthy that it was as the bright young things of the early century reached old age that this generational process became particularly pronounced, and the censure of those feigning youth gained a more pitiless tenor. This was not simply a generation refusing to see themselves as elderly or old at an age they might previously have considered to be so. It was a generation who had fashioned themselves on their youthful attributes reassessing what it was to be an older adult at the same time as younger adults were redefining what it meant to be young. Neither the fogram nor the rising generation can be understood in isolation. To locate adulthood in the eighteenth century is, therefore, as much about age relations as it is about any particular phase in the life course.

Notes

1. For a wider discussion of the links between age relations and the processes of historical change, see Barbara Crosbie, *Age Relations and Cultural Change in Eighteenth-Century England* (Woodbridge: Boydell Press, 2020).

2. Philippe Ariès, *Centuries of Childhood* (Harmondsworth: Penguin Books, 1979) is a problematic book but his underlying claim that childhood had changed fundamentally at this time is stubbornly persistent. For an overview, see Crosbie, *Age Relations*, 19–51. For a counter-claim, see Anthony Fletcher, *Growing Up in England: The Experience of Childhood, 1600–1914* (London: Yale University Press, 2008).

3. Amanda Vickery, 'Mutton Dressed as Lamb? Fashioning Age in Georgian England', *Journal of British Studies*, 52, no. 4 (2013): 858–86; Susannah R. Ottaway, *The Decline of Life: Old Age in Eighteenth-Century England* (Cambridge: Cambridge University Press, 2004); Helen Yallop, *Age and Identity in Eighteenth-Century England* (London: Routledge, 2013).

4. Crosbie, *Age Relations*.

5. See especially Alexandra Shepard, *Meanings of Manhood in Early Modern England* (Oxford: Oxford University Press, 2006); Sara Mendelson and Patricia Crawford, *Women in Early Modern England, 1550–1720* (Oxford: Clarendon Press, 1998).

6. Lynn Botelho, 'Old Women in Early Modern Europe: Age as an Analytical Category' in *The Ashgate Research Companion to Women and Gender in Early Modern Europe*, eds. Jane Couchman and Allyson M. Poska (London: Taylor & Francis, 2013), 305; also see Crosbie, *Age Relations*.

7. Crosbie, *Age Relations*, 1.

8. Botelho, 'Old Women in Early Modern Europe', 296; also see Yallop, *Age and Identity*, 4–5.

9. For useful discussions of this topic, see Deborah Simonton, 'Earning and Learning: Girlhood in Pre-Industrial Europe', *Women's History Review*, 13, no. 3 (2004): 363–86; Ilana Ben-Amos, *Adolescence and Youth in Early Modern England* (London: Yale University Press, 1994), especially 208–35.

10. Sarah Toulalan, '"Elderly Years Cause a Total Dispaire of Conception": Old Age, Sex and Infertility in Early Modern England', *Social History of Medicine*, 29, no. 2 (2016): 333–59; Helen Yallop, 'Representing Aged Masculinity in Eighteenth-Century England: The "Old Man" of Medical Advice', *Cultural and Social History* 10, no. 2 (2013): 191–210.

11. *The Infants Lawyer* (London, 1726), 45, 50, 21, 49.

12. Sir Matthew Hale, *Historia placitorum coronæ*, vol. 1 (London, 1736), 17.

13. Sir William Blackstone, *Commentaries on the laws of England*, vol. 1 (Oxford, 1770), 437–8.

14. John Kersey, *A New English Dictionary* (London, 1702).

15. Edward Cocker, *Cocker's English Dictionary* (London, 1704).

16. Nathan Bailey, *An universal etymological English dictionary* (London, 1721).

17. 'British Maids, who in the Times of our Henries were not held marriageable til turn'd of Twenty, are now become falling ripe at twelve.' J. Dennis, *Essay upon Publick Spirit* (1711), 15, cited in the *Oxford English Dictionary*.

18. Samuel Johnson, *A dictionary of the English language* (London, 1755).

19. Daniel Fenning, *The royal English dictionary* (London, 1761).

20. John Ash, *The New and Complete Dictionary of the English language* (London, 1775).

21. John Bentick, *The spelling and explanatory dictionary of the English language* (London, 1786).

22. William Perry, *A General Dictionary of the English Language* (London, 1795).

23. Kay Heath, *Aging by the Book: The Emergence of Midlife in Victorian Britain* (Albany, NY: State University of New York Press, 2009), 1–2.

24. Vickery, 'Mutton Dressed as Lamb?', 859–60.

25. Ella Sbaraini, '"Those That Prefer the Ripe Mellow Fruit to Any Other": Rethinking Depictions of Middle-Aged Women's Sexuality in England, 1700–1800', *Cultural and Social History*, 17, no. 2 (2020): 165–87.

26. Henry Fielding, *The history of Tom Jones*, vol. 1 (London, 1749), 9; *The history of Charlotte Summers*, vol. 2 (London, 1753), 317.

27. Francis Mauriceau, *The Diseases of Women with Child, and in Child-Bed*, translated by Hugh Chamberlen (London, 1710), 112, 122.

28. Crosbie, *Age Relations*, 144–6.

29. *The Berwick museum, or, Monthly literary intelligencer*, vol. 2 (Berwick, 1785–7), 144.

30. 'Of Modern Inventions' in Thomas Gordon, *The Humourist*, 3rd ed. (London, 1724), 82–90.

31. *The Lounger*, no. 51. Saturday, 21 January 1786 (London, 1787), vol. 2, 147–8.

32. Katarzyna Bronk-Bacon, '"It Is Scandalous at My Age": Horace Walpole's Epistolary Aging', *Eighteenth-Century Studies*, 55, no. 4 (2022): 497–516 (see esp. 500–502).

33. Peter McNeil, *Pretty Gentlemen: Macaroni Men and the Eighteenth-Century Fashion World* (London: Yale University Press, 2018), 55.

34. Vickery, 'Mutton Dressed as Lamb?'

35. *The Lounger.*

36. A phrase used by Mary Wollstonecraft, cited in Vickery, 'Mutton Dressed as Lamb?', 868.

37. Mattina Darly was the daughter of the famous producers of prints, Mary and Matthias (Matthew) Darly. For details, see the curator's comments from M. Dorothy George: www.britishmuseum.org/collection/object/P_J-5-109.

38. Eliza Fowler Haywood, *Epistles for the ladies*, vol. 2 (London, 1749–50), 2–4, 7.

39. See especially Vickery, 'Mutton Dressed as Lamb?'

40. Vicesimus Knox, *Essays Moral and Literary* (London, 1782), No. LXXVIII. 'On the Fear of Growing Old', 337–8.

41. Knox, *Essays Moral and Literary*; Yallop, *Age and Identity*, 14.

42. Knox, *Essays Moral and Literary.*

43. Crosbie, *Age Relations*, 158.

44. Bronk-Bacon, 'It Is Scandalous at My Age', 506.

45. Daniel Defoe, *The Protestant monastery: or, a complaint against the brutality of the present age* (London, 1727), iv, 1, 2, 19, 20.

46. Bernard Mandeville, *The virgin unmask'd: or, female dialogues betwixt an elderly maiden lady and her niece* (London, 1731), 1, 7, 2.

47. Christopher Anstey, *An Election Ball*, 3rd ed. (Bath, 1776), 31.

48. Anstey, *An Election Ball*, 40.

49. Anstey, *An Election Ball*, 42–3.

50. For a wider discussion of the generational divisions of the 1770s, see Crosbie, *Age Relations.*

51. Bronk-Bacon, 'It Is Scandalous at My Age', 507.

52. Anstey, *An Election Ball*, 47; see also Francis Grose, *A classical dictionary of the vulgar tongue* (London, 1785); Fogram is defined in the *Oxford English Dictionary* as 'an old person, with very old-fashioned or conservative ideas or attitudes'.

53. Crosbie, *Age Relations*, chapter 5.

54. Bronk-Bacon, 'It Is Scandalous at My Age', 506.

55. Crosbie, *Age Relations*, 33, 174–7, 192–201.

56. Vickery, 'Mutton Dressed as Lamb?', 865.

References

Primary sources

'Of Modern Inventions'. In Thomas Gordon, *The humourist*, 3rd ed. London, 1724.

The Berwick museum, or, monthly literary intelligencer, vol. 2. Berwick, 1785–7.

The history of Charlotte Summers, vol. 2. London, 1753.

The infants lawyer. London, 1726.

The lounger, no. 51, vol. 2. London, 1787.

Anstey, Christopher. *An election ball*, 3rd ed. Bath, 1776.

Ash, John. *The new and complete dictionary of the English language*. London, 1775.

Bailey, Nathan. *An universal etymological English dictionary*. London, 1721.

Bentick, John. *The spelling and explanatory dictionary of the English language*. London, 1786.

Blackstone, Sir William. *Commentaries on the laws of England*, vol. 1. Oxford, 1770.

Cocker, Edward. *Cocker's English dictionary*. London, 1704.

Defoe, Daniel. *The Protestant monastery: or, a complaint against the brutality of the present age*. London, 1727.

Fenning, Daniel. *The royal English dictionary*. London, 1761.

Fielding, Henry. *The history of Tom Jones*, vol. 1. London, 1749.

Grose, Francis. *A classical dictionary of the vulgar tongue*. London, 1785.

Hale, Sir Matthew. *Historia placitorum coronæ*, vol. 1. London, 1736.

Haywood, Eliza Fowler. *Epistles for the ladies*, vol. 2. London, 1749–50.

Johnson, Samuel. *A dictionary of the English language*. London, 1755.

Kersey, John. *A new English dictionary*. London, 1702.

Knox, Vicesimus. *Essays Moral and Literary*. London, 1782.

Mandeville, Bernard. *The virgin Unmask'd: or, female dialogues betwixt an elderly maiden lady and her niece*. London, 1731.

Mauriceau, Francis. *The diseases of women with child, and in child-bed*, translated by Hugh Chamberlen. London, 1710.

Perry, William. *A general dictionary of the English Language*. London, 1795.

Secondary sources

Ariès, Philippe. *Centuries of Childhood*. Harmondsworth: Penguin Books, 1979.

Ben-Amos, Ilana. *Adolescence and Youth in Early Modern England*. London: Yale University Press, 1994.

Botelho, Lynn. 'Old Women in Early Modern Europe: Age as an Analytical Category'. In *The Ashgate Research Companion to Women and Gender in Early Modern Europe*, edited by Jane Couchman and Allyson M. Poska, 297–315. London: Taylor & Francis, 2013.

Bronk-Bacon, Katarzyna. '"It Is Scandalous at My Age": Horace Walpole's Epistolary Aging', *Eighteenth-Century Studies*, 55, no. 4 (2022): 497–516.

Crosbie, Barbara. *Age Relations and Cultural Change in Eighteenth-Century England*. Woodbridge: Boydell Press, 2020.

Fletcher, Anthony. *Growing Up in England: The Experience of Childhood, 1600–1914*. London: Yale University Press, 2008.

Heath, Kay. *Aging by the Book: The Emergence of Midlife in Victorian Britain*. Albany, NY: State University of New York Press, 2009.

McNeil, Peter. *Pretty Gentlemen: Macaroni Men and the Eighteenth-Century Fashion World*. London: Yale University Press, 2018.

Mendelson, Sara and Crawford, Patricia. *Women in Early Modern England, 1550–1720*. Oxford: Clarendon Press, 1998.

Ottaway, Susannah R. *The Decline of Life: Old Age in Eighteenth-Century England*. Cambridge: Cambridge University Press, 2004.

Sbaraini, Ella. '"Those That Prefer the Ripe Mellow Fruit to Any Other": Rethinking Depictions of Middle-Aged Women's Sexuality in England, 1700–1800', *Cultural and Social History*, 17, no. 2 (2020): 165–87.

Shepard, Alexandra. *Meanings of Manhood in Early Modern England*. Oxford: Oxford University Press, 2006.

Simonton, Deborah. 'Earning and Learning: Girlhood in Pre-Industrial Europe', *Women's History Review*, 13, no. 3 (2004): 363–86.

Toulalan, Sarah, '"Elderly Years Cause a Total Dispaire of Conception": Old Age, Sex and Infertility in Early Modern England', *Social History of Medicine*, 29, no. 2 (2016): 333–59.

Vickery, Amanda. 'Mutton Dressed as Lamb? Fashioning Age in Georgian England', *Journal of British Studies*, 52, no. 4 (2013): 858–86.

Yallop, Helen. *Age and Identity in Eighteenth-Century England*. London: Routledge, 2013.

Yallop, Helen. 'Representing Aged Masculinity in Eighteenth-Century England: The "Old Man" of Medical Advice', *Cultural and Social History*, 10, no. 2 (2013): 191–210.

Chapter 5

Seduction suits and gendered adulthood in the civil court systems of the early United States, 1820–50

Holly N.S. White

On 18 February 1828, weeks after her twenty-first birthday, wealthy Virginian Elizabeth Ruffin picked up her pen to ask her brother 'a peculiar favor'. Recognising that her birthday meant the termination of her formal guardianship, she wrote to her older half-brother and legal guardian Edmund Ruffin: 'This legal independence – what a mistaken notion is entertained of it: what an undesirable possession it is in my opinion.'[1] In a second, undated letter, Elizabeth broached the subject again: 'If you would just forget what age and law have entitled me and act precisely as my guardian still in the management of all my business I should deem it a peculiar favor.'[2] Rather than allow her guardianship to come to its natural conclusion, Elizabeth wanted to extend her legal guardianship longer; a request no American male ward would have made in the early United States.

Elizabeth's father died when she was young, and he left her enough of an inheritance that she could be financially independent as an adult. Unlike most American women at the time, Elizabeth would not need to work, depend on family or marry to have her economic survival needs met. Without having to worry about money, Elizabeth was theoretically free to do as she pleased. And yet, even as Elizabeth's wealth and elite white status bolstered what her 'legal independence' could mean for her, her gender diminished her identity as an adult in early American culture (1820–50).

For women in the early United States, especially those who were impoverished, reaching the age of legal adulthood deliberately offered them no real opportunities or rights. Unable to vote or participate in government, women were intentionally denied access to full adult status.[3] Consequently, American families and communities often ignored the fact that a woman had reached a legal milestone at all. Because of their gender, American women were always assumed to be someone's dependant, regardless of their age, race or class.[4] This expectation of female dependence was so prevalent that it was used as a legal strategy to undermine age laws that defined adulthood and independence.

Laura Tisdall and Maria Cannon note in the Introduction to this collection that adulthood is an intersectional category. When examining age-relevant cases heard in early American courts, the intersectionality of American adulthood was clear; the significance of one's age and status were always negotiated within the context of one's race and gender.[5] It is important to recognise that people of African and American Indian descent suffered even more from stratified definitions of adulthood. However, this chapter's purpose is to consider the role that gender, age and marital status played in either elevating or circumscribing an unmarried, white woman's claim to adult identity in the early United States.

Beginning with a brief overview of early American definitions of adulthood, this chapter concludes with an examination of five age-relevant civil court cases called 'seduction suits'. Each case was heard in the first half of the nineteenth century; three in Pennsylvania and two in North Carolina. Originally, a seduction suit revolved around the claim of a loss of service and was meant to be a dispute between two employers. The English law of servitude 'recognized the loss a master might suffer if another individual improperly "seduced" away one of his servants'.[6] English law also defined the status of children as legal dependants, or 'servants', to their fathers. Thus, by legally claiming a series of 'necessary fictions', seduction suits allowed fathers to sue for a 'loss of service' when their unmarried, underaged daughters became pregnant, even if the daughter never actually laboured for the household. Used in this way, early American seduction suits were inherently gendered, as only daughters, not sons, could become pregnant.

Early American definitions of gendered adulthood

The identities of 'adult' and 'child' have always been strategically ascribed to some Americans and kept from others. In 1828, the same year that Elizabeth wrote her letters to Edmund, Noah Webster's *American Dictionary of the English Language* defined an 'adult' as 'a person grown to full size and strength, or to the years of manhood ... a person between fourteen and twenty-five years of age'.[7] Defining adult status by chronological age as well as physical traits and abilities still made sense to early Americans, even as the concept of independence firmly worked its way into newer definitions of adulthood.

Prior to the American Revolution, dependence was a fact of life for colonists. From marriage to monarchy, dependence and power were defined and balanced through mutual obligation in all relationships. For example, the relationship between the king and a male British subject was one of dependence; so was the relationship between a trades master and his apprentice. It was not until the Declaration of Independence that 'the meaning of dependence shifted ... [and] ceased to be a construct with positive connotations'. It was only over the course of the last two decades of the eighteenth century that the concept of dependence became 'highly gendered', 'feminized' and 'imbued with a sense of powerlessness'.[8]

As American legislators redefined the cultural and social meanings of dependence, they also leaned into the use of age to define legal independence. As independence became equated with adulthood which became equated with age, it seemed Americans might solve some of the problems associated with monarchy. But it could not be so simple as 'turning dependent subjects into republican citizens'.[9] The reality of America's racialised and gendered social hierarchies required thoughtful qualifiers to define who was allowed to hold full adult status and what that status meant. Although property ownership was initially required to vote, this requirement was dropped in the first decades of the nineteenth century. As a result, full legal adulthood became available to any white male over the age of twenty-one.[10]

Comparatively, unmarried 'adult' women were expected to remain socially, physically and financially dependent upon male family members. The first American legislatures did little to facilitate a change in these expectations. Historian Jacqueline Beatty notes that the law of the early United States 'recognized women's personhood, and, to a certain degree, their citizenship, but it also presumed their dependence, which codified them as legally vulnerable and passive'.[11] This expectation that women were either in a state of dependence or actively trying to move back into one served as justification for denying women the right to vote. For many women of the working or lower classes, adult status meant more risk than reward. Some scholars have even argued that 'legal independence for young single women in the nineteenth century often meant greater vulnerability to sexual predation'.[12]

In most states, girls reached legal adulthood before their brothers. In theory, these gendered age differences reflected an expectation that girls reached puberty two to three years earlier than boys. Early American lawmakers reasoned that because girls could theoretically reproduce at younger ages than boys, this meant that they should be ready for marriage at earlier ages as well. However, as historian Nicholas L. Syrett argues, the lower age of consent for women also 'served to move girls more smoothly as dependents between different men's households and to ensure that a male head of household always governed their property'.[13] American daughters were expected to marry at the age of legal adulthood and be subsumed under their husband's identity, transformed back into dependants akin to children.

Once a woman married, her wealth and any property she owned became her husband's and her independent legal identity ceased to exist. This was because of the English common-law practice of coverture, a legal doctrine that the United States maintained after its break from Great Britain. Coverture meant that once a woman married, her legal existence was merged with that of her husband's. Coverture also meant that it was illegal for a married woman to enter contracts, own her own property, make a will, be sued, sue others, press charges on her own or be a witness in court. American women, regardless of race or class, were never intended to attain social and legal independence, the cornerstone concepts of full adulthood in the early United States.[14]

American 'adult' daughters were expected to remain at home as dependants (and servants) of their families until their inevitable marriage. Veiled as gendered protection, a more accurate representation of the relationship that existed between unmarried adult daughters and their families was economic and legal interdependence. This was especially true for those who came from lower- and working-class backgrounds. Elite parents might have expected deference, largely because of their continued financial and social support, but they did not depend on their children for labour or income the way that lower-class families did. The influence of gender on adulthood and legal independence can be best seen in the labour arrangements of lower-class families.[15] More specifically, when a family actually lost something if they recognised a daughter's legal adulthood, we see the clearest examples of challenges to the laws that defined independence by age.

Even as the experience and understanding of work and labour changed over the course of the nineteenth century, the traditional expectation that children's labour would contribute to the household's productivity continued seamlessly after the American Revolution.[16] This was particularly true for families that did not rely on wage-based work arrangements in addition to many families who did work for wages but still relied on family labour to maintain the household. Legally, fathers had the right to benefit from their children's labour, male or female, until their child turned eighteen or twenty-one.[17] However, culturally, many families expected this arrangement to continue so long as their child was unmarried and dependent in some way on the household for survival. Daughters suffered this reality exponentially more than sons, indicating that gender and marital status rather than legal adulthood influenced how families defined extended dependence and servitude.

Evidence of how common it was for working- and lower-class daughters to maintain at least a façade of extended dependence can be found in seduction suits and loss-of-service cases tried and appealed in the first half of the nineteenth century. Courts allowed these cases to be heard even though the women involved were legal adults. This is significant because it demonstrates how culturally pervasive this idea of perpetual female dependence was. By looking at a small sample of appealed seduction suits, important insight is gained into how working-class families strategically ignored the significance of their female members' legal adulthood. Additionally, these cases reveal the struggle jurors and justices experienced when faced with upholding laws that defined adult status but that also conflicted with communal expectations of perpetual female dependence.

Seduction suits in the early United States

How and why 'seduction suits' were filed in the early United States had evolved significantly by the nineteenth century. Over the course of the eighteenth century, rape and bastardy charges became exceedingly difficult to press and prove in American courts.[18] Families living in the early United States needed a way to secure redress for the social and sexual harm done to their unmarried, and now non-virginal, female members. Over time, with the help of 'inventive lawyering', the seduction suit became a form of civil action that families could pursue when the criminal courts failed them.[19]

The five seduction suits to be discussed revolved around a presumed dependent relationship. It is important to remember that being defined as someone's child or dependant did not make them *a child*, even if a family attempted to portray them as such. Based on chronological age, each woman to be discussed was a legally independent adult. But, because these women were unmarried, their families viewed and claimed them as dependants. The testimonies and rulings found in these suits shed light on how white families negotiated evolving legal definitions of adulthood against cultural realities of female dependence and marital status in the early United States.

The 1822 Pennsylvania appellate case *Hornketh v. Barr* offers a straight-forward example of how seduction suits in the early United States generally worked.[20] According to trial records, sometime in 1816, with his consent, Hugh Barr's younger daughter moved to Philadelphia to work and to live with her older, married sister. While in Philadelphia and before she turned twenty-one, 'the seduction and confinement of [Barr's] daughter took place'. The defence appealed the case and argued that because Barr's daughter lived with her sister, technically her sister was her master. This meant that the sister should be the one to sue for a loss of service, not the father. However, as the initial court as well as the appeals court ruled, because the girl was a minor, 'the father could command the services of his child at any time. Therefore, during her pregnancy and confinement, he lost, because he could not have had her services if he had required them'. Consequently, Barr won the case.

The two factors that made the ruling in *Hornketh v. Barr* so clear cut were that Hugh Barr's daughter was under the age of twenty-one and that he was her 'natural' father. But not all seduction and loss-of-service cases were like this. This chapter concludes by analysing four additional court cases, two in Pennsylvania and two in North Carolina, to explore how some American families negotiated legal definitions of adulthood against cultural realities of female dependence in the early United States. It is important to note that this micro case study is meant to be illustrative and evocative, not reflective or representative of all American families' experiences at the time.

Each state in the United States defined adulthood by age; and in each case to be discussed, the 'seduced' was a legal adult by that measure. It would seem, then, that all four cases should be straightforward; because the 'seduced' were legal adults, there should have been no case. And yet these four cases were all tried, indicating that early American court systems recognised adulthood as a more fluid status, one that was informed by gender, race, class and status rather than strictly chronological age.

The seduction suit *Logan v. Murray*, filed in 1820 Pennsylvania, first began as a rape case heard in Westmoreland County. James Murray was accused of sexually assaulting and impregnating Sarah Logan on the night of 16 September 1815. According to the testimony, Sarah 'was above the age of twenty-one years' when the rape occurred but she was unmarried and still resided with her parents. Her father had died on 28 November that same year, after which Sarah continued to live with her mother 'who became the head of the family'. The baby was born on 2 June 1816, forty weeks after the rape. Margaret insisted that after the birth, Sarah 'was never well' again.

In January 1817, Sarah passed away, leaving behind a child that her mother was now forced to raise.[21] It took nearly three years, but Margaret, Sarah's mother, managed to file a seduction suit against Murray in 1820. Margaret argued that the pregnancy, caused by James Murray's sexual assault, resulted in Sarah's death. Because Sarah never left her parents' household, her 'lying in' and death deprived Margaret of her daughter's labour. Margaret wanted to be financially compensated for this loss.

The outcome of *Logan v. Murray* is not surprising: Margaret lost her case due to Sarah's age at the time of her pregnancy. Sarah had been a legal adult, and the court was quick to point this out. Despite Sarah's legal independence, Margaret insisted that Sarah never transitioned into social adulthood and remained a dependent daughter. More than likely, Sarah had an interdependent relationship with her parents as she continued to live and work in the family home after ageing into adulthood. The court suggested it would have considered the argument more seriously had the Logan patriarch not died. As justices explained, usually 'the slightest evidence of service is sufficient, where the daughter resides with the parent, and has arrived at years of maturity'. That assumed dependency did not transfer to Sarah's mother once her father died. Instead, when her mother took on Sarah's dependence, she was already pregnant and thus, the court argued, Margaret had knowingly acquired that risk.

In September 1831, Robert Sproul filed a seduction suit in Pennsylvania against John Wilson for impregnating his sister-in-law, Polly Porter. Polly had given birth in the Sproul home in November 1826 when she was twenty-eight years old. Like Sarah, Polly was unmarried and had aged into her legal independence. However, by the time of the trial, both Polly's parents had died, which severed her ability to claim she was a dependent daughter, still living and working at home. Instead, Polly leaned into her reality, even as she left out critical details about her life.

Under oath, Polly admitted that she had lived with the Sprouls since she was about twenty years old. Polly's sister and her husband Robert had opened their home to her in exchange for 'weaving' and other work around the household. Based on these informal exchanges, Robert argued that Polly was his servant. Once Polly gave birth in the Sproul home, he argued that she also became his dependant as 'she was nursed by his wife ... for two weeks and worked but little for four weeks'.[22]

Jurors found Robert Sproul's initial argument convincing, perhaps thinking about their own family dynamics and who they considered dependants within their own households. However, John Wilson appealed the verdict and won. In the new ruling, justices agreed that biological parents were not the only family members who could sue for a loss of service. However, 'in such cases, the child must be underage, and actually employed in the service of the plaintiff'. Neighbours had confirmed that Polly came and went from the Sproul household and that when she did stay for extended lengths of time, she paid Robert as a boarder. At one point, Robert even owed her money. Consequently, justices ultimately dismissed the suit against John Wilson because 'the seduced was twenty-eight years of age ... and was in every respect her own mistress'.[23]

To the community, Polly lived and earned as an independent adult woman. And yet, Polly and Robert filed a seduction suit as if she were a dependent daughter-like figure in his household. More importantly, they had at least initially convinced others of this argument. It's important to remember that Robert Sproul was not a father, an uncle or even a biological brother to Polly. But because he was related to her by law and she had a history of living in his household, the case moved forward despite law and logic. This is significant to note because it indicates how deeply embedded the belief that regardless of age, if a woman was unmarried, society assumed she was some household's childlike dependant.

In the first seduction suit discussed, *Hornketh v. Barr*, Hugh Barr quickly won his case because he was the dependant's father, and because the dependant was still legally a child. In comparison, Margaret Logan and Robert Sproul lost their cases because the dependants they claimed were legally independent, adult women. The fact that Logan and Sproul were not fathers further weakened their suits. However, the last two seduction suits to be discussed, *Phipps v. Garland* and *Briggs v. Evans*, were a bit more complicated. Both Phipps and Briggs were the fathers of those they filed suits for; however, in each case the daughter was a legal adult. The communities in which they each lived clearly expected unmarried women to live in perpetual dependence, deference and servitude to their families. Concluding with these cases underscores how arbitrary age and law were in defining independent adulthood in the early United States.

On an autumn day in 1837 in Yancy County, North Carolina, thirty-year-old single mother Jane Phipps testified about where she had lived and worked prior to her pregnancy.[24] Jane swore that 'her father's house was her home; her bed and furniture and all her other property, except some clothing, remained there'. However, 'with her father's consent', she had worked and lived in the Garland household for the past several years as a 'hireling'. While working for the Garland family, Jane regularly moved between the two households, and when she returned to her

SEDUCTION SUITS AND GENDERED ADULTHOOD 119

father's home, she 'performed the ordinary duties in his family of washing, cooking, and milking'.[25]

Jane's testimony was carefully worded; she made clear that despite being a legal adult, she deferred to her father, Jacob Phipps, for consent on life choices and considered his house as her home. Jane described herself as a dependent daughter because like Elizabeth Ruffin mentioned at the start, legal independence offered little to Jane as an unmarried woman. Had she acknowledged herself as an independent adult, Jacob Phipps's seduction suit would have had no chance of moving forward.

Jacob Phipps filed the seduction suit against his grandchild's father, John W. Garland, in 1837. In the original trial, the jury found in favour of Phipps; however, Garland won the appeal. Familial and legal interpretations of father–daughter relationships were clearly at odds with one another in this North Carolina community. The initial trial was ruled upon by a jury, or members of the community that Phipps and Garland lived in. Made up of similarly aged and life-staged men, jurors likely took into consideration their own family circumstances. Although their children legally became independent adults once they turned twenty-one, they often remained at least semi-dependent beyond that age. Recognising that the transition into full adulthood was more fluid and conditional on other factors besides age, jurors may have been swayed to overlook the law in favour of supporting Phipps.

However, the appeals case was ruled upon by justices who were more interested in adhering strictly to the law. Justices argued in the final case that because 'the daughter was of full age and did not live with her father at the date of the debauchery', there was 'no legal obligation on the father to maintain and take care of her'. In other words, Jacob Phipps chose to take his daughter back into his household when he no longer had a legal obligation to do so. Consequently, Phipps had no right to sue John Garland for loss of service.

Lewis Briggs filed a writ of seduction in 1842 against John J. Evans for a loss of service due to the pregnancy of his daughter, Rosanna.[26] In September 1841, when the seduction was alleged to have occurred, Rosanna was twenty years old and living with her grandmother. One month after conception, she turned twenty-one. Jurors were meant to determine what right Lewis Briggs had to sue for a loss of service given that Rosanna was in her minority at the time of conception but an adult for most of the pregnancy and the subsequent birth.

The trial judge recognised the uniqueness of the case and broke the decision down for jurors based on the father–child relationship and the master–servant relationship. First, the judge instructed the jury to decide whether Lewis Briggs as Rosanna's father had lost any services because of the pregnancy before she had turned twenty-one. Then, the jury was to decide whether he had lost any services as her master after Rosanna became a legal adult. Once these two aspects of the case were determined, the jury could then 'take into their consideration the anguish and disgrace brought upon the plaintiff and his family, in order to enhance the damages'.[27]

The jury found for Lewis Briggs. John Evans appealed the case, and it made its way to the state Supreme Court where justices upheld the original verdict. John Evans argued that Lewis Briggs could not sue for loss of services 'without proof of an actual contract for services after the daughter became of age'. Justices disagreed, arguing that because it was clear that she lived with her family and provided services at the time of the seduction, an assumed master–servant relationship existed. Justices explained:

> Before the child attains the age of twenty-one years, the law gives the father dominion over her, and, after, the law presumes the contract, when the daughter is so situated, as to render services to the father, or is under his control; and this it does for the wisest and most benevolent purposes, to preserve his domestic peace, by guarding from the spoiler, the purity and innocence of his child. If this were not so, in those cases ... the unfortunate parent would be without redress if his daughter were over twenty-one years of age.[28]

The assertion that a legally recognised master–servant relationship was not dependent on a contract was surprising. Setting the pregnancy aspect aside, had Rosanna been a man, a court would never have considered the case. The age of twenty-one meant full legal independence for sons, but, as this suit clearly shows, it only sometimes meant that for daughters.

All four cases revolved around the issue of lost service due to pregnancy; however, in none of the cases was the unmarried woman in question under the age of twenty-one or a contracted servant. Even as they were all legally recognised as independent adults due to their chronological age, the fact that these women were unmarried was precisely what caused their families and communities to view them as dependants. A murder case, *The People v. Matthew Wood*, provides another example of this presumption. In 1849 in New York, Matthew Wood was found guilty of murdering his wife of two years, Susan. Susan's brother took the stand and explained how the pair met, describing Susan as a 'girl' who was 'enticed away' by Matthew. However, the court record also specified that Susan was 'forty-two years of age' at the time of their marriage.[29] Clearly, for many families and the communities they lived in, one's marital status and gender was more important than one's chronological age in determining a person's status in life. Women could be well over the age of legal adulthood, yet if they were unmarried, they were still considered a child-like dependant who owed deference and service to their families.

Although each of the seduction suits discussed ultimately failed, the testimonies captured in the trial records give insight into how adulthood was defined in the early United States. Both sides often moved their definitions of adulthood away from age and towards a person's other forms of identity, like gender or race, to win their cases. Prosecution and defence alike alternated between the terms adult and independent or dependant and child. This intentional word slippage was more than just a legal strategy; these negotiations over who was a child, who was an adult and when age mattered reflected and informed wider debates about the evolving definitions of adulthood in the early United States.

Conclusion

Edmund Ruffin never responded to Elizabeth's 'peculiar request'. It turns out he did not need to as just a few months later, Elizabeth slipped comfortably into the role of wife, losing her legal independence and identity altogether. No longer needing to be protected by her brother, Elizabeth lived out the rest of her life legally 'covered' by her husband. For many women, like Elizabeth Ruffin, dependency was so embedded into their understanding of self that age meant nothing to them. This was because white American females lived in a liminal state between childhood and adulthood. Their bodies changed and aged even as their status never truly did. Should their guardians deem it necessary, girls could be 'adult' enough to bear and raise children as young as ten or twelve.[30] Once 'women', they could just as easily be transformed back into symbolic children who were assumed to be perpetually dependent upon someone – whether family or husband.

And yet, so long as a woman remained unmarried, the law insisted they were legal adults, capable of business transactions and informed consent. Early Americans reconciled these opposing concepts strategically; contradictions were ignored when convenient and deeply acknowledged when it was necessary. Adulthood in the early United States, then, was not a static category of being. Just like childhood, it was a murky, sometimes age-defined status. The concept of adulthood, in general, was manipulated by early Americans to best protect themselves and their family members. However, those who were white, female and unmarried seemed to have been able to move in and out of these two life-stage statuses most easily. The filing of seduction suits offers a clear example of just that as white families increasingly used these suits to benefit their sexually wronged, unmarried, female members.

Notes

1. Elizabeth Ruffin to Edmund Ruffin, 18 February 1828, 'Edmund Ruffin Papers', Southern Historical Collections, Richmond, Virginia, United States. The Ruffin family were members of Virginia's planter aristocratic class; they owned large swathes of land and financially benefited from the enslavement of hundreds of Black Virginians.

2. Elizabeth Ruffin to Edmund Ruffin, undated letter, 'Edmund Ruffin Papers', Southern Historical Collections, Richmond, Virginia, United States. The letter had to have occurred sometime shortly after the first letter written on 18 February 1828 as Elizabeth was married later that same year.

3. Corinne T. Field, *The Struggle for Equal Adulthood: Gender, Race, Age, and the Fight for Citizenship in Antebellum America* (Chapel Hill, NC: University of North Carolina Press, 2014), 52–3. Women in the United States were not guaranteed the right to vote until the 19th Amendment was passed by Congress on 4 June 1919 and ratified on 18 August 1920.

4. There is a long history of scholarship on female (in)dependence in the early United States. For two of the most recent works, see Jacqueline Beatty, *In Dependence: Women and the Patriarchal State in Revolutionary America* (New York: New York University Press, 2023); Mary Sarah Bilder, *Female Genius: Eliza Harriot and George Washington at the Dawn of the Constitution* (Charlottesville, VA: University of Virginia Press, 2022).

5. See Ariela J. Gross, *What Blood Won't Tell: A History of Race on Trial in the Early United States* (Cambridge, MA: Harvard University Press, 2010); Holly N.S. White, 'Judging the Bodies of Children: Racial Science and Double Age as Legal Strategy in the Early United States', *Journal of the History of Childhood and Youth*, 15, no. 3 (2022), 399–409.

6. John Wood Sweet, *The Sewing Girl's Tale: A Story of Crime and Consequences in Revolutionary America* (New York: Henry Holt and Company, 2022), 225.

7. Noah Webster, *American Dictionary of the English Language* (1828): 'Adult'.

8. Beatty, *In Dependence*, 7.

9. Field, *The Struggle for Equal Adulthood*, 23.

10. Field, *The Struggle for Equal Adulthood*, 6–7.

11. Beatty, *In Dependence*, 7.

12. Lea VanderVelde, 'The Legal Ways of Seduction', *Stanford Law Review*, 48, no. 4 (1996), 871.

13. Nicholas L. Syrett, *American Child Bride: A History of Minors and Marriage in the United States* (Chapel Hill, NC: University of North Carolina Press, 2016), 17.

14. Field, *The Struggle for Equal Adulthood*; see also Jon Grinspan, *The Virgin Vote: How Young Americans Made Democracy Social, Politics Personal, and Voting Popular in the Nineteenth Century* (Chapel Hill, NC: University of North Carolina Press, 2016).

15. See Anya Jabour, *Scarlett's Sisters: Young Women in the Old South* (Chapel Hill, NC: The University of North Carolina Press, 2007), esp. chapter 3: Single Life.

16. See Frances M. Clarke and Rebecca Jo Plant, *Of Age: Boy Soldiers and Military Power in the Civil War Era* (Oxford: Oxford University Press, 2023); Mary Ann Mason, *From Father's Property to Children's Rights: A History of Child Custody* (New York: Columbia University Press, 1994); Jeanne Boydston, *Home and Work: House-work, Wages, and the Ideology of Labor in the Early Republic* (Oxford: Oxford University Press, 1994); Holly Brewer, *By Birth or Consent: Children, Law, and the Anglo-American Revolution in Authority* (Chapel Hill, NC: University of North Carolina Press, 2007).

17. Frances M. Clarke and Rebecca Jo Plant argue that parental rights, especially regarding their ownership of minor children's labour, became of special concern to the American public during the War of 1812 through the American Civil War. Because of a need for soldiers, the American government lowered the age of enlistment from twenty-one to eighteen. Parents responded with an onslaught of legal challenges to enlistment contracts of their underaged sons on the grounds that they still owned their labour for three more years. Clarke and Plant argue that these military lawsuits demonstrate 'the endurance of a communal vision of the household' and expose 'parents' economic reliance on minor children'. Clarke and Plant, *Of Age*, 19.

18. For changes to bastardy laws in colonial British North America, see John Ruston Pagan, *Anne Orthwood's Bastard: Sex and Law in Early Virginia* (Oxford: Oxford University Press, 2001). For changes to rape laws in colonial British North America, see Sharon Block, *Rape and Sexual Power in Early America* (Chapel Hill, NC: University of North Carolina Press, 2012) and Alexander Smyth, *A Rape in the Early Republic: Gender and Legal Culture in an 1806 Virginia Trial* (Lexington, KY: University of Kentucky, 2017).

19. For the most recent scholarship on early American seduction suits, see Sweet, *The Sewing Girl's Tale* (quote: p. 225). For a thorough legal explanation of seduction suits in the nineteenth century, see VanderVelde, 'The Legal Ways of Seduction'.

20. *Hornketh v. Barr*, 8 Serg. & Rawle 36 (1822).

21. *Logan v. Murray*, 9 A.M. Dec. 422 (1820).

22. *Wilson v. Sproul*, 3 Pen. & W. 49 (1831). This case is also mentioned in M.B.W. Sinclair, 'Seduction and the Myth of the Ideal Woman', *Minnesota Journal of Law & Inequality*, 5, no. 1 (March 1987), as well as VanderVelde, 'The Legal Ways of Seduction'.

23. *Wilson v. Sproul*, 3 Pen. & W. 49 (1831).

24. Trial records do not name Phipps's daughter. However, based on ancestral records, Phipps's eldest daughter was born in 1806 and was named Jane. That would have made her about thirty or thirty-one at the time of the trial. Phipps's next daughter was not born until 1817, making her too young.

25. *Jacob Phipps v. John W. Garland*, 20 N.C. 38 (1838).

26. *Lewis Briggs v. John J. Evans*, 27 N.C. 16 (1844). Trial records do not name Briggs's daughter. However, based on ancestral records, Briggs had a daughter born in 1820 named Rosanna.

27. *Lewis Briggs v. John J. Evans*, 27 N.C. 16 (1844).

28. *Lewis Briggs v. John J. Evans*, 27 N.C. 16 (1844).

29. *The People v. Matthew Wood*, 2 Edm. Sel. Cas. 71 (1849).

30. Syrett, *American Child Bride*.

References

Primary sources

'Edmund Ruffin Papers', Southern Historical Collections, Richmond, Virginia, United States.

Hornketh v. Barr, 8 Serg. & Rawle 36 (1822).

Lewis Briggs v. John J. Evans, 27 N.C. 16 (1844).

Logan v. Murray, 9 A.M. Dec. 422 (1820).

Phipps v. Garland, 20 N.C. 38 (1838).

The People v. Matthew Wood, 2 Edm. Sel. Cas. 71 (1849).

Wilson v. Sproul, 3 Pen. & W. 49 (1831).

Webster, Noah. *American Dictionary of the English Language* (1828).

Secondary sources

Beatty, Jacqueline. *In Dependence: Women and the Patriarchal State in Revolutionary America*. New York: New York University Press, 2023.

Bilder, Mary Sarah. *Female Genius: Eliza Harriot and George Washington at the Dawn of the Constitution*. Charlottesville, VA: University of Virginia Press, 2022.

Block, Sharon. *Rape and Sexual Power in Early America*. Chapel Hill, NC: University of North Carolina Press, 2012.

Boydston, Jeanne. *Home and Work: Housework, Wages, and the Ideology of Labor in the Early Republic*. Oxford: Oxford University Press, 1994.

Brewer, Holly. *By Birth or Consent: Children, Law, and the Anglo-American Revolution in Authority*. Chapel Hill, NC: University of North Carolina Press, 2007.

Clarke, Frances M. and Plant, Rebecca Jo. *Of Age: Boy Soldiers and Military Power in the Civil War Era*. Oxford: Oxford University Press, 2023.

Field, Corrine T. *The Struggle for Equal Adulthood: Gender, Race, Age, and the Fight for Citizenship in Antebellum America*. Chapel Hill, NC: University of North Carolina Press, 2014.

Grinspan, Jon. *The Virgin Vote: How Young Americans Made Democracy Social, Politics Personal, and Voting Popular in the Nineteenth Century*. Chapel Hill, NC: University of North Carolina Press, 2016.

Gross, Ariela J. *What Blood Won't Tell: A History of Race on Trial in the Early United States*. Cambridge, MA: Harvard University Press, 2010.

Jabour, Anya. *Scarlett's Sisters: Young Women in the Old South*. Chapel Hill, NC: The University of North Carolina Press, 2007.

Mason, Mary Ann. *From Father's Property to Children's Rights: A History of Child Custody*. New York: Columbia University Press, 1994.

Pagan, John Ruston. *Anne Orthwood's Bastard: Sex and Law in Early Virginia*. Oxford: Oxford University Press, 2003.

Smyth, Alexander. *A Rape in the Early Republic: Gender and Legal Culture in an 1806 Virginia Trial*. Lexington, KY: University of Kentucky, 2017.

Sweet, John Wood. *The Sewing Girl's Tale: A Story of Crime and Consequences in Revolutionary America*. New York: Henry Holt and Company, 2022.

Syrett, Nicholas L. *American Child Bride: A History of Minors and Marriage in the United States*. Chapel Hill, NC: University of North Carolina Press, 2016.

VanderVelde, Lea. 'The Legal Ways of Seduction', *Stanford Law Review* 48, no. 4 (1996), 817–904.

White, Holly N.S. 'Judging the Bodies of Children: Racial Science and Double Age as Legal Strategy in the Early United States', *The Journal of the History of Childhood and Youth*, 15, no. 3 (2022), 399–409.

Chapter 6

'They're not children anymore': Juveniles as adult defendants in US criminal justice, 1786–2000

Jack Hodgson

On 24 March 2023, sixteen-year-old Joshua Keith Beasley Jr died by suicide at Jester State Prison in Fort Bend County, Texas. The *Texas Tribune* reported that 'Texas imprisoned Joshua ... when he was 11, purportedly for his own good. Five years later he returned home in a casket', six months after being transferred to adult jail. He died while Texan officials were asking judges to transfer more juveniles to adult prisons. The Texas Special Prosecuting Unit's Jack Choate argued such transfers removed the most challenging inmates from juvenile facilities, especially 'dangerous youths who had assaulted staff'. Investigative journalism revealed that prematurely transferred inmates included others like Beasley Jr who had diagnosed mental health difficulties and trafficking victims. Meanwhile, Texas Department of Juvenile Justice inmates inhabited toilet-less cells for up to twenty-three hours per day amid acute staffing shortages. Critics accused Texan officials of 'throwing away kids' to hide institutional failings.[1]

The first Texan facility for 'delinquent' youths opened in 1889 and specific juvenile courts began opening across the US in 1899. Yet in 2023 juveniles were still dying in adult jails. This chapter argues that American juvenile justice systems were only ever intended to cater for *some* children. Biological age has not been the decisive factor in determining if defendants are processed as adults or children. Children are still sent to adult facilities despite research suggesting they are up to thirty-six times more likely to die by suicide than their peers in youth custody. They have a disadvantageous form of adulthood thrust upon them. 'Adult' status often comes with greater power, autonomy and social standing, but here the 'adult' label is weaponised by the state and wielded against specific children of whom it disapproves. Theoretically this involves a subjective judgement of a child's character, but decision-making is vulnerable to structural racism which oppresses entire groups of children.

The histories of children in 'adult' US criminal justice are important, not least because they expose how seemingly neutral laws discriminate against specific racial groups. For historians of adulthood or childhood, this history shows how distinctions between these categories are unclear. What do we mean by 'adult' if a child can be deemed an 'adult' in proceedings important enough to shape the rest of their life? Considering this, as Winthrop Jordan comments, 'in our culture, adulthood, as a condition used to be simply assumed' but now it demands 'an explanation'.[2] Legally, clear divisions between adult and child exist in the US but despite these apparent boundaries, children much younger than the age of majority are charged, incarcerated and punished as 'adults'. This chapter argues that to be deemed an 'adult' in US criminal justice children were often judged to have betrayed the innocence commonly associated with childhood and to have a capacity for evil or criminal intent which society deems adult-specific. It examines cases where children accused of murder faced either the death penalty or life imprisonment, paying attention to how their race influenced their treatment by analysing remarks by judges, law enforcement and journalists. In these cases, adulthood was conferred based upon an evaluation of an individual's behaviour, but judgements were influenced by other factors including race, gender and class.

Children and the death penalty

From the colonial era through to the early nineteenth century, US criminal codes were written to apply to everyone, irrespective of age. For example, during the famous Salem Massachusetts 1692 witch trials, Sarah and Thomas Carrier were accused of witchcraft alongside their mother, Martha. They were aged seven and nine. Thomas's likely coerced confession that his mother had taught him witchcraft but that he had only practised it for one week helped to secure his reprieve.[3] The Carrier children's involvement demonstrates how in Puritan New England children alongside adults were deemed capable of the evil occult. In that heightened religious environment there were not separate categories of juvenile delinquency and adult criminality but one type of wrongdoer:

the sinner. Nevertheless, the public and authorities recognised that young children were different to adults. This was uncodified, so some youths were afforded more leniency than others. Some were treated as if they were miniature adults – receiving the same severe punishments as adult offenders including public whippings, imprisonment and even death, whereas in other cases youthfulness was recognised as a mitigating factor.

On 20 December 1786, twelve-year-old Hannah Ocuish, a mixed-race Pequot Native with a Black father, was hanged in New London, Connecticut, after being convicted of murdering six-year-old Eunice Bolles. Crystal Webster and Holly N.S. White disagree over the strength of evidence implicating Ocuish.[4] One alleged motive was a quarrel between the two girls over strawberries several months prior. Prosecutors' case included conjecture and blatantly racialised testimony where Ocuish's Native mother was described as an alcoholic 'creature'. The 1752 Murder Act mandated punishment by death by hanging. The judge refused to consider Ocuish's age in mitigation, stating 'the sparing of you on account of your age would ... be of dangerous consequence to the public, by holding up an idea, that children might commit such atrocious crimes with impunity'.[5] White analyses numerous cases where predominantly Black youths were executed having faced near-impossible battles to prove criminal innocence or diminished responsibility and contrasts these against cases involving white children where early American courts carefully considered age, maturity and innocence. Gender, race and class were decisive in adjudicating children's criminal responsibility – themes that continue to arise in the early twentieth-century cases analysed later.

Rather than operate as impartial authorities, courts were oppressive tools leveraged against colonised people. The court endorsed a racialised view that Ocuish was inherently savage and sanctioned the state's desire to kill her. It is no coincidence that Ocuish remains the youngest-known executed convict in US history and that James Arcene, a ten-year-old Cherokee convicted of assisting an 1872 murder-robbery, remains the youngest-known child sentenced to die. He escaped post-sentencing but was executed after recapture in 1885.[6] Both cases were frequently invoked by opponents of the juvenile death penalty and speak to the harsh treatment of Native Americans by courts and a federal government which did not consider them citizens until 1924. Aged ten and twelve respectively, authorities deemed them 'adult' enough to die at an executioner's hand.

Between 1642 and 1959 colonies, states and the federal government executed at least 394 juveniles. One of the starkest indications that American juvenile justice was never designed to cater for all youths is that this continued long after reforms established differentiated juvenile justice systems. The last minor executed in the US was seventeen-year-old African American Leonard Shockley who died in a Maryland gas chamber in 1959.[7] The twentieth-century history of youths and capital punishment is one of discrimination against Black boys. George Stinney Jr was fourteen when South Carolina electrocuted him in 1944. His trial spanned two hours. The all-white jury deliberated for ten minutes. Carl Suddler's analysis of postwar New York reveals how Black youths were condemned with a stigma of assumed criminality at odds with a justice system purporting to presume defendants' innocence, showing that this was not a purely Southern issue.[8] Stinney's conviction for murdering two younger white girls was posthumously vacated in 2014 when a South Carolina court ruled that his trial was unfair.[9] Habiba Ibrahim's work demonstrates how Black age was seen as malleable and contingent in a way which has affected youths accused of crimes like Stinney but also Black youths when they are victims of adult violence. Ibrahim points to the killings of Emmett Till and Trayvon Martin as examples of the adultification of Black youths in victimhood. These twentieth- and twenty-first-century cases are linked to the longer history of Black subjugation by Ibrahim, including the longer history of manipulating Black age for the purpose of enslavement.[10] In this sense, Black age has historically been linked to white perceptions of appearance and presumed capacities rather than biological age, something which remained evident in the treatment of Black youths within criminal justice.

The US Supreme Court (SCOTUS) temporarily halted the death penalty in 1972's *Furman v. Georgia* but it was reinstated in 1976. Post-1976, twenty-two males were executed for crimes committed as juveniles. In *Thompson v. Oklahoma* (1988) SCOTUS prohibited capital punishment where the defendant was under sixteen when committing the crime, overturning the death penalty imposed upon fifteen-year-old William Thompson for the revenge killing of his former brother-in-law over abuse perpetrated against Thompson and his sister.[11] SCOTUS expanded its ruling from *Thompson* in *Roper v. Simmons* (2005). The majority cited adolescent brain development science and prohibited the death penalty in cases where the defendant was under eighteen at the time of the crime. After *Roper*, 'evolving standards of decency' meant juvenile capital punishment amounted to unconstitutional cruel and unusual punishment.[12]

The rise of juvenile courts

Despite allowing executions for juvenile-committed crimes until 2005, the US had long differentiated children from adults in other aspects of criminal justice. Prior to nineteenth-century reforms, this was discretionary, but the longstanding recognition that children were different to adults and needed different treatment eventually informed separate juvenile justice infrastructure. But children continued to be charged, tried and incarcerated as adults. Officials sorted youths into two discrete categories: those deemed worthy of protection from the vices of the adult criminal justice system and those deemed 'adult' enough to be exposed to them. This 'adulthood' was not about biological age or physical and mental maturity but a value judgement on potential to reform. Children deemed to have flawed characters or whose alleged crimes were too severe were stripped of their child status by authorities pursuing harsher punishment.

During the Progressive era, loose coalitions of 'child-saving' activists, often upper- and middle-class white women, achieved various piecemeal child-focused reforms. Janet Wilson details how historical appraisals of their motivations vary: child-savers are regarded as humanitarians who extended their domestic care-giving roles into the public sphere; meanwhile, critical accounts highlight attempts to impose values on impoverished and immigrant families, using the state to enforce order on their terms to control youthful behaviours. Furthermore, even some of the staunchest advocates for a separate juvenile system raised comparatively little opposition to Black children's experiences of Jim Crow justice.[13] Geoff Ward details how Black Americans mounted their own child-saving campaigns while Black youths continued to encounter a parallel Jim Crow justice system after a Progressive rehabilitative approach had begun shaping white children's experience of justice.[14] Child-savers disagreed on issues but agreed on foundational principles that children were innocent, uniquely vulnerable and deserved more compassionate treatment. Children whose actions betrayed notions of innocence and vulnerability were frequently denied access to the separate juvenile justice system these reformers helped to shape.

From 1863, Massachusetts law meant that 'children of tender years' were not criminally responsible for their actions and in 1878 the Bay State passed the first American probation law. By 1910, thirty-eight states and the District of Columbia had similar laws. The 1898 Illinois Juvenile Court Act reflected child-saving reformers' attitudes in establishing the country's first juvenile court. Its primary mandate was to save predelinquent children from lives of adult criminality, though it did hear serious cases including murders. Protestant minister and Children's Aid Society founder Charles Loring Brace described the type of children juvenile courts routinely served as *enfants perdus* (lost children).[15] Juvenile justice architects envisioned it as prescribable treatment for predelinquent youths. In 1905, Pennsylvania's Supreme Court ruled that authorities could commit children to reformatories to 'save a child from becoming a criminal, or from continuing a life of crime'.[16] Children who displayed too much criminality to be 'saved' were still processed as 'adults'. The historic attitude that children can reach a point of no return regarding 'adult' criminality long remained in legislation; in 2023, thirty-five states had so-called once/always laws, meaning that once a youth faces adult charges, all subsequent charges are filed in adult court, even in non-violent minor cases.[17]

Juvenile courts did not evenly spread across America's complex myriad of legal jurisdictions. In 1923, the US Children's Bureau's Katherine Lenroot observed that urban youths were likely to have their cases heard in youth courts but juveniles in smaller towns and rural areas frequently lived in jurisdictions without a children's court. Lenroot also noted a concerning lack of minimum national standards for juvenile courts which increased the risk of unfairness. That persisted. In 1967's *In re: Gault*, SCOTUS asserted that juveniles had the constitutional right to due process; 1970's *In re: Winship* raised the burden of proof in juvenile proceedings to 'beyond reasonable doubt', mirroring adult criminal justice. Previously juvenile court defendants had no guarantee of due process and could lose their liberty based on a mere balance of probabilities.[18]

The charging, trying and incarceration of juveniles as adults is mainly a state-by-state issue as youths usually face state charges but federal courts do try children's cases; there is no federal juvenile court. US attorneys have the power to charge children as adults. The federal system resisted Progressive-era reforms and continued to process all children as if they were adults. For example, *Ex Parte Beaver* (1921) considered a writ of *habeas corpus* over custody of a youth who had lied about his age to join the army before deserting. His lawyers pleaded for his case to be treated differently but he was prosecuted for desertion in federal court despite being too young to legally serve. Despite more recent SCOTUS case law, the federal prosecutors' manual continued favouring a 1989 case asserting that older youths should be charged as adults because the 'more mature a juvenile becomes, the harder it is to reform the juvenile's values and behaviour'. Similarly, it states that youth with 'streetwise intellect or precociousness' should similarly be candidates for trial as an adult.[19] A 'streetwise intellect' is a subjective judgement that invites class-based and racialised prejudice against specific youths previously exposed to violent crime who adapted their behaviour because of traumatic experiences. Appearing 'streetwise' does not mean that a child can follow federal criminal proceedings.

Herbert Niccolls Jr

Aside from federal courts and rural areas lacking youth-specific provision, a separate juvenile justice system of juvenile courts and reformatory schools had spread across the US by the Depression era. Children accused of serious crimes like murder were still tried in adult courts and accommodated in adult jails. Authorities recognised that young children could not practically live in adult jails. In 1929, six-year-old Carl Newton Mahan of Paintsville, Kentucky, became the youngest murder defendant in American history. Mahan, a middle-class white boy, shot eight-year-old playmate Cecil van Hoose following an argument over scrap metal. Days after the killing, Mahan described to the court how he had killed his friend during a day-long trial which continued even as the tired defendant napped on a courtroom desk. After half an hour of deliberations, the jury convicted him of an alternative manslaughter charge. A county judge sentenced Mahan to fifteen years' imprisonment to be served in a reformatory rather than county jail, prompting public outcry and legal appeals. To some a manslaughter conviction was not enough. Others thought it excessive. Newspapers ran photographs of the skinny Mahan in a suit, clutching his toy doll. Kentucky attorney general James Cammack reviewed the case and upheld a circuit judge's writ of prohibition preventing Mahan serving his custodial sentence. He was 'bailed' to the custody of his parents.[20]

Mahan was unusually young but homicides involving older children have proven semi-frequent. These defendants' race shaped their treatment, as did press coverage, judicial assignments and accessibility of quality legal counsel. In 1931, Asotin, Washington, was rocked by the fatal shooting of the small town's long-serving sheriff John Wormell as he investigated a late-night shop burglary. The killer was eleven-year-old Herbert Niccolls Jr, a local white boy with a reputation as 'Mary Addington's delinquent grandson'. Before living with Addington, Niccolls had spent time in reformatories for offences including tricycle theft, joyriding and setting fire to a church. Within hours an angry mob formed outside the courthouse where Niccolls was held and began shouting for him to be hanged. Outnumbered, and fearing for his and their safety in a town with a history of lynching, officers hastily transferred him across county lines. At first the case appeared uncontroversial; public opinion seemed set against Niccolls.[21]

Before his trial Niccolls was held in an adult jail, segregated from other prisoners. Without counsel, he gave prosecutors a confession which quickly appeared in the *Lewiston Morning Tribune*. When the case came to trial, it proved impossible to find jurors who had not read it. Two potential jurors were discharged for stating opposition to the 'drastic penalties' prescribed by law, given Niccolls's age.[22] Again without accompaniment, Niccolls was evaluated at Eastern State Hospital and underwent psychological questioning and invasive medical procedures, including having spinal fluid drawn for analysis. This lack of regard for juvenile defendants' constitutional rights was commonplace prior to 1960s SCOTUS cases but Niccolls's rights were repeatedly violated before an 'adult' trial. Defending Niccolls was a necessary but unpopular task; the court appointed him out-of-town attorneys. The trial hinged on whether Niccolls was sane and responsible for his actions as the facts were agreed. Niccolls testified: 'I was so scared I just fired my pistol to scare him. I didn't know which way I pointed it, but I shot Mr Wormell.'[23]

The case drew national publicity and crowds gathered in Asotin ahead of *State v. Niccolls*. An enterprising Methodist Church sold fried chicken lunches to people keen to catch a glimpse of the boy dubbed 'the barefoot killer', a reference to his owning no shoes. Public opinion had shifted. Rather than baying for blood like the crowd that had gathered on the night of the killing, this crowd included well-wishers. One woman gave Niccolls homemade gingersnaps. Local farmer J.B. Tucker paid to outfit him in a tailored suit and sporty red bowtie. Niccolls did not resemble the monstrous descriptions that had saturated the press immediately after the murder. He looked 'more like eight than twelve, with his long delicate face, long eyelashes, and a very thin frame'. A *Seattle Post-Intelligencer* journalist commented that Niccolls could have stepped straight from the pages of Booth Tarkington's *Penrod* tales. In doing so they compared him to a popular representation of rugged American boyhood which followed the fictional pre-World War I adventures of eleven-year-old Midwesterner Penrod Schofield, a character frequently likened to Mark Twain's Tom Sawyer.[24]

Judge Elgin Kuykendahl opened the trial by asking if 'Mr Niccolls' was present. The defendant answered as he would for morning roll at school, prompting laughter from the public gallery. His actions and appearance gave the impression of a lost little boy who did not understand the proceedings around him. Nobody denied that he had killed Wormell. The uncertainty regarded prosecutors' abilities to convince Kuykendahl that he should die. Colonel Fulton, from whom Niccolls had stolen the murder weapon, testified to that effect, saying, 'He's a murdering little thief. He should be hanged.' At this Niccolls urgently tugged on his attorney's shirt and as the judge called recess the boy ran to the lavatory and vomited. Fulton was in the minority. Niccolls's growing number of sympathisers

'THEY'RE NOT CHILDREN ANYMORE'   135

pointed to traumatic childhood experiences to argue that the state owed him protection, not punishment.[25]

Niccolls spent his early childhood on the family ranch in Star, Idaho. His mother Hazel was 'neglectful' to her children amid her violent and dysfunctional marriage to Herbert Sr. Herbert Jr recalled 'Papa hitting Mama' and how his father's fists 'split flesh'. Idaho removed the children after their father was committed to an asylum for killing a neighbour. Herbert Jr found the body and suffered regular night terrors where he saw a woman's corpse lying 'like a broken toy'. Life with his grandmother was also difficult. After his arrest, jailers summoned doctors to treat him for 'trench mouth', signifying longstanding malnutrition and neglect. His playmate Murphy Watkins described how Addington locked her grandson in a room without food or water. Watkins's mother Jean recalled that if Herbert was late, Addington beat him with a club. In an era where white children were seen as having a right to a childhood, Niccolls's experience of neglect and violence went against ideals of what childhood should be.[26] His sympathisers argued that the failings of his guardians, society and the authorities who were expected to intervene in matters of child welfare made the prospect of the death penalty unfair.[27]

The jury deliberated for three hours to convict Niccolls of murder but did not recommend the death penalty. Kuykendahl drew criticism from all sides for sentencing Niccolls to life imprisonment at Washington's Walla Walla state penitentiary. Washington State Supreme Court justice Kenneth Mackintosh commented that Niccolls 'should have hung' and that he would always be a 'menace' to society.[28] New York's Sing Sing prison's warden disagreed, arguing that he could be rehabilitated into a productive citizen. Newspaper opinion sections were vitriolic. One letter-writer described a child receiving a life sentence as 'an ungodly, rotten stain' on the judiciary's intelligence and a 'rank foul miscarriage of justice'. Another called the jury which convicted him 'uncivilized barbarians'. Oakland's St Celia Society even prayed that 'every bad fortune' be visited on Kuykendahl and his family.[29] Guards at Walla Walla described Niccolls as a 'problem', explaining 'we can't treat him as we would a man'. Niccolls liked checkers and dominoes, frequently asking, 'Maybe you could play with me?' He also enjoyed performing tunes like 'Home on the Range' on his harmonica.[30] His behaviour, perhaps deliberately, conformed to expectations of childishness and influenced how jailers and inmates treated him. When deadly riots engulfed the prison, concerned inmates sheltered him from violence.

Seattle socialite and child welfare campaigner Armene Lamson petitioned for Niccolls's release and invited father Edward Flanagan of Boys

Town, Nebraska fame to join her campaign. Flanagan argued that Niccolls had 'never been given a chance' in life and used the airwaves to criticise Governor Roland Hartley's non-intervention. Hartley retaliated, attacking Flanagan in the press.[31] Taking the principle that one who does not prevent a crime is also guilty to an extreme, Flanagan contended that a preadolescent boy can only be as guilty as the community around him. The *Seattle Star* published readers' letters condemning Hartley's stance. One wrote that 'pest houses never cured diseases'. Another declared, 'Governor Hartley will not be so inhuman as to deny that poor boy a chance in life. If he does, he will lose the respect of all Seattle people.'[32] In 1932 Hartley suffered a heavy defeat to his lieutenant governor John Gellatly in the Republican primary.[33] Democrat Clarence Martin defeated Gellatly as Roosevelt-led Democrats dominated nationally. Martin shared a birthday with Niccolls and took an interest in his case. Niccolls was moved from a cell to a hut by a guard tower, ate his meals with the guards and graduated from high school after being supplied with schoolwork. Martin conditionally pardoned him in 1941 and after his release he lived a crime-free life working as an accountant for Twentieth Century-Fox in Hollywood.

The babes of San Quentin

The same year that Herbert Niccolls Jr arrived at Walla Walla, fourteen-year-old Jesus Borja arrived at California's notorious San Quentin prison. Borja had fatally stabbed twenty-two-year-old Pedro Garcia at Garcia's wedding reception. Ethnicity will have shaped how Borja's case progressed through the justice system. Miroslava Chavez-Garcia's *States of Delinquency* exposes how racist ideas and pseudoscience shaped juvenile experiences of criminal justice in California. This involved categorising youths as either reformable or dismissing them as feebleminded or criminally degenerate. Mexican American, Black and ethnic Euro-American youths resisted and endured state-sanctioned abuses and harsh punishments including involuntary sterilisation as the state appropriated the disciplinarian role from families and communities.[34]

Garcia married thirteen-year-old Rose Guerrero, a girl who Borja considered his 'sweetheart'; the two children had formed a playground pact to marry when grown up. Police originally arrested Garcia for 'child-stealing' after he drove Guerrero from Fresno to Bakersfield. Once lodged in the county jail, Garcia began negotiating with Guerrero's father who gave him permission to marry her and dropped the charges. Press coverage worked to legitimise Garcia's romantic interest in a child with the

'THEY'RE NOT CHILDREN ANYMORE'   137

Selma Enterprise telling readers Guerrero 'looked at least sixteen' and to vilify Borja by describing his 'uncanny and deadly aim'.[35]

This capacity for calculated violent criminality was presented as 'adult' to support Borja's arraignment in adult court. State law meant he would not receive the death penalty. Prosecutors sought permission to try Borja as an adult to pursue life imprisonment. As a juvenile, Borja faced a maximum of six years in a reformatory, which Judge T.R. Thompson described as 'clearly insufficient'. Trying Borja as an adult came from a desire to punish him more severely rather than any judgement of his personal qualities. His attorney Tom Okawara entered a not guilty plea at the Superior Court, withdrawing a confession Borja had given to police without counsel present. Borja stated, 'I was feeling so bad my mind was blank. Right now, I remember making only one or two of the statements you have there. If I made all those statements, I didn't know what I was talking about.' When the trial opened, he 'appeared frightened and cried often during the first hour he was in court'.[36]

Okawara commissioned Stockton State Hospital's assistant superintendent to assess Borja. He concluded that Borja had the mental age of a ten-year-old. Judge H.Z. Austin dealt a significant blow to the defence by barring the physician from testifying, opining it 'not relevant'. To Austin, the severity of Borja's 'adult' crime outweighed considering his mental capacity. After unsuccessful appeals, Borja focused on his education at San Quentin, hoping to be released and able to pursue a career. He became ill with appendicitis and tuberculosis. Governor James Rolph denied Borja's estranged father's plea for a pardon to allow the terminally ill boy to spend his final days with family. Jesus Borja died at San Quentin in May 1933, aged sixteen.[37] While Washington's executive showed Herbert Niccolls Jr leniency, California's denied that to Borja, even when approaching death.

San Quentin's juveniles received intense press interest. Journalists referred to the youngest inmate as the 'babe of San Quentin'. In 1941 that title belonged to fifteen-year-old Achomawi Native Lee Vernon Gibson who had confessed to the murder-arson of sixty-eight-year-old Robert Burke, a disabled mill caretaker in Modoc County. Gibson's confession came after two weeks of unsupervised questioning from police and the district attorney. He arrived at San Quentin days after his fifteenth birthday where jailers described him as acting like a younger boy typically would, exemplified by him bringing his precious bag of marbles to jail.[38]

Journalists and officials involved in Gibson's case moved quickly to justify his treatment. Sheriff John Sharp described a 'plenty tough boy'. The *Sacramento Bee* emphasised Gibson's physical strength as an adultifying quality: 'Lee is large for his age', it explained, describing how 'his black eyes took in every detail of the prison yard' and how he had a 'deep knife scar across his neck'. Gibson's injuries were used to portray him as someone well acquainted with criminal violence, far from childish or naive. He was in fact a victim of violence that had left him permanently disfigured with debilitating stiffness in his neck. Gibson understood his situation enough to tell reporters that he would 'rather be dead' than serve life at San Quentin, but other comments suggest he did not understand the prison environment. He told one reporter, 'I plan to learn how to play the Hawai'ian guitar; that's one of my ambitions.' Beyond that, 'Well, I'd like to be able to read a little better, write more handedly, and maybe learn arithmetic.'[39]

Did a boy attached to his marbles and preoccupied with the Hawai'ian guitar belong in San Quentin? Similar to how Washington jailers felt they could not treat Herbert Niccolls Jr as a man, San Quentin's progressive governor Clinton Duffy felt uneasy with Gibson's presence. Duffy could not change Superior Court Judge A.K. Wylie's mind but ordered that Gibson be separated from the institution's 'hardened' criminals. Duffy considered Gibson a boy in a man's prison despite California considering him 'adult' enough. Duffy responded to authorities placing small numbers of juveniles at San Quentin by attempting to replicate the reformatory within the prison complex, opening a schoolhouse and permitting Gibson and other youths to eat with the guards and their families.

Assessing Gibson's case retrospectively is difficult because of the prejudices he encountered. The circumstances of the confession render it meaningless. Journalists and law enforcement assumed him to be inherently 'savage' as an Achomawi and manipulated his injuries and disability to exploit such assumptions. Police and the press emphasised Gibson's prior police records. Initial reports that he had committed bicycle and automobile thefts proved erroneous. Gibson's criminal record stemmed from his numerous escapes from Nevada's Stewart Residential Indian School. Evidence of the worst psychological, physical and sexual abuses which have emerged from similar institutions have not yet emerged from Stewart, but some former residents describe hating their time there. Stewart still played a role in systematically removing Native youths from their families to strip them of their cultural identities. Historian David Adams describes boarding schools as 'education for extinction'.[40] Gibson's running away from Stewart was an act of resistance against colonial oppression which authorities leveraged against him to construe a pattern of criminality. This contributed to him receiving an adult life sentence as a minor.

The tough-on-crime era

For decades after Progressive-era reforms, juvenile courts dealt with most juvenile criminal cases. Only exceptionally serious cases like homicides were routinely transferred to adult courts. There were differing degrees of leniency for youths within the adult system, seemingly dependent on race, which is exemplified by the contrasting treatment of Herbert Niccolls Jr and Jesus Borja. By the 1950s, the US was experiencing a panic over juvenile crime and youthful violence. Withstanding pressure, the federal government initially responded with rehabilitation-focused policies, prioritising prevention over punishment. The Senate Judiciary committee's subcommittee investigating juvenile delinquency remained friendly to progressive ideas promoted by the US Children's Bureau and the National Institute of Mental Health.[41] But by the 1980s, a 'tough on crime' approach to juvenile justice garnered support and the Reagan presidency saw what Russell van Vleet describes as an outright 'attack on juvenile justice'.[42]

Between the mid-1980s and the mid-1990s, there was a 70 per cent increase in the number of juveniles being transferred to adult court. Legislators made 'get tough' reforms, reacting to concerns over increasing juvenile homicide rates. They re-wrote state laws which previously stressed 'rehabilitation' and 'the best interests of the child' to prioritise 'punishment' and 'protection of the public'. In 1994 Brooklyn District Attorney Cardea Goldfarb explained, 'These [juvenile] laws were drafted at a time when kids were throwing spitballs ... now they're committing murders.' Similarly, Cook County Attorney Eileen O'Neil remarked, 'Our juvenile criminal act was written at a time kids were knocking over outhouses, not killing people. We're looking at a whole new breed now.' Republican Florida Congressman Bill McCollum introduced a 1996 bill to allow police and jails to place thirteen-year-olds in cells with adult convicts, stating, 'They're not children anymore. They're the predators out there. They're the most violent criminals on the face of the Earth.'[43] To these officials the assumed threat posed by youths determined if the law should treat them as an adult. Their justifications were demonstrably false. Children have, as this chapter details, been implicated in murders throughout US history.

'Tough on crime' reforms gave officials significant discretion over whether juveniles are tried as children or adults with the intention of weighting unique case facts and judgements on defendants' characters. Jason Carmichael's research suggests that other factors influence decisions. Judges in counties with Republican-leaning electorates are more likely to send juveniles to adult prison, as are those who are elected to the bench. States with larger non-white populations admit greater proportions of juveniles to adult prisons. Rather than any quality or characteristic of the accused, local politics and judicial elections influence the chances of juveniles being tried or jailed as adults.[44] As it was in the era of the early Republic, race remains crucial in determining children's experiences of criminal justice. In the early 2000s, despite using drugs at a lower rate than white youths, Black youths constituted 75 per cent of children charged as adults over drug offences. In Florida between 2020 and 2021, 46 per cent of the 19,086 juveniles arrested were Black but Black juveniles accounted for 61 per cent of children transferred to adult court. From a Critical Race Theory perspective, laws allowing discretionary transfer of juveniles to adult courts are discriminatory in practice. Black and Hispanic youth are more likely to be treated harshly by having a disadvantageous form of adulthood imposed upon them.[45]

Conclusion

The long history of American juvenile justice has not ended the practice of children being tried as adults because American juvenile justice systems were only ever intended to serve the select children who adults deemed worthy of differentiated treatment. The juvenile system was idealised as a treatment for predelinquent youths who still exhibited the vulnerability and innocence commonly associated with childhood. Since the colonial era, only some children have been able to reliably rely on their youthfulness in defence or mitigation. There have been fluctuations, with the Progressive era and subsequently a 'tough on crime' era, the latter of which has culminated in growing numbers of youths being incarcerated in adult prisons for non-violent offences. Historically it is evident that there has never been a neat dividing line between 'adult' and 'child' within American criminal justice. Children's treatment in American adult jails and their large-scale processing as adult defendants is a major contemporary human rights and safeguarding concern. Society perceives adults as capable of evil and extreme criminality and perceives children as innocent. Where children's alleged behaviour violates this ideal, they are deemed overmature and are treated as adults to reflect the 'adult' nature of their behaviour. White children's behaviour in those cases has been more likely to be judged sympathetically. For historians examining the concept of adulthood, this history is particularly important. This unwanted disadvantageous form of adulthood does not come with power. It has no definite biological or legal boundary. It is a subjective character appraisal which is often unchallengeable, with far-reaching consequences, and is wielded against specific children of whom the state disapproves.

Notes

1. Lisa Armstrong, 'Texas Imprisoned Joshua Keith Beasley Jr. When He Was 11, Purportedly for His Own Good. Five Years Later, He Returned Home in a Casket', *Texas Tribune*, 25 April 2023; Jolie McCullogh, '"A Way to Throw Kids Away": Texas' Troubled Juvenile Justice Department Is Sending More Children to Adult Prisons', *Texas Tribune*, 1 May 2023.

2. Winthrop D. Jordan, 'Searching for Adulthood in America', *Daedalus* 105, no. 4 (1976), 1–11.

3. 'Examination of Thomas Carrier Jr Taken before Dudly Broadstret Esq'r', 10 August 1692. Essex Institute Collection, no. 24–5v, Peabody Museum, James Duncan Philips Library, Rowley, MA.

4. Crystal Webster, '"Hanging Pretty Girls": The Criminalization of African American Children in Early America', *Journal of the Early Republic* 42, no. 2 (2022), 253–76; Holly N.S. White, *Negotiating American Childhood: Age-Based Laws and the Illusion of Protection in the Early United States* (Charlottesville, VA: University of Virginia Press, Forthcoming).

5. Henry Channing, *God Admonishing His People of Their Duty, as Parents and Masters. A Sermon, Preached at New-London, December 20th, 1786 Occasioned by the Execution of Hannah Ocuish, a Mulatto Girl* (New London, 1786).

6. 'Hanged on the Gallows', *New York Times*, 27 June 1885; Victor L. Streib, *Death Penalty for Juveniles* (Bloomington, IN: University of Indiana Press, 1987): 72; James Joy, *States of Confinement: Policing, Detentions, and Prisons* (New York: Palgrave Macmillan, 2000), 23.

7. Shockley's sentence was upheld by Maryland's Court of Appeals. See *Shockley v. State*, 218 Md. 491, 148 A.2d 371 (1959).

8. Carl Suddler, *Presumed Criminal: Black Youth and the Justice System in Postwar New York* (New York: New York University Press, 2019).

9. Eli Faber, *The Child in the Electric Chair: The Execution of George Junius Stinney Jr. and the Making of a Tragedy in the American South* (Columbia, SC: University of South Carolina Press, 2021).

10. Habiba Ibrahim, *Black Age: Oceanic Lifespans and the Time of Black Life* (New York: New York University Press, 2021).

11. *Furman v. Georgia*, 408 U.S. 238 (1972); *Thompson v. Oklahoma*, 487 U.S. 815 (1988).

12. *Roper v. Simmons*, 543 U.S. 551 (2005). This case over-ruled *Stanford v. Kentucky*, 492 U.S. 361 (1989) where SCOTUS ruled that Kentucky could execute Stanford for a murder he committed as a seventeen-year-old. Stanford's sentence was commuted by Governor Paul Patton.

13. Janet K. Wilson, 'Child Savers Movement' in F.P. Bernat and K. Frailing, eds., *The Encyclopaedia of Women and Crime* (Hoboken, NJ: Wiley, 2019), n.p.

14. Geoff K. Ward, *The Black Child-Savers: Racial Democracy and Juvenile Justice* (Chicago, IL: University of Chicago Press, 2012).

15. Charles Loring Brace, *The Dangerous Classes of New York, and Twenty Years' Work Among Them* (New York, 1872), 26–8, 90–93. Appears in James Marten, ed., *Childhood and Child Welfare in the Progressive Era: A Brief History with Documents* (Boston, MA: Bedford St Martins, 2005), 29–33.

16. Joseph B. Sanborn Jr, 'Ex parte Crouse' in C.J. Schreck, M.J. Leiber, H.V. Miller and K. Welch, eds., *The Encyclopaedia of Juvenile Delinquency and Justice* (Hoboken, NJ: Wiley, 2017), n.p.

17. Ayra Neelum, *Getting to Zero: A 50-State Study of Strategies to Remove Youth from Adult Jails.* (Los Angeles, CA: UCLA School of Law, 2018).

18. Katherine F. Lenroot, 'The Evolution of the Juvenile Court', *Annals of the American Academy of Political and Social Science* 105 (1923), 213–22; *In re Gault*, 387 U.S. 1 (1967); *In re Winship*, 397 U.S. 358 (1970).

19. Esther K. Hong, 'The Federal Juvenile System', *Boston University Law Review* 102 (2022), 2025–87; Emily Buss, 'Response: What Can We Learn from the Federal Approach to Prosecuting Juvenile Crime?', *Boston University Law Review* 102 (2022), 2089–100.

20. 'Mahan Case Finished in Kentucky, Is Belief; Boy Apparently Free', *Cincinnati Enquirer*, 27 June 1929, 1.

21. Nancy Bartley, *The Boy Who Shot The Sheriff: The Redemption of Herbert Niccolls Jr* (Seattle, WA: University of Washington Press, 2013); 'Sheriff of Asotin Slain by Boy Burglar in Store', *Seattle Times*, 5 August 1931.

22. 'Boy, 12, Unmoved in Murder Trial', *San Francisco Examiner*, 27 October 1931, 5; 'Young Murderer Shows No Sign of Remorse; Sleeps after Tragedy', *Lewiston Morning Tribune*, 5 August 1931.

23. 'Boy, 12, Tells Court How He Killed Sheriff', *San Francisco Examiner*, 28 October 1931, 6.

24. Bartley, *The Boy Who Shot the Sheriff*, 36. For *Penrod*, see Frederic I. Carpenter, 'The Adolescent in American Fiction', *The English Journal* 46, no. 6 (1957), 313–19.

25. Bartley, *The Boy Who Shot the Sheriff*, 47–8.

26. Bartley, *The Boy Who Shot the Sheriff*, 42–5, 49–55. For the concept of a right to a childhood, see Kriste Lindenmeyer, *'A Right to Childhood': The U.S. Children's Bureau and Child Welfare* (Urbana, IL: University of Illinois Press, 1997).

27. 'Tragic Side to Case Is Bared', *Walla Walla Daily Bulletin*, 30 October 1931, 1; 'Home Life of Boy Enters Trial', *Daily Northwestern*, 28 October 1931.

28. 'Boy Guilty of Murder', *Los Angeles Times*, 29 October 1931, 1; 'Jurist Would Hang Boy Given Life for Murder', *Sheboygan Press*, 5 November 1931.

29. Bartley, *The Boy Who Shot the Sheriff*, 42–5, 49–55.

30. Bartley, *The Boy Who Shot the Sheriff*, 93; 'Slayer, 12, Plays Harmonica, Waits Decision by Jury', *Seattle Times*, 23 October 1931.

31. 'Noted Priest to Try to Help Boy Slayer', *Helena Independent*, 22 November 1931.

32. 'Governor Refuses Parole for Herbert Niccolls and Assails Father Flanagan for Sensational Campaign', *Bellingham Herald*, 21 December 1931, 1; 'Readers Urge Lad's Parole', *Seattle Star*, 26 November 1931, 7.

33. Washington Secretary of State, 'September 1932 Primary Election Results'.

34. Miroslava Chavez-Garcia, *States of Delinquency: Race and Science in the Making of California's Juvenile Justice System* (Berkeley, CA: University of California Press, 2012).

35. 'Bridegroom Dies at Hand of Rival after Wedding', *Selma Enterprise*, 3 September 1931, 1.

36. 'Fresno Killer in Court Today', *Los Angeles Post-Record*, 1 September 1931, 2; 'Trial of Youthful Slayer Is Up to Juvenile Court', *The Hanford Sentinel*, 1 September 1931, 3; 'Court Bars Low Mental Age as Murder Defence', *The Fresno Bee*, 31 October 1931, 15.

37. 'Boy Prisoner from Fresno Has Operation', *Fresno Bee*, 13 January 1933, 14; 'Killer's Ambitions Balked by Disease', *San Bernardino County Sun*, 13 May 1933, 17, 'Boy's Dream to Atone for Killing Blasted by Death', *Fresno Bee*, 16 May 1933, 15.

38. 'Indian Boy Life Termer Says He Will Not Worry', *Sacramento Bee*, 10 October 1941, 10.

39. 'Indian Boy Life Termer Says He Will Not Worry', 10; 'Young Lifer Brings No Worries to Pen', *Spokane Chronicle*, 10 October 1941, 13; 'San Quentin's "Baby" Glum: No Whiskey!', *San Francisco Examiner*, 10 October 1941, 10.

40. David Wallace Adams, *Education for Extinction: American Indians and the Boarding School Experience, 1875–1928* (Lawrence, KS: University of Kansas Press, 1997).

41. Jason Barnosky, 'The Violent Years: Responses to Juvenile Crime in the 1950s', *Polity* 38, no. 3 (2006), 314–44.

42. Russell K. van Vleet, 'The Attack on Juvenile Justice', *The Annals of the American Academy of Political and Social Science* 564 (1999), 203–14.

43. David S. Tanehous and Steven A. Drizin, '"Owing to the Extreme Youth of the Accused": The Changing Legal Response to Juvenile Homicide', *Journal of Law and Criminology* 92, no. 3 (2002), 641.

44. Jason T. Carmichael, 'Punishing Juvenile Offenders as Adults: An Analysis of the Social and Political Determinants of Juvenile Prison Admissions across the United States', *Sociological Focus* 44 no. 2 (2011), 116.

45. Florida statistics: Dwayne Fatherree, 'Criminal Injustice: States Unfairly Prosecute Children as Adults', Southern Poverty Law Centre, 21 January 2022, www .splcenter.org/news/2022/01/21/criminal-injustice-states-unfairly-prosecute-children -adults (accessed 7 June 2023); Rodney K. Hopson and Jennifer E. Obidah, 'When Getting Tough Means Getting Tougher: Historical and Conceptual Understandings of Juveniles of Color Sentenced as Adults in the United States', *Journal of Negro Education* 71, no. 3 (2002), 171–2.

References

Archives

California State Archives, Sacramento.
Essex Institute Collection, James Duncan Philips Library, Rowley, MA.
Justia.com.
Newspapers.com.

Primary sources

Armstrong, Lisa. 'Texas Imprisoned Joshua Keith Beasley Jr. When He Was 11, Purportedly for His Own Good. Five Years Later, He Returned Home in a Casket', *Texas Tribune*, 25 April 2023.
'Boy, 12, Unmoved in Murder Trial', *San Francisco Examiner*, 27 October 1931, 5.
'Boy, 12, Tells Court How He Killed Sheriff', *San Francisco Examiner*, 28 October 1931, 6.
'Boy Guilty of Murder', *Los Angeles* Times, 29 October 1931, 1.
'Boy Prisoner from Fresno Has Operation', *Fresno Bee*, 13 January 1933, 14.
'Boy's Dream to Atone for Killing Blasted by Death', *Fresno Bee*, 16 May 1933, 15.
Brace, Charles Loring. *The Dangerous Classes of New York, and Twenty Years' Work among Them* (New York, 1872).
'Bridegroom Dies at Hand of Rival after Wedding', *Selma Enterprise*, 3 September 1931, 1.
Channing, Henry. *God Admonishing His People of Their Duty, as Parents and Masters. A Sermon, Preached at New-London, December 20th, 1786 Occasioned by the Execution of Hannah Ocuish, a Mulatto Girl* (New London, 1786).
'Court Bars Low Mental Age as Murder Defence', *The Fresno Bee*, 31 October 1931, 15.
'Examination of Thomas Carrier Jr Taken before Dudly Broadstret Esq'r', 10 August 1692. Essex Institute Collection, no. 24–5v, Peabody Museum, James Duncan Philips Library, Rowley, MA.
'Fresno Killer in Court Today', *Los Angeles Post-Record*, 1 September 1931, 2.
'Governor Refuses Parole for Herbert Niccolls and Assails Father Flanagan for Sensational Campaign', *Bellingham Herald*, 21 December 1931, 1.
'Hanged on the Gallows', *New York Times*, 27 June 1885.

'Home Life of Boy Enters Trial', *Daily Northwestern*, 28 October, 1931.

'Indian Boy Life Termer Says He Will Not Worry', *Sacramento Bee*, 10 October 1941, 10.

'Jurist Would Hang Boy Given Life for Murder', *Sheboygan Press*, 5 November 1931.

'Killer's Ambitions Balked by Disease', *San Bernardino County Sun*, 13 May 1933, 17.

Lenroot, Katherine F. 'The Evolution of the Juvenile Court', *Annals of the American Academy of Political and Social Science* 105 (1923), 213–22.

'Mahan Case Finished in Kentucky, Is Belief; Boy Apparently Free', *Cincinnati Inquirer*, 27 June 1929, 1.

McCullogh, Jolie. '"A Way to Throw Kids Away": Texas' Troubled Juvenile Justice Department Is Sending More Children to Adult Prisons', *Texas Tribune*, 1 May 2023.

'Noted Priest to Try to Help Boy Slayer', *Helena Independent*, 22 November 1931.

'Readers Urge Lad's Parole', *Seattle Star*, 26 November 1931, 7.

'San Quentin's "Baby" Glum: No Whiskey!', *San Francisco Examiner*, 10 October 1941, 10.

'Sherrif of Asotin Slain by Boy Burglar in Store', *Seattle Times*, 5 August 1931, 1.

'Slayer, 12, Plays Harmonica, Waits Decision by Jury', *Seattle Times*, 23 October 1931, 1.

'Tragic Side to Case Is Bared', *Walla Walla Daily Bulletin*, 30 October 1931, 1.

'Trial of Youthful Slayer Is Up to Juvenile Court', *Hanford Sentinel*, 1 September 1931, 3.

Washington Secretary of State. 'September 1932 Primary Election Results'.

'Young Lifer Brings No Worries to Pen', *Spokane Chronicle*, 10 October 1941, 13.

'Young Murderer Shows No Sign of Remorse; Sleeps after Tragedy', *Lewiston Morning Tribune*, 5 August 1931.

Secondary sources

Adams, David Wallace. *Education for Extinction. American Indians and the Boarding School Experience, 1875–1928*. Lawrence, KS: University of Kansas Press, 1997.

Agyepong, Tera Eva. *The Criminalization of Black Children: Race, Gender and Delinquency in Chicago's Juvenile Justice System, 1899–1945*. Chapel Hill, NC: University of North Carolina Press, 2018.

Barnosky, Jason. 'The Violent Years: Responses to Juvenile Crime in the 1950s', *Polity* 38, no. 3 (2006), 314–44.

Bartley, Nancy. *The Boy Who Shot the Sheriff: The Redemption of Herbert Niccolls Jr.* Seattle, WA: University of Washington Press, 2013.

Bernat, F.P. and K. Frailing. *The Encyclopaedia of Women and Crime.* Hoboken, NJ: Wiley, 2019.

Bush, William S. '"A Situation That Has Existed for Generations": Double Age, Race, and American Juvenile Justice', *The Journal of the History of Childhood and Youth* 15, no. 3 (2022), 410–21.

Buss, Emily. 'Response: What Can We Learn from the Federal Approach to Prosecuting Juvenile Crime?', *Boston University Law Review* 102 (2022), 2089–100.

Carmichael, Jason T. 'Punishing Juvenile Offenders as Adults: An Analysis of the Social and Political Determinants of Juvenile Prison Admissions across the United States', *Sociological Focus* 44, no. 2 (2011), 102–23.

Carpenter, Frederic I. 'The Adolescent in American Fiction', *The English Journal* 46, no. 6 (1957), 313–19.

Chavez-Garcia, Miroslava. *States of Delinquency: Race and Science in the Making of California's Juvenile Justice System.* Berkeley, CA: University of California Press, 2012.

Faber, Eli. *The Child in the Electric Chair: The Execution of George Junius Stinney Jr. and the Making of a Tragedy in the American South.* Columbia, SC: University of South Carolina Press, 2021.

Fatherree, Dwayne. 'Criminal Injustice: States Unfairly Prosecute Children as Adults', Southern Poverty Law Centre, 21 January 2022, www.splcenter.org/news/2022/01/21/criminal-injustice-states-unfairly -prosecute-children-adults (accessed 7 June 2023).

Forst, J. Fagan and T.S. Vivona. 'Youth in Prisons and Training Schools: Perceptions and Consequences of the Treatment-Custody Dichotomy', *Juvenile and Family Court Journal* 40 (1989), 1–14.

Frost, Jennifer. '"On Account of Age": The Youth Franchise Movement and the Twenty-Sixth Amendment', *Australasian Journal of American Studies* 50, no. 2 (2021), 49–70.

Hong, Esther K. 'The Federal Juvenile System', *Boston University Law Review* 102 (2022), 2025–87.

Hopson, Rodney K. and Jennifer E. Obidiah. 'When Getting Tough Means Getting Tougher: Historical and Conceptual Understandings of Juveniles of Color Sentenced as Adults in the United States', *Journal of Negro Education* 71, no. 3 (2002), 158–74.

Ibrahim, Habiba. *Black Age: Oceanic Lifespans and the Time of Black Life.* New York: New York University Press, 2021.

Jordan, Winthrop D. 'Searching for Adulthood in America', *Daedalus* 105, no. 4 (1976), 1–11.

Joy, James. *States of Confinement: Policing, Detentions, and Prisons*. New York: Palgrave Macmillan, 2000.

Lindenmeyer, Kriste. *'A Right to Childhood': The U.S. Children's Bureau and Child Welfare, 1912–1946*. Urbana, IL: University of Illinois Press, 1997.

Marten, James, ed. *Childhood and Child Welfare in the Progressive Era: A Brief History with Documents*. Boston, MA: Bedford St Martins, 2005.

Mysogland, Erin. '"Where's Your Birth Certificate, Pilgrim?": Analyzing Double Age in Immigration Policing and Chicano Community Organizing, 1975–1985', *The Journal of the History of Childhood and Youth* 15, no. 3 (2022), 422–33.

Neelum, Ayra. *Getting to Zero: A 50-State Study of Strategies to Remove Youth from Adult Jails*. Los Angeles, CA: UCLA School of Law, 2018.

Sanborn Jr, Joseph B. 'Ex parte Crouse' in C.J. Schreck, M.J. Leiber, H.V. Miller and K. Welch, eds., *The Encyclopaedia of Juvenile Delinquency and Justice* (Hoboken, NJ: Wiley, 2017), n.p.

Schreck, C.J., M.J. Leiber, H.V. Miller and K. Welch, eds. *The Encyclopaedia of Juvenile Delinquency and Justice*. Hoboken, NJ: Wiley, 2017.

Streib, Victor L. *Death Penalty for Juveniles*. Bloomington, IN: Indiana University Press, 1987.

Suddler, Carl. *Presumed Criminal: Black Youth and the Justice System in Postwar New York*. New York: New York University Press, 2019.

Tanehouse, David S. and Steven A. Drizin. '"Owing to the Extreme Youth of the Accused": The Changing Legal Response to Juvenile Homicide', *Journal of Law and Criminology* 92, no. 3 (2002), 641–706.

van Vleet, Russell K. 'The Attack on Juvenile Justice', *The Annals of the American Academy of Political and Social Science* 564 (1999), 203–14.

Ward, Geoff K. *The Black Child-Savers: Racial Democracy and Juvenile Justice*. Chicago, IL: University of Chicago Press, 2012.

Webster, Crystal. '"Hanging Pretty Girls": The Criminalization of African American Children in Early America', *Journal of the Early Republic* 42, no. 2, (2022), 253–76.

White, Holly N.S. *Negotiating American Childhood: Age-Based Laws and the Illusion of Protection in the Early United States*. Charlottesville, VA: University of Virginia Press, forthcoming.

Wilson, Janet K., 'Child Savers Movement' in F.P. Bernat and K. Frailing, eds., *The Encyclopaedia of Women and Crime* (Hoboken, NJ: Wiley, 2019), n.p.

Chapter 7

'Childish, adolescent and recherché': Psychoanalysis and maturity in psychological selection boards, c.1940s–60s[1]

Grace Whorrall-Campbell

The mood of the room was apprehensive. The men eyed each other up uneasily, each waiting for another to speak first. Suddenly, one of them cried out, 'grenade!' The young men threw themselves to the floor in a burst of nervous energy, hitting the ground with awkward thuds that were not masked by the sound of an explosion. The room remained silent and still. Unharmed, the men picked themselves up off the floor, making self-conscious conversation. One man remained unmoved throughout. Watching the action unfold, perhaps the observing psychologist raised an eyebrow or made an approving scribble on his notepaper.[2]

This exercise took place at an assessment centre to select suitable men for an officer commission in the British Army. Following concerns about the objectivity and effectiveness of the old interview method for selecting officers, from 1942 Army Commands across Britain established assessment centres. These centres, known as War Office Selection Boards, assessed candidates over three days using experimental methods taken from psychoanalysis and clinical psychology. In 1945, these military selection techniques moved into the public sector when the head of the Civil Service Commission, Sir Percival Waterfield, adapted War Office methods for selecting senior civil servants. By 1953, psychodynamic job selection made its way into private industry; Unilever's Management Development Scheme selected university graduates for junior management positions.

In all three boards, selectors used maturity as a framework to guide their decisions; unsuccessful candidates were rejected on the basis of their immaturity. The boards evaluated young men and, in the two civilian schemes, women aged in their late teens and early twenties. For many candidates, this was their first entry into a professional career. It was perhaps no surprise that selectors assessed candidates according to their maturity. Work was and is still one of the main markers of distinction between adults and children. Therefore, in selecting candidates who were ready for work, it made sense that the assessors chose individuals who conformed to their ideal of adulthood.

Historians have uncovered how the psychological sciences in Britain shaped ideas about childhood in the inter- and postwar years.[3] This reflects the psychoanalytic belief in childhood as the central site of personality development, an idea that became widely accepted over the twentieth century.[4] However, there is a paucity of literature on how the psy-sciences constructed an ideal of adulthood. In this chapter, I argue that psychological theories of child development also impacted how the science constructed ideas of normative adulthood, something Laura Tisdall also finds in her contribution to this volume. Moreover, my chapter also demonstrates that the state of adulthood was subject to psychologisation and expert adjudication, just as historians have demonstrated for childhood.

In this chapter, I outline three dimensions of maturity used by the three selection boards. Firstly, I argue that maturity, as a normative state of adulthood, was used to describe an appropriate performance of authority: what I call plausible leadership. Secondly, I demonstrate that the language of maturity was used to smuggle psychoanalytic theories of psychosexual development and personality formation into the boards, circumnavigating the strong social taboo regarding frank discussions of sexuality. Thirdly, maturity necessitated emotional restraint, calling for a relationship to one's emotions that was associated with normative masculinity. As Thomas Dixon has argued, emotional restraint became a cornerstone of English masculinity in the late Victorian and Edwardian period of imperial expansion. The call for emotional control, however, reached a high point in the mid-twentieth century, following the valorisation of stoicism as a uniquely British value during World War II.[5]

Taken together, these components indicate that maturity was a social characteristic, made manifest through interactions with others, rather than a purely interior state of being. I argue that the premium placed on mature and emotionally restrained authority resulted from the wartime and postwar commitment to democratic leadership. In the immediate postwar years, psychiatrists insisted that the best defence against authoritarianism was an emotionally mature population. Mature citizens would resist the pull of a paternalistic dictator, and instead be capable of robust participation in democratic society.[6]

In this chapter, I focus on how the selection board experts understood maturity, and the different meanings psychological and lay selectors brought to the concept as it operated in the boards. I can say much less about the candidates' experience of going through the boards, and how far the boards shaped their understanding of behavioural norms they ought to carry with them into the workplace. It is difficult to know how much candidates and board members shared a common definition of maturity; however, it is unlikely many candidates were familiar with maturity's psychoanalytic connotations.

The selection boards

All three boards replaced the traditional biographical interview with a multi-day psychological selection process. Candidates now faced questionnaires about their life and family history, intelligence tests, psychological projective tests, group discussions, job simulation tasks and, in the case of the War Office Boards, an obstacle task and a psychiatric interview.

The psychoanalysts responsible for the boards were associated with the Tavistock Clinic in London, the premier centre for psychodynamic psychiatry in Britain. The boards were later supervised by the Tavistock Clinic's sister organisation, the Tavistock Institute of Human Relations, founded in 1947 to pursue socio-psychiatric research.[7] The psychotherapist Hugh Crichton-Miller opened the Tavistock Clinic in 1920 to continue in peacetime the treatment he had provided at hospitals for shellshocked soldiers during the war. The historian of military psychiatry Ben Shephard described the Tavistock as 'the struggling poor relation of psychological medicine ... where the old Great War traditions of psychotherapy co-existed with a mild, British form of Freud'.[8] While Freud's theories of infant sexuality were treated with suspicion and fear in Britain, psychoanalysis exerted a clear, if eclectic, influence across British medical and popular culture.[9] Psychoanalysts' influence was only to increase during World War II, boosted by refugee analysts fleeing antisemitic persecution on the continent and the discipline's capacity to provide solutions to the problems of civilian stress and population mobilisation during total war.[10]

Maturity and leadership

Assessors labelled as immature candidates who were not fit to be army officers, civil servants or managers. Immaturity seems to have a simple negative relationship to leadership: but what exactly did board members mean when they dismissed candidates for being immature? One unsuccessful candidate for the civil service was rejected on the basis of being 'A bit immature – in fact very young and raw and inclined to be supercilious.'[11] Staff on the Civil Service Selection Board therefore understood immaturity to be connected both to inexperience and to the improper performance of superiority.

The candidate's haughtiness ruled him out as a plausible leader. Selection boards were interested in candidates' maturity because seniority legitimated authority. The young men, and in the civil service and Unilever boards occasionally women, were in their late teens and early twenties. They were young adults, newcomers to the world of work. However, they were being chosen for senior leadership positions. Success in the War Office boards would earn a young man an officer commission; those who passed the civil service boards were appointed as senior administrators; and the Unilever scheme was designed to select people who would be at upper management level by their mid-thirties.[12] Successful candidates would therefore be expected to manage people older than themselves. Disrupting the naturalised hierarchy of age required authority to be legitimated via different means. Candidates were therefore required to don a seniority that was appropriate for their position, regardless of their chronological age.

Maturity was valued not just because it gave candidates an internal aptitude for leadership. Maturity was also a visual, superficial quality that existed in how that person was perceived. Tavistock psychoanalysts instructed Unilever selectors to pay attention to candidates' physical maturity. Board members were asked to comment on whether candidates looked 'older than [their] years', a positive attribute, or 'boyish', to be marked negatively.[13] Maturity rested on an understanding of the workplace as a social system, where it mattered that leaders were perceived as having a plausible claim to authority.

Because the selection boards chose candidates who they assumed would be more readily accepted as leaders within the workplace, they necessarily conformed to a conservative model of leadership. This undercut their claims that psychological selection was a more democratic way of choosing leaders. Psychological tests of personality and aptitude were apparently 'not concerned with distinctions of rank or social status' and were therefore 'more democratic' than the traditional system of selection via interview and personal recommendation.[14] Nevertheless, psychological selection retained the old biases.

The postwar boards made less progress towards democratisation than the War Office boards. The unprecedented expansion of the armed forces as a result of conscription necessitated recruiting officers from a broader social base than the traditional officer class.[15] However, in peacetime, the civil service and Unilever's practice of only considering applications from university graduates, in the decade before the expansion of higher education, weakened their supposed commitment to democratic selection.[16] Moreover, the army desperately needed officers, meaning that even candidates who were graded 'doubtful' were still passed by the board; the civil service and Unilever could afford to be more exclusive.[17]

Maturity and sexuality

For the psychoanalysts on selection boards, homosexuality indicated an immature personality that rendered one unfit for leadership positions. The psychoanalytic theory of psychosexual development, originating with Freud but remaining popular into the mid-century, held that homosexuality was a condition of arrested development, the result of an infant becoming stuck, or fixated, at one of the earlier stages of psychic evolution.[18] Homosexuality was therefore evidence of psychopathology, and psychological experts argued they needed to screen against this form of mental instability. The psychiatrist John Bowlby, best known for his postwar work on attachment theory, warned the Royal Army Medical Corps that certain 'characteristics' indicated 'Mental Defect or Temperamental Instability' among recruits. Alongside men who exhibited nervousness, depression or 'stupidity', Bowlby also listed 'feminine types and confirmed homosexuals' as men who were especially likely to 'break down in the face of action'.[19] Bowlby placed homosexual men alongside 'bedwetters' as examples of undesirable candidates, demonstrating the link in psychoanalysts' minds between deviant sexuality, immaturity and psychic trouble.

War Office board psychoanalysts therefore took an interest in candidates' sexualities. As part of the officer selection process, men were given a series of psychological tests called 'personality pointers'. The pointers were used to filter out candidates with 'dull' or 'immature' personalities.[20] One such test was the Thematic Apperception Test, in which candidates were presented with a series of images and invited to write a short story based on the illustration. The images were adapted by board psychologists from the clinical version of the test, created by American psychologists

Henry A. Murray and Christiana Morgan.[21] Images were selected to show 'an undefined social situation', onto which the candidate could 'project his own dominant phantasies'.[22] One illustration depicted two sets of hands, belonging to an elderly man and a younger man, supposed to be around the same age as the candidates.[23] The image was designed to reveal candidates' attitude towards authority and leadership. In doing so, it connected authority to age, underscoring the fragility of the young candidates' claims to the leadership role.

The Thematic Apperception Test was also intended to expose deviant or morbid sexual tendencies. One slide, designed to draw out oedipal conflicts, depicted an older woman standing behind a man around the same age as the candidates.[24] Another showed a young man standing fully clothed with his back to a young woman lying supine in bed, the covers sitting just under her exposed breasts.[25] The Thematic Apperception Test, administered at both the War Office and civil servant boards, was intended to weed out candidates who displayed an immature sexuality.

Probing candidates' sexuality could take a very direct form. One candidate recounted his success at a War Office board in a letter to his sweetheart. Richard Williams described the luxurious surroundings of the board, hosted at Brockham Park in Surrey. The men gawped at the Monets, Cezannes and Manets still hanging on the walls ('Some of the nudes shook us ... All excused like strip-tease, under "ART"'). This was not the only salacious aspect of the boards Williams shared with his beloved. His psychiatric interview started with the shocking question, 'How many women have you slept with?' Williams reassured his girlfriend that he was horrified by the line of questioning, calling the experience 'rotten'.[26]

For psychoanalysts, sexuality was key evidence of an immature personality. However, psychiatric attempts to make candidates' sexualities knowable chafed against the wishes of the non-psychological staff. For them, it was more important that selection boards adhered to norms of privacy and respectability. The mere presence of psychoanalysts, with their alarming associations with madness, sexuality and other taboos, threatened to undo the propriety of this project. The comments by MP for Westminster Abbey Harold Webbe at the 1946 Estates Committee, where Percival Waterfield explained his new scheme for selecting civil servants, represented a more colourful version of the widespread suspicion of psychoanalysts. Webbe ridiculed the selection board as

> three days in a sort of glorified hotel with a 'snooper' behind every palm tree, and a man liable at every point to hop out and ask you: 'How round is a cricket ball?' ... many of these people must finish up their

'CHILDISH, ADOLESCENT AND RECHERCHÉ' 155

three days thinking that they must really have been, by mistake, sent to a lunatic asylum.[27]

Probing into candidates' sex lives was therefore a scandal waiting to happen.

Psychiatric and non-psychiatric board members firmly disagreed on the appropriateness of enquiring into candidates' sexual experiences. Psychoanalysts felt these questions were a natural element of their duties as 'medical psychologists' trained in 'sensitivity to the graduations in personality' from normal to abnormal.[28] However, non-psychiatric staff were squeamish about such prurient investigations. In 1943, the War Office forbade psychiatrists from asking candidates questions on sex and religion.[29] Later that year, psychiatrists were restricted to interviewing no more than 50 per cent of candidates, and in December 1946 they were completely removed from the boards. From then on, the psychological staff were represented only by psychologists employed to administer and interpret the intelligence and personality tests.[30] Irreconcilable tension over the place of sexuality in the boards resulted in the exclusion of the very experts who had devised the selection scheme. Psychoanalysts were also unwelcome in the civil service scheme: Waterfield saw from the scandal over psychoanalysts' interest in sexuality in the War Office boards that they were not worth the 'political storm'.[31]

Regardless of the psychiatrists' exclusion, the link between maturity and candidates' psychosexual development remained encoded in the personality pointers. The Civil Service Selection Board used adapted versions of the Thematic Apperception and Word Association Tests that were administered at the War Office boards. Even without the psychiatrists' interview, where explicit questions about sexuality were asked, the meanings of maturity across these two boards remained consistently tied to theories of psychosexual development. The departure of the psychiatrists halted the development of new personality tests, fossilising the meaning of maturity within the Thematic Apperception and Word Association Tests.

The language of maturity allowed psychoanalytic theories of sexuality to be incorporated obliquely. For example, the Word Association Test could be used to assess candidates' level of psychosexual development without direct questioning. First used by Carl Jung, the Word Association Test provided carefully selected words intended to reveal candidates' phantasies. The quality of the candidate's response indicated their maturity: a 'mature' candidate would be 'able to express his emotions in an integrated fashion' in contrast to 'inhibited' candidates.[32] Moreover, word association was supposed to reveal desirable or problematic personality traits. The list of words testing 'ego-centrism' demonstrated an interest in homosexuality conceptualised as a pathological personality associated with narcissism, feebleness and emotional immaturity.[33] The test also asked candidates to respond to words such as 'childhood', 'mother' and 'father', stimuli to indicate candidates with unresolved oedipal complexes. The psychoanalytically designed tests scrutinised candidates' psychosexual development, all the while couching their investigation in the more neutral language of maturity.

The concept of maturity did important work for psychoanalysts, who turned to euphemism to evaluate candidates' psychosocial development. Maturity was a concept around which both the psychological and non-psychological selection board members could align. It sat at the boundary between the two groups, each bringing their own definitions to the term.[34] For the non-psychological staff, immaturity described an instinctive feeling that the candidate would not be able to plausibly wield authority in the workplace. The psychological staff invested the same term with the framework of psychosexual development that their fellow board members found so distasteful.

In the Unilever scheme, established in 1953, psychiatrists from the Tavistock Institute of Human Relations returned to job selection, working as specialist advisors on the board. The analysts continued to use maturity to exclude candidates who did not adhere to norms of respectable heterosexuality. The psychoanalysts instructed assessors to score the hobbies candidates included on their application form according to the level of maturity their interests demonstrated. Candidates who mentioned 'childish, adolescent or recherché' pastimes, such as 'model railways, tiddly-winks, women, jiving [and] astronautics' were marked down.[35] Selectors didn't just disapprove of childish enthusiasm for trains, space travel and games, but also of racier playboy types. Adulthood was contrasted against both childhood naivete and adolescent sexuality. Unilever's list of unacceptable interests also included 'carving shepherds crooks, telling fortunes [and] Victorian gothic architecture'.[36] This list of peculiar hobbies (how many candidates actually spent their days carving shepherd's crooks?) referenced a certain kind of queer fastidiousness and campy eccentricity. The bizarre list, which was seemingly a sly joke on the part of the psychoanalysts, enabled assessors to intuit what kind of man these hobbies implied. Assessors could therefore use their own discretion to exclude candidates without requiring gender nonconformity or sexual deviance to be any more than a spectre.

Maturity and emotions

The framework of maturity was used to refer to a candidate's adherence to norms of masculine adulthood. As we have seen, this included respectable heterosexuality. It also included emotional control. Emotional restraint was an important social norm for both men and women in early to mid-twentieth-century Britain. Hera Cook has argued that the mid-twentieth century saw a strong insistence on emotional control, limiting acceptable emotional expression to 'sensible and reasonable' displays of feeling.[37] Although, as Deborah Youngs's, Maria Cannon's and Emily E. Robson's chapters in this volume show, the association between adulthood and emotional control has a history stretching back to the Middle Ages, the expectation upon adults to exercise considerable emotional restraint began in the nineteenth century. Calls for emotional control intensified during World War II, during which time understatement and distaste for extremes became a prized part of the national character, in contrast to the mass displays of political fervour in Nazi Germany.[38] This was a culture of respectability, in which the expression of strong, and especially strongly negative, emotions violated the norm of privacy.

Emotional control remained important after the war. The 'emotional politics' of reconstruction Britain, as Claire Langhamer has chronicled, rested on the assumption that political and social stability stemmed from 'the ability of each citizen to manage their own emotions'.[39] Although emotional reticence was an androgynous social norm, it had special importance for men. 'Emotional reticence', Sonya Rose argues, was 'quintessentially masculine'. If women indulged in emotional outbursts, they were silly fools: if men failed to maintain a level head, they lost their manliness.[40] Martin Francis also identified 'unflappability' as one of the 'dominant codes of masculine emotional culture' in 1950s Britain.[41] Self-possession was not only required in the task of postwar reconstruction, it also needed reasserting as a normatively masculine emotional style in the context of supposed threats to British masculinity, both in the figure of the homosexual and the racialised immigrant.[42]

One assessor's description of a young civil servant demonstrates the association between adulthood, masculinity and emotional control. The observer felt this young man was hindered by his 'inexperience and comparative youth', but also remarked approvingly that he 'spoke like a man of thirty – balanced, sensible and with steady common-sense'.[43] Adulthood was, in this remark, associated with good judgement and emotional stability. Despite not having the wisdom of age, the candidate could at least conjure up the corresponding gravitas through his performance of emotional restraint.

Board members were more likely to find women lacking in maturity. As both Maria Cannon and Kristin Hay note in their chapters in this volume, women have frequently been excluded from markers of adulthood. One selector described a female civil servant as 'markedly immature, gauche and lacking in confident judgement'.[44] Another young woman gave 'the impression of never having quite grown up, although in fact she has fairly heavy domestic responsibilities which might have been expected to make her old beyond her years'.[45] Selection boards found it more difficult to understand women as mature. While male candidates could demonstrate experience in 'man management' through their time in National Service, women's maturity was derived from their domestic responsibilities.[46] Unlike the inexperienced young man who still managed to speak with the 'sensible' authority of a thirty-year-old, women's distance from conventional forms of authority prevented them from being read as plausible leaders. The civil service supported the inclusion of exceptional women into their ranks in the interests of democratisation. However, they simultaneously retained their commitment to a definition of maturity that positioned masculine adulthood as normative, sustaining the exclusion of those who were not contained within that gendered norm.

Emotional restraint not only marked hegemonic masculinity, it also indicated psychological normality. Screening for psychic stability was one of the primary goals of the selection boards, and the reason for the psychological presence in the first place. The War Office boards were created over concerns that the previous system of officer selection did not sufficiently guard against selecting men who would break down in the face of conflict, creating both inefficient leadership and a burden for on military pensions.[47] However, the two civilian selection schemes maintained the War Office's interest in psychic resilience, even though civil servants and Unilever managers faced none of the psychological strain of war.

The enmeshed nature of maturity, masculine emotional restraint and psychological normality is evident in a psychiatric interview staged for the information film *Personnel Selection in the British Army* (1944). The film was part of a Ministry of Information series titled 'Report from Britain', which Arthur Elton, director of the Ministry's Films Division, described as 'prestige propaganda' illustrating the 'efficiency of the British war effort'. The series aimed to challenge the 'deep-seated' American impression that Britain was 'inefficient' and 'muddl[ing] through' by showcasing the modern psychological selection scheme to a specialist audience.[48] Although shot in documentary style, all of the candidates had already passed through the War Office boards and were simulating the process for the cameras.

Nevertheless, the film remains useful as evidence of how selectors assessed candidates' personalities. In *Personnel Selection*, one young man was given a psychiatric interview after his responses in the Thematic Apperception Test raised concerns about his mental state. In the interview, the candidate disclosed that he had suffered from a recurring nightmare since he was a child. He described waking up in the middle of the night, not knowing 'the least where I am' in the darkness. This was accompanied by a claustrophobic feeling, as if he was 'being entombed'.[49] In a discussion about the interview with the psychologist, the board psychiatrist noted that the candidate's recurring nightmare demonstrated a 'state of inner tension' that he needed to 'master' before he could be considered 'fully mature'.[50]

The psychoanalyst's call for the candidate to 'master' his nightmare revealed gendered emotional norms. The dream was a subconscious emotional leakage that the candidate needed to control in order to be considered a man, rather than a boy. The candidate's disclosure of this recurring night terror got him graded poorly by the board; he barely scraped through on the lowest pass grade. The nightmare itself was only part of the problem. The psychoanalyst, reporting on the psychiatric interview to the rest of the board, described the candidate as 'cooperative and naïve, disclosing nervous traits almost too readily'.[51] Despite the context of the psychiatric interview, where honesty and cooperation might be expected, this candidate was penalised for displaying these qualities. Honesty instead looked childishly naïve if it led a candidate to disclose the more morbid parts of their personality, however normal the experience in the grand scheme of human emotion.

For psychoanalysts in particular, fear was associated with childhood.[52] Tavistock analysts were familiar with Melanie Klein's theory of early childhood as a time of intense anxiety, fears that the infant must learn to integrate as part of the process of healthy psychological development.[53] The fact that the candidate still experienced a nightmare which first occurred in childhood indicated his incomplete maturity. Although historians have held psychoanalysts responsible for a loosening of emotional restraint and a less moralising attitude towards negative emotions such as fear, this was not the case in the War Office boards.[54] The military psychiatrist approved of emotional control, seeing the candidate's expression of fear through nightmares as a troubling sign of psychological immaturity.

Maturity and democracy

The war against Nazi Germany and its allies raised questions regarding the nature of leadership in a democratic society. Democracy was an animating principle in the War Office boards. Labour councillor Emrys Jones called for an egalitarian overhaul of selecting officers in light of the war, arguing that 'the simple liberal proposition that men should have equal opportunities is one of the things we surely are fighting for against the German idea of the master class and the master race'.[55] Postwar reconstruction also sought to embed democracy in Britain as a bulwark against the re-emergence of fascism and the current threat of Communist authoritarianism. Moreover, as the postwar labour shortage put pressure on productivity and the power of the trade unions rose, management by consent became an increasingly important principle.

The immediate postwar decades were characterised by an expectation that to secure the peace, groups with differing interests needed to work together in pursuit of the common good.[56] The civil service and Unilever selection boards were imbued with this spirit: candidates were selected for their ability to lead by consent and to demonstrate a democratic, rather than dictatorial, authority. Maturity referenced this considerate and emotionally contained style of leadership. The Tavistock psychoanalysts hired by Unilever defined maturity in 1968 as 'a combination of practical wisdom, of steady and socially acceptable emotional behaviour and of effective social techniques'.[57] Adulthood was defined by the ability to relate to others in a socially appropriate manner, which involved the avoidance of emotional extremes. Psychologists understood adulthood as the peak of an individual's psychosocial development: when one could moderate one's own selfish drives and instincts according to social norms and expectations.

The definition of maturity from 1968 stayed remarkably consistent with the meaning of the term two decades prior. In the War Office boards, too, candidates who failed to demonstrate 'effective social techniques' were penalised for being immature. One candidate was graded poorly by the board psychiatrist for his 'pushing rather than constructive attitude to the group'.[58] Domineering men who were 'individualist' or had a 'selfish streak' were not praised by the boards.

Rather, the selection board was looking for candidates who made acceptable leaders within the group. The Leaderless Group discussion, where candidates had to select and debate a topic collectively with no input from the testers, and group physical tasks, such as getting a team of men over a barbed-wire fence, were designed to simulate a group setting in which the role of leader was not fixed, and 'passe[d] easily from one [candidate] to the other'.[59] By allowing candidates to organically take turns as leaders of the group, the tests hoped to show not just which men had leadership abilities but, more importantly, which of the men were accepted as leaders by the group.

The Unilever selectors were also interested in whether candidates behaved well in a group. The interests that candidates listed on their application form were allocated a plus or minus score depending on the social quality they evidenced. Candidates were scored one point for a hobby that was 'sound, creative, maturing' and minus one for a 'faulty interaction' or an 'immaturing' interest.[60] The hobbies were not important in themselves. Instead, the boards considered whether candidates' interests, and the way men spoke about them, showed mature or immature social interactions. The board psychologists considered there to be 'no (or little) difference between a solitary ... activity or a social one which is apparently viewed from a solitary standpoint'.[61] Therefore, a candidate who wrote 'I play tennis' on his application form would only be awarded a point if he mentioned playing tennis with his friends. Solitary interests were only marked positively if they helped 'mature the personality'. For instance, wood carving was deemed a suitably mature hobby because it taught problem-solving skills; although, as discussed earlier, apparently not if the candidate carved shepherd's crooks.[62]

Psychologists asked examiners to consider 'what kind of relationship' the candidate enjoyed with other participants in their interests. Assessors were required to take note of whether candidates displayed a 'dependent' or 'aggressive' relationship to others in the pursuit of their hobby.[63] Selectors were interested in candidates' pastimes as a means to ascertain the quality of their social relationships. A mature candidate was one who demonstrated an easy sociability, who was amiable rather than authoritarian. An easy-going manner and a proclivity for groups, what the Civil Service Selection Board called 'clubability [sic]', were believed to constitute the ideal personality for leadership in a democratic society, in which the modern manager was supposed to attend to his subordinates' wants and feelings.[64]

Conclusion

Maturity remained a resilient concept, moving between military, public sector and private industry recruitment without much modification. Despite the psychiatrists' ejection from War Office boards in 1946, the language of maturity remained encoded in the tests they left behind, tests that were adopted by the Civil Service Selection Board in 1945. The psychoanalysts returned to advise on the Unilever Companies Management Development Scheme in 1953. All three schemes lasted well into the twentieth century. Even today, the renamed Army Officer Selection Board assesses candidates using psychometric tests and similar group tasks to those devised in 1942. Despite reforms to civil service selection following the 1968 Fulton Report, the Civil Service Selection Board remained into the early twenty-first century. Aspiring civil servants in 2023 continue to take cognitive and personality tests. Although the language of maturity is obscured, successful candidates remain those who are able to make calm and intelligent decisions, exhibit leadership skills and cultivate appropriate social relations.[65] Tavistock psychoanalysts continued to work as consultants on the Unilever Management Development Scheme until at least the 1980s. Today, the Unilever Future Leaders Programme still tests candidates' 'cognitive, emotional, and social traits'.[66]

All three schemes used psychoanalytic theories of personality development to sustain adulthood as a privileged state. Throughout the chapter, we've seen that board members more often described candidates as 'immature' than 'mature'. The language of maturity was used as a means of exclusion, rejecting candidates who did not conform to psychosexual, emotional or social standards. Maturity was a resilient concept because it was capacious, capable of containing different meanings for the psychological and non-psychological staff. The non-psychological staff understood maturity as a common-sense requirement for successful applicants. For the young men and occasionally women to be plausible leaders, they needed to conduct themselves with the authority on which their young age provided a tenuous grip.

Maturity's stability as a concept over time and across the three boards provides an object lesson in how dominant norms of adulthood are reproduced. Although the boards promised that scientific methods would democratise job selection, they failed to challenge dominant norms of adulthood that made some candidates appear readier for leadership positions than others. Paradoxically, the democratic impulse incentivised rewarding candidates who conformed to a conventional model of adult authority that was deemed acceptable by the group.

This chapter started with a game of pretend. The boards asked candidates to explore their imaginations, tackle obstacle courses and play at being an army officer, civil servant or manager. Despite, or more likely because of, this 'house party' atmosphere, the young people who passed through the boards were watched carefully for signs of juvenility that would disqualify them from the role.[67] The language of maturity was used to legitimate the authority that successful candidates would wield in the workplace. Psychoanalysts strengthened the longstanding association between adulthood and power by linking immaturity with a libidinal and anxious infant psyche. Psychoanalysts might have transformed the meanings of childhood in the twentieth century, but their work in job selection showed they retained a conservative model of the powers and privileges of adulthood.

Notes

1. Research for this chapter was funded through an Oxford-Open-Cambridge AHRC Doctoral Training Partnership. Thank you also to Alice White for sharing her expertise on the Tavistock Institute of Human Relations.

2. 'Indoor Leaderless Group Situation', RTC Information Bulletin No. 3, June 1943, SA/TIH/B/2/1/1/1/3, Tavistock Institute collection, Wellcome Library, London.

3. John Stewart, '"The Dangerous Age of Childhood": Child Guidance and the "Normal" Child in Great Britain, 1920–1950', *Paedagogica Historica* 47, no. 6 (December 2011): 785–803; Michal Shapira, *The War Inside: Psychoanalysis, Total War, and the Making of the Democratic Modern Self in Postwar Britain* (Cambridge: Cambridge University Press, 2013); Mathew Thomson, *Lost Freedom: The Landscape of the Child and the British Post-War Settlement* (Oxford: Oxford University Press, 2013).

4. Thomson, *Lost Freedom*.

5. Thomas Dixon, *Weeping Britannia: Portrait of a Nation in Tears* (Oxford: Oxford University Press, 2015).

6. Teri Chettiar, 'Democratizing Mental Health: Motherhood, Therapeutic Community and the Emergence of the Psychiatric Family at the Cassel Hospital in Post-Second World War Britain', *History of the Human Sciences* 25, no. 5 (December 2012): 107–22.

7. Henry Victor Dicks, *Fifty Years of the Tavistock Clinic* (London: Routledge & Kegan Paul, 1970).

8. Ben Shephard, *A War of Nerves: Soldiers and Psychiatrists in the Twentieth Century* (London: Jonathan Cape, 2000), 168. It is true that the Tavistock Clinic was often overshadowed by its rival, the Maudsley, which had a more psychobiologic slant. Edgar Jones, Shahina Rahman, and Robin Woolven, 'The Maudsley Hospital: Design and Strategic Direction, 1923–1939', *Medical History* 51, no. 3 (2007): 357–78.

9. Rhodri Hayward, 'The Pursuit of Serenity: Psychological Knowledge and the Making of the British Welfare State', in *History and Psyche: Culture, Psychoanalysis, and the Past*, ed. Sally Alexander and Barbara Taylor (Basingstoke: Palgrave Macmillan, 2012), 283–304; Rhodri Hayward, *The Transformation of the Psyche in British Primary Care, 1970–1970* (London: Bloomsbury Academic, 2014); Sarah Phelan, 'A Commonsense Psychoanalysis: Listening to the Psychosocial Dreamer in Interwar Glasgow Psychiatry', *History of the Human Sciences* 34, no. 3–4 (2021): 142–68; Dean Rapp, 'The Early Discovery of Freud by the British General Educated Public, 1912–1919', *Social History of Medicine* 3, no. 2 (1990): 217–43; Dean Rapp, 'The Reception of Freud by the British Press: General Interest and Literary Magazines, 1920–1925', *Journal of the History of the Behavioural Sciences* 24, no. 2 (1988): 191–201; Graham Richards, 'Britain on the Couch: The Popularization of Psychoanalysis in Britain 1918–1940', *Science in Context* 13, no. 2 (2000): 183–230.

10. Shapira, *The War Inside*; Mathew Thomson, *Psychological Subjects: Identity, Culture and Health in Twentieth Century Britain* (Oxford: Oxford University Press, 2006), 209.

11. 'Follow-Up Notes on Reconstruction Assistant Principals Administration Course at T.E. Division of H.M. Treasury', 13–29 May 1944, CSC 5/394, Records of the Civil Service Commission, National Archives, Kew.

12. 'Unilever Companies Management Development Scheme: Notes for Selectors', 1969, SA/TIH/B/2/9/9/7, Tavistock Institute collection, Wellcome Library, London.

13. 'Unilever Companies Management Development Scheme'.

14. *Personnel Selection in the British Army 1944: Officers*, 1944; letter from John Pinsent to Percival Waterfield, 30 January [1946], CSC 5/394, Records of the Civil Service Commission, National Archives, Kew.

15. Ben S. Morris, 'Officer Selection in the British Army: 1942–1945', *Occupational Psychology* 12, no. 4 (1949): 219–34.

16. See chapter 5 of Peter Mandler, *The Crisis of the Meritocracy: Britain's Transition to Mass Education since the Second World War* (Oxford: Oxford University Press, 2020).

17. *Personnel Selection in the British Army 1944: Officers*.

18. Melanie Klein, *The Psycho-Analysis of Children*, trans. Alix Strachey, revised (London: Hogarth Press, 1975), 240; Paul Robinson, 'Freud and Homosexuality', in *Homosexuality and Psychoanalysis*, ed. Tim Dean and Christopher Lane (Chicago, IL: University of Chicago Press, 2001), 92; Jonathan Ned Katz, *The Invention of Heterosexuality* (Chicago, IL: University of Chicago Press, 2007), 72–4.

19. Emma Vickers, *Queen and Country: Same-Sex Desire in the British Armed Forces, 1939–45* (Manchester: Manchester University Press, 2013), 122; notes on selection and diagnosis in the Armed Forces, 1942, PP/BOW/C.5/2/3, Papers of John Bowlby, Wellcome Library, London.

20. Selection board notes on personality pointers, c.1942, SA/TIH/B/2/1/1/2/2, Tavistock Institute collection, Wellcome Library, London.

21. Christiana D. Morgan and Henry A. Murray, 'A Method for Investigating Fantasies: The Thematic Apperception Test', *Archives of Neurology & Psychiatry* 34, no. 2 (1 August 1935): 289.

22. *Personnel Selection in the British Army 1944: Officers*.

23. Alice White, 'From the Science of Selection to Psychologising Civvy Street: The Tavistock Group, 1939–1948' (PhD thesis, University of Kent, 2016).

24. White, 'From the Science of Selection to Psychologising Civvy Street', 98.

25. White, 'From the Science of Selection to Psychologising Civvy Street', 99.

26. Chotie Darling, 'How Many Women Have You Slept With?', 25 February 2013, www.chotiedarling.co.uk/my-blog/2013/02/how-many-women-have-you-slept-with -thursday-25th-february.html, accessed 17 July 2024.

27. Richard A. Chapman, *Leadership in the British Civil Service: A Study of Sir Percival Waterfield and the Creation of the Civil Service Selection Board* (London: Croom Helm, 1984), 100.

28. 'Preliminary Technical Appreciation of the Problem of Selecting Higher Grade Civil Servants during the Reconstruction', Eric Trist and J.D. Sutherland, 20 November 1944, CSC 5/397, Records of the Civil Service Commission, National Archives, Kew.

29. Robert H. Ahrenfeldt, *Psychiatry in the British Army in the Second World War* (London: Routledge & Kegan Paul, 1958), 64.

30. Ahrenfeldt, *Psychiatry in the British Army in the Second World War*, 67.

31. Percival Waterfield's notes following his meeting with Brigadier Buchanan Smith, 7 October 1944, CSC 5/397, Records of the Civil Service Commission, National Archives, Kew.

32. Selection board notes on personality pointers.

33. Elizabeth Lunbeck, 'The Narcissistic Homosexual: Genealogy of a Myth', in *History and Psyche: Culture, Psychoanalysis, and the Past*, ed. Sally Alexander and Barbara Taylor (Basingstoke: Palgrave Macmillan, 2012), 49–67.

34. Susan Leigh Star and James R. Griesemer, 'Institutional Ecology, "Translations" and Boundary Objects: Amateurs and Professionals in Berkeley's Museum of Vertebrate Zoology, 1907–1939', *Social Studies of Science* 19, no. 3 (1998): 387–420; Susan Leigh Star, 'The Structure of Ill-Structured Solutions: Boundary Objects and Heterogenous Distributed Problem Solving', in *Distributed Artificial Intelligence*, ed. Les Gasser and Michael N. Huhns, vol. 2 (London: Pitman, 1989), 37–54; Susan Leigh Star, 'This Is Not a Boundary Object: Reflections on the Origins of a Concept', *Science, Technology, & Human Values* 35, no. 5 (2010): 601–17. For the application of Star's concept to the War Office boards, see White, 'From the Science of Selection to Psychologising Civvy Street'.

35. 'Criteria for the Second Section of the Recruitment and Screening Study', 24 February 1960, SA/TIH/B/2/9/3/3, Tavistock Institute collection, Wellcome Library, London.

36. 'Criteria for the Second Section of the Recruitment and Screening Study'.

37. Hera Cook, 'From Controlling Emotion to Expressing Feelings in Mid-Twentieth-Century England', *Journal of Social History* 47, no. 3 (1 March 2014): 628.

38. Sonya Rose, *Which People's War? National Identity and Citizenship in Britain 1939–1945* (Oxford: Oxford University Press, 2003).

39. Claire Langhamer, 'An Archive of Feeling? Mass Observation and the Mid-Century Moment', *Insights* 9, no. 4 (2016): 142.

40. Rose, *Which People's War?*, 157.

41. Martin Francis, 'Tears, Tantrums, and Bared Teeth: The Emotional Economy of Three Conservative Prime Ministers, 1951–1963', *Journal of British Studies* 41, no. 3 (July 2002): 355.

42. Francis, 'Tears, Tantrums, and Bared Teeth'.

43. 'Follow-Up Notes on Assistant Principals on Course at T.E. Division of H.M. Treasury', 7–24 August 1946, CSC/5 394, Records of the Civil Service Commission, National Archives, Kew.

44. 'Thumbnail Sketches of Failure in the Administrative Grade of the Civil Service', January 1946, CSC 5/394, Records of the Civil Service Commission, National Archives, Kew.

45. 'Thumbnail Sketches of Failure in the Administrative Grade of the Civil Service'.

46. On the importance of National Service to managers' sense of themselves as leaders, see Michael Roper, *Masculinity and the British Organisation Man since 1945* (Oxford: Oxford University Press, 1994), 112.

47. Shephard, *A War of Nerves*, 139–40.

48. Edgar Jones, 'Neuro Psychiatry 1943: The Role of Documentary Film in the Dissemination of Medical Knowledge and Promotion of the U.K. Psychiatric Profession', *Journal of the History of Medicine and Allied Sciences* 69, no. 2 (2014): 302.

49. *Personnel Selection in the British Army 1944: Officers*.

50. *Personnel Selection in the British Army 1944: Officers*.

51. *Personnel Selection in the British Army 1944: Officers*.

52. Stearns and Haggerty have argued that the influence of psychology and psychoanalysis in American child guidance literature from the 1920s to the mid-century emphasised fear as a childhood emotion that needed significant

parental attention. Peter N. Stearns and Timothy Haggerty, 'The Role of Fear: Transitions in American Emotional Standards for Children, 1850–1950', *The American Historical Review* 96, no. 1 (1991): 63–94; Peter N. Stearns, *American Fear: The Causes and Consequences of High Anxiety* (Abingdon: Routledge, 2006). In Britain, Michal Shapira has also identified psychoanalysts' influence in lay attitudes to fear, including the belief that adult anxieties were rooted in childhood fears. Shapira, *The War Inside*, 55, 57.

53. Melanie Klein, *Love, Guilt and Reparation and Other Works, 1921–1945* (London: Hogarth Press, 1975); Klein, *The Psycho-Analysis of Children*.

54. Shapira, *The War Inside*, 35; Cook, 'From Controlling Emotion to Expressing Feelings in Mid-Twentieth-Century England'.

55. White, 'From the Science of Selection to Psychologising Civvy Street', 32.

56. Ben Jackson, 'Corporatism and Its Discontents: Pluralism, Anti-Pluralism and Anglo-American Industrial Relations, c. 1930–80', in *Modern Pluralism: Anglo-American Debates since 1880*, ed. Mark Bevir (Cambridge: Cambridge University Press, 2012), 105–28; Daniel Ussishkin, 'Morale and the Postwar Politics of Consensus', *Journal of British Studies* 52, no. 3 (2013): 722–43.

57. 'Unilever Companies Management Development Scheme Notes on Screening', 23 February 1968, SA/TIH/B/2/9/9/3, Tavistock Institute collection, Wellcome Library, London.

58. *Personnel Selection in the British Army 1944: Officers*.

59. *Personnel Selection in the British Army 1944: Officers*.

60. 'Notes on Assessment for the Unilever Companies Management Development Scheme', c.1960, SA/TIH/B/2/9/3/3, Tavistock Institute collection, Wellcome Library, London.

61. 'Notes on Assessment for the Unilever Companies Management Development Scheme'.

62. 'Notes on Assessment for the Unilever Companies Management Development Scheme'.

63. 'Notes on Assessment for the Unilever Companies Management Development Scheme'.

64. 'Job Analysis', 1944, CSC 5/394, Records of the Civil Service Commission, National Archives, Kew.

65. 'Preparing for the Civil Service Judgement Test', Civil Service HR, 11 February 2022, www.gov.uk/guidance/preparing-for-the-civil-service-judgement -test; 'Preparing for the Civil Service Work Strengths Test', Cabinet Office, 9 June 2022, www.gov.uk/guidance/preparing-for-the-civil-service-work-strengths-test.

66. 'Unilever Future Leaders Programme', Unilever UK, 2023, https://careers .unilever.com/unilever-future-leaders-programme, accessed 17 July 2024.

67. Our Special Correspondent, 'Qualities for a Civil Servant', *The Times* (London), 24 May 1948, 2.

References

Archives

Tavistock Institute collection, Wellcome Library, London.
Records of the Civil Service Commission, National Archives, Kew.

Primary and secondary sources

Ahrenfeldt, Robert H. *Psychiatry in the British Army in the Second World War*. London: Routledge & Kegan Paul, 1958.

Cabinet Office. 'Preparing for the Civil Service Work Strengths Test'. 9 June 2022. www.gov.uk/guidance/preparing-for-the-civil-service-work-strengths-test.

Chapman, Richard A. *Leadership in the British Civil Service: A Study of Sir Percival Waterfield and the Creation of the Civil Service Selection Board* (London: Croom Helm, 1984).

Chettiar, Teri. 'Democratizing Mental Health: Motherhood, Therapeutic Community and the Emergence of the Psychiatric Family at the Cassel Hospital in Post-Second World War Britain'. *History of the Human Sciences* 25, no. 5 (December 2012): 107–22.

Chotie Darling. 'How Many Women Have You Slept With?' 25 February 2013. www.chotiedarling.co.uk/my-blog/2013/02/how-many-women-have-you-slept-with-thursday-25th-february.html, accessed 17 July 2024.

Civil Service HR. 'Preparing for the Civil Service Judgement Test', 11 February 2022, www.gov.uk/guidance/preparing-for-the-civil-service-judgement-test.

Cook, Hera. 'From Controlling Emotion to Expressing Feelings in Mid-Twentieth-Century England'. *Journal of Social History* 47, no. 3 (1 March 2014): 627–46.

Dicks, Henry Victor. *Fifty Years of the Tavistock Clinic*. London: Routledge & Kegan Paul, 1970.

Dixon, Thomas. *Weeping Britannia: Portrait of a Nation in Tears*. Oxford: Oxford University Press, 2015.

Francis, Martin. 'Tears, Tantrums, and Bared Teeth: The Emotional Economy of Three Conservative Prime Ministers, 1951–1963', *Journal of British Studies* 41, no. 3 (July 2002): 354–87.

Hayward, Rhodri. 'The Pursuit of Serenity: Psychological Knowledge and the Making of the British Welfare State'. In *History and Psyche: Culture, Psychoanalysis, and the Past*, edited by Sally Alexander and Barbara Taylor. Basingstoke: Palgrave Macmillan, 2012, 283–304.

Hayward, Rhodri. *The Transformation of the Psyche in British Primary Care, 1970–1970*. London: Bloomsbury Academic, 2014.

Jackson, Ben. 'Corporatism and Its Discontents: Pluralism, Anti-Pluralism and Anglo-American Industrial Relations, c. 1930–80', in *Modern Pluralism: Anglo-American Debates since 1880*, ed. Mark Bevir (Cambridge: Cambridge University Press, 2012), 105–28.

Jones, Edgar. 'Neuro Psychiatry 1943: The Role of Documentary Film in the Dissemination of Medical Knowledge and Promotion of the U.K. Psychiatric Profession', *Journal of the History of Medicine and Allied Sciences* 69, no. 2 (2014): 302.

Jones, Edgar, Shahina Rahman, and Robin Woolven. 'The Maudsley Hospital: Design and Strategic Direction, 1923–1939', *Medical History* 51, no. 3 (2007): 357–78.

Katz, Jonathan Ned, *The Invention of Heterosexuality*. Chicago, IL: University of Chicago Press, 2007.

Klein, Melanie. *Love, Guilt and Reparation and Other Works, 1921–1945*. London: Hogarth Press, 1975.

Klein, Melanie. *The Psycho-Analysis of Children*. Translated by Alix Strachey. Revised. London: Hogarth Press, 1975.

Langhamer, Claire. 'An Archive of Feeling? Mass Observation and the Mid-Century Moment', *Insights* 9, no. 4 (2016): 142.

Lunbeck, Elizabeth. 'The Narcissistic Homosexual: Genealogy of a Myth', in *History and Psyche: Culture, Psychoanalysis, and the Past*, ed. Sally Alexander and Barbara Taylor (Basingstoke: Palgrave Macmillan, 2012), 49–67.

Mandler, Peter. *The Crisis of the Meritocracy: Britain's Transition to Mass Education since the Second World War*. Oxford: Oxford University Press, 2020.

Morgan, Christiana D. and Henry A. Murray. 'A Method for Investigating Fantasies: The Thematic Apperception Test', *Archives of Neurology & Psychiatry* 34, no. 2 (1 August 1935): 289.

Morris, Ben S. 'Officer Selection in the British Army: 1942–1945', *Occupational Psychology* 23, no. 4 (1949): 219–34.

Our Special Correspondent. 'Qualities for a Civil Servant'. *The Times* (London), 24 May 1948.

Percival Waterfield's notes following his meeting with Brigadier Buchanan Smith, 7 October 1944, CSC 5/397, Records of the Civil Service Commission, National Archives, Kew.

Personnel Selection in the British Army 1944: Officers, 1944. www.iwm .org.uk/collections/item/object/1060025108, accessed 17 July 2024.

Phelan, Sarah. 'A Commonsense Psychoanalysis: Listening to the Psychosocial Dreamer in Interwar Glasgow Psychiatry'. *History of the Human Sciences* 34, no. 3–4 (2021): 142–68.

Rapp, Dean. 'The Reception of Freud by the British Press: General Interest and Literary Magazines, 1920–1925'. *Journal of the History of the Behavioural Sciences* 24, no. 2 (1988): 191–201.

Rapp, Dean. 'The Early Discovery of Freud by the British General Educated Public, 1912–1919'. *Social History of Medicine* 3, no. 2 (1990): 217–43.

Richards, Graham. 'Britain on the Couch: The Popularization of Psychoanalysis in Britain 1918–1940'. *Science in Context* 13, no. 2 (2000): 183–230.

Roper, Michael. *Masculinity and the British Organisation Man since 1945*. Oxford: Oxford University Press, 1994.

Rose, Sonya. *Which People's War? National Identity and Citizenship in Britain 1939–1945*. Oxford: Oxford University Press, 2003.

Shapira, Michal. *The War Inside: Psychoanalysis, Total War, and the Making of the Democratic Modern Self in Postwar Britain*. Cambridge: Cambridge University Press, 2013.

Shephard, Ben. *A War of Nerves: Soldiers and Psychiatrists in the Twentieth Century*. London: Jonathan Cape, 2000.

Star, Susan Leigh. 'The Structure of Ill-Structured Solutions: Boundary Objects and Heterogenous Distributed Problem Solving', in *Distributed Artificial Intelligence*, ed. Les Gasser and Michael N. Huhns, vol. 2 (London: Pitman, 1989), 37–54.

Star, Susan Leigh. 'This Is Not a Boundary Object: Reflections on the Origins of a Concept', *Science, Technology, & Human Values* 35, no. 5 (2010): 601–17.

Star, Susan Leigh and James R. Griesemer. 'Institutional Ecology, "Translations" and Boundary Objects: Amateurs and Professionals in Berkeley's Museum of Vertebrate Zoology, 1907–1939', *Social Studies of Science* 19, no. 3 (1998): 387–420.

Stearns, Peter N. *American Fear: The Causes and Consequences of High Anxiety*. Abingdon: Routledge, 2006.

Stearns, Peter N. and Timothy Haggerty. 'The Role of Fear: Transitions in American Emotional Standards for Children, 1850–1950'. *The American Historical Review* 96, no. 1 (1991): 63–94.

Stewart, John. '"The Dangerous Age of Childhood": Child Guidance and the "Normal" Child in Great Britain, 1920–1950', *Paedagogica Historica* 47, no. 6 (December 2011): 785–803.

Thomson, Mathew. *Psychological Subjects: Identity, Culture and Health in Twentieth Century Britain*. Oxford: Oxford University Press, 2006.

Thomson, Mathew. *Lost Freedom: The Landscape of the Child and the British Post-War Settlement*. Oxford: Oxford University Press, 2013.

Unilever UK. 'Unilever Future Leaders Programme'. 2023, https://careers.unilever.com/unilever-future-leaders-programme, accessed 17 July 2024.

Ussishkin, Daniel. 'Morale and the Postwar Politics of Consensus', *Journal of British Studies* 52, no. 3 (2013): 722–43.

Emma Vickers, *Queen and Country: Same-Sex Desire in the British Armed Forces, 1939–45* Manchester: Manchester University Press, 2013.

White, Alice. 'From the Science of Selection to Psychologising Civvy Street: The Tavistock Group, 1939–1948' (PhD thesis, University of Kent, 2016).

Chapter 8

'The Pill for an unmarried girl is hardly going to improve her character': The impact of changing sexual behaviours on the construction of adulthood in Scotland, c.1968–80[1]

Kristin Hay

> I was starting university in Edinburgh, and I was going to be nearly 19 ... It was exciting, and everything was new, and I was young, and in love and on the pill![2] (Deborah, b. 1956)

Deborah, who was born to a coal miner and an office clerk, was raised in Dunfermline, a city in the north-west of Scotland. As part of the so-called 'baby boomer' generation, considered those born between 1945 and 1965, Deborah and her peers were the purported beneficiaries of a transformation in British society and culture. As alluded to in the above epigraph, this generation were the first to be fully nurtured under the postwar welfare state and were the beneficiaries of a number of socio-economic benefits: including the end of postwar austerity, low unemployment, greater access to university education and, of course, the creation of the National Health Service (NHS).[3] Moreover, this cohort bore witness to a dramatic shift in attitudes towards sex and accepted sexual behaviours. In 1967, an article in the *Aberdeen Evening Express* wrote that a 'relentless social and Sexual Revolution' had occurred in Scotland.[4] The article stressed a correlation between the sweeping permissive reforms of the late 1960s and a new, purportedly sexually liberated, Scottish public.

However, this narrative obscures the fact while changes were occurring on a legislative level, attitudes towards the increasing availability of birth control in Scotland remained hostile, culminating in a strong countermovement against the so-called sexual revolution. Most of the backlash to the 'permissive society' emerged in Scotland due to the increasing availability of birth control for the unmarried. Gradually throughout the 1960s, the use of contraceptives came to be blamed for 'corrupting' a younger, more 'promiscuous' generation who were increasingly at odds with the traditional values of their parents. Between 1950 and 1970 there was a perceivable increase in premarital sexual activity and a notable decline in traditional religious practices, what cultural historian Callum Brown describes as a 'transformation in the nature of human respectability'. Young adults were purportedly engaging in sexual activities before marriage more frequently and with more partners. They were also engaging less often with the Christian church and its associated customs.[5] These demographic shifts occurred as a result of (or in tandem with) technological developments in contraception and legislative developments in family planning provision. In many ways, then, the generation of Deborah and her peers was indeed distinctive to their predecessors, who had often viewed sex as reserved for marriage; relied on philanthropy to access family planning; did not have access to reliable contraception or legal abortion; and could not access birth control unless in a marital relationship. A gulf between generations had emerged, signifying a change in transitions to adulthood.

The perceived socio-cultural distinctions between the dominant and emergent generations garnered significant interest during this time. As early as 1976, American historians and sociologists John Modell, Frank F. Furstenberg and Theodore Hershberg argued that 'the process of growing up has become more prevalent, less prolonged, and more concentrated than it was a century ago'. In coming to this conclusion, the authors highlighted contradictions in the popular belief that 'the period of youth has been moved later in the life course, extended, removed for better or for worse from meaningful contact with the adult world'.[6] This suggests that the parameters and timing of adulthood were in a state of instability in the 1970s; stuck in a paradox wherein those over the age of sixteen were simultaneously perceived as growing up too fast (in regards to obtaining economic independence and engaging in premarital sexual behaviours) and too slowly (in regards to marriage, homeowning, completing education, obtaining a career and procreating). As this chapter will show, these perceptions did not always align with demographic or chronological change, but rather reflected cultural understandings of the point at which one became 'adult'.

Latterly, in 2010, Furstenberg suggested that the changing status of women via the increasing availability of birth control in particular 'complicated the passage to adulthood', but lamented that 'researchers still know far more about the demography and economics of the change than about its implications for family life and practices'.[7] In studies of the history of sex, gender and youth culture, Claire Langhamer has convincingly argued that premarital 'courtship' changed in the postwar period and 'constituted a transitional stage between gendered youth and gendered adulthood'.[8] As highlighted in the Introduction to this collection, Carol Dyhouse has also looked at the infantilisation of young women, particularly in relation to their sexual autonomy, through the lens of youthfulness.[9] However, little research has been conducted on the anxieties surrounding the increasing availability of contraception as a lens to examine the construction of adulthood, despite the centrality of birth control in changing family and gender dynamics.

This chapter attempts to reconcile the present gap in the literature by examining attitudes towards the increasing availability of contraception in Scotland and its use by unmarried people through the lens of adulthood. Through archival evidence, this chapter will demonstrate that the moral panic over the provision of contraception for the unmarried was rooted in concerns over the agency and capacity of young adults, with a disproportionate emphasis placed on unmarried women and their sexual behaviours. As this chapter will show, unmarried women were disproportionately represented as inherently juvenile – regardless of their age – and lacking the key social indicators which made them independent adults. This demonstrates the enduring centrality of marriage as a linchpin signifier of adulthood despite the changing cultural climate around marriage as an institution during this time. This case study further demonstrates the ways in which changing access to contraception and sexual behaviours coincided with wider changes in understandings about adulthood in post-1960s Scotland.

This chapter will begin with a brief overview of the development of family planning contraceptive provision for the unmarried and its reception in Scotland. Attention will then turn to representations of young adults and their sexual practices, highlighting the ways in which adulthood remained elusive until marriage and procreation, despite demographic shifts in the dynamics of the family throughout this time. Finally, this chapter will examine debates surrounding contraceptive use by unmarried women as a particularly problematised category. It will identify the ways in which they were denied adult status, representing them as incapable of making informed choices and making their sexual and reproductive autonomy the responsibility of the family, the state and the medical profession.

The development of family planning services in Scotland

The twentieth century witnessed a transformation in family planning and its place within British society. Perhaps the most significant development was the invention and introduction of the oral contraceptive pill. Developed by Drs Gregory Pincus and John Rock, the combined oral pill represented the first biomedical method of preventing conception.[10] The drug surpassed all previous methods of contraception in quality and usability: it was novel, discrete, stylish, non-intrusive and reportedly had a 'virtually 100 per cent' effectiveness rate in preventing conception.[11] By 1964, around 480,000 married women across Britain were being regularly prescribed one of the fifteen brands of oral contraceptives available, each offering their own tailored balance of progestogen and oestrogen in order to prevent pregnancy.[12]

As emphasised by Elizabeth Siegel-Watkins, the pill represents a magic bullet of birth control, with the 1960s bearing witness to a 'contraceptive revolution' in which reproduction was medicalised and controlled by triumphs in science.[13] However, the invention of oral contraceptives was precipitated by a broader shift in attitudes towards sex and family planning which gained momentum in the late nineteenth century and accelerated following World War I.[14] In the decades prior to the oral contraceptive pill, family planning had gradually become normalised as a feature and emblem of healthy, middle-class married life. This was due, in part, to the efforts of birth control campaigners – including Marie Stopes, Stella Browne and Joan Malleson – and the uncomfortable alliances between eugenicists and first-wave feminism.[15] The provision of family planning services further limited any public concern about new contraceptive technologies. Until the late 1960s, the NHS played no organised role in family planning. The majority of family planning clinics were operated by charities such as the Family Planning Association (FPA), who at their height were the second largest healthcare provider and the largest private healthcare organisation in Britain, providing 90 per cent of family planning services in Scotland in 1969.[16] Lastly, in the early 1960s, the pill was only available for married women for medical reasons, such as to prevent a medically dangerous pregnancy.[17] As a result, the technological revolution of the oral contraceptive did little to disrupt the established cultural status quo in Scotland.

'THE PILL FOR AN UNMARRIED GIRL'   175

However, following the introduction of the oral contraceptive pill, legislative changes occurred throughout the 1960s that gradually eroded barriers to contraceptive access, described by Audrey Leathard – a former chairperson of the FPA – as a 'rationalisation of family planning provision – a slow movement from confusion to order'.[18] The NHS Family Planning Act of 1967 removed the barrier of marital status on contraceptives and allowed doctors to include societal factors for prescribing the pill in England and Wales. It also compelled local health authorities to pay and provide for family planning. Shortly thereafter, the Health and Public Services Act of 1968 provided the same family planning provisions for Scotland, which had delayed implementation until 1972. In 1974, the NHS Reorganisation Act formally enshrined family planning under the umbrella of the NHS – removing the private prescription fee and transferring all FPA clinics to the health service. The state was formally responsible for providing family planning services. Family planning, even for the unmarried, became state sanctioned. Unlike most forms of healthcare in Britain, family planning remained a dually provided service: women could access prescription birth control services either via their general practitioner (GP) or through NHS-funded family planning clinics.

Yet, while the initial introduction of oral contraception garnered little public outrage, the shift from third-sector provision to state-funded provision – and, more significantly, the increased availability of contraceptives for the unmarried for social purposes – created a moral panic across mainland Britain. Tensions were heightened in Scotland: a nation described in 1969 by Mass Observation, a prominent British social research organisation, as at the 'other end of the moral scale' in comparison with 'London – the centre of permissive society'.[19] As Roger Davidson and Gayle Davis note, 'within the British context, the Scottish public was the least supportive of free birth control and a more proactive role by the state in the provision of family planning'.[20]

In part, this was the result of the increasing conflation made between contraceptive use and increased sexual activity by the unmarried. Moreover, the unmarried were increasingly represented as juvenile in debates around their contraceptive use. This served a political purpose: as perpetually adolescent, the unmarried were viewed as incapable of making their own decisions and asserting their own sexual and reproductive autonomy. As Marcus Collins colourfully argues, the pill came to be viewed as a means for unmarried men and women 'to engage in guilt-free, conception-free, no-strings-attached sex'.[21] By removing the fear of an unwanted pregnancy, the assumption was that unmarried people would engage in greater promiscuous activity, sanctioned by the state. In a letter written in 1970 to the secretary of state for Scotland, William Ross, one Miss. E. Lewis – not her real name – from Glasgow commented:

> I deplore deeply that fornication is encouraged among the unmarried by the giving of contraceptives and by the most evil of all the murder of the unborn ... Scotland retains enough of its Christian principles to prevent it from sinking to the depths of permissiveness and evil.[22]

Her correspondence highlights that the removal of marital status as a barrier to contraception was seen to promote premarital sex. As further demonstrated, reactions were often intersected with concerns over religious values, with clergy members of both Protestant and Catholic Churches arguing that giving the pill to the unmarried was a 'threat to the Christian way' and was sending Scotland into 'a post-Christian age in an increasingly Pagan society'.[23] However, even outside of secular spaces, there were anxieties about the 'destructive' effect of contraception on the unmarried, with newspaper articles arguing that 'sex on the rates' – a euphemism for contraceptives on the NHS – was 'a licence for widespread immorality'.[24] These accounts demonstrate that it was the provision of contraceptives for the unmarried which caused the backlash to oral contraception, and its conflation with promiscuity led to panic around the age and conditions at which sex was, or should be, permissible.

Who were 'the unmarried' in 1970s Scotland?

Although the term could refer to anyone of any age, the majority of opposition to birth control for the unmarried was both implicitly and explicitly focused on young people throughout the 1970s. This was not exclusive to Scotland: as Caroline Rusterholz has shown, journalists 'used "unmarried" and "young people" interchangeably' in discussions of unmarried promiscuity in England.[25] Yet, this phraseology obscured the small but significant distinctions between a broad and varied category of people who concurrently garnered increased legal attention in Scotland following the late 1960s. Specifically, increasing attention was being paid to the age at which young people were given the legal status of 'adult' during this time.

In 1969, the 'age of majority' – the threshold at which a person is granted legal status as an adult – was reduced in Britain from twenty-one to eighteen.[26] Yet, the age of consent and the age at which a young person could marry remained at sixteen, and in 1972 the school leaving age was raised to this age as well. Thus, young people were in secondary education for longer, but attained legal adulthood status much earlier at the turn of the 1970s. Between the ages of sixteen and eighteen, they could get a job, get married, have sex and have children, yet would still not be regarded as 'adult' in the eyes of the law. Moreover, Scots law further distinguished young people into two categories of legal capacity – minors and pupils. This was a distinctive legal system from England and Wales. While 'pupils' – 'boys under the age of 14 and girls under the age of 12' – were deemed to have 'no legal capacity whatsoever', minors – 'boys and girls between those ages and 18' – had 'limited' capacity and could act on their own behalf in certain situations without the consent of a parent or guardian. This included medical consent. Moreover, unlike in England and Wales, a sixteen-year-old did not need the permission of their parents to marry in Scotland. Ultimately, this created an ambiguous and malleable legal climate for defining an 'adult', as demonstrated in a Memorandum by the Scottish Law Commission in 1985:

> The law ignores the fact that many young people become economically active before they reach the age of 18, either simply by having pocket money to spend, or by taking a full-time job and becoming financially independent of their parents, or by getting married and leaving home.[27]

In the above conclusion, the Scottish Law Commission epitomised the difficulty of defining an adult in the late 1960s, owing to societal expectations which did not always align with the legal framework. Their conclusion reflects Jordan Stanger-Ross, Christina Collins and Mark J. Stern's assessment that:

> Beginning in the mid-1970s, young people ... were the first twentieth-century generation to make decisions about marriage and establishing procreative households in positions of relative autonomy ... reinvent[ing] their transitions to adulthood ... [and reflecting] how the world around them had changed.[28]

The increased access to both higher education and oral contraception purportedly led to delays in obtaining a career, getting married and starting a family by having children without a delay to sexual activity.

However, this assessment has been critiqued by Jeffrey Weeks, who asserts that 'Changes were apparently taking place largely within traditional frameworks of marriage ... rather than breaking them.'[29] Weeks suggests that while premarital sex was demographically on the rise, it was reconfigured within a conservative, heteronormative moral framework. Indeed, despite the fact that the age of first marriage in Scotland increased dramatically in the second half of the twentieth century, there was a distinctive dip in the aftermath of the so-called 'sexual revolution'. Between 1951 and 1960, the mean age at first marriage for men decreased from 26.4 to 24.3 by 1970. Respectively, the mean age at first marriage for women declined from 24.0 between 1951 and 1960 to 22.8 by 1970. Between 1971 and 1980, there was only marginal change in the average age for both men and women.[30] This suggests that young adults were getting married earlier than in previous decades. However, the heightened affluence and social mobility of this generation did provide them with an opportunity to move out of their parental home and live independently from their parents. As Lindsay Paterson has shown, 'the proportion [of young adults] living in their parental home decreased from 57 per cent in 1950 to 41 per cent in the 1970s'.[31] Consequently, the mid-1970s represented a time of legal and social tensions surrounding what constituted an adult in Scotland. Yet, as this section will show, concern over the changing attitudes of young people did not always align with demographic reality.

Within the broader context of changing legal and social understandings of what constituted an 'adult', marriage remained a keystone event which solidified and concluded transitions to adulthood in Scotland. Consequently, the 'unmarried' remained a person who had not obtained adult status. This had a significant impact on debates and attitudes towards increasing contraceptive access for the unmarried. Indeed, the issue with conflating 'unmarried' with 'young person' was epitomised by a letter to the editor written by Valerie Riches to *The Times* in 1974. Riches was a prominent anti-abortion campaigner and then-secretary of the Responsible Society, a social hygienist pressure group formed in 1971. In the letter, Riches used a case study from Aberdeen to argue that 'the wider availability of contraceptives has not been proved beyond a doubt to have reduced the number of unwanted pregnancies and may have had the reverse effect', echoing broader sentiments circulating during this time. Yet, more significantly, Riches further argued that:

> Perhaps the most important factor in the controversy is the implied approval, almost amounting to *encouragement* by the Government of sexual relations outside of marriage and below the *age of consent*.[32]

Her statement egregiously depicted the unmarried not only as young people but as teenagers under the age of sixteen. This transformed the issue from unmarried sexual behaviours to the sexual activity of minors still under the legal protection of their guardians. The conceptualisation of unmarried people as juvenile was also shown in debates in Edinburgh in 1971, when it was reported that 'several thousand anxious parents' had signed a petition to oppose plans by Edinburgh Town Council to prescribe the oral contraceptive to 'unmarried girls over 16'. Despite the fact that the age of consent for both sex and marriage at the time was also sixteen,

'THE PILL FOR AN UNMARRIED GIRL' 179

the petition's organisers argued that 'parents who feel responsible for the moral and physical welfare of their family consider it very irresponsible for the council to pass legislation which obviously undermines their authority'.[33] The quote explicitly places parents of young adults in a power role, with ultimate control over their children. These examples show that the unmarried were disproportionately represented as non-adults, heightening the anxieties surrounding the availability of birth control for this demographic. Within these debates, marital status remained the linchpin of adulthood.

The emphasis on adolescence within growing opposition towards the availability of birth control in the late 1960s is of further significance because teenagers represented only a small portion of total family planning service users. Scotland had a unique system of family planning service distribution, within which unmarried young people faced particular issues of access that were distinct to the rest of Britain. This can be shown by the lack of specific family planning services for teenagers in Scotland, which in England and Wales were delivered largely by the third sector. In 1966, the Brook Advisory Service was set up specifically to provide young people with sexual health advice and support and was particularly attractive to those under sixteen. However, Scotland only had one Brook Advisory Service clinic, located in Edinburgh. The only other Scottish clinic operated by Brook, located in Glasgow, was absorbed by the FPA in 1970.

Because of their lack of locations in Scotland, the FPA clinics were the only option for most unmarried persons until the mid-1970s. After this point, clinics remained the most popular family planning provider, as many unmarried people were reluctant to visit their GP. In the FPA's 1968 Annual Report, the Scottish branch showed that just 10 per cent of all attendees were under twenty, with 40 per cent aged between twenty and twenty-four, and 25 per cent twenty-five to twenty-nine.[34] It was not until 1970 that the FPA formally provided family planning support to unmarried men and women; however, it is clear that many individual clinics offered advice and products clandestinely. By 1974, the percentage of those attending FPA within the twenty to twenty-four age range had increased to 75 per cent.[35] Thus, the vast majority of pill takers obtaining the pill from the FPA in Scotland, married and unmarried, were over the age of twenty. This demonstrates that teenagers, particularly those of school age, represented only a small minority of those accessing hormonal contraceptives, in part due to the inherent issues of accessibility.

A further factor which emphasises the persistent centrality of marital status in transitions to adulthood during this time was that teenagers were not the only category to be disproportionately focused on in debates around contraception for the unmarried. Just as teenagers caused alarm during increasing contraceptive availability, students were also the focus of both anxiety and vitriol. Between 1960 and 1970 in Scotland, the number of students at university doubled as a result of the introduction of state grants and the expansion of universities.[36] While the pill was seen to corrupt and harm minors, students who were using contraceptives were conversely seen as sexually indulgent and reckless, further contributing to increased promiscuity. This rendered 'the unmarried' as either incapable of consenting or incapable of making responsible choices surrounding sex and reproduction. Concerns over their sexuality grew throughout this period as many began to question the moral welfare of university campuses.

Yet, equally, students were presented in the Scottish press as selfish and hedonistic, as one anonymous columnist named 'Alma Mater' in 1968 stereotyped:

> The student population appears to be a collection of social misfits, hippies, ill-dressed, ill-mannered louts, living off the charity provided by the working population, and intent only on spending a few promiscuous years at university, living on drink and The Pill.[37]

This statement reflects the intergenerational tensions and opposition to oral contraceptives during this time. Class also featured heavily in this attitude, as broader resentments surrounding the growing affluence and social mobility of young people in this period clearly influenced the bitterness surrounding their access to contraceptives. Scottish education was defined by its 'democratising' nature, with Lindsay Paterson highlighting that over a quarter of all university students were from working-class families by the mid-1970s.[38] Although not insignificant, it nevertheless highlights that the majority of students were middle class. Perhaps because of this higher affluence and assumed homogeneity, Jane O'Neill argues that in Scotland 'students of the period were often assumed to be at the forefront of liberalisation in sexual behaviour'.[39] This compounded the disdain towards students.

Commentators saw contraception as a means of escaping the 'punishment' of premarital sex – namely, an unexpected pregnancy – and its socio-economic consequences. This was further shown in another response to a petition against opening a family planning clinic on an Edinburgh University campus in 1967:

> This time they [students] have gone too far. Not the married ones ... the 'Pill' is for the unmarried couples on the campus who feel that it is needed because there have been so many illegitimate births among

> university students ... May I suggest another way of curing the increase in illegitimacy? A good hard kick on the posterior for you and all your kind!
>
> I am not going to pay good money so that you can spend four years of your life having sex with a few of your fellow students, with the blessing of the country and a free supply of contraceptives.[40]

The author explicitly focused on unmarried students in their discussion. It is clear that the state provision of family planning, coupled with a general resentment of the student population, fuelled the anger permeating through the article. In contrast, married students were excluded from the author's haranguing. Consequently, unmarried university students – the vast majority of whom were over the age of eighteen – were denied the status of adulthood.

Ultimately, unmarried men and women were presented either as innocent children in need of protecting or reckless, affluent adolescents who had little regard for the community social mores. Teenagers, despite being a broad category, were almost always considered minors, thus deemed impressionable and asexual, thus in need of protection. University students, in contrast, were typically of the 'age of majority', and yet were still considered inherently juvenile. Scottish university students were frequently presented as indulgent and reckless in the press, thus limiting their adulthood status. As argued by J.J. Arnett in the context of American youth culture during the 1990s, 'making the transition to adulthood [meant] avoiding behaviour that might be harmful to others ... [including] reckless behaviour concerning crime and sexual behaviour'. Within this definition, unmarried university students were dispossessed of adulthood status by 'character qualities [viewed] as part of adolescence' such as 'egocentrism and selfishness'.[41] These two categories demonstrate that marital status above all else acted as the delineation between adult and non-adult, in spite of the demographic changes occurring throughout Britain during this time.

Gender and the unmarried

While the unmarried were universally considered to be non-adult, unmarried women were disproportionately represented within debates around the consequences of permissive society. On one hand, the fact that the pill was the first effective contraceptive for women played a significant role in the heightened emphasis on female sexuality, as the responsibility for family planning reversed from male-controlled birth control to female-controlled.[42] However, it is evident that unmarried women's sexual activity remained highly stigmatised socially, with Carol Dyhouse commenting that 'young women [were] represented as the victims of all manner of social trends' including 'sexualisation' during this time.[43] Their presumed victimisation presented unmarried women as perpetually adolescent and in need of protection, thus further denying their passage into adulthood.

In debates around unmarried women's contraceptive and sexual practices, an over-emphasis on their 'girlhood' emerged. This infantilisation of unmarried women within the Scottish context was demonstrated in 1972 through comments made by the Conservative MP for East Aberdeenshire, Patrick Wolridge-Gordon. In a newspaper interview, he argued that 'the Pill ... for an unmarried girl is hardly going to improve her character'.[44] Wolridge-Gordon's comment conflated the pill with sex and promiscuity and demonstrated the concerns over the degeneration of Scottish youth during this time. In fact, rarely were young women over the age of sixteen represented as adults in the Scottish press. As shown previously, in 1971 parents protested against Edinburgh Town Council for making 'family planning services available to unmarried girls over 16'. Later on in the article, it was stated that 'to provide these facilities is to encourage girls to engage in physical relationships which they would otherwise avoid'.[45] Similarly, in Banffshire, in the north-east of Scotland, a local councillor unsuccessfully opposed the opening of a family planning clinic because they felt that 'the fact that a school girl could go to the clinic and get the pill, without this being disclosed to her parents, was "horrible"' and that the clinic would be 'a place to license immorality' for 'problem girls'.[46] There is a slight shift in emphasis between these two case studies, with one presenting unmarried women as ignorant and in need of protection and another presenting them as a social issue.

This dichotomy was further represented throughout the Scottish press. Girls who engaged in premarital sex were either presented as 'bad girls' and 'problem girls' – who were being given 'a place to licence immorality' through family planning clinics – or 'bewildered girls' and 'lonely ... young unmarried girl[s]'.[47] Often, this emerged in tandem with discussions surrounding illegitimacy: while 'bad girls' were 'too selfish to take risks and know too much about birth control' to have an unexpected pregnancy outside of marriage, other girls were 'girls ... with a real sense of shame' or 'real, ordinary girls ... faced with a tragic personal problem'.[48] This again denoted the class differences between middle- and working-class women: presumptuously organised as those with purported knowledge of, and access to, contraception and those without, respectively. This reflects Dyhouse's assessment that 'in the minds of the moral right, girls tended to appear as either victims or sluts ... they were chaste or they were promiscuous'.[49] Yet, in all cases, unmarried women were defined as 'girls' regardless of age. Even in cases where age could be determined – such as one instance concerning university students – 'girl' was still used throughout.[50] In contrast, unmarried boys were rarely mentioned. In 1962, the general secretary for the National Council of the Unmarried Mother and Her Child (latterly Gingerbread and the National Council for One Parent Families) wrote that:

> We might well consider how best to help the teenage schoolboy father whose complicated reactions to the predicament in which he has placed his girl may jeopardise his whole future.[51]

Here, the emphasis of the emotional conflict experienced by the unmarried boy lay not in premarital sex, but in managing the presumedly volatile reaction of his partner. The agency in the above quote remained with the 'schoolboy' who had led his partner into a stigmatised 'social problem'.[52] Thus, differences existed in accepted sexual behaviours between unmarried men and unmarried women.

The use of the term 'girl' to describe unmarried women during this period denoted the lack of maturity and agency placed upon single, sexually active women, suggesting that they had not yet reached adulthood in the eyes of Scottish society. As Michael Messner, Margaret Carlisle Duncan and Kerry Jensen note, the use of 'girls' linguistically 'reflects the lower status of women'. It is used to 'sexualise ... trivialise [and] ... infantilise women', as well as 'to (often subtly) re-construct gender and racial hierarchies'.[53] By putting unmarried women in the position of a minor, women remained sexually subordinate – or even asexual – and so remained vulnerable, requiring the guardianship of their parents until marriage. Consequently, the status quo of the immediate postwar period was maintained through denying women the right to assert their contraceptive choices.

The gendered differences between attitudes to unmarried women's sexual activity in contrast to unmarried men further suggested that sexual activity before marriage was seen as potentially more 'dangerous' for single women. Women were seen to face not only greater consequences by becoming pregnant but also greater emotional consequences for engaging in sex outside of a stable relationship. Indeed, medical doctors often pathologised what was perceived to be a growing prevalence of female promiscuity at this time, including one Dr Murdoch from Glasgow, who wrote a letter in 1972 to the *British Medical Journal* titled 'Sex and the Single Girl'. In this letter, he argued that:

> They say that the patient must get what she came for ... There are so many doctors who believe that obedience to the moral law of God is as important as obedience to His physical law ... they act, therefore, in their patient's best interests when they advise her to contain her sexual experience.[54]

As shown by his letter, Murdoch opposed 'single girls' having the legal ability to access contraceptives because of the moral consequences of women having the ability to engage in sex freely outside of marriage. He explicitly viewed the role of the doctor as providing moral 'treatment' to their patients as well as physical care, and so saw the prescription of contraceptives to the unmarried as antithetical to his profession and against the value of 'do no harm'. His letter demonstrates the consequences of perceiving unmarried women as inherently juvenile: they were unable to consent to medical intervention and required moral, emotional treatment.

Even in spaces where contraceptives for the unmarried were advocated for, unmarried women's sexuality was disproportionately problematised. During a conference on family planning in Scotland in 1968, Professor Ian MacGillivray, an obstetrician-gynaecologist and vocal advocate of contraception for the unmarried in Aberdeen, stated:

> We cannot ignore the rising incidence of extramarital and premarital sexual intercourse. It seems fairly certain that more schoolgirls have coitus today than did a similar group in the early years of this century.

His opening statement pervasively demonstrated the correlation between age, gender and marital status during this time. The interchangeable use of 'premarital' and 'schoolgirl' conjures the image of a minor within his discussion. Although ultimately in favour of increasing access to family planning – combined with a sex education programme focused on abstinence – MacGillivray's final comment was:

> I have deliberately concentrated on the unmarried girl in my talk ... this is now a very permissive society and there is a great deal of sexual provocation in dress, and we can think in particular, of course, of the mini skirt ... It should be emphasised to them that it is dangerous to experiment, not just because of the risk of pregnancy and venereal disease but because of the psychological hurt which they might suffer.[55]

The paternalism which has been proven to be typical in debates surrounding female sexuality at this time is notable in MacGillivray's speech, emphasising that premarital sex was seen as problematic for them. Dyhouse notes that 'the style revolution ... had obvious links to the widening gap between generations'.[56] Thus, MacGillivray's analogising of the 'mini skirt' further genders his discussion, making a connection between women's fashion, sexuality and the differences between his generation and the generation being discussed. The reference to the psychological harm – which he considers equal to the dangers of sexually transmitted disease – also suggests a pathologising of female sexual desire in the late 1960s. As he continues:

> It should be pointed out to the girl that a feeling of guilt sometimes follows premarital intercourse and sexual unhappiness in marriage sometimes occurs because of this guilt associated with premarital experience.[57]

His comments reflect the shame that women were expected to feel by engaging in sex outside of marriage. In contrast, there is no mention of the emotional or psychological harm of young boys engaging in sexual activity. The role of men is only discussed in relation to their sexual experience and knowledge in comparison to women's sexual ignorance, as he states, 'in a teenage affair the boy who asks the girl to have intercourse is willing to subject her to pain and grief from which he cannot rescue her'.[58] Within these discussions, unmarried women were continuously represented as lacking autonomy and sexual expression in comparison with their male contemporaries. Their naivety and vulnerability made them particularly significant in discussions around the dangers of increasing premarital sex. Yet, this construction and subsequent paternalism also denied them the independence characteristically necessary to develop into an adult during this time.

As Furstenberg notes, women played a significant role in shifting transitions to adulthood throughout the 1970s, due to a great extent to the availability of reliable birth control. The pill allowed women not only to enjoy sex without the fear of pregnancy but also to delay marriage and child-bearing in pursuit of education and a career. This 'complicated the passage to adulthood' but also led to a disproportionate reaction from Scottish society in which unmarried women were constructed as even less adult than unmarried men.[59] This demonstrates that gender further influenced and complicated the construction of adulthood in 1970s Scotland.

Conclusion

As this edited collection as a whole has argued, the contemporary transition to adulthood is an intently subjective and emotional experience. The status of 'adult' is not met according to the arbitrary age limits defined by law, nor is it a goal which can be achieved in a singular moment. Rather, it is a gradual progression of life events which intersect legal capacity with emotional maturity and culminates in the creation of a contributory, socially responsible citizen. Yet, an adult is not simply the act of 'being'; it is a performance. Adulthood can be observed, assessed, ascribed and denied by others within the community, and so plays a crucial role in the formation and functioning of society. While simultaneously being an inherently personal, private process, in the modern period key social indicators continue to designate a person the status of adult: having a career, getting married, owning a house, having children. More abstractly, characteristics such as responsibility, conscientiousness and altruism further differentiated the adult from the adolescent in the twentieth century, which in turn aligned with the accepted moral framework of a given nation.

In the context of changing social, economic and familial structures during the 1960s, the popular indicators of adulthood remained static, particularly the perception that marriage represented the apex of adulthood. Yet, the perception that young people were not mapping themselves neatly onto this enduring paradigm led to a conservative backlash against a seemingly 'novel' generation. This was heightened in Scotland, which had a distinctive legal and cultural framework to the rest of mainland Britain. The pill for the unmarried – provided by the British state – facilitated premarital sex and in so doing raised questions about the purpose of marriage as an institution. By removing marriage as a 'culminating event' which previously 'provided an easy (though not always a successful) route out' of adolescence, questions about the ability of 'the unmarried' to assert their sexual and reproductive (thereby medical) autonomy emerged.[60]

Young people were disproportionately emphasised within debates about 'the unmarried', as they represented a tiny portion of total family planning users. Further and higher education students, most of whom were over eighteen – the new age of majority – were also infantilised and viewed as in need of paternalism, further demonstrating that age played a limited role in the construction of an adult. Rather, marriage socially remained a keystone event which delineated an independent adult from a dependent adolescent. The backlash to the pill for the unmarried thus acted as an extension of resisting the increasing autonomy and individualism within Scottish society and a rejection of changing familial structures and patterns.

Yet, even within the cohort of the unmarried, gender dynamics further resulted in a spotlight being placed on unmarried women to a greater extent than unmarried men. This demonstrates a consistency from earlier time periods: as Deborah Youngs noted earlier in this collection, gender has played a significant role in the construction of adulthood since at least the medieval period. The unmarried were almost universally represented as either a gender-neutral monolith or as the 'single, unmarried girl'. Rarely were 'unmarried boys' named in the press or debated in medical journals. This influenced the construction of sex as a particularly hazardous activity for women, who were represented as lacking total knowledge of the physical, emotional and moral dangers of premarital sex. Women's perceived 'vulnerability' and inability to assert their own sexual and reproductive autonomy reflected the characteristics of a non-adult who was incapable of making responsible choices, thus denying them adult status.

Notes

1. This research was funded by the Wellcome Trust.

2. Interview with Deborah conducted by author (23 November 2020), 9.

3. Tom Devine, 'The Sixties in Scotland: A Historical Context' in Elizabeth Bell and Linda Gunn (eds.), *The Scottish Sixties: Reading, Rebellion, Revolution?* (Amsterdam: Rodopi, 2013), 21.

4. 'The New Sexual Freedom', *Aberdeen Evening Express* (13 December 1967).

5. See Callum G. Brown, *Religion and the Demographic Revolution: Women and Secularisation in Canada, Ireland, UK and USA since the 1960s* (Cambridge: Cambridge University Press, 2013).

6. John Modell, Frank F. Furstenberg and Theodore Hershberg, 'Social Change and Transitions to Adulthood in Historical Perspective', *Journal of Family History* 1, no. 1 (1976), 7–19.

7. Frank F. Furstenberg, 'On a New Schedule: Transitions to Adulthood and Family Change', *The Future of Children* 20, no. 1 (2010), 69.

8. Claire Langhamer, 'Love and Courtship in Mid-Twentieth-Century England', *The Historical Journal* 50, no. 1 (2007), 196.

9. Carol Dyhouse, *Girl Trouble: Panic and Progress in the History of Young Women* (London: Zed, 2013).

10. For a comprehensive history of the development of the oral contraceptive pill, see Laura Marks, *Sexual Chemistry: A History of the Contraceptive Pill* (New Haven, CT: Yale University Press, 2001).

11. GWL FP-11-6, FPA pamphlet, 'The Pill' (1973).

12. Hera Cook, *The Long Sexual Revolution: English Women, Sex and Contraception, 1800–1975* (Oxford: Oxford University Press, 2004).

13. Elizabeth Siegel-Watkins, *On the Pill: A Social History of Oral Contraceptives 1950–1970* (London: Johns Hopkins University Press, 1998), 2.

14. For more on the late nineteenth century, see Tanya Cheadle, *Sexual Progressives: Reimagining Intimacy in Scotland, 1880–1914* (Manchester: Manchester University Press, 2020).

15. Lesley Hall, *Sex, Gender and Social Change in Britain since 1880* (Basingstoke: Macmillan, 2000) provides a thorough account of Stopes's work. See also Angus McLaren, *A History of Contraception: From Antiquity to the Present Day* (Oxford: Blackwell, 1990) and Lesley Hoggart, *Feminist Campaigns for Birth Control and Abortion Rights in Britain* (Lewiston, NY: Edwin Mellen Press, 2003).

16. ML, HB77/3/12, 'Annual General Meeting, North of Scotland Branch: Chairman's Address' (1969); Jane Silvermann and Elise Jones, 'The Delivery of Family Planning and Health Services in Great Britain', *Family Planning Perspectives* 20, no. 2 (1988), 69.

17. Cook, *The Long Sexual Revolution*, 297.

18. Audrey Leathard, *The Fight for Family Planning: The Development of Family Planning Services in Britain, 1921–1974* (London: Macmillan, 1980), 157.

19. Wellcome Library SA/FPA/C/E/16/2/3MO Press Release, 'Morals Aren't What They Used to Be' (1969).

20. Roger Davidson and Gayle Davis, *The Sexual State: Sexuality and Scottish Governance, 1950–1980* (Edinburgh: Edinburgh University Press, 2015), 144.

21. Marcus Collins, *Modern Love: An Intimate History of Men and Women in Twentieth-Century Britain* (London: Atlantic, 2003), 177.

22. NRS, HH61/1208 'Letter to Scottish Home and Health Department from [Miss. E. Lewis] Glasgow' (21 December 1970).

23. 'Christ Gave No Licence to Sin', *Aberdeen Evening Express* (19 December 1967).

24. 'Sex on the Rates: "A Licence for Widespread Immorality" Say Some', *Aberdeen Evening Express* (9 August 1968).

25. Caroline Rusterholz, 'Youth Sexuality, Responsibility, and the Opening of the Brook Advisory Centres in London and Birmingham in the 1960s', *Journal of British Studies* 61, no. 2 (2022), 20.

26. Age of Majority (Scotland) Act (1969), www.legislation.gov.uk/ukpga/1969/39/body.

27. Scottish Law Commission, 'Consultative Memorandum No. 65 Legal Capacity and Responsibility of Minors and Pupils' (June 1985).

28. Jordan Stanger-Ross, Christina Collins and Mark J. Stern, 'Falling Far from the Tree: Transitions to Adulthood and the Social History of Twentieth-Century America', *Social Science History* 29, no. 4 (2005), 627.

29. Jeffrey Weeks, *The World We Have Won: The Remaking of Erotic and Intimate Life* (London: Routledge, 2007), 67–71.

30. 'Annual Report of the Registrar General of Birth, Deaths and Marriages for Scotland' (General Registrar Office for Scotland, 1996), 124.

31. Lindsay Paterson, *Scottish Education in the Twentieth Century* (Edinburgh: Edinburgh University Press, 2003), 159.

32. Valerie Riches, 'Letter to the Editor', *The Times* (1974). Emphasis included by author.

33. 'Parents Protest Family Planning Bid', *Aberdeen Press and Journal* (14 March 1971).

34. ML, HB773/12, FPA, 'Second Annual Report, 1968' (1968).

35. ML, HB773/12, FPA, 'Annual Report, 1974'.

36. Paterson, *Scottish Education in the Twentieth Century*, 156.

37. 'Readers' Letters: Hypocrisy, I Detest!', *Aberdeen Evening Express* (21 February 1968).

38. Paterson, *Scottish Education in the Twentieth Century*, 158.

39. Jane O'Neill, '"Education Not Fornication"? Sexual Morality among Students in Scotland, c. 1955–75', in Jodi Burkett (ed.), *Students in Twentieth Century Britain and Ireland* (London: Palgrave Macmillan, 2018), 77.

40. 'So You Want the Pill?', *West Lothian Courier* (1 December 1967).

41. J.J. Arnett, 'Learning to Stand Alone: The Contemporary American Transition to Adulthood in Cultural and Historical Context', *Human Development* 41, nos. 5–6 (1998), 309.

42. See Cook, *The Long Sexual Revolution*.

43. Dyhouse, *Girl Trouble*, 2.

44. 'Why Patrick Is Afraid of the Pill', *Aberdeen Press and Journal* (26 June 1972).

45. 'Parents Protest Family Planning Bid'.

46. 'Pill Clinic Is Defeated', *Aberdeen Press and Journal* (16 February 1971).

47. 'We Are All to Blame: Our Modern Sickness Apathy', *Aberdeen Evening Express* (24 October 1966); 'Pill clinic is defeated'.

48. 'We Are All to Blame'; 'Unwed Mums and Elderly Face Homes Crisis', *Evening Express* (23 August 1973); 'The Loneliness of the Unmarried Mother', *Aberdeen Press and Journal* (1 December 1965).

49. Dyhouse, *Girl Trouble*, 182.

50. 'Edinburgh Pill Issue: Students Back Rector', *Aberdeen Evening Express* (13 December 1971).

51. 'Social Problem No. 2: The Unmarried Mother', *Aberdeen Press and Journal* (26 July 1962).

52. 'Social Problem No. 2'.

53. Michael A. Messner, Margaret Carlisle Duncan and Kerry Jensen, 'Separating the Men from the Girls: The Gendered Language of Televised Sports', *Gender and Society* 7, no. 1 (1993), 128–33.

54. J. Campbell Murdoch, 'Sex and the Single Girl', *British Medical Journal* 22, no. 3 (1972), 235–6.

55. WL, SA/FPA/A16/24/62A; Ian McGillivray, 'Opening Address', in *Family Planning for Scotland: Proceedings of the Conference, Glasgow, 1968* (Bristol: John Wright and Sons, 1969), 14–15.

56. Dyhouse, *Girl Trouble*, 154.

57. MacGillivray, 'Opening Address', 15.

58. MacGillivray, 'Opening Address', 15.

59. Furstenberg, 'On a New Schedule', 69.

60. Furstenberg, 'On a New Schedule', 81.

References

Archives

British Newspaper Archive.
Glasgow Women's Library, Glasgow.
Interview with Deborah conducted by author (23 Nov 2020).
Mitchell Library, Glasgow.
National Records of Scotland, Edinburgh.
Wellcome Library, London.

Primary and secondary sources

Age of Majority (Scotland) Act (1969), www.legislation.gov.uk/ukpga/1969/39/body.

'Annual Report of the Registrar General of Birth, Deaths and Marriages for Scotland' (General Registrar Office for Scotland, 1996).

Arnett, J.J., 'Learning to Stand Alone: The Contemporary American Transition to Adulthood in Cultural and Historical Context', *Human Development* 41, nos. 5-6 (1998), 295–315.

Brown, Callum G., *Religion and the Demographic Revolution: Women and Secularisation in Canada, Ireland, UK and USA since the 1960s*, Cambridge: Cambridge University Press, 2013.

Campbell Murdoch, J., 'Sex and the Single Girl', *British Medical Journal* 22, no. 3 (1972), 235–6.

Cheadle, Tanya, *Sexual Progressives: Reimagining Intimacy in Scotland, 1880–1914*, Manchester: Manchester University Press, 2020.

'Christ Gave No Licence to Sin', *Aberdeen Evening Express* (19 December 1967).

Collins, Marcus, *Modern Love: An Intimate History of Men and Women in Twentieth-Century Britain*, London: Atlantic, 2003.

Cook, Hera, *The Long Sexual Revolution: English Women, Sex and Contraception, 1800–1975*, Oxford: Oxford University Press, 2004.

Davidson, Roger and Davis, Gayle, *The Sexual State: Sexuality and Scottish Governance, 1950–1980*, Edinburgh: Edinburgh University Press, 2015.

Devine, Tom, 'The Sixties in Scotland: A Historical Context' in Elizabeth Bell and Linda Gunn (eds.), *The Scottish Sixties: Reading, Rebellion, Revolution?*, Amsterdam: Rodopi, 2013, 23–46.

Dyhouse, Carol, *Girl Trouble: Panic and Progress in the History of Young Women*, London: Zed, 2013.

'Edinburgh Pill Issue: Students Back Rector', *Aberdeen Evening Express* (13 December 1971).

Furstenberg, Frank F., 'On a New Schedule: Transitions to Adulthood and Family Change', *The Future of Children* 20, no. 1 (2010), 67–87.

Hall, Lesley, *Sex, Gender and Social Change in Britain since 1880*, Basingstoke: Macmillan, 2000.

Hoggart, Lesley, *Feminist Campaigns for Birth Control and Abortion Rights in Britain*, Lewiston, NY: Edwin Mellen Press, 2003.

Langhamer, Claire, 'Love and Courtship in Mid-Twentieth-Century England', *The Historical Journal* 50, no. 1 (2007), 173–96.

Leathard, Audrey, *The Fight for Family Planning: The Development of Family Planning Services in Britain, 1921–1974*, London: Macmillan, 1980.

'The Loneliness of the Unmarried Mother', *Aberdeen Press and Journal* (1 December 1965).

Marks, Laura, *Sexual Chemistry: A History of the Contraceptive Pill*, New Haven, CT: Yale University Press, 2001.

McGillivray, Ian, 'Opening Address', in *Family Planning for Scotland: Proceedings of the Conference, Glasgow, 1968* (Bristol: John Wright and Sons, 1969), 14–15.

McLaren, Angus, *A History of Contraception: From Antiquity to the Present Day*, Oxford: Blackwell, 1990.

Messner, Michael A., Carlisle Duncan, Margaret and Jensen, Kerry, 'Separating the Men from the Girls: The Gendered Language of Televised Sports', *Gender and Society* 7, no. 1 (1993), 121–37.

Modell, John, Furstenberg, Frank F. and Hershberg, Theodore, 'Social Change and Transitions to Adulthood in Historical Perspective', *Journal of Family History* 1, no. 1 (1976), 7–32.

'The New Sexual Freedom', *Aberdeen Evening Express* (13 December 1967).

O'Neill, Jane, '"Education Not Fornication"? Sexual Morality among Students in Scotland, c. 1955–75', in Jodi Burkett (ed.), *Students in Twentieth Century Britain and Ireland*, London: Palgrave Macmillan, 2018, 77–98.

'Parents Protest Family Planning Bid', *Aberdeen Press and Journal* (14 March 1971).

Paterson, Lindsay, *Scottish Education in the Twentieth Century*, Edinburgh: Edinburgh University Press, 2003.

'Pill Clinic Is Defeated', *Aberdeen Press and Journal* (16 February 1971).

'Readers' Letters: Hypocrisy, I Detest!', *Aberdeen Evening Express* (21 February 1968).

Riches, Valerie, 'Letter to the Editor', *The Times* (1974).

Rusterholz, Caroline, 'Youth Sexuality, Responsibility, and the Opening of the Brook Advisory Centres in London and Birmingham in the 1960s', *Journal of British Studies* 61, no. 2 (2022), 315–42.

Scottish Law Commission, 'Consultative Memorandum No. 65 Legal Capacity and Responsibility of Minors and Pupils' (June 1985).

'Sex on the Rates: "A Licence for Widespread Immorality" Say Some', *Aberdeen Evening Express* (9 August 1968).

Siegel-Watkins, Elizabeth, *On the Pill: A Social History of Oral Contraceptives 1950–1970*, London: Johns Hopkins University Press, 1998.

Silvermann, Jane and Jones, Elise, 'The Delivery of Family Planning and Health Services in Great Britain', *Family Planning Perspectives* 20, no. 2 (1988), 68–74.

'Social Problem No. 2: The Unmarried Mother', *Aberdeen Press and Journal* (26 July 1962).

'So You Want the Pill?', *West Lothian Courier* (1 December 1967).

Stanger-Ross, Jordan, Collins, Christina and Stern, Mark J., 'Falling Far from the Tree: Transitions to Adulthood and the Social History of Twentieth-Century America', *Social Science History* 29, no. 4 (2005), 625–48.

'Unwed Mums and Elderly Face Homes Crisis', *Evening Express* (23 August 1973).

'We Are All to Blame: Our Modern Sickness Apathy', *Aberdeen Evening Express* (24 October 1966).

Weeks, Jeffrey, *The World We Have Won: The Remaking of Erotic and Intimate Life*, London: Routledge, 2007.

'Why Patrick Is Afraid of the Pill', *Aberdeen Press and Journal* (26 June 1972).

Chapter 9

African-Caribbean and South Asian adolescents, adulthood and the 'generation gap' in late Cold War Britain, c.1970–89

Laura Tisdall[1]

In post-war and Cold War Britain, new ideas about adulthood were shaped both by the psy sciences and by demographic, economic and social change. The average age of first marriage and first child dropped from the early 1950s to the early 1970s, while rising affluence allowed young adults access to financial independence and homes of their own. Meanwhile, schools increasingly grouped pupils by chronological age rather than by ability, indicating how tightly age was now linked with internal psychological maturity.[2] Achieving external, relational markers of adulthood like marriage, parenthood and secure employment there-fore became even more important in signalling that you were continuing along the 'correct' path, as Kristin Hay's chapter in this collection demon-strates.[3] Even during the 1980s, when rising unemployment threatened young people's economic security and 'transitions' to adulthood, these ideals remained unshaken. However, this hegemonic model of adulthood was based on white British norms, and did not take account of the experi-ences of immigrants or of people of colour.

Changing age norms in modern Britain emphasised the importance of passing through a sequence of developmental stages in order to attain maturity. This both hardened existing divisions between these age stages and suggested that children and teenagers lacked key adult qualities – like empathy, self-control, logical thinking and selflessness – because of their phase of psychological development, as Grace Whorrall-Campbell has shown in her chapter. Accelerating through age stages, or skipping out stages, was seen as abnormal, as was proceeding through the stages too slowly.[4] While these ideas affected all children and teenagers, they were especially oppressive for teenagers of colour because they allowed older ideas about race and age to be justified in new psychological language.[5]

Black adolescents, especially African-Caribbean adolescents, were depicted by teachers and by other professionals like social workers as accelerated in their physical development but 'retarded' in their intellectual and emotional development, often classified as 'educationally sub-normal' and seen as loud, excitable and immature.[6] South Asian adolescents were viewed as emotionally backward in a different way because of their supposed quietness and passivity; the ideal adolescent was gregarious and confident. They were stereotyped as 'unrealistic' because of their educational ambitions, language which both questioned their intellectual capabilities and pinned them to an earlier stage of development, as adolescents, unlike children, were meant to be able to adjust their dreams to the 'real world'.

Tammy-Charelle Owens has argued, in relation to her work on black girlhood in the United States during the period of slavery, that white people refused to recognise black girls as either children or adults, which denied them 'time privilege'.[7] As Jack Hodgson argues in his chapter in this collection, black children are often 'adultified' in situations where white people of their age would be framed as children, and this could have punitive consequences for them.[8] However, Owens's insight is that black children and teenagers are not just harmed by being seen as adults but because they are never permitted to be children, so they can never move through a 'proper' sequence of developmental stages and attain maturity.

Similar ideas were at play in the treatment of South Asians. As Satadru Sen argued, considering juvenile reform in British India between 1850 and 1945, 'if the native child was not truly a child, then the native adult could not be a true adult ... because he was the culmination of a flawed childhood'.[9] Radhika Natarajan's recent article on South Asian migration to Britain in the early 1960s demonstrates how this colonial logic was translated into the metropole, as young male migrants were both framed as older than they looked – and hence not eligible to enter the country as 'dependants' – and younger than they looked – and so vulnerable to exploitation from older South Asian men. Whether they were understood as children or as adults, young male South Asian migrants were unwelcome.[10] Therefore, to understand how African-Caribbean and South Asian teenagers in late Cold War Britain experienced adulthood, we must also know how they experienced childhood and adolescence, and how these life stages were interpreted for them.

In this chapter, African-Caribbean and South Asian adolescents' understandings of adolescence and adulthood in 1970s and 1980s Britain will be explored almost entirely through accounts written or spoken when they were still under twenty-one. Teenagers were the social group who were most likely to be asked to think about adulthood in postwar and Cold War Britain, either through imagining their own adult futures or writing about the future of the world. While African-Caribbean and South Asian adolescents were likely under-represented in larger cohort studies or in certain smaller sociological investigations, their testimonies were actively sought out by Black-led organisations from the 1970s onwards. Rob Waters has argued that the collection of teenage testimonies was seen as important by the black community for several reasons. First, it offered young people a chance to write in Creole languages, which helped them to assert a positive identity while facing racism. Second, the act of writing was viewed as politically significant for young black people, who were framed as 'agents of history' as well as 'the repository of past struggle'.[11] This emphasis on self-narrative was framed by the rise of black supplementary schools and the introduction of 'black studies' into mainstream secondary school curriculums.

This chapter therefore draws from a wide range of anthologies and archives that collected the writings of young people of colour during this period, although the young people represented are predominantly African-Caribbean and South Asian.[12] The testimonies of other racially minoritised teenagers in late Cold War Britain, such as Black Africans and Chinese and East Asians, are rarer, although the experiences of Indian-Caribbean and African Asian teenagers are briefly considered in this chapter. The Afro-Caribbean Education Resource Project (ACER) was set up in 1976 and it established the Black Youth Annual Penmanship Awards from 1978. This essay competition offered a selection of titles for black young people to choose from, and published anthologies of the winning entries into the late 1980s.[13] Alongside these collections of essays from (mostly) African-Caribbean young people, this chapter draws on a range of other sources: archived material from the Black Cultural Archives and George Padmore Archives that preserves the writings of young people of colour, especially those attending supplementary schools; the occasional pieces of writing by teenagers that were published in radical and educational magazines and journals; and sociological studies of African-Caribbean and South Asian teenagers that record their spoken words.[14]

As with white adolescents, the 'real views' of black and South Asian adolescents are difficult to discern using this source material. Much of it was either written for an imagined white, adult audience or spoken to white sociologists. Even when the adult audience addressed was Black, teenagers might have felt compelled to put forward certain narratives, especially for the ACER essay competition, which often set leading titles like 'Reggae Music Is a Source of Strength Because ...'. Although African-Caribbean adults may have intended respondents to write in patois or in Creole, as Waters suggests, this rarely happened in practice, which may have been for several reasons: teenagers may have wanted to emphasise their ability to write 'proper' English; they may not have been confident writing in other languages or dialects; or they may have been discouraged by other African-Caribbean adults from talking or writing in this way because it was seen as a barrier to success in Britain. A taped and transcribed discussion about speaking 'West Indian' dialect between some African-Caribbean fifth-form girls at a comprehensive school in Ealing in 1976 indicated the tensions here: Sonya commented, 'I don't think parents approve it so much because they think you're trying to act bad' and Meryl said, 'I think it's a good thing' but 'if my mum heard me talking like that she'd bust my little ass ... My parents talk like that but if I do they try and stop me'.[15]

As Waters has argued, Black people in Britain were especially suspicious of sociological studies, even those that were not conducted under the auspices of the state, and even those that were conducted by people from the same ethnic group. This could be especially true of young people, who were under intense scrutiny from both white adults and adults of colour, as the Grenadian sociologist Gus John discovered when he encountered 'anger and frustration' during his research in Manchester youth clubs.[16] Teenagers of all races refused to take part in research projects during this period. However, the adult-led projects featured in this chapter seem to have elicited certain kinds of responses because they were either conducted in mainstream schools or channelled through black supplementary schools or educational programmes. Young people in school had a different relationship to authority than they did when they were outside school, and might have less latitude to openly resist.

These records, therefore, remain vital sources for historians of age and adulthood not because they always give us access to the true 'voices' of African-Caribbean and South Asian young people but because of what they tell us about what these writers believed adults wanted to hear. By professing certain opinions in these writings, young people were either able to demonstrate their maturity by emphasising how closely they conformed to adult norms of respectability, independence and hard work or challenge prevailing norms, as African-Caribbean girls did when they resisted marriage and motherhood. Through these sources, we can understand how African-Caribbean and South Asian adolescents constructed adolescence and adulthood in relation to each other, and how they rewrote white British understandings of both life stages.

Schooling and education

The structural racism that both African-Caribbean and South Asian teenagers faced in school was framed by the belief that they were unable to grow up into psychologically and emotionally healthy adults. To a degree, this affected white working-class adolescents as well, as it was assumed they would never reach the more advanced developmental stages of abstract reasoning, an idea that has affected the treatment of non-elite people since at least the early modern period. However, African-Caribbean and South Asian teenagers were framed as more deviant, diverging even further from the 'correct' developmental pathway. African-Caribbean or 'West Indian' students were stereotyped as loud and disruptive, with a disproportionate number labelled as 'educationally sub-normal', an issue that sparked activism among black communities.[17] D.L. Edmondson, the headteacher of Holyhead secondary school in Handsworth, in Birmingham, where 85–90 per cent of the students were teenagers of colour, reflected in 1977 in the journal *Multiracial School*, published by the National Association for Multicultural Education (NAME): 'one's first impression of Jamaican children is that they are noisy, volatile and excitable ... I have noticed a good deal of bitchiness among the girls ... When stirred up and in full flow, many of these children seem to abandon all restraint ... They can be extremely offensive'.[18]

An article in the same journal published in 1983 highlighted similar views held by teachers in a Yorkshire comprehensive school where a third of the pupils were African-Caribbean: one teacher commented, 'I am prepared to expect louder or noisier behaviour from West Indian pupils than Asians or other groups' and another said that they gave West Indians more oral work as 'even the able West Indians become agitated when not writing well'. They encouraged them to participate in sport, where they had a 'chance of success' as 'West Indian pupils seem to be more muscular, more physically developed and have better physical skills than white children of the same age'.[19] These racist ideas framed teenage African-Caribbean students as precociously physically advanced but essentially childlike, unable to demonstrate the greater self-control expected in adolescence. Sometimes they were intended 'benevolently', suggesting that African-Caribbean students needed to be cut more slack than white or Asian students, but this only emphasised the idea that they would never be able to attain maturity.

African-Caribbean and Indian-Caribbean students challenged these ideas when given the opportunity to write about their experiences. They were acutely aware of where these stereotypes came from. In the 1980s, they cited popular television programmes like *Grange Hill* that, as sixteen-year-old Mike, an African-Caribbean boy at school in South East London, commented in 1982 in his ACER essay, presented black pupils as 'extremely stupid and/or disruptive'.[20] Sharon, an African-Caribbean girl, wrote in an ACER essay on 'What It Means to Be Black and British' in 1981, when she was seventeen, that, at school

> there is already built-up by the teacher (who is usually white) a comical view of black children ... Feeling now, alienated, you sit quietly brooding in the corner, or as you realise that you got the class laughing, you continue playing the Black comedian. Gradually, you get behind in your work and sent to the remedial unit.[21]

Another way of challenging racist ideas linked to the language of age and maturity was to point out that the racist behaviour of white peers indicated that they were the ones who were truly immature. Fifteen-year-old Paul, whose surname suggested that he was likely Indian-Caribbean, wrote in his ACER essay in 1982, 'Has Racism Been a Factor in School-Life for Me in Britain?', that 'Racism plays such an active role in my school-life that it is rarely possible for me to travel between my school's two buildings without being physically or verbally assaulted.' When he started secondary school, 'I naively imagined my fellow inmates to be responsible, mature young adults ... they soon proved me wrong.'[22]

A play written by an African-Caribbean teenage boy, Michael McMillan, which was published by the Black Ink Collective in 1978, attacked these stereotypes. In 'The School Leaver', Lester is introduced in these terms: 'A TEENAGE BLACK BOY sits at a desk, academic and brilliant, doing his physics.'[23] Nevertheless, McMillan recognised the social and cultural costs of trying to achieve on the terms set by white British society; Lester is bullied by his peers and doesn't feel 'truly' West Indian. When his dad asks him, 'has your teacher asked you if you're going to stay on [at school], boy, you nah want fuh go out on the streets', Lester replies, 'Yes, Daddy, I've told him that I intend to stay on, but you should try and learn to speak proper English', indicating that he has rejected his family's language and heritage.[24] In contrast, another black teenage boy, Errol, finds school pointless and leaves as soon as possible, but listens to Bob Marley and adopts Rastafari clothing. The play ends on an uncomfortable note, when Lester ends up working for Social Security and refuses to help Errol when he applies for unemployment benefit. McMillan suggested that neither adult path chosen by these two boys was a fulfilling one because of the way their choices were restricted.

The wider black community saw education as a central issue in this period. As Jessica Gerrard has shown, black supplementary schools and Saturday schools expanded from the late 1960s in reaction to the inadequate education being provided by British state schools. Local activist groups, like Camberwell's Black Parents Association, also united around the ways black children and black parents were being treated by the school system.[25] Students developed their own activist groups, such as the Black Students' Activism Collective founded at Tulse Hill in 1974.[26] In Chapeltown in Leeds, Olivia Wyatt has argued that older women temporarily supported more militant forms of resistance during a playgroup takeover in 1972 and a school strike in 1973 because of the importance they placed on the interests of children.[27] What was happening to African-Caribbeans in schools was identified by the black community as crucial to the ways in which white supremacy functioned in Britain, and part of that was the way they were framed as both adultified children and childlike adolescents.

South Asian teenagers navigated issues around age in different but parallel ways. South Asian girls were framed by the school system as permanently childlike in a different sense, passive and acquiescent. Sometimes they were seen as the helpless victims of an oppressive religion. Edmondson recited an accepted narrative about Indian girls being caught between two cultures, which inhibited appropriate adolescent development because this involved socialising: 'Any child naturally wants to associate with his or her peer group.'[28] Pratibha Parmar, a young Kenyan Asian woman, argued alongside Nadia Mirza in *Spare Rib* in 1981 that 'Asian women are portrayed as either sexually erotic or completely passive', and linked these assumptions to TV representations, where Asian women were depicted as 'pathetic' people who couldn't speak English or 'smiling air hostesses'.[29]

South Asian boys and girls tended to have better educational outcomes than their black peers, despite being framed by white teachers as having 'unrealistic aspirations'.[30] Some early research from the 1970s, as Sally Tomlinson has argued, 'may have unwittingly colluded in ensuring that Asian pupils were offered a fairer deal in education than pupils of West Indian origin' because their achievements were so much more significant.[31] This interpretation, as well as distorting South Asians' struggles, views childhood experience solely from the perspective of adulthood and assumes it was good because these students managed to hit traditional milestones of social mobility. However, this ignores the ways in which teenage South Asians were treated as naïve children in schools, and how adult South Asian women, in particular, continued to be framed as ignorant and childlike. As Amrit Wilson argued in 1978, the Grunwick strike (1976–8), led by East African Asian women, was so 'exceptional' precisely because it was assumed that Gujarati women could not face the world and demand their rights, in other words, that they were too weak to act as 'true' adults would.[32]

Girls, marriage and motherhood

Marriage and motherhood were crucial milestones for heterosexual white female adolescents in modern Britain, as Hay's chapter has shown, but did not mark a pathway to adulthood in the same way for African-Caribbean and South Asian teenage girls.[33] For either first- or second-generation migrant girls from the Caribbean, early marriage and childbearing might represent danger, and they were much more likely to resist these expectations than their white counterparts. Evelyn G. Christie published 'Lissen Sisters' in the journal of the *Ahfiwe* school in 1974, when she was still only nineteen. She warned other black girls:

> A black girl have to think about life not just having babies and boy-friends ... I hear a lot of girls saying to hell with 'A' level, 'O' level, CSE and GCE but it will help get you somewhere in life ... But no, you believe you're 20 when you're just 14 or 15, and men use young black girls for they say she fool and don't have any sense ... We should have ambition, education and a career in front of us.[34]

In a series of studies conducted with school-age African-Caribbean girls in the 1970s and 1980s, this point was continually emphasised. Michelle, a sixteen-year-old African-Caribbean girl attending a London comprehensive school, stated in 1976:

> I want a proper job first and some kind of skill so that if I do get married and have children I can go back to it; don't want just relying on him for money, 'cause I've got to look after myself ... Maybe I'll be a housewife or something like that, but I always picture myself working.[35]

Like Michelle and Evelyn, many African-Caribbean girls explicitly stated that they would put work above marriage, whereas white girls were more concerned with figuring out how to fit work around domestic responsibilities and childbearing.[36] Kathryn Riley worked with a small group of fifteen- to eighteen-year-old girls from Jamaica attending an inner-city girls' school in South London, publishing her findings in *Multiracial Education* in 1982. Unlike working-class white girls, who overwhelmingly gravitated towards traditionally female jobs, these working-class black Jamaican girls wanted 'male' jobs. Christine commented, 'It's good if you're getting a job that men usually do. You're achieving something', while Annette said, 'I couldn't do that job of being a secretary sitting at a desk every week.'[37] These kinds of accounts indicated the pressures on African-Caribbean girls, who needed to 'prove' their worth in a racist society. However, ironically, by achieving these very goals, they were setting themselves at odds with the traditional milestones of female adulthood in post-war and Cold War Britain.

Sharon, now twenty years old, reflected on these issues in another essay written for the ACER black young writers' competition in 1984. She started her essay by vividly illustrating that, although black girls themselves might not want marriage or early motherhood, this was not the way they were viewed by outsiders: '"Is it true that all West Indian girls leave school and have babies?" the white girl in the office asks.' Sharon felt that black women were

> still living in the same trap of having children when we are not physically, mentally or economically prepared for them ... This results in the stereo-typical view by the indigenous population that the problems really stem from the home. How often do we hear the familiar echoes from teachers now, 'well, she's probably rebelling against a strict West Indian upbringing ...'[38]

This trapped African-Caribbean girls in a double bind, unable to reflect upon the problems they felt their communities faced because these would be used as evidence that they, and their families, were unfit adults and parents.

South Asian girls negotiated a different set of cultural and social expectations around womanhood. It was assumed by the institutions they encountered that they would be 'forced' into arranged marriages that they did not want.[39] Some South Asian girls directly challenged this stereotype by pointing out, like some African-Caribbean girls, that they were not interested in marriage and were focused on their careers. South Asian girls often used school instrumentally as a place where they might experience greater freedom than they did at home, and which could supply them with the qualifications they needed to achieve their goals. They became increasingly likely to stay on at school past the official leaving age between 1972 and 1991.[40]

Amajit Kaur explored some of the tensions she experienced in 'An Indian Girl Growing Up in England', which was published in *Multiracial School* in 1973:

> At fourteen I had decided that whatever happened I was not going to leave school and get a dead-end job ... I wanted to separate myself emotionally from my parents, to find out what I wanted to be, and also to gain independence ... I began to become jealous and bitter and wished I was English ... The majority of my friends were rejecting school and they lived only for the weekends, while I lived for the school days.

Amajit was afraid that her Sikh parents would make her have an arranged marriage, and wished she could experience the 'series of intense infatuations' that her white friends were having, which she saw as one of the 'necessary stages of adolescence', employing developmental psychological language.[41] Wilson argued that arranged marriages were particularly oppressive for Sikh or Muslim girls, suggesting that Hindu girls were more likely to be able to continue in education after marriage.[42]

However, not all South Asian girls, religion notwithstanding, felt the same way as Amajit. Another way of challenging white British expectations was to point out that arranged marriages were no more oppressive than the emphasis placed on romantic love by teenage magazines, pop music and society, or the expectations of white British parents.[43] Parmar and Mirza argued in their *Spare Rib* article in 1981 that 'nobody seems to question the fact that the marriages of [working-class] white girls are "arranged", in that those who marry will do so with boys of a very similar class background, from the same area, and generally with their parents' consent'. They quoted Pragna, who rejected the trappings of white teenage girlhood: 'What is the freedom in going to a disco, frightened in case no boy fancies you, or no one asks you to dance?'[44] Fifteen-year-old Kamaljit, in contrast, 'loved the discos and the parties' but felt that, for her, familial love was more important than romantic love. She expected to organise her own marriage alongside her parents, as 'all my sisters have married who they wanted to', but understood that this would be a problem if the boy was not of her faith.

> I think [my mum] would mind ... she would tell me not to see him. Then it would be up to me to decide whether to see him or not. But I am the sort who can't leave a family but can leave a boy.[45]

Teenage South Asian girls were also keen to emphasise that this was a conversation that needed to be had within their communities rather than imposed upon them. In 1981, a group of sixteen- to eighteen-year-old Asian girls responded critically to a Conservative White Paper of 1979 which proposed restricting the immigration of Indian men who intended to marry women in Britain. Abida commented, 'They are making too much out of arranged marriages and using it for their own purpose. We have to realise that', whereas Daxa said, 'It's for us, the girls and our families, to work out our problems and issues of marriage.'[46] These young women emphasised that, even if they did not agree with everything their parents wanted for them, intergenerational solidarity was still important, as tension within South Asian communities would be exploited by outsiders for their own ends. This became crucial in how young people of colour understood their relationships with adults in their communities, as well as their own future adulthoods.

The 'generation gap'

Popular narratives about postwar Britain often focus on the 'generation gap' that supposedly emerged between white British parents and their offspring from the 1950s onwards, with the rise of a sequence of youth subcultures emphasising the difference between teenagers and adults.[47] Later historical work has argued that this 'generation gap' has been over-emphasised.[48] Nevertheless, white British adolescents writing in this period found that the 'generation gap' was a useful rhetorical tool. White teenagers used the language of age and generation to criticise their parents' attitudes to the nuclear bomb, for example, constructing adolescence and adulthood as categories that were in opposition to each other, and had no shared goals.[49] Youth-led activist organisations like the Youth Campaign for Nuclear Disarmament (CND) picked up on this language in the 1980s, arguing that young people's idealism and energy was what was needed to combat the geopolitical crisis.[50]

For African-Caribbean and South Asian adolescents, relationships between generations were markedly different, and this shaped their understandings of what it meant to be a 'teenager' or an 'adult'. While not denying the presence of intergenerational conflict, teenagers of colour often emphasised what they shared with their parents, especially when they themselves had been born in Britain and did not have direct experience of their country of origin. In 1983, fifteen-year-old Farida, who was probably Indian-Caribbean, wrote in her ACER essay, '"Education" Rather Than "Schooling" Is the Key to Liberation': 'Our parents and family life form a stable background which gives us the confidence to achieve ... Our parents will offer comfort and reassurance and the strength to combat the racism of society as a whole.'[51] A nineteen-year-old African-Caribbean boy suggested to ACER in 1984 that 'parents should try and understand ... that children of today, whatever race, colour or creed, face more pressures, temptations and responsibilities than they ever did ... [but] children should understand the problems of their parents, especially in times of a depressing economic situation'.[52]

As the titles offered to these young black writers by ACER suggest, they were guided towards a certain narrative about black identity and intergenerational solidarity, and the winning essays may reflect this agenda. However, a dissenting voice came from fifteen-year-old Debbie, in a 1983 essay entitled 'What Carnival in Notting Hill Means to Me as a Young Black Person in Britain':

> I had an idea from the beginning the Carnival was for the older generation of black people, to me the Steelband seemed to be an old sort of music ... A lot of my age group were just walking with the crowd and looking at older people dancing ... Maybe it is because I was born in England and not in the West Indies, I don't think the Carnival means a lot to me.[53]

Debbie did not feel that this kind of event, or this kind of music, was central to her generation's identity in the same way as it was for 'the older generation'.

These narratives also emerged in other settings that were less controlled by adults and where young people may have felt more able to speak freely, suggesting that they weren't simply an artefact of this essay competition. *Step Forward Youth* was a film produced by Menelik Shabazz in Brixton in 1977; at the time, Shabazz himself was only twenty-three. In one section of this film, a nineteen-year-old black Jamaican girl who had been born in Britain said that reggae music was important to her because 'we're here in England, we're born here, OK, never having been to Jamaica ... we're having to eat school dinners because our parents are out all day, so we have to get used to English food OK, West Indian food is gone ... there's just music'.[54] This suggested that parents did not always provide the easy connections to one's own heritage that might be expected, but that Jamaican culture was still vital to understanding her identity, and part of that culture was respecting the older generation so you might become an adult who was fully aware of their own inheritance.

While South Asian teenagers also acknowledged that family expectations could be restrictive, they were often acutely aware of the reasoning behind their family's rules, and presented a complex picture of family relationships rather than a simplified narrative of intergenerational conflict. Harjinder was in her first year of secondary school when she wrote for 'Scotland My New Country', produced by the Glasgow branch of NAME in 1977. She felt that her family was slightly unusual: 'My dad allows me to go to school discos and pictures alone, whereas other Asian parents probably would not let their children go out. I think this is the influence of my big brother Gurmeet, who is happily married to a Scottish girl.' However, she recognised that the fears of other Asian families might be justified: 'Also, because we have a restaurant, we meet a lot of Scottish people, and through this I think my dad is confident that I will not be attacked by somebody who is colour prejudiced.'[55]

Colonial histories were another way that teenagers of colour connected with their parents, especially second-generation adolescents who relied on their parents' experiences of living in colonised countries. Anwar, a second-generation teenager from Kashmir who had grown up in Bradford, remembered in the late 1970s

> coming home one day after a history lesson at school and sharing the information with my father about what I'd just been taught that day and my father, sort of, corrected me, not because he was that educated in historical facts of India but – his own experiences. And I was taught in my history lesson how good the Empire was for India, and 'we built the roads for the uncivilised people out there' etc. When I came and shared that with my father, my father says, 'well most of the roads were already there', right, 'some roads were built by the Raj, but they weren't built for the benefit of the Indians, they were built so that they could get the stuff out of India a lot quicker and more conveniently, and as far as civilisation is concerned, we were running around in silks when this lot was still in animal skins!'[56]

These kinds of narratives both strengthened intergenerational connections and challenged white colonial assumptions about the 'backwardness' of the countries they exploited, which were often related to ideas about the inherent childishness of the people they had colonised. Anwar's conversation with his father emphasised that Indian people were not 'uncivilised', and subtly challenged the racist assumptions made by schools about the 'immaturity' of South Asian children.

As African-Caribbean, South Asian and African Asian activists increasingly worked together from the 1970s onwards, youth were often seen as the vanguard of radical change by both the white British media and within their own communities. Attention turned from the education system to the abuse of young black men by the police, with protests focusing on racist 'stop and search' laws from the late 1970s onwards, plus the targeting of youth clubs and dance halls by police raids. Waters has argued that publications like *Race and Class*, *Race Today* and *Black Liberator* increasingly focused on the revolutionary potential of black youth from the mid-1970s, arguing that their refusal of 'shitwork' was crucial for the undermining of capitalism. But, he suggests, black young people remembered a 'weight of expectation' that came from both the state and from within their own communities. These ideas also fed into stereotypes about teenagers as naturally rebellious and politically radical.[57]

Young Asian people's activism also became prominent from the 1970s onwards, as Anandi Ramamurthy has shown in her important history. Asian Youth Movements (AYMs) emerged across Britain, influenced by earlier activism among their parents' generation, such as the Imperial Typewriters and Grunwick strikes. Direct action by Asian teenagers also challenged the stereotype that South Asians were meek and passive, as Ramamurthy argues. *Race Today* published an article called 'Are Asian Youth Breaking the Mould?' However, young Asian activists reframed this idea, arguing this was not about a generational rift. Mohsin Zulfiqar from Manchester said, 'it was not a question of us breaking the mould, we had always said there have been two kinds of movements within the South Asian community in this country, one is revolutionary, one is compromising and moderate'.[58] Similarly, looking at black communities in Handsworth in the 1980s, Kieran Connell argues that divisions between older and younger generations over Rastafarianism 'have been exaggerated', given the older generation's commitment to establishing Pan-Africanist organisations. Although family tensions emerged over religious commitment in Pentecostal households, 'younger generations were able to move between the apparently contradictory worlds of church and sound system'.[59]

Indeed, young people of colour argued, it might be the racist attitudes of older white adults that drove divisions within white families, rather than the activism of teenagers of colour driving divisions within their families. Fourteen-year-old African Caribbean Elaine made this argument in her ACER essay of 1984: 'Some white youths (13–15) have become visibly different from the white society. In so doing they are taking an anti-adult and anti-racist stand against the groups like the National Front.'[60] Here, Elaine may have been referring to the activities of mixed-race groups like the National Union of School Students (NUSS) and School Kids Against the Nazis, which opposed the recruitment drive of the National Front in secondary schools. One anti-Youth National Front leaflet produced by NUSS in the late 1970s, for example, read: 'Now these hate-peddlers are trying to bring their anti-black hysteria into our schools.'[61] These generational tensions were also noted by white adolescents. Fifteen-year-old Sarah, from Middlesex, wrote in a *Just Seventeen* anthology in 1987 that '[racism] does not seem to be as severe among the youth as it does among the older generation ... I notice more racist remarks being said by (especially) OAPs'.[62] Many white adolescents were as culpable as their parents in upholding racism and white supremacy, but some believed that their different views on race contributed to a 'generation gap'.

In her work on indigenous families and child removal in North America, Margaret D. Jacobs has argued that 'Continuity across generations ... became a form of resistance to settler colonial state policies' so we should not 'create binaries that connect youthful generational rebellion to radical change and intergenerational continuity to stasis'.[63] This reflects the intergenerational activism employed by communities of colour in late Cold War Britain, and their investment in challenging binary categories of childhood and adulthood. This is not to suggest that there was no intergenerational conflict within African-Caribbean and South Asian communities, but that it was negotiated differently than in white communities. Community activists recognised that a hostile media was keen to play into tropes of rebellious youth and rifts within families because this supported racist assumptions about the need for immigrant families to 'adapt' to British norms.

Conclusion

Normative ideals of both adolescence and adulthood were difficult for young people of colour to achieve in late Cold War Britain. They often rejected these dominant depictions of life stages, asserting that their families, their communities and they themselves were different. At school, African-Caribbean and South Asian adolescents were framed as childlike, but without the saving quality of malleable innocence possessed by 'real', white children; instead, they were seen as deviant and irredeemable. African-Caribbean and South Asian girls, in particular, struggled with expectations around marriage and motherhood. When African-Caribbean girls rejected early marriage, they travelled further from the life path that white female adolescents expected to follow. But if South Asian girls accepted arranged marriages, this was used to 'confirm' that they were helpless and passive, even when the girls themselves argued in their favour.

White adolescents, especially those involved in activist groups, often invested in the idea of a 'generation gap', which allowed them to depict adolescents and adults as having specific identities, and to argue for the virtues of the 'idealism' possessed by young activists in contrast to adult apathy. African-Caribbean and South Asian adolescents were much more likely to be involved in intergenerational activism and to argue for intergenerational solidarity. When conflicts emerged, they were handled differently, which changed understandings of what it meant to be a 'teenager' or an 'adult'. Adult values were not necessarily seen as different from those of teenagers. Even when teenagers of colour did not share their parents' values, understanding them was an important way of developing new visions of what it meant to be 'mature', especially when they knew they did not want to follow the white British path to adulthood that was both mandated, and withheld.

Notes

1. The research for this chapter was funded by the Leverhulme Trust, grant number ECF-2017-369.

2. Laura Tisdall, *A Progressive Education? How Childhood Changed in Mid-Twentieth-Century English and Welsh Schools* (Manchester: Manchester University Press, 2020), 74–5.

3. See also Teri Chettiar, *The Intimate State: How Emotional Life Became Political in Welfare-State Britain* (Oxford: Oxford University Press, 2023).

4. Tisdall, *A Progressive Education?*, 178–84.

5. See Habiba Ibrahim, *Black Age: Oceanic Lifespans and the Time of Black Life* (New York: New York University Press, 2021).

6. 'Black' was a contested term during this period, rendered both as 'Black' to indicate solidarity between all oppressed groups of colour and as 'black' to refer to those of African descent. Writers used the term in both ways. I use 'Black' in this chapter only when I mean 'politically Black' and 'black' only where I am referring to all people of African descent.

7. Corinne T. Field, Tammy-Charelle Owens, Marcia Chatelain, Lakisha Simmons, Abosede George and Rhian Keyse, 'The History of Black Girlhood: Recent Innovations and Future Directions', *Journal of the History of Childhood and Youth*, 9, no. 3 (2016), 385–6.

8. See also Tera Eva Agyepong, *The Criminalization of Black Children: Race, Gender and Delinquency in Chicago's Juvenile Justice System, 1899–1945* (Chapel Hill, NC: North Carolina University Press, 2018).

9. Satadru Sen, *Colonial Childhoods: The Juvenile Periphery of India, 1850–1945* (London: Anthem Press, 2005), 213.

10. Radhika Natarajan, 'The "Bogus Child" and the "Big Uncle": The Impossible South Asian Family in Post-Imperial Britain', *Twentieth Century British History*, 34, no. 3 (2023), 440–66.

11. Rob Waters, *Thinking Black: Britain, 1964–1985* (Berkeley, CA: University of California Press, 2018), 142, 154.

12. These umbrella terms cover a wide range of different racial, cultural and religious heritages. 'African-Caribbean' teenagers in Britain might primarily be from Jamaica, given the demographics of the 'Windrush' wave of immigration, but could also be from many other countries including Dominica, Barbados and Trinidad and Tobago; teenagers of 'South Asian' descent could be from India or Pakistan, or from African countries like Kenya or Uganda, and could be Sikh, Muslim or Hindu. Often, in primary sources, race is only recorded as 'Black', 'West Indian' or 'South/Asian', and religions, if any, are not recorded at all.

13. Waters, *Thinking Black*, 152.

14. I have identified these teenagers only by their first names when they are participants in studies or in anthologies. Last names are used when they have clearly published in their own right and through their own decisions, such as authoring articles or publishing scripts.

15. Geraldine McGuigan, 'Talking and Writing by Black Fifth Formers', *Multicultural Education*, 4, no. 3 (1976), 3–4.

16. Rob Waters, 'Race, Citizenship and "Race Relations" Research in Late-Twentieth-Century Britain', *Twentieth Century British History*, 34, no. 3 (2023), 504.

17. Tisdall, *Progressive Education?*, 193–4.

18. D.L. Edmondson, 'Working in a Multicultural School: Some Early Impressions', *Multiracial School*, 5, no. 3 (1977), 11.

19. Bruce Carrington and Edward Wood, 'Body Talk: Images of Sport in a Multiracial School', *Multiracial School*, 11, no. 2 (1983), 31–2.

20. *Black Youth Annual Penmanship Awards: Winning Essays 1982* (London: ACER, 1982), 38.

21. *Black Youth Annual Penmanship Awards: Winning Essays 1981* (London: ACER, 1981), 9.

22. *Black Youth Annual Penmanship Awards: Winning Essays 1982*, 13.

23. Michael McMillan, *The School Leaver* (Brixton: Black Ink Collective, 1978), 11.

24. McMillan, *The School Leaver*, 35.

25. Jessica Gerrard, *Radical Childhoods: Schooling and the Struggle for Social Change* (Manchester: Manchester University Press, 2014), 157–8.

26. Waters, *Thinking Black*, 166.

27. Olivia Wyatt, '"The Enemy in Our Midst": Caribbean Women and the Protection of Community in Leeds in the 1970s' in Hakim Adi ed., *Many Struggles: New Histories of African and Caribbean People in Britain* (London: Pluto Press, 2023), 303–304.

28. Edmondson, 'Working in a Multicultural School', 10.

29. Pratibha Parmar and Nadia Mirza, 'Growing Angry, Growing Strong' in Susan Hemmings ed., *Girls Are Powerful: Young Women's Writings from Spare Rib* (London: Sheba Feminist Publishing, 1982), 146.

30. Tahir Abbas, *The Education of British South Asians: Ethnicity, Capital and Class Structure* (Basingstoke: Palgrave Macmillan, 2004), 30.

31. Sally Tomlinson, *Race and Education: Policy and Politics in Britain* (Maidenhead: Open University Press, 2008), 35.

32. Amrit Wilson, *Finding a Voice: Asian Women in Britain* (London: Virago Press, 1978), 59, 63–5.

33. Laura Tisdall, '"What A Difference It Was to Be a Woman and Not a Teenager": Adolescent Girls' Conceptions of Adulthood in 1960s and 1970s Britain', *Gender and History*, 34, no. 2 (2022), 495–513.

34. Evelyn G. Christie, 'Lissen Sisters', *Ahfiwe: Journal of the Ahfiwe School and Abeng*, Issue 1 (1974), 8–9, BCA, WONG/2/1-2.

35. Mary Fuller, 'Black Girls in a London Comprehensive School' in Rosemary Deem ed., *Schooling for Women's Work* (London: Routledge and Kegan Paul, 1980), 52–65.

36. Tisdall, 'What a Difference It Was to Be a Woman'.

37. Kathryn Riley, 'Black Girls Speak for Themselves', *Multiracial Education*, 10, no. 3 (1982), 5–6.

38. Paul McGilchrist ed., *Black Voices: An Anthology of ACER's Black Young Writers Competition* (London: ACER, 1987), 226.

39. Christine Griffin, *Typical Girls? Young Women from School to the Job Market* (London: Routledge and Kegan Paul, 1985), 54.

40. Sue Sharpe, *Just Like a Girl: How Girls Learn to Be Women – From the Seventies to the Nineties*, 2nd ed. (London: Penguin, 1994), 103.

41. Amajit Kaur, 'An Indian Girl Growing Up in England', *Multiracial School*, 2, no. 2 (1973), 1–4.

42. Wilson, *Finding a Voice*, 101.

43. Angela McRobbie, '*Jackie* Magazine: Romantic Individualism and the Teenage Girl' (1977) in Angela McRobbie, *Feminism and Youth Culture*, 2nd ed. (Basingstoke: Palgrave Macmillan, 2000), 67–117.

44. Parmar and Mirza, 'Growing Angry, Growing Strong', 149.

45. Parmar and Mirza, 'Growing Angry, Growing Strong', 142.

46. Valerie Amos and Pratibha Parmar, 'Resistances and Responses: The Experiences of Black Girls in Britain' in Angela McRobbie and Trisha McCabe eds., *Feminism for Girls: An Adventure Story* (London: Routledge and Kegan Paul, 1981), 134.

47. Dominic Sandbrook, *Never Had It So Good: A History of Britain from Suez to the Beatles* (London: Little, Brown, 2006).

48. Selina Todd and Hilary Young, '"Baby-Boomers" to "Beanstalkers": Making the Modern Teenager in Post-War Britain', *Cultural and Social History*, 9, no. 3 (2012), 451–67; Gillian A.M. Mitchell, 'Reassessing the "Generation Gap": Bill Haley's 1957 Tour of Britain, Inter-Generational Relations and Attitudes to Rock 'n' Roll in the Late 1950s', *Twentieth Century British History*, 24, no. 4 (2013), 573–605.

49. Laura Tisdall, '"We Have Come to Be Destroyed": The "Extraordinary" Child in Science Fiction Cinema in Early Cold War Britain', *History of the Human Sciences*, 34, no. 5 (2021), 8–31.

50. LSE Archives, YCND, 'Tomorrow's Conscience Today', CND/1993 7/1, YCND Publications 1984–9.

51. *Black Youth Annual Penmanship Awards: Winning Essays 1983* (London: ACER, 1984), 2.

52. McGilchrist ed., *Black Voices*, 224.

53. *Black Youth Annual Penmanship Awards: Winning Essays 1983*, 1.

54. *Step Forward Youth*, dir. Menelik Shabazz (1977), https://the-lcva.co.uk/videos/594bb2a60609e223a0d38a6b, accessed 17 August 2023.

55. George Padmore Institute (GPI), AME/5/3/3/1-2, 'Scotland My New Country', 6.

56. Quoted in Anandi Ramamurthy, *Black Star: Britain's Asian Youth Movements* (London: Pluto Press, 2013), 19.

57. Waters, *Thinking Black*, 182–206.

58. Ramamurthy, *Black Star*, 28.

59. Kieran Connell, *Black Handsworth: Race in 1980s Britain* (Berkeley, CA: University of California Press, 2019), 117, 143.

60. McGilchrist ed., *Black Voices*, 267.

61. Martin Hoyles ed., *Changing Childhood* (London: Writers and Readers Publishing Co-Operative, 1979), 251, 254.

62. Leonore Goodings ed., *Bitter-Sweet Dreams: Girls' and Young Women's Own Stories* (London: Virago, 1987), 194.

63. Abosede George, Clive Glaser, Margaret D. Jacobs, Chitra Joshi, Emily Marker, Alexandra Walsham, Wang Zheng and Bernd Weisbrod, 'AHR Conversation: Each Generation Writes Its Own History of Generations', *American Historical Review*, 123, no. 5 (2018), 1528.

References

Archives

Black Cultural Archives, London.
George Padmore Institute, London.

Primary and secondary sources

Abbas, Tahir. *The Education of British South Asians: Ethnicity, Capital and Class Structure*. Basingstoke: Palgrave Macmillan, 2004.

Agyepong, Tera Eva. *The Criminalization of Black Children: Race, Gender and Delinquency in Chicago's Juvenile Justice System, 1899–1945*. Chapel Hill, NC: North Carolina University Press, 2018.

Amos, Valerie and Parmar, Pratibha. 'Resistances and Responses: The Experiences of Black Girls in Britain' in Angela McRobbie and Trisha McCabe eds., *Feminism for Girls: An Adventure Story*. London: Routledge and Kegan Paul, 1981. Black Cultural Archives, London.

Black Youth Annual Penmanship Awards: Winning Essays 1981. London: ACER, 1981.

Black Youth Annual Penmanship Awards: Winning Essays 1982. London: ACER, 1982.

Black Youth Annual Penmanship Awards: Winning Essays 1983. London: ACER, 1984.

Carrington, Bruce and Wood, Edward. 'Body Talk: Images of Sport in a Multiracial School', *Multiracial School*, 11, no. 2 (1983), 29–36.

Chettiar, Teri. *The Intimate State: How Emotional Life Became Political in Welfare-State Britain*. Oxford: Oxford University Press, 2023.

Connell, Kieran. *Black Handsworth: Race in 1980s Britain*. Berkeley, CA: University of California Press, 2019.

Edmondson, D.L. 'Working in a Multicultural School: Some Early Impressions', *Multiracial School*, 5, no. 3 (1977), 10–13.

Field, Corinne T., Owens, Tammy-Charelle, Chatelain, Marcia, Simmons, Lakisha, George, Abosede and Keyse, Rhian. 'The History of Black Girlhood: Recent Innovations and Future Directions', *Journal of the History of Childhood and Youth*, 9, no. 3 (2016), 383–401.

Fuller, Mary. 'Black Girls in a London Comprehensive School' in Rosemary Deem ed., *Schooling for Women's Work*. London: Routledge and Kegan Paul, 1980, 52–65.

George Padmore Institute (GPI), London, AME/5/3/3/1-2, 'Scotland My New Country', 6.

George, Abosede, Glaser, Clive, Jacobs, Margaret D., Joshi, Chitra, Marker, Emily, Walsham, Alexandra, Zheng, Wang and Weisbrod, Bernd. 'AHR Conversation: Each Generation Writes Its Own History of Generations', *American Historical Review*, 123, no. 5 (2018), 1505–46.

Gerrard, Jessica. *Radical Childhoods: Schooling and the Struggle for Social Change*. Manchester: Manchester University Press, 2014.

Goodings, Leonore ed. *Bitter-Sweet Dreams: Girls' and Young Women's Own Stories*. London: Virago, 1987.

Griffin, Christine. *Typical Girls? Young Women from School to the Job Market*. London: Routledge and Kegan Paul, 1985.

Hoyles, Martin ed. *Changing Childhood*. London: Writers and Readers Publishing Co-Operative, 1979.

Ibrahim, Habiba. *Black Age: Oceanic Lifespans and the Time of Black Life*. New York: New York University Press, 2021.

Kaur, Amajit. 'An Indian Girl Growing Up in England', *Multiracial School*, 2, no. 2 (1973), 1–4.

McGilchrist, Paul ed. *Black Voices: An Anthology of ACER's Black Young Writers Competition*. London: ACER, 1987.

McGuigan, Geraldine. 'Talking and Writing by Black Fifth Formers', *Multicultural Education*, 4, no. 3 (1976), 2–5.

McMillan, Michael. *The School Leaver*. Brixton: Black Ink Collective, 1978.

McRobbie, Angela. '*Jackie* Magazine: Romantic Individualism and the Teenage Girl' (1977) in Angela McRobbie, *Feminism and Youth Culture*, 2nd ed. Basingstoke: Palgrave Macmillan, 2000, 67–117.

Mitchell, Gillian A.M. 'Reassessing the "Generation Gap": Bill Haley's 1957 Tour of Britain, Inter-Generational Relations and Attitudes to Rock 'n' Roll in the Late 1950s', *Twentieth Century British History*, 24, no. 4 (2013), 573–605.

Natarajan, Radhika. 'The "Bogus Child" and the "Big Uncle": The Impossible South Asian Family in Post-Imperial Britain', *Twentieth Century British History*, 34, no. 3 (2023), 440–66.

Parmar, Pratibha and Mirza, Nadia. 'Growing Angry, Growing Strong' in Susan Hemmings ed., *Girls Are Powerful: Young Women's Writings from Spare Rib*. London: Sheba Feminist Publishing, 1982, 143–50.

Ramamurthy, Anandi. *Black Star: Britain's Asian Youth Movements*. London: Pluto Press, 2013.

Riley, Kathryn. 'Black Girls Speak for Themselves', *Multiracial Education*, 10, no. 3 (1982), 3–6.

Sandbrook, Dominic. *Never Had It So Good: A History of Britain from Suez to the Beatles*. London: Little, Brown, 2006.

Sen, Satadru. *Colonial Childhoods: The Juvenile Periphery of India, 1850–1945*. London: Anthem Press, 2005.

Sharpe, Sue. *Just Like a Girl: How Girls Learn to Be Women – From the Seventies to the Nineties*, 2nd ed. London: Penguin, 1994.

Tisdall, Laura. *A Progressive Education? How Childhood Changed in Mid-Twentieth-Century English and Welsh Schools*. Manchester: Manchester University Press, 2020.

Tisdall, Laura. '"We Have Come to Be Destroyed": The "Extraordinary" Child in Science Fiction Cinema in Early Cold War Britain', *History of the Human Sciences*, 34, no. 5 (2021), 8–31.

Tisdall, Laura. '"What A Difference It Was to Be a Woman and Not a Teenager": Adolescent Girls' Conceptions of Adulthood in 1960s and 1970s Britain', *Gender and History*, 34, no. 2 (2022), 495–513.

Todd, Selina and Young, Hilary. '"Baby-Boomers' to "Beanstalkers": Making the Modern Teenager in Post-War Britain', *Cultural and Social History*, 9, no. 3 (2012), 451–67.

Tomlinson, Sally. *Race and Education: Policy and Politics in Britain*. Maidenhead: Open University Press, 2008.

Waters, Rob. *Thinking Black: Britain, 1964–1985*. Berkeley, CA: University of California Press, 2018.

Waters, Rob. 'Race, Citizenship and "Race Relations" Research in Late-Twentieth-Century Britain', *Twentieth Century British History*, 34, no. 3 (2023), 491–514.

Wilson, Amrit. *Finding a Voice: Asian Women in Britain*. London: Virago Press, 1978.

Wyatt, Olivia. '"The Enemy in Our Midst": Caribbean Women and the Protection of Community in Leeds in the 1970s' in Hakim Adi ed., *Many Struggles: New Histories of African and Caribbean People in Britain*. London: Pluto Press, 2023, 177–97.

Chapter 10

Marriage, intimacy and adulthood in disabled people's lives and activism in twentieth-century Britain[1]

Lucy Delap

In 1972, Margaret, an adult resident of a home for people with cerebral palsy, reflected bitterly on national television concerning her attempts to marry her boyfriend, Willy. Willy and Margaret were an attractive couple – capable, funny, in love and determined to live together. Their parents and carers did not, however, welcome their partnership, and Margaret reflected:

> The parents of a handicapped child have got a good excuse to keep their dear little babies with them until they die ... [pause], the parents die that is. It's just an excuse to hang on to them, they treat them as children, wrap them up in cotton wool. I can't ... I can't express how much it adds to the handicap.[2]

Their televised plight, depicted by BBC investigative journalism programme *Man Alive*, demonstrated that adult status – epitomised by the intimacies of marriage and sexual activity – was a significant privilege denied to many disabled people. This chapter suggests some of the ways in which adulthood became closely linked to marriage and (sexual) intimacy in the twentieth century, and how disabled people experienced and contested their uncertain access to adulthood. It uses sources from policymakers, social workers and disabled people located in life writing, psychosocial surveys and broadcast media. These are deliberately selected to foreground experience and personal testimony, countering the intrusive control and scrutiny disabled people have experienced in their intimate lives. In keeping with a turn to self-narratives in the mid-twentieth century, disabled people found new means to explore their feelings and desires, even in surveys or films that did not always have this as their goal.

Mental or physical impairment gained through military service or industrial accidents could led to the affirmation of adulthood through connotations of warrior and worker, at least in the immediate aftermath of injury.[3] But those born with developmental, intellectual and sensory impairments, or acquiring them in childhood, often found the status of adult to be elusive. In 1930, George Thomas, a working-class slum dweller in his late twenties whose muscular dystrophy confined him to a crumbling rented tenement in Soho, was given a charity seaside holiday and access to a wheelchair. His diary noted, 'I feel very strange ... seeing [people] from the level of an invalid chair. I felt like a child looking up at grown-ups, and I am a child in such experiences, for I have forgotten what it is like to meet another and look the person straight in the face at eye level'.[4] Others reported being prematurely forced into adulthood; Louis Battye, born with cerebral palsy in 1923, noted how rarely he spent time with other children: 'My world, both outer and inner, was more adult than childlike.'[5]

Through disablement, adulthood could be delayed, denied, removed or imposed, particularly for those disabled people further minoritised by intersections of gender, class, race and ethnicity. This effect was exacerbated by the growth of specialised or segregated infrastructure for disabled people from the late nineteenth century, such as 'special' schools, mobility aids, sheltered employment and large-scale confinement in asylums and colonies. Disabled people were more socially integrated in prior epochs, more acceptable as marital partners and less likely to be infantilised.[6] Early twentieth-century of ideas of mental age as an alternative to chronological age proved a powerful means of denying some adults the choice and adequate support to shape their lives. This was often backed up by eugenic assumptions about fitness to reproduce which persisted into the later twentieth century.[7]

The sense of life course among disabled people has frequently been messy, subversive and unpredictable. As scholars of 'crip time' have argued, disability disrupts linearity.[8] Expected transitions towards maturity, modernity, productivity or progress cannot be aligned with disabled lives that experience constraint and regression, or which cannot be slotted into available temporal templates. Time moves slowly or is sped up by experiences of pain, fatigue, distress and recuperation. Disability has a 'braking effect ... because any disablement must slow down activity [and] is such an appalling waste of time', commented Reginald Ford, a disabled writer, in 1966. Elsa, a wheelchair user writing in the 1980s, used a striking metaphor of rebirth that again subverts linear ideas of life course. Writing in her forties, she observed that 'being able-bodied was my larval or pupal stage and being disabled is the real me now'.[9]

The disruptive effects of unpredictable embodiment were accompanied by a powerful cultural positioning of disabled people as eternal children or as old before their time. Employers routinely referred to disabled workers as 'girls and boys', whatever their age. Institutions such as asylums, hospitals and convalescence homes imposed rigid bedtimes and routines associated with the very young or the elderly. Campaigning organisations, largely led by non-disabled people until the 1980s, used images of children to fundraise for disabled adults, and found it hard to adjust to growing demands for choice, control and autonomy made by disabled people. Parents and other relatives also found it extremely hard to allow disabled family members the space to grow into adulthood, judging them unable to bear its burdens and therefore also excluded from its privileges. Fluctuating or insecure adult status was not simply a subjective experience or materially expressed in the design of mobility aids, as George Thomas had encountered. It was hardwired into statutory interventions, institutional practices, social attitudes and the campaigning methods of advocacy groups.

Understanding disability as discrimination and disadvantage located in social, economic and material environments, the focus of the chapter spans different forms of impairment. It gives close scrutiny to those whose rights to intimacy were particularly harshly policed. This includes those with intellectual impairment, commonly seen as an inherited condition and associated with forms of 'moral danger' and fecundity, alongside those with stigmatising forms of impairment such as cerebral palsy and epilepsy. The Board of Control, established in 1913 to oversee institutional care and guardianship in the community for those deemed 'mentally defective', described marriage of 'defectives' as 'the negation of the aims of a civilized community'. But they were forced to acknowledge that 'many parents do not recognize that their children are defective, or even if they do, they believe that the best thing for them is to marry'.[10] Clearly, its civilisational concerns were not widely shared.

The chapter argues that disabled people displayed resistance to stereotypes of tragic singleness, asexuality and child-like sexual innocence and insisted upon rights to (sexual) intimacies.[11] Their determination to marry is consonant with the turn historians have identified towards the central importance of sex and love in the mid- to late twentieth century, largely expressed through the institution of marriage.[12] Sean Brady has argued that heterosexual marriage had become a key life-course event by the early 1900s.[13] Poverty still kept marriage out of reach of many working-class people in the first half of the twentieth century. Selina Todd and Hilary Young have traced the falling age of marriage in the 1940s to 1970s, as affluence allowed young people to achieve greater autonomy from their parents.[14] Hannah Charnock argues that sexual experimentation in adolescence became an important postwar rite of passage to adulthood, though often still with marriage as an idealised destination.[15]

It is no surprise therefore that marriage formed a key means of claiming adult status among disabled people in the twentieth century. The later twentieth-century trends towards relationship informality and instability, charted by Kristin Hay in her chapter, were less visible among disabled people. Many found marriage to be practically and emotionally valuable, though their marriages were still barely tolerated by those around them. Lack of secure access to marriage meant that feminist insights into intimate partner violence were only slowly registered in disabled people's organisations, and the focus of anti-abuse campaigning remained on institutional and carer practices rather than the violence sometimes experienced in marriage and intimate relationships.

Intimate testimonials

The musings and concerns of policymakers and medical practitioners can be relatively easily seen in historical archives; the experiences and desires of disabled people are much less well represented. Their hopes for intimacy, their experiences of love and sexual (dis)satisfaction, and their marriages were sometimes recorded in the memoirs and diaries which describe their experiences in the decades after 1925. Most of these were organised around narratives stressing personal adversity and courage in tackling it – at least this is how reviewers and publishers routinely presented them. The public had an appetite for sensational stories of poverty and bodily difference, and many such memoirs also reflected on faith as a source of resilience.[16] George Thomas's *A Tenement in Soho* described his impoverished family of seven, of whom four experienced muscular dystrophy and were mostly confined to their home or bed. This made intimate relationships extending beyond the family difficult, though the family were notably emotionally close. In his forties, Thomas married a penfriend – unusually, the couple did not meet in person before becoming engaged, and their correspondence and courtship were closely mediated by their shared Catholic faith. Other disabled people who published memoirs in the 1930s such as John Gray's *Gin and Bitters* describe only friendships and are silent on sexual intimacies.[17]

MARRIAGE, INTIMACY AND ADULTHOOD IN DISABLED PEOPLE'S LIVES

The numbers of disabled people writing about their lives grew exponentially in the 1960s, spurred by a wider growth of life writing, community publishing and the oral history movement.[18] The increasing contestation of the marginalisation, abuse and control experienced by disabled people also sparked a rash of life writing, including by the 1980s many women, whose voices had been previously somewhat muted.[19] Perhaps the earliest example of this more politicised mode of life writing was the pioneering collection of essays on the stigma of disability edited by Paul Hunt in 1966. This was an important book which marked the early phases of disabled-led campaigning in the UK. Paul Hunt received over sixty essays after an appeal in newspapers and magazines for contributions, and eventually published twelve.[20] All contributors had physical impairments, and most wrote about the effect on their intimate relationships and aspirations.

Hunt (1937–79) had a particularly sharp experience of social segregation. He turned sixteen in 1953 whereupon his access to care and education at Queen Mary's Children's Hospital, Carshalton ended abruptly. Becoming (as defined by the hospital administrators) an adult was an abrupt transition and meant immediate uprooting. Hunt's muscular dystrophy and wheelchair use made it impossible for him to live at home; he was sent instead to the 'chronic ward' at St John's Hospital, Battersea. As Luke Beesley and Tony Baldwinson document, this was a neglectful, hopeless environment in which chronically ill, mostly elderly patients were dumped.[21] Disability was confused with ill-health, and many disabled 'patients' were unnecessarily confined to bed, or used as ward labour, feeding and dressing other residents without pay. The label 'Young Chronic Sick' was attached to anyone under sixty-five on these wards to distinguish them from geriatric patients, indicating the distorted age categories commonly applied to disabled people; one activist, Pamela La Fane, described it as 'growing up geriatric' in a newspaper exposé of her own experiences of nearly thirty years in a 'chronic sick' ward from age sixteen.[22]

Hunt became a determined advocate for himself and others, managing to get released at age nineteen when he moved into Le Court, a home run by the Leonard Cheshire Foundation. In this adapted environment that claimed to provide a genuine home, Hunt continued to battle petty restrictions that tried to limit residents' bedtimes and silence dissent. He embarked on a journalism campaign, advocating freedom to make life choices for disabled people in both the national press and Le Court's own journal, the *Cheshire Smile*. In 1970, he married Judy Hunt, a former worker employed at Le Court; the couple moved into their own home and continued their joint involvement in disabled people's activism.[23]

In *Stigma*, Hunt included those born with disabling conditions and those who acquired them in adulthood. The latter had sometimes already established marriages, but these could not be taken for granted. Rosalind Chalmers, for example, was married with two children when she contracted polio in 1950. She became much more dependent on her husband and described her experience of illness as 'nothing less than a second birth, another expulsion from the womb. ... The iron lung [her respirator in hospital] contained its foetus'.[24] The cost to Chalmers's marriage was evident, and she was painfully aware of husbands who simply walked away from disabled wives, while children were put into care. Her own husband, in her words, 'had lost his wife, but she was not conveniently dead and buried. ("Daddy has three children," said our daughter pertinently, "Me, Peter and Mummy.")'. She moved into a nursing home in 1964 and described her marriage as 'com[ing] to a full stop. Or it could be a semi-colon; we don't know yet'.[25] Chalmers's life demonstrated the uncertain or reversible age status of someone who was dependent on the care of others.

Louis Battye (1923–77) had been disabled his entire life, and his contribution to Hunt's collection described his stark sense of detachment from personal intimacies: 'The bitterest truth of all [is] that we are forever barred from the deepest and most intimate levels of human intercourse.'[26] Like others, Battye felt this to be an exclusion from the status of adulthood: 'The congenital cripple ... passes straight from the subworld of childhood to the subworld of the cripple.' Battye's own experiences of heterosexual contact were infused with emotional discomfort, with intimate relationships 'inevitably containing a certain amount of pity and curiosity. ... Bitterly he will begin to realise that he is in for the lonely, perverted life of the enforced celibate'.[27] This bleak assessment was characteristic of the tone of *Stigma*. None of the contributors found marriage straightforward, and came to it late or never. Marriage or intimacy between disabled people was not discussed – relationships were consistently framed in terms of contact between disabled and non-disabled (or 'normal') individuals.

The 1970s witnessed quite a sharp change in the tone of disabled people's life writing. Earlier testimony about disability had been dominated by ideas of mental adjustment to be made by disabled people. Margaret Gill, a *Stigma* contributor, for example, described experiencing a twin disability of 'the obvious disfigurement of body, and the hidden disfigurement of personality'.[28] In the 1970s, talk of suffering, isolation and disfigurement were replaced by more positive languages of pride, rights and revolutionary change. Paul Hunt was at the heart of this shift through his prominent involvement with the Union of the Physically

Impaired Against Segregation (UPIAS), and his championing, along-side figures such as Vic Finkelstein and Mike Oliver, of the 'social model' that located disablement in the social environment rather than a medi-calised or embodied condition.[29] Rights to marriage, sex and intimacy become more centre stage in disabled people's activism, with Hunt arguing in 1970 that relationships provided leverage to disrupt the insti-tutional order:

> the emotional and sexual relationships which can arise in mixed [dis-abled and non-disabled] communities, particularly when accompanied by strong bonds of affection and commitment, are an anti-institutional factor which makes it more difficult for people to be controlled by authority. This problem has been the bane of more than one authori-tarian or paternalistic administrator's life.[30]

At this point, however, Hunt was still keen to cast marriage as a route to emotional maturity for disabled people who had been institutionalised, rather than a right and legitimate expectation. An alternative approach that was more focused on practical fulfilment of sexual and emotional needs came from the 'normalisation movement', prominently associated with institutional care of people with intellectual disabilities in Nordic countries.

Normalisation

Ideas of 'normalisation' began to be voiced by those working with intellec-tually disabled people in the 1960s. Niels Erik Bank-Mikkelsen (1919–90) was closely involved in policy and voluntary action for disabled people in Denmark and pioneered their inclusion in all aspects of life. His approach, in opposition to medicalised approaches, was widely influential across Nordic countries. It helped shape the United Nations through its 1971 Declaration of the Rights of Mentally Disabled Persons, and was taken up in North America by prominent advocate Wolf Wolfensberger. Wolfensberger (1934–2011) insisted that service providers should use 'culturally valued means in order to enable people to live culturally valued lives'. This would produce, he argued, personal competencies and positive social images to counter the low expectations and often unconscious devaluation of dis-abled people. Age appropriateness was stressed, with Wolfensberger noting the damaging stigma of being an 'eternal child or child-once-again'. Devalued people, he argued, must be 'in age configurations that match those in culturally valued analogues'.[31] Normalisation advocates such as campaigner Ann Shearer strongly supported a 'right to love'; if emotional and sexual needs are suppressed, she argued, 'the position of the individual as an adult, no matter what his age, is apt to be tenuous'.[32]

These ideas were promoted in the United Kingdom by a series of conferences organised by the Campaign for the Mentally Handicapped. 'Our Life' (1972) and 'Listen' (1973) were unusual in offering intellectually disabled people full delegate status and the chance to have a say in their lives. The approach was taken up by the more established and sedate voluntary action group Mencap in a 1974 pamphlet titled 'Sexual Rights of the Retarded'. Mencap had originally been titled 'The National Association of Parents of Backwards Children' when founded in 1946; in 1955, reflecting updated terminology, it became the National Society for Mentally Handicapped Children. Its name was officially shortened to Mencap in 1969, but earlier stigmatising language and its well-known logo of a sad-faced child were incongruously featured on the 'Sexual Rights' pamphlet, suggesting institutional inertia when it came to cementing the shift away from paternalism.

Nonetheless, new thinking on 'normalisation' was foregrounded in Mencap's publication. Its goal was to speed up the slow pace of change in the UK which still operated 1,000-plus-bed Victorian-built institutions that were notorious for their abuse and poor standards of care. Wolfensberger had worked in Britain in the early 1960s with Jack Tizard, and both helped sponsor culture change that led policymakers to begin to aspire to 'home-like settings'.[33] But such 'homes' often remained quite segregative, leading disability activist Peter Townsend to talk of 'fake normalisation'. Social and spatial segregation were particularly durable for people with intellectual disabilities.[34] Sex continued to be approached in terms of their sexual vulnerability or sexual threat to others. Nonetheless, the process of deinstitutionalisation opened up spaces for new approaches, documented within a spate of studies into sexually active and married couples who had been labelled 'handicapped'.

Janet Mattinson (1927–2011), an influential social worker and from 1969 a psychoanalyst at the Tavistock Institute of Marital Studies, published a study in 1970 that tracked marital relationships among former residents of the Royal Western Counties Institution (later Hospital) at Starcross, Devon. Finally closed in 1986, this institution still housed its full complement of 1,800 residents in 1970. Its long waiting list suggested that 'care' options for people with intellectual disabilities were still scanty. Mattinson's study tracked thirty-two married relationships, mostly begun while one or both parties were resident at Starcross. While earlier studies of people with intellectual disabilities had focused on the cognitive status of their children, Mattinson was more interested in the quality of their intimate relationships. Unusually, she cited, in their own words, the views of those she wrote about. Drawing on the language of the normalisation movement, she also stressed social competencies and dismissed Intelligence Quotient (IQ) as a useful tool. Her portrayal of couples was warm, depicting them as sometimes combative with quarrels and physical violence, though couples were quick to make up. Tensions around adult status, however, remained even for those who had successfully achieved marriage. One couple discussed their relationship:

[Wife] I give him his credit, 'cos he's a good boy really.

[Husband] I'm not a boy.

[Wife] Well, he is to me. Well, he's not acting like a man, is he? He comes and gives me a hand if I'm busy. He never hits me, if we have a tiff – well, anybody do, don't they?

[Husband] She treats me like as if I were her son at times ... I looked a right idiot. I won't go out with my missus, not very often.[35]

This exchange is revealing of the behaviour and boundaries that conventionally cemented both gender and marital status; a husband who helped with domestic chores and did not hit his wife did not perform normative adult masculinity, even though a wife might be expected to be grateful. Both parties to this marriage were aware of the disruption of age-gender norms in their past lives and current relationship.

Inspired by Mattinson, a further study was conducted by Ann and Michael Craft in the late 1970s. Ann was a social worker at a relatively new and progressive Welsh 'subnormality' hospital, Bryn-y-Neuadd, and she had pioneered sex education and relationship support for residents. Her husband was a psychologist interested in research into sexual offending. From 1976, they surveyed forty-five couples where one or both had been deemed 'subnormal'. They found a surprising degree of relationship success, with a voluntary break-up rate of 2 per cent. Given support, couples could successfully care for each other, though parents were sometimes very opposed and hospitals had on occasion instructed solicitors to safeguard the rights of over-twenty-ones to marry. The legal status of adult did not consistently govern family attitudes, though institutions were more willing than in prior years to safeguard autonomous choice-making. The Crafts were clear that relationships should be supported not because of any policy goals or cost implications but because it was a source of happiness to individuals.[36]

The medical profession and wider public opinion continued to contest sex and marriage as features of normalisation; as one former staff member at Starcross recalled in the late 1980s, 'the idea of actually having a room where people could go to be private, those sorts of issues. Well, what would the *Dawlish Gazette* say if they knew we were allowing this to happen? I thought to hell with what the *Dawlish Gazette* says! It was never resolved. It still isn't resolved!'[37]

The right to marry remained controversial; the Crafts' study stimulated an extended rebuttal from Dr J. Oliver, a consultant psychiatrist, in the *Journal of the British Institute of Mental Subnormality*. He rejected the findings and methodology, arguing that the Crafts had over-emphasised successful marriages by their call-out for established couples, and thus created a false picture of competence and stability. His contact with children's homes and Care Orders, by contrast, put him intimately in touch with children whose care had broken down through the cruelty and neglect that he associated with low IQ. Oliver felt that marital happiness was subsidiary to effective childrearing which remained the 'most important aspect of partnership and marriage for the subnormal'. He continued to promote ideas of inheritability of intellectual impairment, and insisted that risks to children meant marriage was inadvisable. His beliefs reflect the strong resistance to 'normalisation', especially if this could be cast on grounds of child welfare.[38]

Despite their optimism, both the Crafts and Mattinson recorded removals of children from couples who were deemed unable to care, as well as forms of contraception being imposed where consent was unclear, including sterilisation. As one participant told Mattinson: 'Then they sterilised me and that was that. I didn't want it; it was forced on me. I thought it over and I thought it over.'[39] Some women in Mattinson's study were unaware that they had been sterilised, suggesting that consent was not clear cut. A 1981 memoir by Jamaican-born Pauline Wiltshire recalled being forcibly sterilised in Jamaica after she gave birth outside of marriage, as well as doctors in the UK who refused to listen to her preferences. Racism interacted with ableism in diminishing her adult status, and she was not permitted to raise her son; she recorded that even in her late twenties, when living in London, her mother 'had beaten me like a child in front of other people not of my family. This hurt me very much emotionally, more than it did physically. If there had not been other people there I would have hit her back'. Both her family and statutory services were controlling and judgemental. Wiltshire concluded, 'it's as if my friends have become my family instead'.[40] Although there were successful experiences of parenthood as well as active choices to remain childless documented in these studies, 'normalisation' agendas delivered by care services proved compatible with sexual and reproductive control and coercion.[41]

Handidate

A more combative, subversive and rights-based approach among mobility-impaired people emerged in the 1970s. Paul Hunt reviewed the Swedish Fokus housing scheme, presented in the UK at the initiative of an early disabled-led campaigning group, the Central Council for the Disabled, in 1973. The Fokus scheme included the active participation of disabled people in planning, leadership and the ongoing life choices of residents. Flats rather than rooms were provided, close to city centres rather than in remote hospitals as had been so common in the UK:

> An important aspect of the full-care service was the attitude of the staff. Fokus staff had to be open minded – for instance, on matters of sex – and must never treat the tenant as a patient. The handicapped person's right to independence and to the management of his private affairs must never be infringed.[42]

A third of Fokus residents were married or cohabiting, and practical assistance was given with sex if needed.

These radical arrangements echoed the BBC's current affairs programme *Man Alive*, which also foregrounded issues around sex and disability. The programme had featured Pamela La Fane in her battle to leave the 'chronic sick' ward through three episodes broadcast in June 1968; she eventually was offered a remodelled council flat and lived independently, with the support of a live-in carer, for the rest of her life. La Fane chose to remain single, celebrating the companionship of her friends and her cat.[43] But in 1972, an episode directed by Paul Morrison and co-produced with the Mental Health Film Council and the charity Scope (then named the Spastics Society) featured the loving relationship between Willy and Margaret, cited at the outset of this chapter. They were depicted as normal lovers, through intimate, tender footage of washing each other's bodies and sharing a bed. The episode revealed that group dormitories and brusque care regimes left little space for privacy, and parental attitudes made sexual relationships complicated. Scope supported calls for change – yet were inconsistent on sex and intimacy, issuing a film in 1973 which continued to maintain that for people with cerebral palsy, 'realising that one is not attractive to the opposite sex is a real and difficult problem'.[44] As a branch-led organisation, judgemental and objectifying beliefs continued to feature at some levels of the organisation, even as change was attempted at others.

Man Alive hosted a studio discussion of the issues raised, and foregrounded disabled people insisting on their rights to marry and live together. They also gave space to the conservative views of a consultant psychologist, Joshua Fox, who continued to maintain that residential care was not compatible with intimate freedoms: 'how much freedom can be allowed?', he asked, and forecast that if any resident was granted more choice, all would demand it. Fox was proved correct. In 1976, a disabled couple, Maggie and Ken Davis, heavily involved in UPIAS, were housed in an accessible flat in the Grove Road housing scheme, Nottinghamshire, Britain's first independent living (later renamed 'integrated living') project. The couple had faced steep opposition. Despite being married in 1974, they were refused permission to share a bed in Maggie's 'Young Chronic Sick' unit (located in a geriatric hospital) in Grays, Essex.[45]

In the same year that Maggie and Ken Davis moved into their flat, medical doctor and tabloid agony aunt Wendy Greengross published a National Marriage Guidance Council report, *Entitled to Love: The Sexual and Emotional Needs of the Handicapped*. Greengross cited Swedish and Danish precedents for 'normalisation', to include marriage, sex aids, pornography and paying for sex. She was also involved in an initiative titled 'Sexual Problems Of Disabled People' (SPOD) to facilitate sex and intimacy by providing sex aids.[46] This wider landscape of intimacies envisaged and sought among disabled people is evident in the well-used dating services for disabled people that emerged in the 1980s, as well as disabled people's participation in mainstream dating. A reader's letter to *Singles* magazine was designated 'letter of the month' for its 'wonderful news' about the success of a service named 'Disdate'. Londoner Fred Brown wrote to describe his courtship, through Disdate, with a partially sighted woman from Gravesend; they were now engaged and expecting a child. Brown did not disclose anything about his own ability, but did cautiously note that his partner 'might not be the girl of my dreams' but was 'the love of my life'.[47]

Specialist disability publications also took up dating. *Disability Now*, a widely read monthly newsletter published by Scope, advertised a dating agency, Handidate, which promised to find penfriends and partners for disabled people. *Disability Now* also hosted 'find-a-friend' listings; the adverts were extremely varied. Unusually, many stressed (or sought) the possession of transport or being a car driver. Cars provided private, intimate spaces for those who often lacked privacy; the status of being a driver was another indicator of adulthood. The adverts also differed from those typical of the non-disabled in giving more details of relatives, such as: 'Man with disabilities, early forties, with elderly mother, wishes to contact lady also disabled, in the Leicestershire area. Preferably a single person with an invalid car.'[48] Complex forms of dependency were visible in the listings, revealing a less individualistic and more open-ended sense of intimacy and relationship-building among disabled people.

Limits to change

Ideas of marriage and sexuality for disabled people had rapidly transformed, and the 1970s were a period of optimism over innovative support options in the community. There were still, however, clear limits to the ability of disabled people to be seen as sexually active adults, and the form their sexuality could take. Normalisation campaigners had perhaps been too optimistic about how easily 'normal' life could be taken up. Lives deformed by institutionalisation were not easily made compatible with adult intimacies. Born in 1925 and judged 'mentally defective', David Barron's memoir of his institutionalised childhood included experiences of sexual abuse. Barron was released from institutional confinement in 1955. He courted and married a woman, but could not consummate the marriage and it was annulled. In his 1996 memoir, he disclosed deep anxiety about his own apparent paedophilic desire. After three suicide attempts, he opted for chemical castration by stilbestrol (or DES) as a means of expunging his libido.[49]

The warmly supportive 1979 study by Ann and Michael Craft still used language of sexual deviancy, noting a range of 'sex offences to which subnormals are prone; namely child sex offences, exposure, and homosexual offences'.[50] It is striking that the very concept of 'normalisation' was still so easily paired with its stigmatising converse, 'subnormal'. Ideas of sexual threat remained present in much commentary, and it proved especially difficult for sexual minorities to gain social acceptance. 'Normalisation' all too easily lent itself to heteronormativity. Ideas of environmentally induced same-sex preferences were often referenced to explain and trivialise same-sex activity within single-sex hospitals and institutions. The Crafts, for example, were confident that all residents would prove heterosexual: 'we have been surprised how rapidly homosexuals evidenced heterosexual behaviour once their single-sex hospital closed, and they entered the new bisexual [i.e. co-residential] unit'.[51] Minoritised sexual preferences were thus subject to policing and attempts at 'reform', or dismissed as 'environmental'. Individuals internalised ideas of sexual conformity. As Elsa, a contributor to the 1981 *Images of Ourselves* collection of life writing by disabled women, put it, 'I felt a bit absurd about being gay *and* disabled'.[52]

Elsa's greater openness about her sexual preferences may have come from her involvement in the women's movement, which by the 1980s had a strong component of activist groups for disabled women. She was a member of Gemma, a group of disabled and non-disabled lesbians. Through groups such as Gemma, the Liberation Network of People with Disabilities and Sisters Against Disablement, women's voices became much more prominent in debates about intimacy. Feminist analysis of disabled women's experiences and vulnerabilities had been distinctly lacking in much of the 1970s reformist social policy and media productions. *Man Alive*'s 1972 episode, 'Like Other People', for example, featured without comment the breezy, objectifying statement from a disabled man that 'There was this bird up in Worcester, decent bitch she was, Christ ... I reckoned I could marry this bird'.[53] Studies of relationships among intellectually disabled people in the 1970s took little interest in the violence disabled women disproportionately experienced in relationships. Echoing the controversial views of domestic violence reformer Erin Pizzey, Janet Mattinson saw both men and women as violent and held that the partner who 'usually sets up and invites the violence is often as much of a protagonist as the partner who is finally charged with assault'.[54] As Beckie Rutherford has charted, disabled women's groups of the 1980s began to challenge patriarchal attitudes and foregrounded disabled women's sexual agency, as well as calling out the abuse they suffered.[55]

The momentum of activism around inclusive sexualities in the 1980s was not secure and suffered reversals. In October 1987, *Disability Now*'s agony aunt Margaret Moran described what she termed the 'double stigma' of homosexuality and disability. She cited testimonies from queer disabled people who, at a SPOD conference, had narrated being shunned by family and institutions for identifying as gay or lesbian. Moran was supportive of inclusivity, though she noted cautiously that 'the present legal situation' made it very difficult for carers, and 'the dividing line between helping young people to be fulfilled and taking advantage of, or abusing, them is a very fine one indeed'.[56] Her caution may have resulted from the differential age of consent for male same-sex and cross-sex relationships until equalisation in 1994. The tense atmosphere was crystallised by the Thatcher government's attack on sexual minorities, codified in the notorious Section 28 of the 1988 Local Government Act that prohibited 'promoting homosexuality' in print or education settings. The Gay Men's Disabled Group's chairman wrote to *Disability Now*, welcoming Moran's attention to sexual diversity but rejecting her focus on stigma. It was an irony, the correspondent acknowledged, that despite his pride in being gay, he was not able to reveal his name.[57] The 1995 Disability Discrimination Act did not mention rights to marriage or a family life; these elements of 'intimate citizenship' were first formulated in the 1998 Human Rights Act. A 1996 study still noted a 'conspicuous silence' on sexual matters in disability activism; SPOD was dissolved in 2004, with the director complaining that disabled groups had not prioritised intimacy and sex, preferring to focus on housing, mobility and employment.[58]

Conclusions

Uncovering the history of intimacies for disabled people is worthwhile in its own right, helping to offset the erasure and forgetting that this minoritised population has often been subject to. It also offers valuable insights into the fluidity and contingency of the status of adult, spanning a twentieth century during which sex, intimacy and marriage were privileged and prominent vehicles for its status. Both in terms of subjective experience and in institutional or structural dimensions, 'othered' and devalued forms of embodiment and cognitive status were widely experienced as a destabilising force that meant adulthood was precarious and precious, removed from its taken-for-granted status by the 'time warp' of disability.[59]

Marriage, usually cast as heterosexual and sexually consummated, became a practical and symbolic means of asserting adulthood that was widely available to an increasing number of Britons in the twentieth century. Marriage also became increasingly unstable and subject to dissolution as divorce rates increased sharply from the early 1960s, though the campaigning of sexual minorities for full marital rights in the 1990s and 2000s suggests that it has regained social centrality in the twenty-first century.

Disabled people, particularly those with intellectual impairments, experienced obstacles to sharing the privileges married status brought. Their sexual desires and needs for intimacy were often ignored, judged deviant or only approached in terms of reproductive potential. Non-disabled commentary swung from denial of sexual desire to a hyper-focus on fertility as a social danger. Disabled people's adolescence, a key time for sexual experimentation, was often curtailed, and many transitioned straight from childhood to adulthood, or to other statuses such as 'dependant'. 'Adultification', a term that developed in critique of racist categorisation, is also relevant to disabled people's experiences. Designation as 'adult' sometimes imposed heavy burdens onto disabled children and adolescents.[60]

If married, many disabled people experienced negative judgements, lack of support and intrusive surveillance. They could not easily afford the marital discord and breakups many non-disabled couples began to experience from the 1960s. Despite conflict, disabled people's marriages were often too valuable to relinquish. Their experiences suggest that for disabled people, experiences of 'life course' were contextually specific rather than linear, capable of seemingly going into reverse, or into hyper-acceleration, as they navigated institutions, cultural templates and social environments. Ideas of second or eternal childhood problematised adulthood.

These subversions and fluidities should be understood as histories of power, in terms of boundary-setting practices, resource allocation and statutory labelling. But disabled people sometimes experienced the unusual pace or flow of their lives as liberating or a source of wonder and pleasure. It lent itself to a radical rethinking of value, relationships and the passage of time. Time might productively slow down, or be experienced more intensely, 'in the moment'. Being accepting of care and dependency might help subvert the accumulative or directive temporalities of relationships, education, personal finances and careers. While the social model of disability has understandably kept discrimination and prejudice in the foreground, the 'social landscapes' of disability are more diverse. Disability histories can document a wider range of emotional experiences and forms of resilience, as well as innovative forms of intimacy that decentred marriage, heterosexuality and penetrative sex.

Notes

1. Thanks to Alice McKimm, Victoria Moreland, Caroline Rusterholz, Beckie Rutherford and Zoe Strimpel for generously sharing sources and ideas with me; I'm also grateful to the participants at the Royal Historical Society's workshop, 'Breakups in Britain', for debating the themes of this chapter.

2. 'Like Other People', *Man Alive*, dir. Paul Morrison, screened on BBC television in 1972 and winner of the Grierson award for documentary, 1973, https://player.bfi.org .uk/free/film/watch-like-other-people-1972-online, accessed 14 August 2023.

3. Julie Anderson, *War, Disability and Rehabilitation in Britain: 'Soul of a Nation'* (Manchester: Manchester University Press, 2011); Joanna Bourke, 'Love and Limblessness: Male Heterosexuality, Disability, and the Great War', *Journal of War & Culture Studies* 9, no. 1 (2016): 3–19; Mike Mantin et al., *Disability in Industrial Britain: A Cultural and Literary History of Impairment in the Coal Industry, 1880–1948* (Manchester University Press, 2020).

4. George Thomas, *A Tenement in Soho: Or, Two Flights Up* (London: J. Cape, 1931), 206.

5. Louis Neville Battye, *I Had a Little Nut Tree: A Reconstruction of Childhood* (London: Secker & Warburg, 1959), 93–4.

6. Simon Jarrett, *Those They Called Idiots: The Idea of the Disabled Mind from 1700 to the Present Day* (London: Reaktion Books, 2020). Julie Livingston's comparative research concluded that this was true of less industrialised societies. Julie Livingston, 'Insights from an African History of Disability', *Radical History Review* 2006, no. 94 (2006): 111–26.

MARRIAGE, INTIMACY AND ADULTHOOD IN DISABLED PEOPLE'S LIVES   231

7. Clémentine Beauvais, 'Ages and Ages: The Multiplication of Children's "Ages" in Early Twentieth-Century Child Psychology', *History of Education* 45, no. 3 (2016): 304–18. On the longlasting presence of ableist eugenic assumptions about reproduction, see Laura Kelly and Caroline Rusterholz, 'Depo-Provera, Medical Authority and the Domiciliary Family Planning Services in Glasgow and Haringey, 1970–1983', *Historical Journal*, forthcoming.

8. Erika R. Katzman, Elizabeth Anne Kinsella and Jessica Polzer, '"Everything Is Down to the Minute": Clock Time, Crip Time and the Relational Work of Self-Managing Attendant Services', *Disability & Society* 35, no. 4 (2020): 517–41.

9. Reginald Ford, 'Quite Intelligent', in Paul Hunt, ed., *Stigma: The Experience of Disability* (London: G. Chapman, 1966), 39–40; Jo Campling, ed., *Images of Ourselves: Women with Disabilities Talking* (London: Routledge & Kegan Paul, 1981), 87.

10. 13th Board of Control Annual Report (London: HMSO, 1927), 43, 41, 42.

11. Tom Shakespeare, Dominic Davies and K. Gillespie-Sells, *The Sexual Politics of Disability: Untold Desires* (London: Cassell, 1996); K. Gillespie-Sells, Mildrette Hill and Bree Robbins, *She Dances to Different Drums: Research into Disabled Women's Sexuality* (London: King's Fund, 1998).

12. Claire Langhamer, *The English in Love: The Intimate Story of an Emotional Revolution*, 1st ed. (Oxford: Oxford University Press, 2013); Teri Chettiar, '"More Than a Contract": The Emergence of a State-Supported Marriage Welfare Service and the Politics of Emotional Life in Post-1945 Britain', *The Journal of British Studies* 55, no. 3 (2016): 566–91.

13. Sean Brady, *Masculinity and Male Homosexuality in Britain, 1861–1913* (Basingstoke: Palgrave Macmillan, 2005), 23.

14. Selina Todd and Hilary Young, 'Baby-Boomers to "Beanstalkers": Making the Modern Teenager in Post-War Britain', *Cultural and Social History* 9, no. 3 (2012): 460.

15. Hannah Charnock, 'Teenage Girls, Female Friendship and the Making of the Sexual Revolution in England, 1950–1980', *The Historical Journal* 63, no. 4 (2019): 1–22.

16. There is little published literature tracing the historical relationship between life writing and disabled status, with the exception of Mantin et al., *Disability in Industrial Britain*.

17. Thomas, *A Tenement in Soho*; John Gray, *Gin and Bitters* (London: Jarrolds, 1938).

18. Ben Jones, 'The Uses of Nostalgia: Autobiography, Community Publishing and Working Class Neighbourhoods in Post-War England', *Cultural and Social History* 7, no. 3 (2010): 355–74.

19. See, for example, Campling, *Images of Ourselves*; Jenny Morris, *Able Lives: Women's Experience of Paralysis* (London: Women's Press, 1989).

20. Judy Hunt, *No Limits: The Disabled People's Movement – A Radical History* (Manchester: TBR Imprint, 2019).

21. Paul Hunt, *Collected Works of Paul Hunt*, edited by Luke Beesley (Manchester: TBR Imprint, 2020).

22. 'Michele Gilbert' [Pamela La Fane], 'Growing Up Geriatric', *The Guardian*, 23 December 1966, cited in Pamela La Fane, *It's a Lovely Day, Outside: An Autobiography* (London: Gollancz, 1981).

23. Hunt, *No Limits*.

24. Hunt, *Stigma*, 20.

25. Rosalind Chalmers, 'Victim Invicta', in Hunt, *Stigma*, 22, 21.

26. Battye, 'The Chatterley Syndrome', in Hunt, *Stigma*, 9.

27. Hunt, *Stigma*, 12, 13–14.

28. Margaret Gill, 'No Small Miracle', in Hunt, *Stigma*, 106.

29. Hunt, *No Limits*; Michael Oliver, *The Politics of Disablement* (London: Macmillan Education, 1990).

30. Paul Hunt, 'Observations on Planning a Home for Spastics', *The Architects' Journal Information Library* (May 1970), in *Collected Works*, 125.

31. Wolf Wolfensberger and Susan Thomas, 'The Principle of Normalization in Human Services: A Brief Overview', *Research Highlights* 2 (1982): 14, 18. On the wider context, see John Welshman and Jan Walmsley, *Community Care in Perspective: Care, Control and Citizenship* (Basingstoke: Palgrave Macmillan, 2006).

32. Ann Shearer, *A Right to Love?*, vol. 1972 (London: Spastics Society and National Association for Mental Health, 1972).

33. Ann Shearer, *Normalisation?*, Discussion Paper 3 (London: Campaign for the Mentally Handicapped, 1972). For an experiment in implementation, see 'Richard' and 'Cathy's' engagement and marriage documented in D.G. Race, D.M. Race and Department of Health and Social Security, *The Cherries Group Home: A Beginning: [Helping the Mentally Handicapped Look after Themselves]* (London: HMSO, 1979).

34. Townsend, cited in Alan Tyne, 'The Impact of the Normalisation Principle on Services for the Mentally Handicapped in the United Kingdom', *Research Highlights* 2 (1982): 24–34.

35. Janet Mattinson, *Marriage and Mental Handicap* (London: Duckworth, 1970), 137.

36. Ann Craft and Michael Craft, *Handicapped Married Couples: A Welsh Study of Couples Handicapped from Birth by Mental, Physical or Personality Disorder* (London: Routledge and Kegan Paul, 1979).

37. Viv McAvoy, Nursing Officer, 'Starcross Hospital: What the Voices Tell Us' (2020), 40, https://citizen-network.org/library/starcross-hospital.html, accessed 2 July 2023.

38. J.E. Oliver, 'Partnership and Marriage for the Subnormal?', *Apex: Journal of the British Institute of Mental Handicap* 22, no. 42 (1976): 31–2.

39. Mattinson, *Marriage and Mental Handicap*, 104. See Elizabeth Tilley et al., '"The Silence Is Roaring": Sterilization, Reproductive Rights and Women with Intellectual Disabilities'. *Disability & Society* 27, no. 3 (May 2012): 413–26.

40. Pauline Wiltshire, *Living and Winning* (London: Centreprise, 1985), 34, 62, 44.

41. Hilary Brown, '"An Ordinary Sexual Life?": A Review of the Normalisation Principle as It Applies to the Sexual Options of People with Learning Disabilities', *Disability & Society* 9, no. 2 (1994): 123–44. Caroline Rusterholz notes the growing interest of sexual and reproductive health clinics in the needs of disabled people from the 1970s: *Responsible Pleasure: Youth Sexuality in Postwar Britain* (Oxford: Oxford University Press, 2024).

42. Paul Hunt, 'Fokus Housing Scheme, Sweden', minutes for Central Council of the Disabled, June 1973, in *Collected Works*, 144.

43. La Fane, *It's a Lovely Day, Outside*.

44. *The Management of Work Centres*, Scope/Heron Film Productions, 1973.

45. Maggie Davis and Ken Davis, *To and From Grove Road* (Manchester: TBR Imprint, 2019).

46. W.F.R. Stewart, 'Sexual Aspects of Disability: Growth of Attention in the UK', *Royal Society of Health* 98, no. 1 (1978): 36–39. SPOD's approach was later criticised

as 'mechanistic' and devised for, rather than by, disabled people. Shakespeare, Davies and Gillespie-Sells, *The Sexual Politics of Disability*, 29, 99.

47. 'Wonderful News', Fred Brown, *Singles* magazine, June 1984, 4.

48. *Disability Now*, October 1987, 15.

49. David Barron, *A Price to Be Born: My Childhood and Life in a Mental Institution* (London: Mencap Northern Division, 1996), 122.

50. Ann Craft and Michael Craft, 'Partnership and Marriage for the Subnormal?', *Apex* 3, no. 2 (1975): 13–15.

51. Craft and Craft, *Handicapped Married Couples*, 124.

52. Campling, *Images of Ourselves*, 86.

53. *Man Alive*, 1972.

54. Mattinson, *Marriage and Mental Handicap*, 138. On Pizzey, see Zora Simic, 'From Battered Wives to Domestic Violence: The Transnational Circulation of Chiswick Women's Aid and Erin Pizzey's Scream Quietly or the Neighbours Will Hear (1974)', *Australian Historical Studies* 51, no. 2 (2020): 107–26.

55. Beckie Rutherford, 'Disabled Women Organising: Rethinking the Political Within British Liberation Movements, 1976–1998' (PhD thesis, University of Warwick, 2023).

56. R. Moran, 'Homosexuality and Disability a "Double Stigma"', *Disability Now*, October 1987, 14.

57. *Disability Now*, January 1988, 2.

58. Shakespeare, Davies and Gillespie-Sells, *The Sexual Politics of Disability*, 6. The 2005 Mental Capacity Act clarified the legal status of decision-making by individuals with intellectual disabilities in questions of marriage, but tensions remained in balancing safeguarding and 'personalisation'. Anna Arstein-Kerslake, 'Understanding Sex: The Right to Legal Capacity to Consent to Sex', *Disability & Society* 30, no. 10 (November 2015): 1459–73.

59. Pam Evans, cited in Jenny Morris, *Pride against Prejudice: A Personal Politics of Disability* (London: Women's Press, 1991), 144.

60. See Jack Hodgson's chapter in this volume.

References

13th Board of Control Annual Report. London: HMSO, 1927.

Anderson, Julie. *War, Disability and Rehabilitation in Britain: 'Soul of a Nation'*. Manchester: Manchester University Press, 2011.

Arstein-Kerslake, Anna. 'Understanding Sex: The Right to Legal Capacity to Consent to Sex'. *Disability & Society* 30, no. 10 (26 November 2015): 1459–73.

Barron, David. *A Price to Be Born: My Childhood and Life in a Mental Institution*. London: Mencap Northern Division, 1996.

Battye, Louis Neville. *I Had a Little Nut Tree: A Reconstruction of Childhood*. London: Secker & Warburg, 1959.

Beauvais, Clémentine. 'Ages and Ages: The Multiplication of Children's "Ages" in Early Twentieth-Century Child Psychology'. *History of Education* 45, no. 3 (2016): 304–18.

Bourke, Joanna. 'Love and Limblessness: Male Heterosexuality, Disability, and the Great War'. *Journal of War & Culture Studies* 9, no. 1 (2016): 3–19.

Brady, Sean. *Masculinity and Male Homosexuality in Britain, 1861–1913*. Basingstoke: Palgrave Macmillan, 2005.

Brown, Fred. 'Wonderful News'. *Singles* magazine, June 1984, 4.

Brown, Hilary. '"An Ordinary Sexual Life?": A Review of the Normalisation Principle as It Applies to the Sexual Options of People with Learning Disabilities'. *Disability & Society* 9, no. 2 (1994): 123–44.

Campling, Jo ed. *Images of Ourselves: Women with Disabilities Talking*. London: Routledge & Kegan Paul, 1981.

Charnock, Hannah. 'Teenage Girls, Female Friendship and the Making of the Sexual Revolution in England, 1950–1980'. *The Historical Journal* 63, no. 4 (2019): 1–22.

Chettiar, Teri. '"More Than a Contract": The Emergence of a State-Supported Marriage Welfare Service and the Politics of Emotional Life in Post-1945 Britain'. *The Journal of British Studies* 55, no. 3 (2016): 566–91.

Craft, Ann and Craft, Michael. 'Partnership and Marriage for the Subnormal?', *Apex* 3, no. 2 (1975): 13–15.

Craft, Ann and Craft, Michael. *Handicapped Married Couples: A Welsh Study of Couples Handicapped from Birth by Mental, Physical or Personality Disorder*. London: Routledge and Kegan Paul, 1979.

Davis, Maggie and Davis, Ken. *To and from Grove Road*. Manchester: TBR Imprint, 2019.

Ford, Reginald. 'Quite Intelligent', in Paul Hunt, ed., *Stigma: The Experience of Disability* London: G. Chapman, 1966, 39–40.

Gillespie-Sells, K., Hill, Mildrette and Robbins, Bree. *She Dances to Different Drums: Research into Disabled Women's Sexuality*. London: King's Fund, 1998.

Gray, John. *Gin and Bitters*. London: Jarrolds, 1938.

Hunt, Judy. *No Limits: The Disabled People's Movement – A Radical History*. Manchester: TBR Imprint, 2019.

Hunt, Paul ed. *Stigma: The Experience of Disability*. London: G. Chapman, 1966.

Hunt, Paul. *Collected Works of Paul Hunt*, edited by Luke Beesley. Manchester: TBR Imprint, 2020.

Hunt, Paul. 'Fokus Housing Scheme, Sweden', minutes for Central Council of the Disabled, June 1973, in *Collected Works of Paul Hunt*, edited by Luke Beesley Manchester: TBR Imprint, 2020, 144.

Jarrett, Simon. *Those They Called Idiots: The Idea of the Disabled Mind from 1700 to the Present Day*. London: Reaktion Books, 2020.

Jones, Ben. 'The Uses of Nostalgia: Autobiography, Community Publishing and Working Class Neighbourhoods in Post-War England'. *Cultural and Social History* 7, no. 3 (2010): 355–74.

Katzman, Erika R., Kinsella, Elizabeth Anne and Polzer, Jessica. '"Everything Is Down to the Minute": Clock Time, Crip Time and the Relational Work of Self-Managing Attendant Services'. *Disability & Society* 35, no. 4 (2020): 517–41.

Kelly, Laura and Rusterholz, Caroline. 'Depo-Provera, Medical Authority and the Domiciliary Family Planning Services in Glasgow and Haringey, 1970–1983'. *Historical Journal*, forthcoming.

La Fane, Pamela. *It's a Lovely Day, Outside: An Autobiography*. London: Gollancz, 1981.

Langhamer, Claire. *The English in Love: The Intimate Story of an Emotional Revolution*, 1st ed. Oxford: Oxford University Press, 2013.

Livingston, Julie. 'Insights from an African History of Disability'. *Radical History Review* 2006, no. 94 (2006): 111–26.

The Management of Work Centres, Scope/Heron Film Productions, 1973.

Mantin, Mike, Bohata, Kirsti, Jones, Alexandra and Thompson, Steven. *Disability in Industrial Britain: A Cultural and Literary History of Impairment in the Coal Industry, 1880–1948*. Manchester: Manchester University Press, 2020.

Mattinson, Janet. *Marriage and Mental Handicap*. London: Duckworth, 1970.

Moran, R. 'Homosexuality and Disability a "Double Stigma"', *Disability Now*, October 1987, 14.

Morris, Jenny. *Able Lives: Women's Experience of Paralysis*. London: Women's Press, 1989.

Morris, Jenny. *Pride against Prejudice: A Personal Politics of Disability.* London: Women's Press, 1991.

Oliver, J.E. 'Partnership and Marriage for the Subnormal?' *Apex: Journal of the British Institute of Mental Handicap* 22, no. 42 (1976): 31–2.

Oliver, Michael. *The Politics of Disablement.* London: Macmillan Education, 1990.

Race, D.G., Race, D.M. and Department of Health and Social Security. *The Cherries Group Home: A Beginning: [Helping the Mentally Handicapped Look after Themselves].* London: HMSO, 1979.

Rusterholz, Caroline. *Responsible Pleasure: Youth Sexuality in Postwar Britain.* Oxford: Oxford University Press, 2024.

Rutherford, Beckie. 'Disabled Women Organising: Rethinking the Political Within British Liberation Movements, 1976–1998'. PhD thesis, University of Warwick, 2023.

Shakespeare, Tom, Davies, Dominic, and Gillespie-Sells, Katherine *The Sexual Politics of Disability: Untold Desires.* London: Cassell, 1996.

Shearer, Ann. *A Right to Love?* London: Spastics Society and National Association for Mental Health, 1972.

Shearer, Ann. *Normalisation?* Discussion Paper 3. London: Campaign for the Mentally Handicapped, 1972.

Simic, Zora. 'From Battered Wives to Domestic Violence: The Transnational Circulation of Chiswick Women's Aid and Erin Pizzey's Scream Quietly or the Neighbours Will Hear (1974)'. *Australian Historical Studies* 51, no. 2 (2020): 107–26.

'Starcross Hospital: What the Voices Tell Us', 2020. https://citizen -network.org/library/starcross-hospital.html, accessed 17 July 2024.

Stewart, W.F.R. 'Sexual Aspects of Disability: Growth of Attention in the UK'. *Royal Society of Health* 98, no. 1 (1978): 36–9.

Thomas, George. *A Tenement in Soho: Or, Two Flights Up.* London: J. Cape, 1931.

Tilley, Elizabeth, Walmsley, Jan, Earle, Sarah and Atkinson, Dorothy. '"The Silence Is Roaring": Sterilization, Reproductive Rights and Women with Intellectual Disabilities'. *Disability & Society* 27, no. 3 (2012): 413–26.

Todd, Selina and Young, Hilary. 'Baby-Boomers to "Beanstalkers": Making the Modern Teenager in Post-War Britain'. *Cultural and Social History* 9, no. 3 (2012): 451–67.

Tyne, Alan. 'The Impact of the Normalisation Principle on Services for the Mentally Handicapped in the United Kingdom'. *Research Highlights* 2 (1982): 24–34.

Welshman, John and Walmsley, Jan. *Community Care in Perspective: Care, Control and Citizenship.* Basingstoke: Palgrave Macmillan, 2006.

Wiltshire, Pauline. *Living and Winning.* London: Centreprise, 1985.
Wolfensberger, Wolf and Thomas, Susan. 'The Principle of
Normalization in Human Services: A Brief Overview'. *Research
Highlights* 2 (1982): 10–22.

Chapter 11

A road of one's own: The rejection of standard adulthood in US emerging adult films[1]

Andrea Sofía Regueira Martín

Two decades separate the slackers of 1990s cinema from the 'Messy Millennial Woman' that populates contemporary cinema and television, but both character types are symptomatic of the same phenomenon: the changes that the transition to adulthood – and adulthood itself – have undergone in the last thirty years.[2] Pop culture holds up a mirror to society, reflecting and shaping its values and expectations as well as tracking its changes. Shifts and trends in popular culture are thus a useful tool through which one can study societal change. At the time, films about slackers and Generation X might have seemed like a passing fad, but some of the characteristics embodied by slackers came to stay. In other words, the protagonists changed, but films about drifting twentysomethings hovering between adolescence and adulthood as they try to figure out who they want to be not only remained, but also grew in number as the millennial generation entered their third decade.[3] The rise of these films coincides chronologically with the moment that Jeffrey Arnett pinpoints as the time when emerging adulthood became commonplace.[4] Arnett defines emerging adulthood as a life stage between adolescence and adulthood during which one has attained some markers of adulthood but is yet to reach others, naming a shift in young people's perception of adulthood as a key element of the prevalence of emerging adulthood. As he explains, most emerging adults reject what he calls 'traditional conceptions of adulthood' – and others refer to as 'standard adulthood' – including adult milestones such as 'marriage, home, and children', which

239

are now seen 'not as achievements to be pursued but as perils to be avoided'.[5]

Even though the concept of emerging adulthood has been questioned by those who believe that it reflects a privileged point of view, ignoring larger socio-economic factors behind the lengthening of the transition to adulthood and the shifting nature of adulthood itself, the term remains useful to designate those films that focus on the latter stages of the coming-of-age process and depict the protagonists' struggle, refusal and reluctance to settle down. Conflict between preconceived ideas of what adulthood should look like and the protagonists' desires permeates these films, independently of whether the protagonists strive to achieve that ideal or reject it. This chapter examines filmic representations of this tension between the conception of standard adulthood that emerged in the US in the mid-twentieth century and emerging adulthood in order to discuss what these films tell us about the changing nature of contemporary adulthood.[6] After a brief outline of emerging adulthood and the challenges faced by emerging adults today, this chapter will focus on onscreen depictions of the conflict between standard adulthood and emerging adulthood, dividing the analysis into three parts that correspond to the character types that most commonly embody standard adulthood: romantic partners, best friends and former classmates and relatives.

Becoming an adult today

In the United States, concern with the lengthening of youth and the consequent postponement of adulthood began in the early 1970s. Since then, there have been several attempts to define a life stage bridging adolescence and adulthood. Before Arnett's emerging adulthood took hold, there was Kenneth Keniston's 'youth', Daniel J. Levinson's 'novice phase' and Susan Littwin's 'postponed generation', all of which are reminiscent of Erikson's 'psychosocial moratorium', a 'sanctioned postponement of definitive commitment' that he initially associated with adolescence but later expanded to include college-age individuals.[7] Arnett and Taber criticised Keniston's conception of 'youth' for being too closely linked to the counterculture and not as mass-scale as he claimed, but Keniston's writings show that some of the societal shifts that led to the postponement of adult commitment had already begun in the late 1960s.[8]

Writing from a US perspective, Keniston directly links longer transitions to adulthood to postwar affluence and the increase of the number of students enrolled in tertiary education to meet 'the enormously high educational demands of a postindustrial society'.[9] The correlation between higher education and a later entry to the workplace is clear and acknowledged by many, but there is more to it than university enrolment. Some authors have connected this educational trend with another factor that led to the lengthening of the transition to adulthood: a delay in the age at which people get married and become parents.[10] This shift is also directly related to feminist advances that made women's life patterns more akin to men's as they began to pursue higher education and enter the workplace in greater numbers. At the same time, the changes in interpersonal relationships brought about by the sexual revolution provided women with more sexual and reproductive agency.[11] Although sexist stereotypes regarding women's roles are by no means eradicated, these advances granted women more freedom and opportunities as far as their transition to adulthood is concerned.[12]

While it is true that today's young adults have more freedom to choose an individualised route to adulthood, the uncertainty and precarity under which this transition takes place must not be ignored. As Jennifer Silva explains in her study of US working-class adulthood, deferring adulthood might be a lifestyle choice for privileged individuals who have the economic and familial support to carry out the soul-searching that characterises emerging adulthood, but that is not the case for everybody.[13] For those with less privilege, adulthood is out of reach and a precarious existence with contingent jobs and relationships is the norm. In these cases, individuals are *forced* to explore, to change roles and identities as their financial circumstances do. Although Silva's work focuses on working-class young adults, some of the insecurity and uncertainty that characterise these transitions has seeped into other social classes. As Beck and Beck-Gernsheim explain in their theory of individualisation, the abundance of choices that characterises contemporary life make each person's biography unique, but this 'do-it-yourself biography' does not come without risks.[14] This freedom to explore is a two-sided coin, as it coexists with increased possibilities of failure, especially given that contemporary society is increasingly characterised by uncertainty and unpredictability.[15] When applied to the workplace, this flexibility encourages what Bauman calls a 'short-term mentality' that leaves no space for meaningful, long-lasting connections or involvement in long-term projects, both of which are essential to adulthood as we know it.[16]

Short-term arrangements feature in Arnett's conceptualisation of emerging adulthood, albeit in a more positive light. Arnett calls emerging adulthood a time of in-betweenness, instability, identity exploration, focus on oneself and possibilities.[17] Although Arnett names a rejection of adult values as one of the factors involved in the rise of emerging adulthood, his theory implies that one will eventually leave these traits behind and attain some sort of standardised adulthood that will involve stability, focus on others, the end of self-searching and knowledge of one's place in the world. In contrast, some have argued that such an end is not actually in sight and that what has changed is not the transition to adulthood but adulthood itself. This 'new adulthood' is characterised by 'the uncertainty, unpredictability and instability that once characterised "youth"'.[18] Similarly, Blatterer argues that what once were features of youth now belong to contemporary adulthood, which he sees as 'perpetually liminal' and without a 'definite destination'.[19] Keeping in mind this context, one can argue that the clash between standard adulthood and emerging adulthood that appears in emerging adult films represents a snapshot of a culture grappling with the redefinition of what it means to be an adult.

When you grow up your heart dies: onscreen rejections of standard adulthood

In films, wherever there is an emerging adult protagonist there is usually someone their own age who has moved on from youthful experimentation and into adult commitment. Eighty-five out of the one hundred and sixteen US emerging adult films included in the corpus of my doctoral dissertation featured narrative tension between emerging adulthood and standard adulthood. Looking at the prevalence of this trope across the three decades that I analysed reveals that its prominence grew as time went on. In the 1990s it appeared in 62.5 per cent of the films, rising to 67 per cent in the 2000s and to 80 per cent in the 2010s.[20] It could be argued, then, that onscreen representations of emerging adulthood reveal a growing concern with a form of adulthood that, as was explained in the previous section, some consider to be outdated, undesirable and unreachable for the majority of young people.[21] The fact that representations of this conflict have increased through the decades can be read as a reflection of the ever-growing struggles faced by the millennial generation in their transition to adulthood. Millennials have been described as entitled and immature, but when writing about this generation one must not forget that they have also been described as 'the unluckiest generation in U.S. history', that their coming-of-age process has been tainted by two recessions – the Great Recession affected older millennials and the COVID-19 recession younger ones – and that they fare poorly as far as intergenerational wealth is concerned.[22]

Through this narrative tension, emerging adult films highlight the fact that the markers of standard adulthood have become *demodé* for some and unattainable for others. As we will see in the analyses that follow, the characters who embody standard adulthood are depicted as antagonists. While the protagonists chase their dreams and struggle to give up what they believe to be the core elements of their personality, adulthood is portrayed as a loss of authenticity, which makes the protagonists view their more grown-up partners, friends and family members as corporate drones who have given up and whose essence is gone, which inevitably poses challenges to their relationship.

Emerging adult protagonists often struggle when their romantic interest has a more adult outlook than themselves. This can be seen from the earliest iterations of emerging adult films. While in some instances the distance between the two characters prevents a relationship from even beginning, in other cases the protagonists find themselves in a relationship with someone who represents standard adulthood and both parties have to compromise parts of themselves in order for the relationship to succeed. Compromise and willingness to change are necessary for the protagonists of *Always Be My Maybe* (Nahnatchka Khan, 2019), a film that represents the differences between emerging adulthood and standard adulthood visually as well as narratively.[23] When two childhood best friends who lost touch after losing their virginity to each other find each other again, their lifestyles could not be any more different. Sasha (Ali Wong) is a successful celebrity chef, but Marcus's (Randall Park) life seems to have been on pause since he was a teenager. Not only has Marcus never left his hometown of San Francisco, he still lives in his childhood bedroom and plays in his high school band. After a montage sequence showing photo booth pictures of the protagonists through childhood and adolescence, a flashback shows the nature of their friendship and the moment when it ended. This is immediately followed by two scenes that introduce the two ex-friends' lives in the present day, presenting them as opposites. The differences between the two are marked not only by the narrative but also by the mise-en-scène, particularly their clothes and the spaces that they occupy. We see Sasha in her successful LA restaurant – where accolades and framed magazine covers adorn the walls – and at a charity gala, wearing a chic red gown and accompanied by her restaurant developer fiancé. The luxury and glamour of her life contrast starkly with the ordinariness of Marcus's, whom we first meet when he is dancing and smoking weed in front of a mirror in his childhood bedroom in San Francisco. His scruffy clothes – tracksuit bottoms, an unbuttoned shirt with a vest underneath and no shoes – and the mess in his room hint towards a lack of discipline in his life, while the decor on his walls and shelves suggests that he has evolved very little since adolescence.

Yet, these two juxtaposed scenes reveal other telling details about the protagonists' personal lives. Sasha's relationships are strained and her priorities are wrong. Her tight schedule does not leave her time to be there for her pregnant friend and assistant but she does have time for her fiancé, whose smiles turn into iciness the very moment camera lenses are not pointed at them. After an event, the couple is shown driving back home while sitting at opposite sides of the car. Their position within the frame reflects his emotional detachment, which is also highlighted by his monosyllabic responses and lack of interest in Sasha. In contrast, the relationship between Marcus and his father is warm and affectionate, which is shown by their actions, as in the previous scene, by framing. Marcus is sitting very close to his father while giving him an injection. As he does this, the camera moves closer until they are both shot from the chest up in a medium close-up, emphasising their bond as well as the very personal nature of both their actions – looking after one another – and their conversation about their gentrifying neighbourhood.

These two scenes contain several elements that appear recurrently in emerging adult narratives. Even though Sasha's adulthood is not exactly standard, the differences between her and Marcus are represented through the same visual elements commonly used to highlight tension between emerging adulthood and standard adulthood: mise-en-scène – particularly costume and setting – and framing. In addition, these scenes provide a good example of the critical lens through which accomplished or successful adulthoods are usually seen in these films. In this film, as in many others, success does not necessarily bring fulfilment. Sasha is rich, famous and glamorous, but her boyfriend does not even look at her when she asks a question and she has no time to devote to those who do care about her. Work has taken over her life and, in the process, she seems to have forgotten who she was and where she came from. This is exactly the outcome that most emerging adult protagonists are trying to avoid when they reject standard adulthood. They often linger as they try to figure out a way to move on in life while remaining true to themselves, which sometimes proves impossible and sometimes requires a readjustment of their expectations. When it comes to their relationship with their past selves, those characters who are too attached to their past need to learn to let go of it, while the ones who have grown up to be completely detached from it need to revisit and reconsider their lives in light of who they were. As mentioned, the two characters reach a compromise by the end of the film: Marcus accepts Sasha's choices and takes a step towards leaving home and improving his life, while Sasha gets back in touch with her origins and rejects *haute cuisine* in favour of the traditional cooking that she learnt from Marcus's mother when she was a child.

But not all films show the protagonists and their more adult-like lovers finding common ground. In some instances, one partner's step into adulthood signals an end for the couple. For example, *For a Good Time Call …* (Jamie Travis, 2012) begins with one of the protagonists (Lauren Miller Rogen) being dumped when her boyfriend is given the chance to move to Milan for work. The opposite occurs in *Someone Great* (Jennifer Kaytin Robinson, 2019), a film in which the protagonist (Gina Rodriguez) is dumped by her boyfriend after she gets her dream job and has to move across the country. These examples show how the 'short-term mentality' mentioned earlier is depicted as an element that affects the professional and personal lives of the protagonists. Whether the root of the break-up is a reluctance to commit, a fear of closing one's options or mere selfishness, it all boils down to an individualised approach to contemporary life that leaves little room for lifelong commitment.[24]

As we have seen, when romantic narratives end on a positive – or, at least, potentially positive – note, the protagonists and their partners need to show self-reflection, growth and mutual understanding, with compromise and letting go of parts of their lifestyle as key elements that allow their union. In these cases, the couple is not united by fate or chance, but by a conscious effort to change to be able to remain compatible, an approach that underscores the fact that interpersonal relationships are the result of hard work and mutual understanding and that they require sacrifices on both sides. In the case of emerging adult films, these sacrifices require the protagonist to take some steps towards maturity and the more 'mature' character to make changes in their lifestyle that bring them closer to who they once were. This does not necessarily mean that they have to become more immature but, rather, that they have to remember who they used to be. In the case of Sasha, this implied using the knowledge she acquired as a child in her new business venture, a more authentic version of success that is not as influenced by preconceived ideas regarding culinary excellence. Emerging adult films therefore see growing up as a process during which one is at risk of losing one's identity, with adult success found not in the rejection of one's past but in the careful calibration of one's personal history and present life.

Even though emerging adults may no longer live with their parents, most of them are still far from becoming completely independent. Many emerging adult films reflect this state of semi-dependence through the relationship of the protagonist with their friends who, in the absence of parental figures, often take on a caretaking role, providing the protagonist with emotional and sometimes even financial support. Living with friends – a common arrangement that reflects the dire financial reality of emerging adults – does not seem to pose a problem as long as all of them are on the same page as far as maturity is concerned. For instance, *Romy and Michele's High School Reunion* (David Mirkin, 1997) focuses on two friends who live together and whose living arrangements cause no drama between them due to their similar status regarding the transition to adulthood. In other cases, people who once disliked one another are forced into friendship when the difficulty to find affordable housing in big cities forces them to share an apartment. For instance, in *For a Good Time Call* ... , precarity forces former college frenemies into an unwanted flatshare that becomes a close friendship.

The relationship between friends becomes more complicated when there is a clear imbalance between the protagonist's position and that of their friend's; that is, when one of the two friends has grown up and the other one is struggling to do so. In some cases, the liminal position of the emerging adult protagonist is depicted through the space they occupy at their friend's house. In *Social Animals* (Theresa Bennett, 2018), the protagonist lives in a camper van parked in her friend's garden, an arrangement that emphasises their different status through a clash between the temporary nature of the protagonist's arrangements and the solidity of home ownership. Another protagonist who is almost a squatter at his friend's place is Dewey (Jack Black) in *School of Rock* (Richard Linklater, 2003). What Dewey calls his 'room' is actually a part of his friend Ned's (Mike White) living room separated by a curtain. Both *School of Rock* and *Social Animals* show a friendship in which the protagonists' friends take on an almost parental role by giving the protagonists shelter, however precarious or temporary their situation may seem.

The settings of these films also emphasise the impossibility of carrying on with a bohemian hipster lifestyle into adulthood. Both feature hipster enclaves where the protagonists' lifestyle cannot continue. In *Social Animals*, Zoe (Noël Wells) cannot afford to live in gentrified Austin, while in *School of Rock* Dewey is kicked out of his band after a show in Williamsburg in which his stage antics hinder the band's performance. Both characters seem to be out of sync with these spaces, which – like their friends – are evolving faster than they are. In gentrified Austin, Zoe's waxing business cannot compete with a laser competitor, while Dewey's penchant for overly long guitar solos and stage diving seems to belong to a different decade and is out of place in Williamsburg, the home of the 2000s hipster.[25] This inability to keep up with the passing of time and evolve, then, sees the protagonists out of sync with spaces that symbolise cultural change as well as with the spaces that their friends occupy, which stand for their personal development and maturity.

In Dewey's case, this incompatibility extends to his relationship with his friend Ned, who embodies standard adulthood and provides a counterpoint to Dewey's recklessness and refusal to move on. What might have seemed like a fun idea to Ned when he let Dewey move in later becomes a major hurdle in his road towards adult commitment. While both friends used to share dreams of becoming rock stars, Ned has acknowledged the fact that rock stardom is out of his reach and has chosen to become a teacher instead. Now, he is studying to become a full-time teacher and he lives with his girlfriend, who is growing increasingly irritated by the intrusiveness of Dewey's living arrangements and the fact that he does not pay any rent. Dewey's corner of the living room is chock-full of music records and other memorabilia that covers most of the walls and windows, which makes his living space look like a teenage bedroom, further accentuating his immaturity and reluctance to step into adulthood. The clash between the two spaces – Dewey's corner and the rest of Ned's flat – is highlighted by the presence of the curtain that separates them and constitutes a physical – but makeshift – boundary between the two friends, whose distance is also emphasised by framing choices that position a pillar or other obstacles standing between them.

As in the examples analysed in the previous section, in *School of Rock* both the emerging adult protagonist and the more mature one need to change to find fulfilment by the end of the film. Through impersonating Ned as a substitute teacher, Dewey finds meaning in teaching music and creativity to the younger generation, adopting a caretaking role himself that signals a substantial step into adulthood.[26] At the same time, Dewey's freer, more anarchic approach to education has an impact on Ned, who quits school teaching and opens an after-school rock music school for kids in his apartment. The closing credits show both friends teaching children, having found a way to reconcile their shared history as rock music fans and performers with a profitable venture that allows them to find adult stability. The same space that was previously divided between Dewey's arrested development and Ned's organised, rule-abiding living has now become an open space where both friends are united by a passion for rock music and for creative approaches to music education. Both characters have had to make adjustments in order for their relationship to flourish, which underscores the fact that in emerging adult films friendships often play a role that is as important as – if not more important than – that of romance, which is often rejected in favour of self-development.

Romantic relationships play a more prominent role in narratives about female friendship. In films like *Walking and Talking* (Nicole Holofcener, 1996), *Frances Ha* (Noah Baumbach, 2012) and *Life Partners* (Susanna Fogel, 2014), the relationship between the protagonists and their best friends is strained after their best friend gets involved in a serious relationship and begins to consider marriage. In these films, the protagonist's best friend's commitment to somebody else results in tension between them that might even separate the two friends for some time, a friendship break-up that resembles a romantic one. In these films, the protagonists feel abandoned and let down by their best friend, whose constant presence they can no longer demand now that they are in serious relationships and their lifestyle has changed. This provokes feelings of loss and anger as they mistakenly believe that their friendship is no longer needed. What all these films share is a marked focus on the depiction of the apparently blissful life of the protagonist and their best friend. While *School of Rock* begins with the protagonist at odds with his friend and the viewer never sees the positive aspects of Dewey and Ned's friendship, films about female friendship take their time to romanticise the relationship between the two friends and to carefully explore both the moments in which the cracks begin to appear on the surface and the clash between the two friends, resulting in a more dramatic friendship break-up that underscores the protagonists' dejection.

These films also share a concern with the institution of marriage, a marker of standard adulthood that the protagonists reject and that affects their relationship with their best friends. The importance of these rites of passage into adulthood is undermined by the narrative, which leaves the door open to other versions of womanhood besides heterosexual couplings, marriage and motherhood. For instance, in *Frances Ha* the apparently idyllic life that follows long-term commitment is not so. *Frances Ha* features a protagonist (Greta Gerwig) who envies the apparently easy life of her best friend Sophie (Mickey Sumner) as she gets engaged to someone with money and moves to a better neighbourhood in Manhattan and, later, to Japan. But the idealised life that Sophie shares on her blog is not real. After some time apart, Sophie drunkenly reveals the truth: she is not happy and she got pregnant by accident. Sophie wanted to have an abortion, but she had a miscarriage before she could arrange the procedure, which caused her a great deal of pain. Sophie's problems deal with life, death and commitment, which makes Frances's problems seem trivial in comparison. This bout of honesty reunites the two friends, who realise that they both have problems of their own regardless of their status and, therefore, they both need their friend by their side.

Through the opposition of friends who are closer to crossing the border into standard adulthood and others who are hovering in emerging adulthood, films position neither of the options as a completely desirable one. Some of the films reaffirm what we saw in the previous section by showing the two friends learning from one another, which results in the emerging adult protagonist gaining some sort of purpose or new responsibility while their more mature friend remembers the importance of staying true to their roots, which are embodied by their longtime friendships and by the hobbies they used to share. In other words, growing up does not necessarily involve letting go of their meaningful relationships or of their passions, both of which should continue to provide joy in adulthood. Adulthood is therefore not seen as a clean break with one's previous self but, rather, as an evolution. Films about female friendship introduce another element into the equation and place the focus on an exploration of the options available to women, questioning the validity of marriage and motherhood as a road to self-fulfilment and positioning alternative paths as equally valid options.

Homecoming narratives are recurrent in emerging adult films, and they have grown in number through the decades, reflecting millennials' tendency to boomerang back home after the Great Recession.[27] In emerging adult films that focus on a return home, the entire narrative structure tends to be organised around a trip during which the protagonist revisits their youth by physically returning to the site of their childhood and adolescence and by reuniting with those people who knew them back then. In some cases, the return or reunion is motivated by a rite of passage like a wedding, a high school reunion or a funeral, but the protagonist's most likely reason for return is personal, more specifically a personal crisis motivated by a failure to live as an independent adult. These crises often result from unemployment, the break-up of a romantic relationship and mental health issues, sometimes from a combination of the three. Most often, breaking up with a partner renders the protagonist unable to support themselves in the big city, which forces them to return home and reassess their situation.[28] These returns force the protagonist to compare their journey into adulthood to that of the people they knew growing up, which is often very different from their own.

High school reunion films place a special emphasis on the connection between one's teenage and adult identity, typically showing how individuals from different high school cliques have fared in the ten years after leaving high school. At twenty-eight, some of them fit the mould of standard adulthood, but the protagonists are still on their way there. The prospect of having to face others who might be more successful generates feelings of anxiety in the protagonists, who sometimes try to embellish the truth about their lives. For instance, in *Romy and Michele's High School Reunion* the protagonists buy an outfit that they believe will make them look professional and make up their own success story claiming that they invented Post-it notes. However, their plan fails to make them fit in when they find that all the former popular girls are defined by marriage and motherhood rather than professional success. Their black power-suits and chic up-dos contrast with the shimmery pastel colours worn by the other girls, as well as with their voluminous hairstyles.

In *Zack and Miri Make a Porno* (Kevin Smith, 2008), the opposite occurs. Zack (Seth Rogen), who is only going to the reunion to repay a favour to his best friend Miri (Elizabeth Banks), is not concerned with performing adulthood at all, to the point that he is the only person at the reunion wearing casual clothes, his flannel shirt and jeans contrasting with everybody else's suits and smart shirts. This film also highlights the contrast between some people's high school persona and their adult selves. Miri's motivation to go to the reunion stems from the unlikely possibility of seducing a former popular boy who, much to her dismay, turns out to be gay. In teen films, those students who fulfil normative conceptions of femininity and masculinity are at the top of the high school hierarchy, but a look at them ten years later often reveals high school popularity to be a façade that neither reflects who an individual really is nor necessarily implies greater chances to succeed as an adult.[29] In the case of *Zack and Miri Make a Porno*, the popular guy's homosexuality confirms that the performance of heteronormativity involved in high school popularity – especially at prom – is a sham.

Additionally, other films show former outcasts as the most successful adults and popular types as stuck in their high school persona, reverting the hierarchical structure of the high school. For instance, in both *Romy and Michele's High School Reunion* and *Grosse Pointe Blank* (George Armitage, 1997), former nerds succeed as adults thanks to the same interest in technology that made them outcasts as teenagers. Despite this commentary on adult success, these films also question what exactly constitutes a successful transition to adulthood. Jobs in sales, insurance and advertising are consistently positioned as undesirable, chosen only by those who are unable to think outside the box. Staying in one's hometown is also depicted as negative. For instance, *Adult Beginners* (Ross Katz, 2014) pokes fun at the life of those who have chosen to stay in their hometown and pursue small managerial roles in local companies, while the protagonist in *The Lifeguard* (Liz W. García, 2013) fails to see her friend's job as assistant principal at their old high school in a positive light.

A temporary move back home forces the protagonists to confront their family. In these cases, both parents and siblings serve as a counterpoint to the protagonist's arrested development. While parents have to deal with their child's failure to fulfil their expectations, siblings – both older and younger – often have to adopt a caretaking role or show greater maturity than the protagonists. *Standing Up, Falling Down* (Matt Ratner, 2019) is a rare example in which the protagonist's younger sibling is in an even worse position regarding the transition to adulthood. While thirty-four-year-old Scott (Ben Schwartz) at least moved to LA and tried to make it as a comedian, his thirty-year-old sister does not seem to have left the parental home. In this film, standard adulthood is embodied by the protagonist's parents, ex-girlfriend and high school friend, who now considers 9 p.m. a late time to be out. Scott's father believes it is time for his son to give up 'this fantasy land bullshit' and get a real job, and he is bitter that he did not manage to get Scott involved in the family business. In other instances, as in *Unicorn Store* (Brie Larson, 2017), parents try to pressure their boomerang child into behaving like someone that they consider an adult role model. In this film parents feel exasperation at their child's return, which often happens in homecoming narratives. Some of them, like *The Lifeguard* and *Unicorn Store*, feature parents who were happy to have a spare room to dedicate to their hobbies and see their plans interrupted by their children's return.

A return home upsets the balance of the household as different family members need to revert into roles that they had already left behind or adapt into new roles. The stagnancy of the emerging adult protagonists' road to adulthood is often underscored by their younger siblings showing greater maturity than them. For instance, in *Tiny Furniture* (Lena Dunham, 2010), Aura (Lena Dunham) returns home after graduation and finds her younger sister Nadine (Cyrus Dunham) ready to take on the world, while Aura is depleted and lost after leaving college. Framing conveys the distance between the two sisters as well as their different outlooks. They are often physically separated by a dividing line or sitting at different levels, with Nadine sitting higher up than Aura. In one occasion, Aura can be seen on the sofa while Nadine runs on a treadmill, a visual metaphor for their respective outlooks on life. While Aura is not ready for adulthood, Nadine cannot wait to get there.

As in the other instances, balance needs to be redrawn for the relationships between family members and old friends to recover from the strain that the protagonists' arrested development causes. More often than not, the protagonists' return home involves the sowing of the seeds of change. That is to say, while the films rarely end with the protagonist's full transition to adulthood, they often end with the beginning of a change in outlook that will help them make progress towards a type of adulthood that works for them while remaining tolerant of those who chose more conventional paths. In any case, the kind of standard adulthood embodied by old classmates and parents remains something to avoid rather than a goal, which once again reflects changing attitudes towards contemporary adulthood as well as changes in the nature of adulthood itself.

Conclusion

As we have seen, filmic representations of the transition to adulthood engage with the same issues as the scholarship on the subject. Through characters who represent standard adulthood, films ultimately reject it, portraying it as too rigid and characterless. This sets the emerging adult protagonists in opposition with standard adulthood and in search of something else. Even though most films do not depict traditional markers of adulthood as completely out of reach, they do position them as undesirable, which in turn forces the protagonists to figure out different ways to grow up. One of the main dilemmas faced by the protagonists in all these films is how to be able to live independently as adults without losing their identity – and their youthfulness – in the process. That is, emerging adult film protagonists are in search of new ways to be an adult that will differentiate them from the previous generations and from those following a standard route. Through this snapshot of the contrast between standard adulthood and emerging adulthood, contemporary film can be argued to support theories of a 'new adulthood' in which adulthood is more fluid than in the past decades and retains certain features that were hitherto associated with youth.[30] The mere existence and prominence of this new type of coming-of-age film that engages with alternative ways to become an adult suggests that the end-point of the coming-of-age process is shifting, and that the entrenched view of adulthood that took hold in the mid-twentieth century no longer constitutes a valid model.

Notes

1. The writing of this chapter was supported by the Spanish Ministry of Science and Innovation under grant PID2021-123836NB-I00 and the Aragonese Regional Government (DGA) under grant H23_20R.

2. Rachel Aroesti, 'How Messy Millennial Woman Became TV's Most Tedious Trope', *The Guardian*, 9 June 2022, www.theguardian.com/tv-and-radio/2022/jun/09/messy-millennial-woman-tv-trope-everything-i-know-about-love-this-way-up, accessed 31 July 2024. Even though Aroesti's article focuses exclusively on television narratives, this character type also became ubiquitous in films from the early 2010s on. Some of these changes began to crystallise – and make their way into American cinema – in the late 1960s, but it was not until the 1990s that longer transitions to adulthood became the norm (Jeffrey Jensen Arnett, *Emerging Adulthood: The Long and Winding Road from the Late Teens through the Twenties* (Oxford: Oxford University Press, 2004)) and narratives about emerging adulthood became more numerous (Andrea Sofía Regueira Martín, 'Growing Up Is Hard to Do: The Emerging Adult Film' (PhD thesis, University of Zaragoza, 2022)).

3. Regueira Martín, 'Growing Up Is Hard to Do'.

4. Arnett, *Emerging Adulthood*.

5. Arnett, *Emerging Adulthood*, 6. Following Harry Blatterer (*Coming of Age in Times of Uncertainty* (New York: Berghahn Books, 2007)) and Nick Lee (*Childhood and Society: Growing Up in an Age of Uncertainty* (Buckingham: Open University Press, 2001)), I use the term 'standard adulthood' to refer to the particular mode of adulthood that became prevalent in the United States in the decades in the mid-twentieth century. Arnett (*Emerging Adulthood*) refers to this model as 'traditional conceptions of adulthood' (208).

6. Even though Arnett (*Emerging Adulthood*) writes about individuals in their twenties, I have not set a specific chronological end-boundary in the films I analyse, allowing the films themselves to guide my classification. Films often engage with the last stages of the transition to adulthood. As a result, although most of the emerging adult protagonists in the films discussed are in their late twenties, a small number of them may be in their thirties. Allusions to the protagonists' age will be made when considered relevant.

7. Kenneth Keniston, 'Youth: A "New" Stage of Life', *The American Scholar* 39, no. 4 (1970): 631–54; Daniel J. Levinson, *The Seasons of a Man's Life* (New York: Knopf, 1978); Susan Littwin, *The Postponed Generation: Why American Youth Are Growing Up Later* (New York: Morrow, 1986); Erik H. Erikson, *Identity and the Life Cycle* (New York: W. W. Norton & Company, 1959); Erik H. Erikson, *The Life Cycle Completed*, extended version (New York: W. W. Norton & Company, 1982), 75.

8. Jeffrey Jensen Arnett and Susan Taber, 'Adolescence Terminable and Interminable: When Does Adolescence End?', *Journal of Youth and Adolescence* 23, no. 5 (1994): 515–37.

9. Kenneth Keniston, *Youth and Dissent: The Rise of a New Opposition* (New York: Harcourt Brace Jovanovich, 1971), 5.

10. John Modell, *Into One's Own: From Youth to Adulthood in the United States 1920–1975* (Berkeley, CA: University of California Press, 1989); Arnett, *Emerging Adulthood*.

11. Modell, *Into One's Own*; Arnett, *Emerging Adulthood*.

12. Even though all the authors cited in this section focus on the United States, similar trends can be observed in other post-industrialised countries. For instance, in the case of Spain these changes can be observed but they took place later than in the United States due to a number of political and socio-economic factors related to the Francoist dictatorship (Joice Melo Vieira and Pau Miret Gamundi, 'Transición a la Vida Adulta en España: Una Comparación en el Tiempo y en el Territorio Utilizando el Análisis de la Entropía', *Revista Española de Investigaciones Sociológicas* 131 (2010): 75–107).

13. Jennifer M. Silva, *Coming Up Short: Working-Class Adulthood in an Age of Uncertainty* (Oxford: Oxford University Press, 2013).

14. Ulrich Beck and Elisabeth Beck-Gernsheim, *Individualization: Institutionalized Individualism and Its Social and Political Consequences* (London: Sage, 2002).

15. Ulrich Beck, *Risk Society: Towards a New Modernity*, trans. Mark Ritter (London: Sage, 1992); Zygmunt Bauman, *Liquid Modernity* (Cambridge: Polity, 2000); Zygmunt Bauman, *Liquid Times: Living in an Age of Uncertainty* (Cambridge: Polity, 2007).

16. Bauman, *Liquid Modernity*, 147.

17. Arnett, *Emerging Adulthood*.

18. Johanna Wyn, Helen Cahill, Dan Woodman, Hernán Cuervo, Carmen Leccardi and Jenny Chesters, eds. *Youth and the New Adulthood: Generations of Change. Perspectives on Children and Young People* (Singapore: Springer Nature Singapore, 2020).

19. Blatterer, *Coming of Age in Times of Uncertainty*, 114.

20. Regueira Martín, 'Growing Up Is Hard to Do'.

21. Blatterer, *Coming of Age in Times of Uncertainty*; Silva, *Coming Up Short*.

22. Andrew Van Dam, 'The Unluckiest Generation in U.S. History', *The Washington Post*, 5 June 2020, www.washingtonpost.com/business/2020/05/27/millennial-recession-covid, accessed 31 July 2024; Kristen Bialik and Richard Fry, 'Millennial Life: How Young Adulthood Today Compares with Prior Generations', Pew Research Center, 2019, www.pewresearch.org/social-trends/2019/02/14/millennial-life-how-young-adulthood-today-compares-with-prior-generations-2, accessed 31 July 2024.

23. Despite the fact that two of the examples mentioned in this section feature non-white protagonists, emerging adult films are overwhelmingly white and fail to represent the racial diversity of the United States. More diverse characters began to appear in these narratives in the late 2010s, but protagonists of colour appear in only 10 per cent of the sixty-one films from the 2010s that made up the corpus of my PhD thesis (Regueira Martín, 'Growing Up Is Hard to Do').

24. Zygmunt Bauman, *Liquid Love: On the Frailty of Human Bonds* (Cambridge: Polity, 2003).

25. Mark Greif, 'What Was the Hipster?', *New York Magazine*, 22 October 2010, https://nymag.com/news/features/69129, accessed 31 July 2024.

26. Even though this may come across as a breaking of gender barriers due to the longstanding association of women and emotional labour, it is worth noting that Dewey's approach uses rock music – a field traditionally dominated by men – to further the self-development of his students. Hints of change may be indicated in the fact that students of all genders are equally empowered by his approach.

27. D. Nicole Farris, *Boomerang Kids: The Demography of Previously Launched Adults* (New York: Springer, 2016); Carl Pickhardt, *Boomerang Kids: A Revealing Look at Why So Many of Our Children Are Failing on Their Own and How Parents Can Help* (Naperville, IL: Sourcebooks, 2011).

28. Regueira Martín, 'Growing Up Is Hard to Do'.

29. Frances Smith, *Rethinking the Hollywood Teen Movie: Gender, Genre and Identity* (Edinburgh: Edinburgh University Press, 2017), 72.

30. Blatterer, *Coming of Age in Times of Uncertainty*; Wyn et al., *Youth and the New Adulthood*.

References

Films

Armitage, George, director. *Grosse Pointe Blank*. Buena Vista Pictures, 1997. 1 hr. 47 min. DVD.

Badham, John, director. *Saturday Night Fever*. Paramount Pictures, 1977. 1 hr. 59 min. DVD.

Baumbach, Noah, director. *Frances Ha*. IFC Films, 2013. 1 hr. 25 min. DVD.

Bennett, Theresa, director. *Social Animals*. Paramount Pictures, 2018. 1 hr. 30 min. DVD.

Dunham, Lena, director. *Tiny Furniture*. IFC Films, 2010. 1 hr. 38 min. DVD.

Fogel, Susanna, director. *Life Partners*. Magnolia Pictures, 2014. 1 hr. 33 min. DVD.

García, Liz W., director. *The Lifeguard*. Focus World, 2013. 1 hr. 38 min. DVD.

Holofcener, Nicole, director. *Walking and Talking*. Miramax Films, 1996. 1 hr. 26 min. DVD.

Katz, Ross, director. *Adult Beginners*. Universal Pictures, 2014. 1 hr. 30 min. DVD.

Khan, Nahnatchka, director. *Always Be My Maybe*. Netflix, 2019. 1 hr. 42 min. www.netflix.com/title/80202874.

Larson, Brie, director. *Unicorn Store*. Netflix, 2017. 1 hr. 32 min. www.netflix.com/title/81034317.

Linklater, Richard, director. *School of Rock*. Paramount Pictures, 2003. 1 hr. 49 min. DVD.

Mirkin, David, director. *Romy and Michele's High School Reunion*. Buena Vista Pictures, 1997. 1 hr. 32 min. DVD.

Rattner, Matt, director. *Standing Up, Falling Down*. Shout! Studios, 2019. 1 hr. 31 min. DVD.

Robinson, Jennifer Kaytin, director. *Someone Great*. Netflix, 2019. 1 hr. 32 min. www.netflix.com/es-en/title/80202920.

Smith, Kevin, director. *Zack and Miri Make a Porno*. The Weinstein Company, 2008. 1 hr. 42 min. DVD.

Travis, Jamie, director. *For a Good Time Call ....* Focus Features, 2012. 1 hr. 25 min. DVD.

Printed texts

Arnett, Jeffrey Jensen. 'Emerging Adulthood: A Theory of Development from the Late Teens Through the Twenties', *American Psychologist* 55, no. 5 (2000): 469–80.

Arnett, Jeffrey Jensen. *Emerging Adulthood: The Long and Winding Road from the Late Teens through the Twenties.* Oxford: Oxford University Press, 2004.

Arnett, Jeffrey Jensen and Taber, Susan. 'Adolescence Terminable and Interminable: When Does Adolescence End?', *Journal of Youth and Adolescence* 23, no. 5 (1994): 515–37.

Aroesti, Rachel. 'How Messy Millennial Woman Became TV's Most Tedious Trope', *The Guardian*, 9 June 2022. www.theguardian.com/tv-and-radio/2022/jun/09/messy-millennial-woman-tv-trope-everything-i-know-about-love-this-way-up, accessed 31 July 2024.

Bauman, Zygmunt. *Liquid Modernity.* Cambridge: Polity, 2000.

Bauman, Zygmunt. *Liquid Love: On the Frailty of Human Bonds.* Cambridge: Polity, 2003.

Bauman, Zygmunt. *Liquid Times: Living in an Age of Uncertainty.* Cambridge: Polity, 2007.

Beck, Ulrich. *Risk Society: Towards a New Modernity*, trans. Mark Ritter. London: Sage, 1992.

Beck, Ulrich and Beck-Gernsheim, Elisabeth. *Individualization: Institutionalized Individualism and Its Social and Political Consequences.* London: Sage, 2002.

Bialik, Kristen and Fry, Richard. 'Millennial Life: How Young Adulthood Today Compares with Prior Generations', Pew Research Center, 2019. www.pewresearch.org/social-trends/2019/02/14/millennial-life-how-young-adulthood-today-compares-with-prior-generations-2, accessed 31 July 2024.

Blatterer, Harry. *Coming of Age in Times of Uncertainty.* New York: Berghahn Books, 2007.

Côté, James E. 'The Dangerous Myth of Emerging Adulthood: An Evidence-Based Critique of a Flawed Developmental Theory', *Applied Developmental Science* 18, no. 4 (2014): 177–88.

Erikson, Erik H. *Identity and the Life Cycle.* New York: W. W. Norton & Company, 1959.

Erikson, Erik H. *The Life Cycle Completed.* Extended version. New York: W. W. Norton & Company, 1982.

Farris, Nicole D. *Boomerang Kids: The Demography of Previously Launched Adults.* New York: Springer, 2016.

Greif, Mark. 'What Was the Hipster?', *New York Magazine*, 22
October 2010. https://nymag.com/news/features/69129, accessed 31
July 2024.

Keniston, Kenneth. 'Youth: A "New" Stage of Life', *The American Scholar*
39, no. 4 (1970): 631–54.

Keniston, Kenneth. *Youth and Dissent: The Rise of a New Opposition.*
New York: Harcourt Brace Jovanovich, 1971.

Lee, Nick. *Childhood and Society: Growing Up in an Age of Uncertainty.*
Buckingham: Open University Press, 2001.

Levinson, Daniel J. *The Seasons of a Man's Life*. New York: Knopf, 1978.

Littwin, Susan. *The Postponed Generation: Why American Youth Are
Growing Up Later.* New York: Morrow, 1986.

Melo Vieira, Joice and Miret Gamundi, Pau. 'Transición a la Vida Adulta
en España: Una Comparación en el Tiempo y en el Territorio
Utilizando el Análisis de la Entropía', *Revista Española de
Investigaciones Sociológicas* 131 (2010): 75–107.

Modell, John. *Into One's Own: From Youth to Adulthood in the United
States 1920–1975.* Berkeley, CA: University of California Press, 1989.

Pickhardt, Carl. *Boomerang Kids: A Revealing Look at Why So Many of
Our Children Are Failing on Their Own and How Parents Can Help.*
Naperville, IL: Sourcebooks, 2011.

Regueira Martín, Andrea Sofía. 'Growing Up Is Hard to Do: The
Emerging Adult Film'. PhD thesis, University of Zaragoza, 2022.

Silva, Jennifer M. *Coming Up Short: Working-Class Adulthood in an Age of
Uncertainty.* Oxford: Oxford University Press, 2013.

Smith, Frances. *Rethinking the Hollywood Teen Movie: Gender, Genre and
Identity.* Edinburgh: Edinburgh University Press, 2017.

Van Dam, Andrew. 'The Unluckiest Generation in U.S. History'. *The
Washington Post*, 5 June 2020. www.washingtonpost.com/business
/2020/05/27/millennial-recession-covid, accessed 31 July 2024.

Wyn, Johanna, Cahill, Helen, Woodman, Dan, Cuervo, Hernán,
Leccardi, Carmen and Chesters, Jenny eds. *Youth and the New
Adulthood: Generations of Change.* Perspectives on Children and
Young People. Singapore: Springer Nature Singapore, 2020.

Afterword: Against adulthood

Kristine Alexander

Adulthood, it turns out, is many things: a relationally constructed social category, a context-specific legal status and (for some people more than others) an empty promise. Not necessarily a milestone and not always a crisis, adulthood – as the contributors to this book make clear – has been imposed, aspired to, denied, rejected and contested in multiple ways over the past six centuries. Focusing on the territories currently known as Great Britain and the United States, this volume charts continuity and change while highlighting the complicated ways in which cultural expectations informed individual lives. Like whiteness, adulthood functions in much historical scholarship as an invisible norm.[1] The entwined and often taken-for-granted histories of adulthood and whiteness need to be understood as outcomes of the 'economy of affirmation and forgetting' that, according to Lisa Lowe, is at the heart of modern liberal humanism.[2] Thinking intersectionally about age and adulthood across time and space, as this book begins to do, offers significant insights about power, lived experience and the construction of hierarchies. It can also encourage us to question the ways of thinking that have, in many contexts, empowered 'adults' at the expense of others.

Ranging chronologically from the medieval period to the (post)modern present, the chapters in this volume historicise adulthood by looking critically and creatively at a wide range of primary documents. From fourteenth-century poetry to early modern visual culture to eighteenth-century dictionaries and satirical texts, the evidence marshalled here reveals a valuable *longue durée* story about time and the multiplicity of life stages. This usefully complicates the still pervasive assumption that the late eighteenth-century 'age of reason' represented a decisive break with popular understandings of adulthood that came before. The chapters that explore the nineteenth and twentieth centuries analyse a still broader range of sources including legal records, news media, life-writing, oral history interviews, feature films and the pronouncements of experts in the fields of medicine, social work, education, psychology and psychiatry. Some of these case studies feature first-person reflections about the meanings and experiences of adulthood, while others focus on how self-proclaimed adults (who were, unsurprisingly, often white men) made claims about the maturity and capacity of others.

A number of the book's chapters discuss lives shaped by what Holly N.S. White and Julia M. Goddard call 'double age' – the process through which some individuals are ascribed a functional age that differs from their chronological one.[3] Two of the most striking examples of this phenomenon appear in case studies by Jack Hodgson and Laura Tisdall, each of which traces the uneven distribution of developmentally defined rights and protections (associated variously with 'childhood' and 'adulthood') among boys and girls who had yet to attain the age of legal majority. Focusing on murder cases in the United States between the eighteenth and twentieth centuries, Hodgson highlights a number of ways in which non-white youngsters have consistently received harsher judicial treatment than their white counterparts. His work demonstrates that the association of (white) childhood with innocence, redeemability and the need for protection could – and often did – have devastating consequences for the young people who were excluded from this category.[4] Tisdall's chapter, meanwhile, addresses the structural racism of British schooling in the 1970s and 1980s by tracing the different ways in which African-Caribbean and South Asian adolescents were pathologised by teachers and social workers for their apparent failure to conform to 'normal' timelines of physical, emotional and intellectual development. White supremacy, Tisdall argues, led these young people – in ways they and their parents often contested – to be seen variously as 'adultified children and child-like adolescents'.

These case studies exemplify the claim, made by Tisdall and Maria Cannon in the Introduction to this volume, that 'understanding adulthood is crucial to understanding power'. They also provide clear evidence that the history of adulthood – like the history of childhood – cannot be disentangled from histories of colonialism and race.[5] The findings of this book as a whole, in fact, need to be understood in the context of a centuries-long Anglo-American chronology of empire, Indigenous dispossession, white settlement and slavery. While medieval Europeans were developing dynamic understandings of 'the ages of man', for example, the original inhabitants of North America – Indigenous peoples who would later be categorised by white settler colonisers as incapable and improvident children – approached ageing and intergenerational relations in ways characterised by collectivity, responsibility and reciprocity.[6] The early modern religious and demographic shifts discussed in Chapters 2 and 3 occurred in tandem with English (and later British) attempts to establish colonies on Indigenous lands in what is now the eastern seaboard of the United States. And by the time the figure of the embarrassing and irrelevant old 'fogram' emerged in late eighteenth-century British society and culture, the United Kingdom had come to dominate the transatlantic trade in enslaved African people.

The permanent migration of millions of white Britons to colonies in the so-called 'New World' began in earnest at the same time, and coincided with a new Anglo-American emphasis (in politics, Protestant Christianity and English common law) on age, reason and consent.[7] The emergence of this Manichean understanding of malleable, vulnerable and incapable children and capable, autonomous, rights-bearing adults culminated, as Holly Brewer has written, in the apparently 'natural' legal incapacitation of children and those who could be compared to children.[8] This unequal and metaphorical understanding of adulthood and childhood was used, as several scholars have written, to justify slavery and empire in a wide range of contexts from the late eighteenth century on.[9] It was also at the heart of what Ishita Pande, writing about late nineteenth- and early twentieth-century India, has called the liberal epistemic contract on age: the 'implicit agreement that age is a *natural* measure of legal capacity for all humans'.[10]

The uneven affordances of the category of adulthood, so clearly linked to histories of race and empire, were also centrally about gender. The association between adulthood and normative masculinity, reinforced through the status given to traits like authority, strength and gravitas, is a consistent thread that runs throughout this volume. These masculine ideals were constructed relationally, often through the infantilisation of women – as demonstrated, for instance, by Holly N.S. White's argument that nineteenth-century American parents and judges often struggled to understand unmarried women as anything other than childlike dependants. The persistence of this way of thinking is evident in Kristin Hay's analysis of Scottish debates about the birth control pill in the decade and a half after 1968; unmarried women, she finds, 'were disproportionately represented as inherently juvenile – regardless of their age – and lacking the key social indicators which made them independent adults'. The association of maturity with masculinity also shaped individuals' employment chances in mid-twentieth-century Britain, as Grace Whorrall-Campbell's chapter shows. The psychological and psychiatric experts hired by the British army, the British civil service and Unilever during the mid-twentieth century, she writes, found it hard to imagine that women, gay men and working-class people might be capable of maturely (or 'convincingly') wielding authority in the workplace.

Looking closely at gender also demonstrates a number of links between the history of adulthood and the history of emotions. The valorisation of masculine emotional restraint as a hallmark of adulthood was central, as Emily E. Robson's chapter shows, to early modern British Protestant ministers' assertions about their superior spiritual maturity. A similar gendered belief in the value of emotional control shaped employment cultures in Britain some 400 years later, as shown by Whorrall-Campbell's analysis of the preferences of mid-twentieth-century psychological selection boards. The idealisation of emotional control as a somehow inherently masculine and 'adult' trait, she writes, 'marked a number of overlapping and mutually reinforcing hierarchies'. Other chapters in the book discuss anger (at supposedly entitled young women enjoying premarital sex without consequences), frustration (as experienced by some disabled Britons in their pursuit of sexual intimacy, love and marriage) and fear – of the decline associated with ageing and of imagined threats to the social order posed by non-white children.

These are strong emotions, and the stakes involved are substantial. Taking an intersectional approach to the history of age and empire is therefore a political as well as an intellectual project, and I agree with Tisdall and Cannon's argument that 'historicising adulthood should not just mean demonstrating the unfairness of the exclusion of non-adults from this category, but questioning the usefulness of the category itself'. The late twentieth- and early twentieth-century 'emerging adult' films discussed in Andrea Sofía Regueira Martín's chapter offer one critique of the project of adulthood, although – as she notes – the viewpoints they represent are firmly rooted in the white American middle class. Queer, antiracist and Black feminist theory offer still more useful tools for questioning the pervasiveness of our attachment to what Habiba Ibrahim describes as the ideal of 'the possessive individual, the free-willed subject, a normative gender binary, [and] a presumptive separation between public and private life'.[11] Embracing interdependence and 'reading sideways' (a method proposed by Ishita Pande, using the work of Kathryn Bond Stockton) are good places to begin, as is a willingness to reckon with failure – in our own 'adult' lives and in the scholarship we produce.[12] As queer theorist Jack Halberstam reminds us, failure (an outcome that Western children and adults are both taught to fear) can sometimes be rewarding – not least because it can allow us 'to escape the punishing norms that discipline behaviour and manage human development with the goal of delivering us from unruly childhoods to orderly and predictable adulthoods'.[13]

Notes

1. Richard Dyer, *White: Essays on Race and Culture* (New York: Routledge, 1997).

2. Lisa Lowe, *Intimacies of Four Continents* (Durham, NC: Duke University Press, 2015), 39.

3. Holly N.S. White and Julia M. Goddard, 'Considering "Double Age" in the History of American Childhood and Youth: An Introduction', *Journal of the History of Childhood and Youth* 15, no. 3 (2022): 355–61.

4. Robin Bernstein, *Racial Innocence: Performing American Childhood from Slavery to Civil Rights* (New York: New York University Press, 2011); Crystal Webster, '"Hanging Pretty Girls": The Criminalization of African American Children in Early America', *Journal of the Early Republic* 42, no. 2 (2022): 253–76.

5. Kristine Alexander and Simon Sleight, 'Introduction', in *A Cultural History of Youth in the Modern Age* (London: Bloomsbury, 2022), 9; Ishita Pande, 'Is the History of Childhood Ready for the World? A Response to "The Kids Aren't All Right"', *American Historical Review* 125, no. 4 (2020): 1304.

6. Sandy Grande, 'The Biopolitics of Aging: Indigenous Elders as Elsewhere', in Rene Dietrich and Kerstin Knopf eds., *Biopolitics, Geopolitics, Life: Settler States and Indigenous Presence* (Durham, NC: Duke University Press, 2023), 67–84; Leanne Betasamosake Simpson, *Dancing on Our Turtle's Back: Stories of Nishnaabeg Re-Creation, Resurgence, and a New Emergence* (Winnipeg: Arbeiter Ring Publishing, 2011), chapter 7; Susan Sleeper-Smith et al., eds., *Why You Can't Teach United States History without American Indians* (Chapel Hill, NC: University of North Carolina Press, 2015).

7. James Belich, *Replenishing the Earth: The Settler Revolution and the Rise of the Anglo-World, 1783–1939* (Oxford: Oxford University Press, 2011).

8. Holly Brewer, *By Birth or Consent: Children, Law, and the Anglo-American Revolution in Authority* (Chapel Hill, NC: University of North Carolina Press, 2007).

9. Ann Laura Stoler, *Race and the Education of Desire: Foucault's History of Sexuality and the Colonial Order of Things* (Durham, NC: Duke University Press, 1995); Uday Singh Mehta, *Liberalism and Empire: A Study in Nineteenth-Century British Liberal Thought* (Chicago, IL: University of Chicago Press, 1999); Anna Mae Duane, ed., *Child Slavery before and after Emancipation: An Argument for Child-Centred Slavery Studies* (Cambridge: Cambridge University Press, 2017); S.E. Duff, *Children and Youth in African History* (Cham: Springer International Publishing, 2022), chapter 4.

10. Ishita Pande, *Sex, Law, and the Politics of Age: Child Marriage in India, 1891–1937* (Cambridge: Cambridge University Press, 2020).

11. Habiba Ibrahim, *Black Age: Oceanic Lifespans and the Time of Black Life* (New York: New York University Press, 2021), 158.

12. My thinking about these questions is inspired by Pande, *Sex, Law, and the Politics of Age*; Kathryn Bond Stockton, *The Queer Child, or Growing Sideways in the Twentieth Century* (Durham, NC: Duke University Press, 2009); Sara Ahmed, *The Promise of Happiness* (Durham, NC: Duke University Press, 2010); and John Wall, 'From Childhood Studies to Childism: Reconstructing the Scholarly and Social Imaginations', *Children's Geographies* 20, no. 3 (2022): 257–70.

13. Jack Halberstam, *The Queer Art of Failure* (Durham, NC: Duke University Press, 2011), 3.

References

Ahmed, Sara. *The Promise of Happiness*. Durham, NC: Duke University Press, 2010.

Alexander, Kristine, and Sleight, Simon. 'Introduction', in *A Cultural History of Youth in the Modern Age*. London: Bloomsbury, 2022, 1–18.

Belich, James. *Replenishing the Earth: The Settler Revolution and the Rise of the Anglo-World, 1783–1939*. Oxford: Oxford University Press, 2011.

Bernstein, Robin. *Racial Innocence: Performing American Childhood from Slavery to Civil Rights*. New York: New York University Press, 2011.

Brewer, Holly. *By Birth or Consent: Children, Law, and the Anglo-American Revolution in Authority*. Chapel Hill, NC: University of North Carolina Press, 2007.

Duane, Anna Mae ed. *Child Slavery before and after Emancipation: An Argument for Child-Centred Slavery Studies*. Cambridge: Cambridge University Press, 2017.

Duff, S.E. *Children and Youth in African History*. Cham: Springer International Publishing, 2022.

Dyer, Richard. *White: Essays on Race and Culture*. New York: Routledge, 1997.

Grande, Sandy. 'The Biopolitics of Aging: Indigenous Elders as Elsewhere', in Rene Dietrich and Kerstin Knopf eds., *Biopolitics, Geopolitics, Life: Settler States and Indigenous Presence*. Durham, NC: Duke University Press, 2023, 67–84.

Halberstam, Jack. *The Queer Art of Failure*. Durham, NC: Duke University Press, 2011.

Ibrahim, Habiba. *Black Age: Oceanic Lifespans and the Time of Black Life*. New York: New York University Press, 2021.

Lowe, Lisa. *Intimacies of Four Continents*. Durham, NC: Duke University Press, 2015.

Mehta, Uday Singh. *Liberalism and Empire: A Study in Nineteenth-Century British Liberal Thought*. Chicago, IL: University of Chicago Press, 1999.

Pande, Ishita. 'Is the History of Childhood Ready for the World? A Response to "The Kids Aren't All Right"', *American Historical Review* 125, no. 4 (2020): 1300–1305.

Pande, Ishita. *Sex, Law, and the Politics of Age: Child Marriage in India, 1891–1937*. Cambridge: Cambridge University Press, 2020.

Simpson, Leanne Betasamosake. *Dancing on Our Turtle's Back: Stories of Nishnaabeg Re-Creation, Resurgence, and a New Emergence*. Winnipeg: Arbeiter Ring Publishing, 2011.

Sleeper-Smith, Susan et al., eds, *Why You Can't Teach United States History without American Indians*. Chapel Hill, NC: University of North Carolina Press, 2015.

Stockton, Kathryn Bond. *The Queer Child, or Growing Sideways in the Twentieth Century*. Durham, NC: Duke University Press, 2009.

Stoler, Ann Laura. *Race and the Education of Desire: Foucault's History of Sexuality and the Colonial Order of Things*. Durham, NC: Duke University Press, 1995.

Wall, John. 'From Childhood Studies to Childism: Reconstructing the Scholarly and Social Imaginations', *Children's Geographies* 20, no. 3 (2022): 257–70.

Webster, Crystal. '"Hanging Pretty Girls": The Criminalization of African American Children in Early America', *Journal of the Early Republic* 42, no. 2 (2022): 253–76.

White, Holly N.S. and Goddard, Julia M. 'Considering "Double Age" in the History of American Childhood and Youth: An Introduction', *Journal of the History of Childhood and Youth* 15, no. 3 (2022): 355–61.

Index

A

Aberdeen, Scotland, 178, 184
ableism, 13, 224, 231n7
abortion, 172, 248
abuse, 130, 205, 218, 219, 222, 228
   sexual, 227
activism, 131, 197, 199, 203, 205–207, 219,
   221, 222, 228–9
Addington, Mary, 133, 135
adolescence, 2–5, 8, 9, 10, 12, 25, 29, 30,
   54, 94, 156, 175, 179, 181, 182, 186,
   194–5, 197, 199, 200, 205, 206, 207,
   240, 243
   and disability, 229
   definitions of, 91–3
   extension of, 13
   opposed to adulthood, 203, 239
   physical signs of, 71
   stages of, 202
adulthood
   and 'ages of man', 45–59
   in American court systems, 111–22,
      127–40
   and chronological age. *See* age
   in disabled people's lives, 215–30
   in eighteenth-century England, 89–105
   emerging, 8, 13, 239–52
   gendered understandings of, 112–15
   historicisation of, 3–5
   in late Cold War Britain, 193–208
   as problematic concept, 259–62
   rejection of, 239–52
   as stage of change and development,
      50–55
   through time, 8–11
   in twentieth-century Scotland,
      171–87
   young. *See* 'young adulthood'
'adultification', 11, 130, 138, 194, 199, 229,
   260
Aeneas, 48
African Americans, 7, 12, 112, 130–31, 136,
   140
African-Caribbeans, 12, 13, 193–208, 260
Afro-Caribbean Education Resource
   Project (ACER), 195–6, 198, 201, 203,
   204, 206

age
   chronological, 1, 2, 4, 5–8, 9–10, 29, 29,
      30, 46, 49, 71, 78, 79, 90, 94, 115, 116,
      121, 152, 193, 216, 260
   cultural, 46, 90
   of discretion. *See* discretion, age of
   'double', 6
   functional, 5, 6, 46, 90, 260
   'mental', 137, 216
   middle. *See* middle age
   old. *See* old age
'age consciousness', 7
ageing, 26, 29, 31, 36, 47, 52, 54, 55, 58,
   73, 90, 93, 96, 97–8, 99, 117, 260, 262
'ages of man', 8, 9, 12, 29, 45–59
   'ages of woman', 55–8
alcohol, consumption of, 1
Alighieri, Dante, 35, 36
Anstey, Christopher, 101
apprentices, 91, 113
Aristotle, 30, 51, 55, 70
Arminianism, 73
Arnett, Jeffrey, 8, 181, 239, 240, 241
asexuality, 217
Ash, John, 92, 93, 94
Asian Youth Movements (AYMs), 206
Asotin, Washington, 133, 134
asthma, 78
Augustine of Hippo, 34, 35
Austin, H. Z., 137
Austin, Texas, 246

B

'baby boomers', 171
Bacon, Francis, 75
Bailey, Nathan, 92, 93
Bainbridge, David, 26, 27
Bakersfield, California, 136
baptism, 72
Barr, Hugh, 116, 118
Barron, David, 227
bastardy, 115, 123n18
Bath, Somerset, 101
Battye, Louis, 216, 220
beards, 47–8
Beasley, Joshua Keith, 127
Bellers, Fulk, 77

267

268   INDEX

Benson, John, 26, 27
Bentick, John, 92, 94
Birgitta of Sweden, 37
birth control. *See* contraception
Board of Control, 217
Bolles, Eunice, 129
Borja, Jesus, 136–7, 139
Botelho, Lynn, 72, 90
Bowlby, John, 153
Boys Town, Nebraska, 135–6
Brace, Charles Loring, 131
Bradford, Yorkshire, 205
Briggs, Lewis, 118, 119–20
Briggs, Rosanna, 119–20
Briggs v. Evans, 118
British Empire, 6, 7, 10, 11, 205
Brockham Park, Surrey, 154
Bronk-Bacon, Katarzyna, 96, 100
Brook Advisory Service, 179
Broughton, Richard, 69
Brown, Fred, 226
Browne, Stella, 174
Bunyan, John, 55
Burgess, Anthony, 70–71, 72

C

California, 136, 137, 138
Calvinism, 67
Cammack, James, 133
canon law, 34
capital punishment. *See* death
    penalty
Carrier, Martha, 128
Carrier, Sarah, 128
Carrier, Thomas, 128
Cartwright, Thomas, 78
Catholicism, 69, 176, 218
Central America, 11–12
cerebral palsy, 215, 216, 217, 225
Chaderton, Laurence, 75
Chalmers, Rosalind, 220
'child-savers', 131
childbirth, 28, 200–201
childhood, 2, 9, 25, 30, 45–6, 50, 56, 92,
    93, 103, 121, 156, 162, 194, 195, 200,
    207, 216, 220, 227, 230, 243, 249, 261,
    262
  concepts of, 3
  end of, 70–71, 90–91
  hazards of, 28
  innocence and, 128, 140, 260
  institutionalised, 229
  'invention of', 89
  piety, 72–5
  political understandings of, 5
  psychoanalytical views of, 150, 159
  right to, 135

stealing of, 10–11
as unstable, 8
childishness, 1, 3, 11, 12, 13, 35, 37, 69–70,
    72, 73, 74, 77, 80, 135, 156, 159, 205
Choate, Jack, 70, 127
Christie, Evelyn G., 200
Christine de Pizan, 36
Cistercians, 4
citizenship, 2, 113
  'intimate', 228
civil service, 149, 152–3, 155, 158, 261
Civil Service Selection Board, 13, 152, 155,
    160, 161–2
Civil War, English, 68
Clark, Hugh, 75
Clarke, Samuel, 68, 75, 78, 79
class, 2, 90, 116, 128, 129, 132, 160, 262
  middle, 10, 131, 133, 174, 180, 182, 262
  upper, 131
  working, 10, 114, 115, 180, 182, 197, 201,
    202, 216, 218, 241, 262
Clever, William, 71
CND (Campaign for Nuclear
    Disarmament), 203
Collins, Christina, 177
colonialism, 10, 11, 14, 260
Columbia, District of, 131
Comenius, John Amos, 57
Communism, 160
conscience, 33
consent, 5, 116, 118, 119, 121, 160, 177,
    180, 184, 202, 224, 261
  age of, 6, 7, 91, 114, 176, 178, 228
contraception, 171–87, 224, 261
control, emotional, 150, 157, 159, 262
conversion, 34–5, 70, 77
Cooper, Thomas, 70
courts, juvenile, 11, 12, 13, 127–40
courtship, 173, 218, 226
Coverdale, Miles, 75
coverture, 114
COVID-19, 242
Craft, Ann, 223, 224, 227
Craft, Michael, 223, 224, 227
Crashaw, William, 69
creole languages, 195, 196
Crichton-Miller, Hugh, 151
criminality, 50, 128, 130, 131–2, 137, 138, 140
'crip time', 216
Critical Race Theory, 140
Cuffe, Henry, 47, 51, 52, 56, 58, 76
Culpepper, Nicholas, 57

D

Dafydd ap Gwilym, 32
Darling, Thomas, 73
Darly, Mattina, 97

INDEX

Darrell, John, 73
dating agencies, 226
Davis, Ken, 226
Davis, Maggie, 226
De Vries, Hans Vredeman, 48
death penalty, 128–30, 135, 137
debt, 1
Declaration of the Rights of Mentally
    Disabled Persons, 221
Defoe, Daniel, 100, 102
deinstitutionalisation, 222
democracy, 6, 159–61
dependants, 30, 112, 114, 115, 117, 118,
    120–21, 194, 229
Depression era, 133
disability, 2, 6, 10, 13, 137, 138, 215–30, 262
discretion, age of, 91, 92
Dod, John, 78
domestic violence, 228
Dove, Mary, 31, 52, 57
drugs, 140
Duffy, Clinton, 138
Dunfermline, Scotland, 171
Dyhouse, Carol, 173, 182, 183, 184

E

early modern period, 4, 5, 8, 10, 12,
    45–59, 67–80, 197, 259, 261, 262
Edinburgh, Scotland, 171, 178, 179, 180,
    182
Edmondson, D. L., 197, 199
education, 4, 10, 36, 51, 57, 72, 80, 137,
    138, 172, 180, 185, 194, 195, 197–200,
    202, 203, 205, 219, 228, 230, 240–41,
    247, 260
  higher, 171, 177, 186
  schooling, 5, 197–200, 260
  sex education. *See* sex education
  spiritual, 75
Elton, Arthur, 158
Elyot, Thomas, 28–9, 30, 45, 46
enslaved people, 10, 11, 122n1, 130, 194,
    260–61
'emerging adult' films, 8, 13, 239–52
employment, 4, 193, 216, 229, 261, 262
epilepsy, 217
eugenics, 174, 216, 231n7
Evans, John J., 119, 120
Ex Parte Beaver, 132
exorcism, 73
exploitation, 11, 12, 138, 194, 203, 205

F

Family Planning Association (FPA),
    174–5, 179
family planning services. *See*
    contraception

fascism, 160
Fathers, Church, 35
Featley, Daniel, 78
femininity, 3, 4, 250
feminism, 174, 218, 228, 241
  Black, 262
Fenning, Daniel, 92, 93
Fenton, Geffray, 51, 52
fertility, 27, 57, 58, 229
Fifth Monarchists, 68
financial crisis (2008), 1, 13, 242, 249
Fisher, Will, 47, 48
Flanagan, Edward, 135–6
Fokus scheme, 225
'fograms', 102, 105, 261
Fortescue, Thomas, 47, 49
Fox, Joshua, 226
Foxe, John, 77
France, 28, 36
Fresno, California, 136
Freudianism, 10, 151, 153
Froissart, Jean, 29, 32
frontal lobes, 2
Fulton Report (1968), 162
Furman v. Georgia, 130
Fürst, Paul, 56
Furstenberg, Frank F., 172, 173, 185

G

Garcia, Pedro, 136
Garland, John W., 119
Gataker, Thomas, 75–6, 79–80
Gellatly, John, 136
gender, 2, 4, 12, 46, 47, 90, 93, 104, 128,
    129, 158, 159, 173, 186–7, 216, 223,
    261–2
  and adolescence, 92
  and adulthood, 111–22
  and life expectancy, 28
  of boys, 48
  nonconformity, 156
  and the unmarried, 181–5
'generation gap', 203–207
Generation X, 239
Generation Z, 1, 13
generations, conflict between, 12, 172,
    185, 206
Georgia (US state), 7
gerontocracy, 59, 73
Gerson, Jean, 34
Gibson, Lee Vernon, 137–8
Gillray, James, 103
Glasgow, Scotland, 176, 179, 183, 204
Goldfarb, Cardea, 139
Good Hope, Cape of, 6
Goodwin, Thomas, 69
Gordon, Thomas, 95, 96, 99

270 INDEX

Gouge, William, 75–6, 78
Goulart, Simon, 74
Government of India Act (1935), 7
Gray, John, 218
Grays, Essex, 226
Great Recession (2008). *See* financial crisis (2008)
Great Reform Act (1832), 6
Grunwick Strike (1976–78), 200, 206
guardianship, legal, 111, 121, 135, 178, 183, 217
Guerrero, Rose, 136–7

H

Hale, Matthew, 91
Handsworth, Birmingham, 197, 206
Hardwick's Marriage Act (1753), 91
Harrison, William, 69
Hartley, Roland, 136
Haywood, Eliza, 97–8
Health and Public Services Act (1968), 175
Heath, Kay, 27, 93
heteronormativity, 177, 227, 250
heterosexuality, 156, 157, 200, 217, 220, 227, 229, 230, 248
high school reunions, 249–50
higher education. *See* education
Hildersham, Arthur, 75, 76
Hinduism, 202, 208n12
Hodges, Thomas, 72
home ownership, 4, 246
homecoming narratives, 249, 251
homosexuality, 10, 13, 153, 156, 157, 227–8, 250, 261
Hoole, Charles, 57
Hoper, R., 48
Hornketh v. Barr, 116, 118
householders, adults as, 4, 50, 54, 56, 58, 59, 90
households, 48, 114, 117, 118, 177, 206
house prices, 1
Human Rights Act (1998), 228
humorism, 47
Hunt, Judy, 219
Hunt, Paul, 219–20, 225

I

Ibn Sīnā (Avicenna), 28, 29
Ibrahim, Habiba, 130, 262
Idaho, 135
Illinois Juvenile Court Act (1898), 131
In re: Winship, 132
independence, legal, 5, 30, 91, 111, 114–15, 117, 118–19, 120–21
Independence, Declaration of, 113

India, 6, 10, 11, 194, 205, 261
Indian Citizenship Act (1924), 7
Indian-Caribbeans, 195, 198, 203
Indigenous populations, 11, 201, 207, 260, 261
infantilisation, 1, 173, 182, 186, 216, 261
intersectionality, 2, 112, 259, 262
intimacy, 9, 13, 215–30, 262
IQ (Intelligence Quotient), 223
Isidore of Seville, 29, 30, 51, 52
Islam, 202, 208n12
Italy, 28

J

Jamaica, 10, 197, 201, 204, 208n12, 224
Jaques, Elliot, 27, 35
Jenkyn, William, 71, 72, 73
Jim Crow laws, 131
Johnson, Samuel, 92, 93–4, 98
Jones, Emrys, 160
Judaism, 32, 35
Julian of Norwich, 36
Jung, Carl, 155
Jurdian, Ignatius, 77

K

Kashmir, 205
Kersey, John, 91, 93
Kilby, Richard, 67, 71
Knox, Vicesimus, 98–9
Kuykendahl, Elgin, 134, 135

L

La Fane, Pamela, 219, 225
labour, 10, 112, 114–15, 117, 123n17, 219, 254n26
Lamson, Armene, 135
Langhamer, Claire, 157, 173
Laurens, André du, 73
leadership, 48, 49, 150, 152–3, 154, 158, 159, 160, 161, 162, 225
Lee, Essex, 70
Leeds, Yorkshire, 199
Lenroot, Katherine, 132
Lenton, Francis, 71
life expectancy, 28, 29
life writing, 215, 219, 220, 227, 260
Loe, William, 78
Logan, Margaret, 117, 118
Logan, Sarah, 34
Logan v. Murray, 116–17
London, England, 28, 95, 175, 198, 200, 201, 224, 226
  Brixton, 204

Ealing, 196
Soho, 216
Tavistock Clinic, 151
Los Angeles, California, 243
lust, 33, 35, 58, 75

M

Macauley, Catherine, 96
MacGillivray, Ian, 184–5
Mackintosh, Kenneth, 135
Mackenzie, Henry, 95, 96, 99
McMillan, Michael, 198–9
Mahan, Carl Newton, 133
majority, age of, 5, 6, 7–8, 25, 30, 186, 260
Malleson, Joan, 174
Manchester, 196, 206
Mandeville, Bernard, 101, 102
manhood, 4, 30, 33, 46, 51, 52, 53, 54, 92, 93, 113
manliness (virility), 33, 48, 51, 157
Marley, Bob, 198
marriage, 4, 9, 13, 33, 46, 54, 56, 58, 91, 95, 113, 120, 135, 172, 173, 177–8, 182, 183, 184, 185, 186, 193, 197, 239, 247, 248, 249, 262
    arranged, 207
    and disability, 215, 217, 218, 220–21, 223, 224, 226, 227, 228, 229, 230
    early, 200–203, 207
    legal age of, 5, 6
Martin, Clarence, 136
Martin, Trayvon, 130
martyrologies, 68, 75, 78, 83n55
masculinity, 3, 4, 46, 48, 49, 54, 150, 157, 158, 223, 250, 261
Massachusetts, 128, 131
Mattinson, Janet, 222, 223, 224, 228
maturity, 1, 2, 3, 4, 5, 9, 13, 29, 31, 33, 34, 93, 117, 129, 150–51, 161–2, 183, 194, 196, 198, 245, 246, 250, 251, 260, 261
    and leadership, 152–3
    emotional, 157–9, 186, 221
    physical, 92, 131
    political, 10, 159–61
    psychological, 131, 193
    and sexuality, 153–6
    spiritual, 12, 49, 59, 67–80, 262
Mencap, 222
menopause, 26, 31, 58, 90, 91, 94
menstruation, 56, 57, 92
mental health, 6, 127, 159, 249
Mexia, Pedro, 47
Mexican Americans, 12, 136
Michals, Teresa, 9, 10
midlife crisis, 3, 27, 32, 35, 37, 93, 97
middle age, 2, 3, 8, 47, 51, 57, 58, 72, 74, 80, 93, 96–7, 98, 99–100, 102, 105

crisis of. *See* midlife crisis
    medieval conception of, 25–37
Middle Ages, 25–37, 157
'middling sort', the, 48
millennials, 1, 13, 239, 242, 249
ministers, Protestant, 49, 67, 68, 74–80, 262
Mintz, Steven, 3–4
Mirza, Nadia, 199, 202
monasteries, 35
mortality, 27
    infant, 28, 63n63
motherhood, 197, 200–203, 207, 248, 249
Murcot, John, 75
murder, 120, 128, 129–35, 137, 139, 176, 260
Murder Act (1752), 129
Murray, James, 116–17
muscular dystrophy, 216, 218, 219

N

National Front, 206
National Health Service (NHS), 171, 174–5, 176
National Service, 158
Native Americans, 7, 12, 112, 129, 137, 138
Nazism, 157, 159, 206
Negus, William, 70
Nevada, 138
New England, 128
New London, Connecticut, 129
New York City, New York, 6, 120, 130, 135
    Sing Sing Prison, 135
New Zealand, 6
Newcomen, Matthew, 76, 78
Newton, Thomas, 76
Niccolls Jr, Herbert, 133–6, 137, 138, 139
Niebrzydowski, Sue, 31, 57
NHS Family Planning Act (1967), 175
nightmares, 159
'normalisation', 221–4, 226, 227
North Carolina, 112, 116, 118, 119
Notting Hill Carnival, 204
Novare, Philippe de, 29

O

O'Neil, Eileen, 139
Ocuish, Hannah, 129
Okawara, Tom, 137
old age, 3, 8, 9, 26, 28, 29, 34, 45, 46, 50, 55–6, 89, 90, 91, 93–4, 95, 96, 98–9, 100, 105
    as decline, 2, 12, 25, 27, 30, 31, 49, 51–3, 54, 59, 72–4, 76–7, 78–9, 80, 262
    and senility, 78–80
Oliver, J., 224
Ovid, 95

272 INDEX

P

Paintsville, Kentucky, 133
Palmer, Herbert, 75
Pan-Africanism, 206
Pande, Ishita, 6, 261, 262
Papillion, David, 71
parenthood, 4, 193, 224
Parlement of the Thre Ages (poem), 32
Parmar, Pratibha, 199, 202
Paterson, Lindsay, 178, 180
patriarchs, biblical, 75
patriarchy, 4, 5, 46, 54, 59, 80, 228
Patrick, Simon, 73
Pentecostalism, 206
Pennsylvania, 112, 116, 117, 132
perfection, 31, 47, 50–55, 57, 72, 92, 98
performance, adulthood as, 150, 152, 157, 186
    heteronormativity as, 250
Perkins, William, 74
Perry, William, 93, 94
Petrarch, Francisco, 35, 36
Philadelphia, Pennsylvania, 116
philosophy, 29, 31, 35
Phipps, Jacob, 118–19
Phipps, Jane, 118–19
Phipps v. Garland, 118
Piers Plowman (poem), 32
pill, the (oral contraceptive pill), 171, 174–5, 176, 179–80, 181, 182, 185, 186, 261
Pincus, Gregory, 174
poll tax, 5
pop culture, 151, 239
Pope, Alexander, 103
Porter, Polly, 117
pregnancy, 116, 117, 118, 180, 182, 183, 184, 185, 244
    in older women, 94
    prevention of. *See* contraception
    underage, 112, 119–20
    unwanted, 175, 178, 248
premarital sex, 172, 176, 177, 180, 182, 183, 184–5, 186, 187, 262
Presbyterianism, 71
Preston, John, 75
Price, Sampson, 71
'prime of life', idea of, 30, 31, 32, 33, 50, 51–2, 53, 54, 55, 74, 76, 93, 96
prisons, 127, 135, 136, 138, 139–40
Progressive era, 131, 132, 139, 140
progressivism, 11
Prohibition, 7
promiscuity, 172, 175, 176, 180, 182, 183
prophecy, 73
Protestantism, 12, 49, 67–80, 131, 176, 261, 262

pseudoscience, 136
psychoanalysis, 27, 149–63, 222
psychology, developmental, 8
psychosexual development, 150, 153, 155, 156, 162
puberty, 8, 92, 114
Pythagoras, 51

Q

Quakers, 68
queer theory, 262

R

race, 2, 112, 113, 114, 116, 121, 132, 157, 194, 204, 216, 261
    and judicial treatment, 128–9, 133, 139–40
racism, 128, 136, 195, 198, 201, 203, 205, 206, 207, 224, 229
    structural, 197, 260
rape, 115, 116, 117
Rastafarianism, 199, 206
Ratis Raving (poem), 30
Reagan, Ronald, 139
Reading, John, 54
reconstruction, postwar, 157
Reggae music, 196, 204
rehabilitation, 131, 135, 139
Reformation, 59
    'second', 68
Reinke-Williams, Tim, 56, 58
religion, 75, 155, 199, 202
Representation of the People
    Act (1918), 7
residential schools, Indian, 138
Revolution, American, 113, 114
Riches, Valerie, 178
rites of passage, 4, 33, 46, 56, 218, 248, 249
Rock, John, 174
Roper v. Simmons, 130
Ross, William, 176
Ruffin, Edmund, 111, 121
Ruffin, Elizabeth, 111, 119, 121

S

saints, 9, 68, 72
Salem, Massachusetts, 128
Saltmarsh, John, 79–80
San Francisco, California, 243
San Quentin, Babes of, 136–8
San Quentin, California, 136, 137, 138
Santiago de Compostella, Spain, 37
satire, 96, 101, 103, 259
Sbaraini, Ella, 58, 93
Schottennius, Hermannus, 48

Scope (charity), 225, 226
Scotland, 7, 12, 171–87, 204
Scottish Law Commission, 177
Seattle, Washington, 135–6
Section 28 (Local Government Act 1988), 228
seduction suits, 111–22
selection boards, psychological, 13, 149–63, 262
Sen, Satadru, 10, 194
senescence, 72, 76, 91
sermons, 34, 54, 68, 74,
   funeral, 71, 72, 75–6
servants, 91, 112, 114, 117, 119–20
sex education, 184, 223
Sexual Offences Act (1967), 7
'Sexual Revolution', 171–2, 174, 177, 241
sexuality, 2, 13, 150, 151, 153–6, 180, 181, 184, 185, 227
Shakespeare, William, 45, 48, 54
Sharp, John, 137
Shearer, Ann, 221
Shepard, Alexandra, 9–10, 46, 49, 59, 72
Shockley, Leonard, 130
Sikhism, 202, 208n12
single mothers, 36, 118
singleness, 113, 183, 184, 187, 217, 225
social mobility, 178, 180, 200
social workers, 194, 215, 222, 223, 260
soldiers, 50, 51, 54, 123n17, 151
South America, 11, 69
South Asians, 12, 13, 194–5, 196, 197, 199–200, 201, 202, 203, 204, 205, 206, 207, 260
South Carolina, 130
sport, 197
Sproul, Robert, 117–18
Star, Idaho, 135
Starcross, Devon, 222, 223
status, social, 4, 5, 9–10, 28, 30, 111–12, 116, 121, 152, 173, 183, 229, 246, 248, 261
stereotypes, 2, 3, 13, 68, 73, 180, 194, 197, 198, 201, 206, 217, 241
sterilisation, involuntary, 136, 224
Stinney Jr, George, 130
Stopes, Marie, 174, 188n15
strength, physical, 9, 30, 49, 50, 52, 77, 137
suicide, 127, 227
Supreme Court, US (SCOTUS), 120, 130, 132, 133, 141n12
Swift, Jonathan, 94–5

T

Tarbin, Stephanie, 50, 55
Tarkington, Booth, 134

teenagers, 8, 179–80, 181, 193–6, 198, 203, 205–206, 207, 250
   African-Caribbean, 208n12
   South Asian, 197, 199, 204, 208n12
Thematic Apperception Test, 153–4, 155, 159
Thomas, George, 216, 217, 218
Thomas of Cantimpré, 29
Thompson, T. R., 137
Thompson, William, 130
Thompson v. Oklahoma, 130
Till, Emmett, 130
'tough on crime' era, 139–40
Townsend, Peter, 222
Tucker, J. B., 134
Twain, Mark, 134

U

unemployment, 1, 171, 193, 199, 249
Unilever, 149, 152–3, 156, 158, 160, 161, 162, 261
Union of the Physically Impaired Against Segregation (UPIAS), 220–21, 226

V

Van Hoose, Cecil, 133
vanity, 58, 99
Vaughan, William, 52
Vickery, Amanda, 93, 96, 104
Vietnam War, 6
Villon, François, 32
virility. *See* masculinity
voting rights, 6, 7, 113

W

Walla Walla, Washington, 135, 136
Walpole, Horace, 96, 98, 100, 102
Walsham, Alexandra, 59, 68, 79
War Office Selection Boards, 13, 149, 151, 153, 154, 155, 158, 160, 161
Waterfield, Percival, 149, 154, 155
Waters, Rob, 195, 196, 205
Webbe, Harold, 154
welfare state, 171
White, Rawlins, 77
widowhood, 56
William of Malmesbury, 28
Williamsburg, Virginia, 246
Wilson, Amrit, 200, 202
Wilson, John, 117, 118
Wiltshire, Pauline, 224
wisdom, 3, 9, 30, 35, 37, 49, 50, 52, 58, 70, 72, 73, 80, 94, 157, 160
witchcraft, 128
Wolfensberger, Wolf, 221, 222
Wolridge-Gordon, Patrick, 182

womanhood, 201, 248
Wood, Matthew, 120
Wood, Susan, 120
Word Association Tests, 155–6
World War I, 134, 151, 174
World War II, 6, 151, 157
Wormell, John, 133, 134
Wright, Thomas, 70

Y

York, England, 28
Yorkshire, 197
'young adulthood', 13, 26, 33, 105

youth, 33–4, 35, 46, 51–4, 55, 57, 58, 71, 73, 74, 79, 80, 93, 95, 97, 101, 104, 157, 182, 205, 206, 207, 240, 242, 249
adulation of, 90, 100, 105
as 'age of man', 29, 30
culture, 172–3, 181, 203
desires of, 36, 48
extension of, 96, 98–100
lost, 27, 31–2
'othering' of, 49

Z

Zulfiqar, Mohsin, 206

Printed in the USA
CPSIA information can be obtained
at www.ICGtesting.com
CBHW060621111224
18608CB00007B/106